SCOTLAND

from the Earliest Times
to 1603

SCOTLAND
from the Earliest Times
to 1603

W. CROFT DICKINSON

Third edition
revised and edited by
ARCHIBALD A. M. DUNCAN

OXFORD
AT THE CLARENDON PRESS
1977

Oxford University Press, Walton Street, Oxford OX2 6DP

OXFORD LONDON GLASGOW
NEW YORK TORONTO MELBOURNE WELLINGTON
IBADAN NAIROBI DAR ES SALAAM LUSAKA CAPE TOWN
KUALA LUMPUR SINGAPORE JAKARTA HONG KONG TOKYO
DELHI BOMBAY CALCUTTA MADRAS KARACHI

British Library Cataloguing in Publication Data

Dickinson, William Croft
    Scotland from the earliest times to 1603—3rd ed.
    1. Scotland—History
    I. Title II. Duncan, Archibald Alexander McBeth
    941.1   DA775
    ISBN 0-19-822453-2
    ISBN 0-19-822465-6 Pbk.

Printed in Great Britain
at the University Press, Oxford
by Vivian Ridler
Printer to the University

Editor's Foreword

THE first edition of W. Croft Dickinson's volume (1961) was followed by a second (1965) (the preface dated April 1963 shortly before his death) which 'embodies a number of modifications in emphasis and interpretation'. This edition was to be a posthumous but proud memorial to his life's work in teaching and research, and whoever reads it now should still sense the scholarly wisdom which inspired each page. The companion volume by Pryde was soon overtaken by other histories of modern Scotland, or histories of Scotland with a modern emphasis. And in some sense both volumes were overtaken by the larger-scale *Edinburgh History of Scotland*. The need for a one-volume history of the ancient Kingdom of Scotland for schools, first-year students, and the general reader none the less remained and remains; it seemed to me that this need could best be met by a thorough revision of the masterpiece of 1963, taking account of subsequent scholarship.

I make no pretence that this is the 1963 book of my old teacher with a few rewordings. It is very thoroughly revised and in many parts wholly rewritten because of new evidence, of new interpretations, and of new attitudes. To outline these changes here would take expensive space; and they are not difficult to discover if the books be set side by side. But I have preserved as one chapter the substance of two on the burghs in the fifteenth and sixteenth centuries, a subject which the author particularly enjoyed and in which therefore the deftness of his pen in summarizing his own research is particularly evident. I cannot hope that elsewhere I have matched that masterly style, and if the new substance be flawed it is in spite of assistance from generous colleagues at Glasgow. I have benefited by many discussions of Scottish history with Dr. Jennifer M. Brown; Dr. Ian B. Cowan; Dr. James Kirk; Professor E. L. G. Stones; Mr. Patrick Wormald, and I thank them here. I also acknowledge a special debt to the Ph.D. thesis of Dr. Norman Macdougall, on the reign of James III, although the interpretation offered here differs somewhat from his.

A. A. M. DUNCAN

The University of Glasgow
March 1976

Foreword to the First Edition

SOME fifty years have now elapsed since Hume Brown published his three-volume *History of Scotland*, which, upon its appearance, was at once accepted as the 'standard' account. Since 'Hume Brown' there have been many books on Scottish history, and, after half a century, a real need has arisen for a new 'History of Scotland', written from a somewhat different approach and taking full account of our advancing knowledge. A new 'History of Scotland', consecutive and comprehensive, but still manageable, seemed to be desirable alike for the general reader, for the university student, and for the advanced school pupil.

On several occasions I discussed this need with Professor George S. Pryde, of the University of Glasgow, and the two of us finally decided to compile a new two-volume History of Scotland ourselves, of which I should write the first volume, 'From the Earliest Times to 1603', while he would write the second, 'From 1603 to the Present Day'. So our joint effort began. In the course of our collaboration we have kept in constant touch with one another, exchanging our chapters, as they were written, not only for comment but also in the hope of securing a reasonable approach to uniformity in scope and treatment.

Because our History is intended for general use, footnotes have been kept to a minimum and there are few references to sources and authorities. For a like reason the Select Bibliography at the end of each volume is intended mainly to furnish details of the works which are referred to in the text or have been used in its preparation, and also to act as a guide to further reading; it does not pretend to be other than a select list of the more essential original authorities and the more important secondary works.

When writing chapters II, III, and V of my own volume I benefited from advice and help freely given to me by Professor Stuart Piggott, Dr. Kenneth Steer, and Mrs. M. O. Anderson; and, when the volume was in draft, my colleagues, Dr. Gordon Donaldson, Mr. A. A. M. Duncan, and Dr. W. Ferguson, generously read through the whole of the typescript and made a number of valuable suggestions for its improvement. I am also indebted to Dr. I. B. Cowan for compiling the Index.

At every stage in the work I have been conscious of the dangers inherent in compression and simplification: in all my generalizations I have been aware of my temerity; in deciding what to include and what to omit I have realized that I might 'content few and displease many'.

Yet if, together, our two volumes stimulate interest and help to further the study of Scottish history we shall be satisfied.

W. Croft Dickinson

The University
Edinburgh
August 1959

Contents

Genealogical Tables

Maps

CHAPTER 1

Introductory—Historical and Geographical

THE history of the Scottish people has been influenced in many ways by geography—not only by the physical structure of Scotland itself, but also by Scotland's position in relation to neighbouring countries.

In the first place, Scotland is the northern part of one island, with England forming the southern part. In prehistoric times there were immigrant movements of the same or similar peoples to both 'Scotland' and 'England', and some settlers moved from 'England' to 'Scotland'. Then, in the second century A.D., a division between the northern and the southern parts of the island was made by the Roman walls; but towards the end of the fourth century Hadrian's Wall was overrun for the last time and never restored, and for centuries the notion of a frontier was almost irrelevant, for men thought rather of the king whom they followed than of the kingdom in which they lived. Yet it was geography and not accident which dictated that the northern Roman wall, the furthest Anglian advance in the sixth and seventh centuries, the firmest and longest English occupation under Edward I and his son and again under Edward III, should all be bounded on the north by the deep inlet of the Forth and the narrow waist of land between Stirling and Loch Lomond. This natural frontier was Flanders Moss, the carse of the Forth and Endrick, *not* the line of the Antonine Wall, the canal, the railway, and the motorway. Flanders Moss was undrained and impassable until the eighteenth century, and must be crossed either at the western end by Drymen and Aberfoyle or at the eastern end where the hills north and south of Forth almost meet at the rock of Stirling Castle. Hence Stirling was truly the nodal point of Scotland. It was comparatively easy for a southern people to advance so far; it was difficult, in the long term impossible even, for them to advance further. The Forth–Clyde isthmus was a 'natural' frontier between peoples and rulers. But it was not to be the frontier between England and Scotland.

For the history of the Scottish people has been influenced in other ways by geography—turn to a map showing the gradations of high land and low land, and we see at once that a great part of the country is high land. The low and fertile land is mainly confined to the 'Midland Valley' (including Lothian) with its continuation up the eastern coastal plain into the 'Laigh o' Moray'.

The Midland Valley, with its fertile soil, has always been Scotland's wealth. In early agrarian times, Picts, Scots, Britons, and Angles all strove for it. In the twelfth and thirteenth centuries many Anglo-Normans were given lands there and colonized it. There (and in the fertile Tweed valley and in the south-west) were founded the principal monasteries. In the industrial age, it was still the wealth of Scotland, not only because of its continuing agricultural fertility, but also because of its valuable mineral deposits, notably coal. Only in the 1970s with the development of oil-extraction from the sea-bed does it seem likely that there will be a shift (at whatever cost) of population and wealth to new areas—and even in Easter Ross the new area is a lowland one.

In the heart of the Midland Valley stands Stirling which, with its castle and its bridge over the Forth, guards all routes, north and south, east and west, the strategic centre of Scotland. In a map drawn by Matthew Paris (died 1259) the estuaries of the Clyde and Forth are shown as practically meeting one another, the country to the north of them is called 'Scotland beyond the Sea', and Stirling is there depicted as a bridge across the 'Sea' and is called *Estrivelin pons.* 'At the Bridge of Stirling', ran the old saying, 'the Forth bridles the wild Highlandman.' Again, any advance northwards from Stirling must go via Strathallan, Strathearn, and Strathmore: and that route, in turn, is guarded by Perth which, with its bridge over the Tay, also guards any southward movement down the east coast plain or down the Perthshire Glengarry and through Dunkeld. To the south, on the Border, Berwick, with its castle and its bridge over the Tweed, is the gateway into Scotland, while Edinburgh, again with its castle on the natural fortress of a rock, guards the gap, nine miles wide, between the Pentlands and the sea, and so acts as a second 'gate' to bar the easiest route of any English advance.

Here we should never forget that rivers and high hills are always difficult barriers to cross. Berwick, Edinburgh, Stirling, and Perth all guarded important routes, and three of them also guarded important river-crossings. Those routes are still the main routes today, and, together with the passes followed in early times through the mountains and hills of the Highlands, are still the routes and passes followed by our modern system of roads and railways. Fifteen miles south of Aberdeen near Dunottar, the foot-hills of the Grampians reach almost to the sea in a range known since the Middle Ages as 'the Mounth' and regarded then as a natural division of Scotland. The eighth-century writer, Bede, speaks of a mountain range which divides the Picts, probably the Mounth, and that division may have persisted until the twelfth century. Thereafter the rulers of Scotland built a string of castles leading to the Mounth, passing freely beyond it, or through it (by the Cairn o' Mount pass) to show their authority in the coastal plain of Moray; traders from Inverness or Aberdeen, hugging the coast in their small vessels, were unaffected by it. For, whereas rivers are difficult barriers for an army to cross, rivers and river-valleys form easy routes of penetration into the interior of the country for the trader. The earliest peoples coming to Scotland moved inland up the river-valleys. At one period in the War of Independence the English were able to hold Stirling and Perth just because they could be reached and supplied by English ships.

In medieval times this fertile Midland Valley, and its continuation up the eastern coastal plain, embraced the cultural, economic, and political life of Scotland. Here Scone (near Perth), with its Moot Hill, was for long regarded as the *caput*, or legal centre of the realm; but the building of Holyrood Palace by James IV and V, and the centralization of the courts of justice in Edinburgh, eventually made Edinburgh the 'capital', the seat of the king and the government. In 1472 and 1492, respectively, St. Andrews and Glasgow were erected into archbishoprics. Universities were founded at St. Andrews (1412), Glasgow (1451), and Aberdeen (1495). Here, too, were many monasteries—at Arbroath, Coupar Angus, Scone, Lindores, Balmerino, St. Andrews, Dunfermline, Culross, and Cambuskenneth.

In this part of Scotland were nearly all Scotland's early trading centres, the burghs, with many of them on the east coast. For, until the seventeenth century Scotland looked east. Her trade was with the Baltic, the Low Countries, and France, and it was a trade mainly in wool, woolfells (that is, sheepskins still bearing their wool), hides and skins from the good land of the Midland Valley, Lothian, and the Tweed valley, and in barrelled fish (salmon, trout, and eels) and cured fish (haddock and herring) from the rivers and the sea—for no part of Scotland is more than fifty miles from sea-water, and the river estuaries and the long sea-lochs encouraged fishing. In return, Scotland imported useful commodities (like iron and salt) or luxuries (like wines and rich cloths).

That 'string' of burghs along the coast of Fife—Kinghorn, Dysart, Wemyss, Largo, Pittenweem, Anstruther, Crail, and St. Andrews (which Andrew Fairservice likened to a 'string o' ingans' but which James VI called a 'golden fringe')—tells part of the tale of Scotland's early trade, largely to the Baltic and the cloth towns of the Low Countries. But today those thriving burghs of the past, which proudly sent their commissioners to the Scottish parliament, are little more than fishing villages, for political and economic changes in the seventeenth and eighteenth centuries turned Scotland's outlook from the east to the west.

For Scotland is close too to northern Ireland, the intervening channel being only fifteen to twenty miles across. From Ireland, in prehistoric times, came the first visitors—fishers and beachcombers—to a 'Scotland' which was still uninhabited after the retreat of the ice sheet; and in the Bronze Age there was a close connection between northern Ireland and western Scotland. From Ireland came the Scots,[1] who established a kingdom in Dalriada (modern Argyll), and to Dalriada, from Ireland, came the missionary Columba, and Scotland's early culture. Many Scots later fought against the English in Ireland in the fourteenth, fifteenth, and sixteenth centuries. In the sixteenth century particularly, there was much co-operation between Scottish and Irish rebels—the Irish helped the Islesmen and Highlanders against the Scottish government; the Islesmen and Highlanders helped the Irish against the English government. In modern times the close proximity of Ireland has led to a vast immigration of Irish labour, particularly into the industrial area around Glasgow.

To the north-east of Scotland lie the island groups of Orkney and Shetland—the first landfall in any western voyage from Scandinavia, as Scotland learned to her cost in the ninth century when the Vikings seized these island groups and held them as a base for further voyaging to Iceland or to Ireland. Then the Vikings, sailing round the north coast of Scotland and down the west coast to Ireland, took and held Caithness, Sutherland, parts of Ross, and the Western Isles and Man. These Vikings established themselves not only in northern Scotland and the Isles but also in Ireland and in northern and central England; and they had command of the sea. As a result Scotland was isolated and driven in upon herself. For more than a century and a half she was virtually cut off from Ireland, England, and Europe; but that period of isolation also helped her to achieve unity in the face of a common foe.

Looking again at our map of Scotland we see how much of the land is poor land. Of the total land area of Scotland, three-fifths are mountain, hill, and wind-swept moor; and one-fifth is woodland, rough grazing, and grass. Thus only one-fifth of the land area is good fertile land, concentrated, as we have seen, in the southwest, the Midland Valley, and the eastern coastal plain. We should remember, too, that in early times, when there was less skilled attention to the land (less draining, less ditching, less dyking), and, earlier still, when there were far wider stretches of forest and scrub and, in the valleys, far more bog and marsh,[2] the proportion of good land was even smaller than it is today.

The poor land lies mainly in the Highlands—a vast region of natural poverty where the hard schist and granite rocks bear only a thin covering of soil which a heavy rainfall, attracted by the mountains, sweeps away or keeps permanently wet.[3] The very nature of the country—small glens amid high hills and the penetrations of sea-lochs—meant isolated communities, each striving to eke out an existence on a limited patch of good land in strath or glen. The communities were small because the supply of food was small; they were isolated because of the great difficulties of communication. They tended to become self-reliant, self-supporting, self-interested.

Here there was nothing to attract the new settler or the colonist. So the people of the Highlands differed from the people of the Lowlands. The Highlander remained the Gael, his economy very largely pastoral, his social organization continued to be the old grouping by family and by kin. The Lowlander might be any mixture of Gael, Saxon, Angle, Norman, Fleming, and Briton; his economy and social organization was based upon grazing but also upon the working of fertile land. He therefore needed protection, and so was more likely to have to pay tribute. Different languages became a further barrier to fusion.

So, for long, Scotland was divided into two: into a Highland zone and a Lowland zone.[4] The distinctions between the two zones were both cultural and geographical. Moreover, the Highlander was apt to think of the Lowlands as land held by 'foreigners', and land where there was 'gear to grip' whenever he was in need, or whenever the occasion offered. The distinction between the Highlander and the Lowlander grew wider with Lowland fear and distrust; and the Lowlander's idea of the Highlander as a wild man dwelling in the woods and mountains, and a born thief, for long ran through Scottish history. Pitscottie, writing in Fife in the middle of the sixteenth century, relates how a MacGregor stole the crown of England at Bosworth Field and, when detected, boldly affirmed that, had he got the crown away to Blair Atholl, the English lords would never have seen it again. Towards the end of the sixteenth century one of the poems attributed to Montgomerie, a court poet,[5] describes how God made a Highlander out of a lump of horse manure, and then

> Quoth God to the Helandman *Quhair wilt thou now?   [*where
> I will doun to the Lowland, Lord, and thair steill a kow.

The Highlander, moreover, was long unwilling to be under the control of the Scottish king. In the twelfth and thirteenth centuries the best that the king could do was to establish his castles at Dumbarton and Inverness at either end of the Highland Line. Dumbarton guarded the route to or from the Highlands via Loch Lomond and Loch Long; Inverness guarded all routes, east and west, south and north. But outside those strongpoints the Scottish kings had little control. Alexander II is said to have made Dumbarton a royal burgh partly because of its services in defending the king's peaceful subjects in Lennox from the oppression of 'men dwelling in the neighbouring mountainous parts'; as late as 1592 James VI speaks of Inverness as 'surrounded on all sides by most aggressive and rebellious tribes, *the clans*'.

Here, in the Highlands, the mountain ranges and 'broken parts' which halted the invader (and no invasion, from the time of the Romans onwards, ever penetrated the Highland west) also arrested the reach of the king's law. In 1527, for example, when James V wished to issue letters against MacLeod of Dunvegan, we read in the records that, 'the said Alexander MacLeod dwells in the Highlands, where none of the king's officers dare pass for fear of their lives'. Moreover, no army could be supplied and maintained in a land of mountains and inland seas; and no roads existed. So, in the later Middle Ages, what law there was, was the unwritten law of the clan. Loyalty to the chief was the only loyalty that was known. Rights and pretensions were maintained by the arbitrament of arms: men fought and died at their chief's command, and in their chief and the unity of the clan found their protection. For long, the Highland chieftains ruled their own lands as a land apart; and we shall see MacDonald of the Isles concluding treaties with English kings. But the clan was a force for cohesion and stability, and feuds are not necessarily more prevalent in the Highlands in the fifteenth century than in the Lowlands.

Here, too, the nature of the land, walled in by mountains and high hills, with deep indentations of the coast, with far-penetrating sea lochs, and with many off-shore islands, made communications by water easier than communications by land. The boat was the natural conveyance. A community was often united by the waters of a loch just as, in the southern Lowlands, a community might be united by a stretch of road. In these north-western Highlands and Islands the Vikings, relying upon sea communications, and finding a land similar to that which they had left, established themselves, and record of their settlements may be read in many place-names and heard in the terms that are used for much of the tackle of a boat. The strongholds at the openings of sea lochs and the positions of the brochs all speak of sea communications. Service to a lord might take the form of providing a galley with so many 'oars'; the sole entrance to Dunvegan Castle was its 'Sea-gate'; and Argyll bore on his arms the galley of Lorn.

Not until the seventeenth century did the Scottish kings begin to have *some* control in these difficult parts, and not until the measures taken after the Risings in 1715 and 1745 did the government secure effective control. Then, in addition to Disarming Acts, and Acts prohibiting the wearing of Highland dress and abolishing the heritable jurisdictions, roads and bridges were constructed to make land communications easier, garrisons were maintained at strategic points including Fort William,[6] Fort Augustus, and Fort George, and, more important still, the officials appointed to administer the estates of those who had been forfeited for their support of the Stewart cause busied themselves with the encouragement of schools, agriculture, fishing, and industry.

Giving one last look at the map we see, close by the Borders, what are known as the Southern Uplands. There, again, the nature of the land and the difficulties of communication made royal control virtually impossible. There the Border 'clans' were as difficult to control as the Highland clans. Moreover, the Borderers, constantly in the forefront of the battle with England, and always the first to be raided and harried, were apt to rely more on the strength of their own right hands than on the slow processes of the courts of law, or the decisions of a distant government. There, in the words of the English historian Camden, 'men knew no measure of law other than the length of their own swords'. There we find the simple plan,

> That they should take, who have the power,
> And they should keep who can.

There the raid and the foray became part of the daily lives of the people. There

> Broken keep and burning farm
> Taught his fathers strength of arm;
> Feud and fight from gate to gate
> Showed them how to nurse their hate.

These men who slept with their swords ready to hand to resist English raids were not averse to using their swords to resist the officers of the Scottish king.

The Union of the Crowns in 1603, however, made the Border counties of both England and Scotland the 'Middle Shires'. And then the appointment of a body of Border Horse to maintain law and order was sufficient, under the spirited leadership of Sir William Cranstoun, to pacify and control a once difficult part—though only after a goodly number of executions and banishings of old Border thieves had been carried out. Old feuds and animosities occasionally flared up anew, but in 1609 the Borders were declared (though with some exaggeration) to be 'as lawful, as peaceable, and as quiet as any part in any civil kingdom in Christianity'.

NOTES

1. Until the tenth century *Scotia* meant Ireland. In the tenth century *Scotia* was being used for the mainland of modern Scotland to the north of the Forth and Clyde, and the Forth was sometimes called 'The Scots Water'. From about the middle of the eleventh century *Scotia* gradually came to mean the whole of modern Scotland, though even at the beginning of the fourteenth century we still find modern Scotland divided into the districts of 'Galloway', 'Lothian', and 'Scotland', this last district embracing the land to the north of the Forth and Clyde.

2. The very many place-names with an element meaning 'bog' or 'marsh' are eloquent of the many stretches of ill-drained land.

3. We should note the (exceptional) fertile soils of the 'Laigh o' Moray'—derived from Old Red Sandstone. Also the lime of the 'machair'—flats of shell sand in certain of the Western Isles—was beneficial for agriculture.

4. It is best to think of the Highland-Lowland line as one dividing the west from the east. The 'Lowlands' extended beyond the Black Isle and into Sutherland and Caithness.

5. Montgomerie (*c.* 1545-1610) is best known for his *The Cherrie and the Slae*, and *The Banks of Helicon*.

6. Though the fort at Inverlochy was first built by General Monck during the Cromwellian regime, it was replaced by a stronger building, and named Fort William, by General Mackay in 1690. There was also a Cromwellian fort at Inverness.

CHAPTER 2

Prehistoric Peoples and Roman Conquerors

DURING the ice age Scotland was covered with glaciers and was uninhabitable. As the ice slowly retreated northwards and the climate became more genial, this uninhabited Scotland was first invaded by plants. Gradually vegetation covered large areas of the land, creeping up from England or coming as wind-borne seed. Then, when this food was available for them, came animals, moving northwards or migrating across the plain which still joined Britain to the continent. Lastly, and much later, came man, who was still dependent upon hunting and fishing for his food.

Meantime the melting waters of the ice had slowly formed a shallow new 'North Sea' and, by flooding the land-ridge between south-east England and the mainland of Europe, had formed the 'Straits of Dover'. Britain had become an island.

During the following thousands of years various peoples came. We know little about them, though from their primitive tools, weapons, pottery, and ornaments that have been found, and from the evidence of their forts, dwellings, and graves, it is possible to reconstruct something of their lives and history.

We speak of different ages—the stone age, the bronze age, the iron age—making these rough classifications according to the material used by each age for its weapons and tools. We can distinguish different cultures—some of these early peoples, for example, followed the custom of burying their dead collectively in tombs over which they erected large cairns of stones; some followed the custom of burying their dead individually in small stone-lined graves; others burned their dead. And these differing customs, we say, reveal different peoples, peoples of different cultures.[1] In a like way even finer distinctions can be made by a close examination of surviving pottery, ornaments, tools, and weapons. When we find pottery of a better clay or of a neater or more ornate design, or when we find the use of a more efficient method of fastening an axe-head to a wooden haft, we deduce that these are the work of later cultures, of peoples who lived nearer to our own time—for we assume that over the long centuries men gradually improved their handiwork. Finally, by associating some particular culture (a type of grave, for example, or a type of pottery or axe) found, shall we say, in the south-west of Scotland or in Fife, with that found in, say, the south of France or the Baltic region, archaeologists have suggested how and whence some of these early peoples came.

Beyond that we know little. We know nothing, for example, of individual men and their actions, of their hopes and aspirations, or of leaders and the events with which they were concerned. All we can say is that for long these peoples must have been few in number, and their lives must have been hard, dangerous, and short. Even when they possessed only crude weapons of stone they had to face bears, wolves, and the wild boar.[2] Until they had learned how to till the land and to raise crops they clung to the sea-beaches, living on fish and shellfish with possibly a little local hunting. Moreover, to venture forth into new territory, even to venture forth in the search for food, was to venture into the unknown. Fear was a constant companion: fear of hunger, fear of nature, fear of strangers; yet peril and want also sharpened man's wits and gave him reliance.

The land, too, was vastly different from the land we know today. The valleys were largely bog and marsh, and much of the higher ground was covered with scrub and forest. Even the levels of sea and land were not the same as they are now. On the floor of a cave near Oban, for example, some of the first visitors to Scotland left a few bone pins and a few serrated bone harpoons, or fish-spears, in amongst the thousands of empty shells of the winkles, limpets, cockles, mussels, and whelks which they had eaten. When those visitors used that cave it was on the sea-shore; when their middens were discovered it was inland and well above the sea-level. It would seem that the whole island of Britain has tilted. In the south-east of England the earlier coastal areas are now beneath the sea, but all round Scotland there are raised sea-beaches, of varying heights above the beaches of today, showing how the land has risen above the earlier level of the sea.

Probably the first people who came to Scotland after the retreat of the ice about 6000 B.C. were visitors from Ireland—fishers and beachcombers, whose flints and barbed harpoons, or fish-spears, made from bone, have been found here and there in the west. Probably they were even regular visitors—if we are to judge by the enormous number of empty sea-shells found on their sites—very small groups coming again and again; but they were hardly settlers. Their tools and weapons show that they were people of the mesolithic age—the middle stone age.

True settlement, however, came with immigrants in the neolithic age—men who brought cereals with them, and who also brought cattle and sheep which they had learned to raise for food; men who were farmers as well as hunters, even though farming and stock-raising only 'in a small way'.[3] The changes they brought were enormous and far-reaching. Grain could be stored against the dangers of winter famine; flocks and herds could provide food and milk and flesh. The hungry hand-to-mouth existence of the hunter and fisher gave way to a more secure and stable existence. Tillage meant settlements; the land was cleared for pasture and arable, and men began to make the first of many changes in the face of the earth.

Because they were still dependent upon stone for their tools moreover, their agriculture was bound to be poor with the few stone implements which they had at their command though large clearances could be made by burning as well as cutting—and some modern experiments in slash and burn clearances have shown that land so cleared was not only improved,[4] but also could be farmed for a considerable length of time. These people brought their families, their cattle and sheep, and their stocks of grain; and their multiple graves in cairns containing burial chambers (found widely in Scotland) suggest successive burials over a long period of time. Another people or culture employed individual burials, the body crouched and often accompanied by distinctively shaped grave-vessels from which these people are known as the beaker folk. Again there were various groups of them, or so the various methods of decorating the beakers suggest; they came it seems by the North Sea route, either direct from the mainland of Europe (probably from the Rhineland and Holland), or by moving further north from settlements they had already made on the coastal areas of eastern England. Like the builders of chambered cairns they were farmers and herdsmen, but unlike them they were also using a little copper—copper knife-daggers and copper ornaments—and the earliest metal objects found in Scotland come from their graves. So the beaker folk are said to belong to the early bronze age.

Last of all came the use of iron. Once men had discovered how to temper iron and so make it as hard as bronze, iron quickly replaced bronze. Moreover, whilst in Europe copper and tin are rare (although the British Isles were fortunate in their deposits of both), iron is abundant everywhere; and abundance meant cheapness. Only the rich and powerful could afford bronze; almost everyone could afford iron.

We do not know much about the dwellings of the earliest peoples, for while their graves were built of stone or covered with earthen mounds, their houses are difficult to locate. Exceptionally, however, a remarkable group of connected stone houses, of the late neolithic age, has been discovered at Skara Brae in Orkney, and gives us some indication of how the people lived. Wood is practically unknown in these northern isles, and these surviving stone houses at Skara Brae with their stone beds, stone cupboards, and stone dressers, may be something like wooden counterparts which were in use in timber houses on the mainland. But we cannot be sure. Prehistoric survivals in Orkney and Shetland are often so different from parallel survivals on the mainland that we cannot draw too close an inference from Skara Brae.

The Skara Brae pastoralists, who lived by breeding sheep and cattle, had built their stone settlement amid the sand-dunes and *beneath* sand and refuse, as a protection from the high winds: and it was exposed when a storm in 1866 cleared the covering sand. In a similar way at Jarlshof (near Sumburgh Head in Shetland) successive drifts of sand over the centuries engulfed successive settlements of the late stone age, the late bronze age, and the iron age, and these have now been excavated to reveal a site that is unique in its evidence of changing 'house styles'.

But while hardly any iron-age graves have as yet been recognized, the dwellings and settlements built by the iron-age people have survived in large numbers both on the mainland and on the western and northern islands; and it is noticeable that from the start of the iron age they were always defensible against attack. In the greater part of the country the iron-age houses, invariably circular in plan, were made entirely of timber. But unlike those of earlier periods, they were enclosed, at first within one or more palisades and later within a wall or a system of ramparts. Possibly the 'lords of the iron age', after invasion and conquest, compelled the local people to work for them, perhaps even to build their strongholds. For while the use of iron made agriculture and all the useful arts more easy, a multiplication of iron weapons may also have made war easier than work. Certainly there is now every indication that attack and defence were part and parcel of the iron-lord's life. Possibly there was now a temptation to try to take a neighbour's lands or cattle by force rather than to open up new land or raise larger herds by work. Moreover, if the iron-lords had subjugated the local people and made them slaves, there was always the risk that the local people might rise in revolt.

The farmsteads, settlements, and 'places of strength' of the iron age occur in great variety. They include single-house homesteads of timber or of stone, farmsteads, small and large settlements, and hill-top towns measuring up to as much as 40 acres in extent. The circular timber houses vary from as little as 20 feet in diameter to more than 60 feet, an example of the largest, found at Scotstarvit in Fife, having a floor space of 3,000 square feet. Timber houses were built throughout the whole period of the pre-Roman iron age, but there is no evidence that the fashion carried on into post-Roman times when houses, though at first still circular, had walls at least founded upon stone, if not indeed wholly constructed of drystone masonry.

The palisades enclosing the earliest iron-age houses were, in their simplest form, merely single fences forming a farmyard boundary; but many much larger and more elaborate forms were developed. These include twin palisades bounding settlements more than one acre in extent, often accompanied by an outlying concentric single or double fence which formed an enclosure for cattle. When more robust defences were demanded, the circular timber houses were enclosed within walls or ramparts. Two of the largest of such defended settlements, the 'hill-forts' or 'towns' on Traprain Law in East Lothian, and on the north-west summit of the Eildon Hills in Roxburghshire, contained hundreds of dwellings and other buildings. At the latter settlement, the final form of the defences was a set of three concentric heavy ramparts which were not, however, maintained after the Roman conquest in the first century A.D. At Traprain Law, an important centre of the Votadini 'tribe' who may have been in treaty with the Romans, the defences were kept in repair until at least the fourth century A.D.

Some of the stone-walled settlements, or hill-forts, had walls of great thickness, strengthened internally with timber beams. It has been shown that, in some cases, the houses or other internal buildings were timber-built lean-to erections attached to the inner face of the wall; and it may be assumed that this was a common arrangement. If such buildings were set on fire, by accident or during an attack, the conflagration would set alight the beams inside the wall. When this happened, many of the blocks of stone in the wall fused together in vitrified masses and even fused on to the underlying rock. Such 'vitrified forts' are to be found in every part of Scotland except the far north. Timber-laced walls, however, are found in southern Britain and in north-west Europe, and their great variety indicates that the technique developed over a long period and among different peoples.

In the west and north, where timber was not available for building, the homesteads were constructed of stone. Communal settlements of the hill-fort kind are not found in these parts, and only individual homesteads occur. Here the two principal varieties are the brochs and the structures now known as duns. The latter are enclosures with very thick walls which often contain galleries and chambers, staircases and cells, and have entrances checked for a door and provided with bar-holes. There are duns of circular, oval, and subrectangular plan; they often measure internally about 3,000 square feet; and it is assumed that within them light-weight lean-to buildings or tent-like shelters were used. The duns occur mainly in the far west, and can sometimes be shown to have been occupied in medieval times.

The broch (found in the west and north and with a much shorter life) was a dry-stone tower with a wall about fifteen feet thick surrounding a circular space usually about thirty feet in diameter. After some six feet or more of solid wall at the base (in which there were often cells), the wall became double with a space of from four feet to a foot or less between an inner and an outer wall, which were tied together by horizontal stone slabs which assisted stability and also served as scaffolding during the work of building. A broch rising to more than forty feet in height, as seen in the best preserved surviving example on the island of Mousa off the east coast of Shetland was exceptional; but in several other cases the wall still stands to a height of more than twenty feet and it may be that this height was common. The few excavations that have been carried out in brochs suggest that the circular interior was covered by a roof, probably thatched and supported on posts set in or on the floor, with its edge resting on a scarcement formed on the inner face of the wall. Only one opening, the entrance, pierced the broch wall.

Like the duns, the brochs are usually found near good land—up the fertile river valleys and along the coastal strip. Like the duns, they were strongholds, and the word *broch* means a fortified dwelling; but their enemy must have been a very special one, and he has been most convincingly identified as the commercial sea-raider looking for slaves for the Roman market.

Finally, as we have seen, the cheapness and abundance of iron meant a steady increase in the amount of land under cultivation and that meant a steady increase in population. Admittedly the archaeological evidence reveals that the economy of the iron age was still mainly pastoral, but only large local groups, or communities, could have built the brochs or, for example, the massive stone ramparts of the fort on Finavon Hill in Angus, with its walls 25 feet thick enclosing an area of some 100 by 300 feet. When the Romans moved north, the population of 'Scotland' was sufficiently large to be a worry to the Romans and to compel them eventually to build a fortified frontier for the protection of southern Britain. Writing of the year A.D. 297 a Roman author, Eumenius, speaks of attacks made on that fortified frontier by 'Picts and Irish [Scots]'. This is the first mention of 'Picts'. Possibly, to the Romans, the Picts were the painted (or tattooed) people attacking from the landmass of Scotland, as opposed to attackers on the west (Scots) from Ireland. Neither archaeologists nor historians can speak with confidence to identify the Picts with a particular earlier culture. It seems likely that no large-scale migration into Scotland took place after 700 B.C. and that the ancestors of the Picts and of the British peoples south of Forth were already here by that date. But that is not to say that their languages were also present, for the conditions of language-transmission may be quite different from those of transmission of cultural traces recoverable by archaeology.

After the successful invasion of England by the Emperor Claudius in A.D. 43, the first real attempt at Roman conquest in Scotland came with Agricola (Governor of the Province of Britain, 78–85) who, in 80, had pushed into Scotland converging upon Inveresk and had reached the narrow neck of land between the Forth and the Clyde. In the following year, Agricola once more advanced to the Forth–Clyde isthmus and there built a chain of small stockaded posts, with strategic roads and forts (like Dalswinton and Newstead) to the south of this new line.

In 82 Agricola carried out a series of campaigns in the south-west, in modern Dumfriesshire, Galloway, and southern Ayrshire, perhaps in preparation for an invasion of Ireland. At this time, too, he sent a fleet to explore the west coast and the western isles—possibly to see whether the Highlands could be outflanked by a landing on the west. But the answer he received must have been unfavourable, for, in 83, when Agricola moved his army north-wards again, he took the route dictated by the geography of the land, the route up Strathallan, Strathearn, and Strathmore—a route signposted by the permanent forts built at Ardoch (at Braco), Strageath (near Innerpeffray), Bertha (near Perth), and Cardean (near Meigle); and in Strathmore he built a legionary fortress at Inchtuthil, about seven miles south-east of Dunkeld, to form a permanent Scottish base. Marching still further north, and keeping in touch with a Roman fleet, he defeated a strong native force at the battle of Mons Graupius in Banffshire or Moray—the site of the battle has not yet been identified.

In 85 Agricola was recalled by Domitian and in 86 the Second Legion Adiutrix was withdrawn from the province of Britain, so that no legion was available for Inchtuthil. That strong and ideally situated fortress commanding the route north and south through Strathmore, guarding both the descent from the hills down through Strathmore, and the descent from the hills down Glengarry, was systematically dismantled and abandoned. And the abandonment of Inchtuthil meant Rome's abandonment of Scotland. There was a slow, contested, but definite Roman retreat. For a time Newstead and Dalswinton appear to have become the main northern Roman bases; then there was further retreat to the line of the Tyne and Solway.

Hadrian's Wall, begun along that line about 122 and completed about 128, was a definite attempt to protect Roman Britain from invasion and attack by the unconquered peoples of the north. It was a Roman frontier, a fortified boundary with a protected road providing a transverse means of communication; it served the double purpose of holding back attacks and of enabling the garrison to move freely in either direction; and it was akin to the Roman frontiers on the Danube and the Rhine. As finally built, the Wall was of ashlar, rubble-filled; its height, to the top of the parapet walk, was about 20 feet; its thickness averaged about 8 feet; and in front of it, to the north, ran a ditch some 15 feet deep, while the upcast from the ditch, thrown out to the north, made the drop even deeper still. With its sixteen large forts, milecastles at regular intervals interspaced with signal-towers or turrets, it was, and still is, a work of stupendous magnificence, eloquent of the ability and might of Rome.

But Hadrian's Wall was apparently too far from the real troublemakers of the north. Less than twenty years later, Lollius Urbicus (Governor of Britain under the Emperor Antoninus Pius), probably influenced by continuing pressure from the north, pushed the Roman arms once more up to the narrow line of the Forth-Clyde isthmus between 139 and 142, and completed a new wall—the Antonine Wall—by about 144. It ran, roughly, from Bo'ness to Old Kilpatrick. In contrast with Hadrian's Wall it was a turf wall erected on a stone pitching. It was about 10 feet high, 15 feet thick at its base, and 6 feet thick at its top, while to the north of it ran a ditch some 36 feet wide and 12 feet deep. Along its course were nineteen forts or garrison strong-points, smaller than those of Hadrian's Wall (that at Duntocher being only half an acre in size, and that at Rough Castle only one acre) and closer to one another for mutual support.[5]

In many respects the Antonine Wall was thus far less strong than Hadrian's Wall. Nevertheless it was intended to be a new permanent line and frontier. The route northwards was again partially opened up; Ardoch was once more occupied; and some twenty or more forts and fortlets were strung along a network of roads to the south. There is also evidence that the Hadrianic forts were held by smaller garrisons, which thus suggests that the tribes of the southern uplands were thought to be no longer dangerous. But the demands of the two walls, together with the demands of the forts to the rear of the Antonine Wall (like Newstead, guarding the important route through Lauderdale), were stretching to its utmost the Roman strength in north Britain.[6]

The new wall, admittedly, was only 37 miles long compared with the 70 miles' length of Hadrian's Wall; but, quite apart from its weaker constructional strength, the Antonine Wall could easily be turned by sea-borne landings (despite the protecting forts on both its flanks), its lines of support (and retreat) through the difficult country of the southern uplands were never good (despite the new Roman roads and forts), and, above all, the new frontier and a large proportion of the Roman forces in Britain were too far north with long and difficult lines of communication.

In about 154 a revolt of the Britons around Hadrian's Wall led to a hasty retreat from Antonine's Wall. There was certainly a reoccupation, the date of which has been the subject of much controversy: 158-63 seem to be the best favoured years, with the final abandonment attributable to that over-thin spreading of scarce resources already remarked.

By the end of the second century the land that is now Scotland was free of Roman arms. More than that, before 207, the Maeatae (north of the Antonine Wall) and the Caledonii (of the central Highlands), having overrun both walls, had joined the Brigantes and, pushing south, had taken part in the sack of York. The rising, however, was eventually crushed; the barbarians were driven back; and in 208 the Emperor Severus himself supervised the restoration of the Hadrianic line and, during the next two years, campaigned in Scotland, as far north as Agricola had done.

Both the Maeatae and the Caledonii were subdued. With the death of Severus at York, in 211 Hadrian's Wall was apparently accepted by Rome as her frontier line and the garrisons were withdrawn from Scotland, though long-range patrols still maintained a certain hold over the country to the immediate north. Yet the success of the Severan campaign was to be seen in the large number of village settlements which flourished in south-eastern Scotland in the third century and which were witness to a period of peace.

For almost 100 years the Hadrianic frontier apparently stayed secure. In 296-7, however, when garrisons of the Wall were taken away by a general seeking to set himself up as Emperor, the Hadrianic line was again broken; and this time we are told by a Roman writer of attacks by 'Picts and Irish [Scots]'. The Wall was repaired and rebuilt (about 305), and Constantius conducted a punitive expedition into the north much as Severus had done.

In 367, however, we are told of Picts sweeping over the Wall, of Scots attacking the west coast, and of Saxons landing in the south-east. Rome's conflict with the barbarians was becoming more difficult. It was no longer possible to man the Wall as of old, and the forts beyond it were never reoccupied. Instead the Romans appear to have tried to set up native buffer states, to take the first shock of attacks from the north. They formed a mobile fleet of light vessels (called *Pictae*), based on harbours in Wales and the west, to spot or even to engage the invading Scots from Ireland. But the attackers were too many and the defenders too few; and the Saxon raids grew more and more serious. The Roman forces, moreover, were again sadly depleted when, in 383, Magnus Maximus took many men from Britain to Gaul in an attempt to set himself up as Emperor. Once more the Wall was overrun, and this time the frontier was never restored. A Roman poet, Claudian, writing in 399 and 400, speaks of a Britain freed from the attacks of Picts, Scots, and Saxons in the first consulate of Stilicho; but, although Stilicho apparently took measures for the defence of Britain, it is doubtful how far Britain was defended north of the vale of York.

Thus, all in all, the Roman occupation of Britain hardly touched the land of modern Scotland. There were brief campaigns, such as those of Agricola and Severus; the land to the south of the Forth and Clyde was held for about fifteen years; but, when the Antonine Wall ceased to be the Roman frontier (before 200 and probably by 163), Scotland (apart from lower Annandale) fell completely outside the Roman province.

This period in Scottish history is largely the history of Scotland's separation from Rome by two frontier walls. Scotland lay beyond the frontier of a wide empire; and Rome's relations with Scotland were much like the relations of the British Empire with the tribes who lived beyond the north-west frontier of India. Scotland can have felt little of the cultural influence of Rome. It has been said, and with truth, that, even in that part of the Province of Britain which is now England, the Romans civilized the south but only occupied the north. In the south of England their occupation was marked by towns and villas and a civil government; in the north of England it was marked only by forts, camps, signal stations, and a military government.

The advent of the Roman legions possibly taught the peoples of Scotland something of new methods in the waging of war: though the very character of the Roman forts, and not merely the strength of Hadrian's Wall, indicates that those peoples had bravery and tenacity of purpose in the defence of their land and in their hatred of the newcomer. The Roman fort at Ardoch, in Strathallan (first built by Agricola, and the best preserved Roman fort in Scotland), eventually had an amazing series of banks and ditches (in some places seven deep) to guard its rampart; the rampart of the fort at Rough Castle, on the line of the Antonine Wall, was protected by a honeycomb of criss-crossed pits in which pointed stakes were concealed. Again, the expeditions of Agricola and Severus may have brought about the first beginnings of a new unity fashioned in alliance against a common foe—Tacitus states that at Mons Graupius, Calgacus was leading a 'confederacy of tribes'. The Maeatae and Caledonians, predecessors and ancestors of the Picts, were also confederacies, and there is some evidence that the third-century peace was bought by subsidizing friendly British states south of Antonine's Wall, and bribing unfriendly Pictish ones north of it.

A little of Rome's culture may have been acquired through trading contacts at the Wall and at posts held for a while, here and there, in advance of it. Roman wares found their way far north of Hadrian's Wall but the volume of trade must have been small and evidently was at its height in the second century; and there is no indication that the native people learned much of the Roman arts and crafts. Above all, however, it may be that the Christian work of Ninian (and possibly of others whose names have not come down to us) was facilitated by Roman stability in the Solway region; certainly the friendly contacts established between Rome and the Votadini (of the Merse and Lothian) secured stability in the east.

Only south of the Forth–Clyde isthmus was Scotland opened up by a system of Roman roads; unlike southern England, Scotland was never 'colonized'. Rome never touched the Highlands; and the Lowlands knew little of Rome apart from the strength of her defensive works and the might of the Roman arms. And yet, in a negative way, Rome may have left a different legacy unawares. Hadrian's Wall, holding until the close of the fourth century, protecting the 'Roman peace' of the south, and barring the onslaughts of the tribes from the north, was the first division between the peoples of one island.

Unfortunately the Roman historians and geographers tell us little of the people to the north of that division. Tacitus, throughout, calls them either *Britanni* or the people inhabiting *Caledonia*; but this does not necessarily mean that the people who, to Tacitus (or Agricola), were the *Britanni* of the north were the same people as the *Britanni* of the south. Ptolemy (about 150) gives the names of a number of tribes and of their strongholds, and places the *Caledonii* in the whole of the central Highland area. An account of the campaign of the Emperor Severus places the *Maeatae* close to a Wall (and since their name is preserved in place-names near Stirling, this would be Antonine's Wall) with the *Caledonii* beyond them. In the fourth century, however, we read of 'the Caledonians,

B

the Picts, and others', or of 'the Caledonians and other Picts'. But the name Caledonians disappears, and then the peoples of the north are called Picts.

NOTES

1. It is important to remember that both 'cultures' and 'ages' could flourish in different places at widely different times; and that, because of its remoteness and its difficult geography, Scotland was late in receiving new cultures and new developments. Even within the limited area of 'Scotland' we find, for example, that in Orkney men were still using stone when, in Lothian, men were using bronze.

2. In the caves at Allt-nan-Uamh, near Inchnadamph in Sutherland, were found fragments of a large number of antlers of reindeer, the bones of wolves, and the bones of bears comparable in size with the grizzly bears of North America. 'Caledonian bears', we are told, appeared in the arena at Rome.

3. By an examination of the bones found in 'middens' it is possible to tell whether an early settlement depended mainly for its food upon hunting or upon stock-raising. If the bones which predominate are, shall we say, the bones of deer and other wild animals, then we know that that settlement was mainly dependent upon hunting; if, on the other hand, the bones which predominate are those of cattle and sheep, then we know that that settlement depended for its food mainly upon stock-raising.

4. We now know that wood-ash is rich in potash, and the 'souring' of the felled wood released ammonia; all that neolithic man knew was that land so cleared yielded better grass and crops. The modern experiments in 'slash and burn' clearances have also shown that alder, hazel, and birch thrive on the cleared land, and from analyses of pollen in the peat bogs we know that oaks, lime, elm, and ash were succeeded by alder, birch, and hazel.

5. The fort at Cramond appears to have been built at this time to act as a supply base.

6. Some 16,000 to 20,000 men would be required for the two walls and the network of intervening forts; and, though it was contrary to Roman practice to use legionaries in front-line garrisons, there is evidence that some legionaries were being used.

CHAPTER 3

The Formation of the Kingdom

THE Venerable Bede, who died in 735, and who had spent his whole life at Wearmouth and Jarrow in 'the land of the Angles', closed his *Historia Ecclesiastica* with the year 731 and with this summary: 'The Picts are at this time at peace with the Angles; the Scots who inhabit Britain, satisfied with their own territories, meditate no hostilities against the Angles; the Britons, although in part they are their own masters, are elsewhere under subjection to the Angles.'

Here Bede refers to four different peoples—Picts, Scots, Britons, and Angles: and, although there were then no definite boundaries, we know that at this time these peoples occupied four separate regions—the Picts, descendants of differing iron-age invaders and of late-bronze-age peoples, in the land from the Forth to the Pentland Firth[1] (and probably also in Orkney, Shetland, and the Hebrides); the Scots in Dalriada or, roughly, modern Argyll; the Britons in Strathclyde, Cumbria, and Wales; and the Angles in Bernicia, the northern part of an Anglian kingdom stretching from the Humber to the Firth of Forth. Elsewhere Bede refers to these four peoples as four 'tongues'. This problem of language is full of difficulties. In the very broadest terms we may say that the Britons, the Scots, and the Picts spoke Celtic languages, whereas the Angles, a Germanic people, spoke a Teutonic language. The Britons spoke a Celtic which has become modern Welsh; the Scots spoke a Celtic which has become modern Gaelic and Irish; and these two dialects (called P-Celtic and Q-Celtic, respectively) may represent two separate Celtic immigrations from Europe in prehistoric times.

These four regions and their peoples were gradually united to form the kingdom of Scotland—though it should be noted that the regions of the Britons and the Angles stretched far down into modern England and that several centuries were to pass before a final boundary, short of the original southern limits of these two regions, was at last fixed and accepted to define the realm of Scotland from the realm of England.

As we have seen, the name Picts does not occur until the end of the third century when a Roman writer speaks of 'Picts and Irish [Scots]' attacking the Roman Wall. If, as we have suggested, the word meant to the Romans simply 'the painted people',[2] it would be an indication that the peoples of the north were still following the custom of painting their bodies at a time when that custom had died out in the south. Probably, too, the Romans used the word as a general term for all the peoples living in the land-mass of Scotland to the north of the Forth: and another Roman writer's phrase 'Caledones and other Picti' seems to show that the term was a collective one. The name 'Picts', however, passed into current use for the peoples of a Pictish kingdom which stretched northwards from the Forth. In Bede we read of 'northern Picts' and 'southern Picts', who, as we shall see, received Christianity at different times, and who, he tells us, were 'separated by a range of steep and desolate mountains', evidently the Mounth. If we take Bede literally their various provinces were by *c.* 700 ruled by or under one king; at best this may have been only a transitory overlordship,[3] though it would explain why the Picts defeated the Angles so decisively at Dunnichen in 685.

But the Irish annals speak of kings of Picts and of kings of Fortriu—which is the name of the most prominent province among the southern Picts and most probably synonymous with a southern Pictish kingdom. There is mention also of a king of Atholl, whom we can take to have been a provincial ruler like the Orcadian kinglet found at the hall of the northern Pictish king by Adomnan. One Pictish kingdom, or two, or many? Probably from the seventh century two, each with many provinces, divided by the Mounth, often warring and one occasionally reduced to clientage by the other. But if the truth be told we cannot be certain of much in Pictland after Bede wrote, and have perhaps read too much certainty about the Picts of his own time into what he wrote.

We rely for much of our knowledge upon lists of Pictish kings which do not always agree with each other, and which, moreover, are scarcely likely to disentangle matters, because they often give a king's name as 'A son of B'—and one thing we know about the Picts is that right to kingship did not pass from father to son. Indeed some of the fathers' names are identifiable as those of Anglian, Dalriadic, or British rulers. This Pictish law of succession, still in force in Bede's time, was unique in Europe, and may have been taken from some system practised by the late bronze-age peoples. Probably the system was matrilinear (that is, descent was reckoned through the mother); and, while the general principle appears to have been that a man became king-worthy because his mother (sometimes married outside Pictish kindreds) was the daughter of an earlier king, and that he was succeeded not by his son but by his mother's son (his brother) or by his sister's son (his nephew), the succession was also subject to choice,[4] probably, that is, to 'choice' of the most powerful and generous brother, cousin, or nephew of the deceased king. Pictish kingship is likely to have been at least as combative as any other in Europe, and we do indeed read in the brief annals kept at Iona of the slaying of kings and seizing and burning of duns, or hill-forts.

No Pictish literature has survived, but the Pictish sculptured stones—usually dressed slabs bearing designs in relief or rough pillars with designs incised[5]—are remarkable works of art. Certain of the designs like the 'V-rod and crescent', the 'pair of spectacles', the 'mirror and comb', and other symbols, are stereotyped; but other designs showing, in relief, warriors, huntsmen, and churchmen, are bold in execution and give us some idea of Pictish costume and armour.

The designs which have these scenes are also associated with a cross—either the simple Latin cross or the more elaborate Celtic cross—and have borders and divisions of intricate interlacing mesh and spiral patterns; they are generally thought to be later (eighth-tenth-century) than the stones which have only symbols (sixth-eighth-century).

The Scots, as we have seen, came from Ireland. Scotia was originally Ireland, and the inhabitants of Scotia were Scotti.[6] Possibly some of them, after helping the Picts against the Romans, decided to settle in the west, in Argyll; possibly at the invitation of the Britons of Strathclyde at first. The Scots of Dalriada in northern Ireland seem to have made a settlement in Argyll early in the fifth century; about 500 Domingart, son of Fergus son of Erc, was apparently king of the Scots of Dalriada in Ireland and Argyll, while in an annal of much later date a like position is accorded to his father.

This Scottish kingdom in Argyll came to be known as Dalriada; and at first it was closely associated with the Scots of Dalriada in Ireland. Fergus, we are told, 'with the people of Dalriada (in

Ireland), held part of Britain'. In strife with the Picts, it was firmly established by Columba[7] and by Aidan, who was made king of Dalriada by Columba about 574. The Scots had already made some penetrations eastwards into the fertile Midland Valley though these cannot have been permanent. Pushing southwards, however, they came into conflict with the Angles who, in turn, had been steadily pushing westwards into the land of the Britons.

The old name for Britain was Albion;[8] but, under the Romans, the name was Latinized to *Britannia* (Britain), the land of the *Britanni* or *Brittones*—the Britons. Then *Alba*, as opposed to *Britannia*, seems to have been used for the non-Romanized part of Britain north of the Roman Wall,[9] for, as we shall see, Alba was used for the united kingdom of the Picts and Scots north of the Forth-Clyde line, and it is now the Gaelic name for Scotland.

After the departure of the Romans, the Britons, apparently divided into various kingdoms, were gradually pushed westwards by invading Angles and Saxons until they held only the western part of Britain from the Clyde to Cornwall. Between 613 and 616, moreover, Ethelfrith, Anglian king of Northumbria, by a victory at the battle of Chester, drove the first wedge between the Britons of the north and the Britons of Wales.[10] A further advance of the Angles up the valley of the Tyne and down the valley of the Irthing not only ended the British kingdom around Carlisle, but made Galloway an Anglian province.

The main strong-point of the Britons of the north limited now to Strathclyde was Dumbarton, which in its British form was Alclut (the rock of the Clyde). Their kingdom of Strathclyde was strong enough to retain its separate identity and even for a period in the tenth century to extend its bounds again until the beginning of the eleventh century.[11]

The Angles, using the Humber as a river-base, moved northwards by sea, establishing themselves in such places as Bamburgh, St. Abb's Head, and Dunbar. Then, driving inland, they built up a kingdom of north-Humber (Northumbria) from the Humber to the Forth. Spreading westwards, the Angles were met by Aidan, king of the Scots, at the battle of (the unidentified) Degsastan in 603, where they gained a complete though costly victory. As a result they were able, during the following decades, to push into the land of the Britons (though not, apparently, into the land of the Scots), and to expand northwards, over the Forth. Eventually, however, they were heavily defeated in 685 by Brude, son of Bili, king of the Picts, at Nechtansmere, the modern Dunnichen, near Forfar, when not only was their northward penetration halted but also, owing to the heavy Anglian losses, their pressure upon the Scots and the Britons was reduced, and, although still powerful, their kingdom, in the words of Bede, thereafter had 'narrower bounds'.

The gradual union of these separate kingdoms with their fluctuating boundaries, and the formation of modern Scotland began about the year 843 when Kenneth MacAlpin, king of the Scots, became also king of Picts and, by crushing Pictish resistance during the period 843-50, firmly established his control over a kingdom of Alba.

How Kenneth MacAlpin gained the Pictish throne is difficult to understand, not least because our sources for this crucial episode are scarcely more than three lines of type in length. This was the last of many interpenetrations; more important, it was lastingly successful. Undoubtedly, however, the union of the Picts and Scots was facilitated by the attacks of the Scandinavians. The Picts may have been weakened through a heavy defeat which they suffered at the hands of the Danes in 839; the Scots may have received assistance from Ireland—and there are references to a continuing relationship and to a reinforcement (in 836) of 'Dalriada in Scotland'. Certainly the union became permanent in the face of a new danger. We are told of Viking raids on the Western Isles, beginning at the very end of the eighth century, but we must remember that our sources written in monasteries would dwell on pagan raids and ignore the settlements revealed by archaeology in lands similar to those left behind in Norway. Over-population on the west coast of Norway was undoubtedly the first cause of these new settlements overseas when they took and held Shetland and the Orkney Islands, Caithness, Sutherland,[12] part of Ross,[13] the Western Isles, and the Isle of Man; from these settlements they moved on to Iceland and Ireland, while Danish Vikings found the conditions they had left behind in establishing themselves in the north and the midlands of England. The Vikings had command of the sea; Scotland was surrounded and isolated.

It is uncertain why there were no Scandinavian settlements in the east of Britain between the Oykel and the Tees, between Sutherland and Yorkshire. Certainly Alba and Strathclyde were raided and churches there suffered heavily for they were known to be storehouses of treasures both secular and ecclesiastical and so were singled out for plundering.[14] But the armies which came did not stay to settle, and like Wessex in England, Alba survived the ninth century to take the offensive in the tenth. True the old link of Dalriada with Ireland was broken; and Scotland was cut off from southern England and the continent. The new kingdom of Alba would seem to have been thrown in upon itself.

Perhaps that kingdom had not included all the mainland Pictish provinces. The Norse occupied Caithness and Sutherland, and we cannot be sure of the standing of Ross, Moray, and Buchan after Kenneth MacAlpin became ruler of the Scots and (at least) the southern Picts. It does seem possible that in northern Pictland another Dalriadic family sometimes provided the provincial ruler, sometimes called *mormaer* (governor) sometimes 'king', of Moray. The degree of independence from the kings of Alba enjoyed by these rulers of Moray (who often had to fend off Norse attacks from the north) perhaps varied from time to time; it has even been claimed that there were two kingdoms, northern and southern, both in Pictish times and through the ninth and tenth centuries, and that the kings of Alba in fact ruled only south of the Mounth or perhaps the Spey. Our sources are scanty but it is certainly the case that in the eleventh century, when Cnut the Dane ousted the Anglo-Saxon royal house, Macbeth of Moray ousted the royal house of Alba. It is just possible that his reign was the real time of unification of northern and southern Alba—three or four hundred years after Bede would have us believe in a single Pictish kingdom. Most historians, however, would probably prefer to accept Kenneth MacAlpin and his successors as kings from Ross to Lothian, kings of a conglomeration of provinces each yielding tribute but some, notably Moray, rebelling, even seeking independence from time to time.

What we know of kingship in the Frankish realms or in England between the eighth century and the eleventh should warn us against expecting 'rules' of succession, say from father to eldest son, among the kings of contemporary Scotland. A king in those times must rule in person by a show of authority and wealth in ceaseless journeyings from one royal estate to another. We should certainly look for a royal kin or house, among whom the royal succession might be claimed by adults but scarcely by a child, and be made

effective by building up support among the magnates of the kingdom. Sometimes two of the royal kin, evenly balanced in following
and resources, might partition the kingdom, as apparently happened
in the late ninth century with Eochaid.

Unfortunately, though we know their dates (approximately) and
interrelationships, we know very little else about the early kings
of Scotland. The 'Lists of the Kings' show that, after Kenneth
MacAlpin until 878, the reigning king of Alba was succeeded by
his brother or his nephew but that thereafter kingship came to
alternate between two main collateral branches of the royal house.

Table 1

KINGS OF ALBA

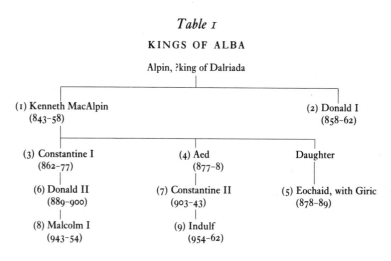

Since no king was succeeded by his brother (and some *must* have
had brothers) this order of succession was apparently known and
agreed: the senior collateral of the alternate branch could expect
to succeed as of right. There is no evidence of any formal election,
but the magnates would acclaim the new king in the ceremonies
attending his inauguration, upon the stone, a symbol of his 'marriage'
to the people of Alba. Not until the eleventh century did dynastic
faction and rivalry lead to insecurity and quick changes in succession
when a third royal line was added to the two alternates; now there
was competition. Moreover Malcolm II was apparently anxious
that Duncan, the son of his daughter, Bethoc, should succeed him.
This was something new, and contrary to custom. And, in his
endeavour to maintain the succession in his own line, Malcolm II

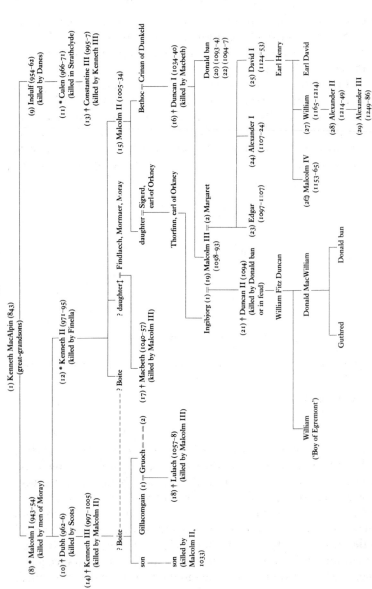

Table 2. SCOTTISH KINGS 943–1286

(1) Kenneth MacAlpin (843)
(great-grandsons)

(8) * Malcolm I (943–54) (killed by men of Moray)

(9) Indulf (954–62) (killed by Danes)

(10) † Dubh (962–6) (killed by Scots)

(12) * Kenneth II (971–95) (killed by Finella)

(11) * Culen (966–71) (killed in Strathclyde)

(14) † Kenneth III (997–1005) (killed by Malcolm II)

(13) † Constantine III (995–7) (killed by Kenneth III)

? Boite

? daughter† = Findlaech, Mormaer, Moray

(15) Malcolm II (1005–34)

? Boite ---------- ? daughter‡

Bethoc = Crinan of Dunkeld

daughter = Sigurd, earl of Orkney

Gillacomgain (1) = Gruoch = (2) (18) † Lulach (1057–8) (killed by Malcolm III)

(17) † Macbeth (1040–57) (killed by Malcolm III)

Thorfinn, earl of Orkney

(16) † Duncan I (1034–40) (killed by Macbeth)

son

son (killed by Malcolm II, 1033)

Ingibjorg (1) = (19) Malcolm III = (2) Margaret (1058–93)

Donald ban (20) (1093–4) (22) (1094–7)

(25) David I (1124–53)

(21) † Duncan II (1094) (killed by Donald ban or in feud)

(23) Edgar (1097–1107)

(24) Alexander I (1107–24)

Earl Henry

William Fitz Duncan

William ('Boy of Egremont')

Donald MacWilliam

Guthred   Donald ban

(26) Malcolm IV (1153–65)

(27) William (1165–1214)

Earl David

(28) Alexander II (1214–49)

(29) Alexander III (1249–86)

* Killed in feud, possibly in favour of his successor.
† Killed by his successor.
‡ The evidence that Macbeth's mother was of the royal house of Alba is late and may have been invented to explain his succession.

'removed' the grandson of Boite (Boite having been either his own brother or a son of Kenneth III), thus cutting out the male heir of the alternate line. But Boite had also a daughter, Gruoch, who had married, first, Gillacomgain, mormaer of Moray, and, secondly, Macbeth, whose father, Findlaech, had been mormaer of Moray, and who was Gillacomgain's cousin. These mormaers[15] of Moray were largely independent of the Scottish king—an independence helped by the barrier of the Mounth;[16] the Irish annalists accord them the title of *ri*, or 'king'; they could claim to be, and perhaps were, kings in their own right; and there was certainly an old feud between them and Malcolm II. Moreover, in Gruoch's two marriages there lay a definite danger that the 'House of Moray' might rule all Scotland, both north and south, unless Malcolm could secure the accession to the throne of Duncan who, through his mother's marriage to Crinan, abbot of Dunkeld, could count on the support of Atholl against Moray.

Duncan in due course succeeded his grandfather in 1034. But Macbeth had a claim to the throne which may well have been a double and a better claim—perhaps going back through his mother to Kenneth II, as well as through his wife to Kenneth III. More important, in 1040 Macbeth succeeded in killing Duncan, near Elgin, in the Moray country (whence doubtless Duncan was seeking to remove his rival), and thereby succeeded to the throne. All 'in the manner of the Scots', but made to appear wild and strange by Hector Boece,[17] and thence made famous by Shakespeare.

Macbeth appears to have ruled well. A reign of seventeen years is also indicative of a strong king; and he and his queen (Gruoch) were generous to the church. But in 1054 he was defeated, and in 1057 slain by Malcolm, son of Duncan I, near Lumphanan, in Mar (near the Moray country to which he may have retreated in the hope of finding support); and in 1058 Malcolm also slew Lulach, the son of Gillacomgain and Gruoch—again in the same northern region, in Strathbogie. He was called king but can have ruled only in northern Alba (perhaps the last of a long line of kings of Moray?). With his death, Malcolm, son of Duncan I, became king as Malcolm III, ruling as Macbeth had done the whole of Alba.

When the new kingdom of Alba was thrown in upon itself by the Viking incursions, it was also welded together as the armies of its various provinces were called out against the common foe. By contrast in the ninth century the kingdom of Mercia was wholly destroyed, and Northumbria fell apart as Norse chiefs from Ireland crossed by the Solway to York and established authority over the Danes already settled in Yorkshire. Galloway slipped from Anglian overlordship and the area between Clyde and Solway called Cumbria or Strathclyde, was the western equivalent of the rump of Anglian Northumbria, now an earldom only, between Tees and Forth. As the tenth-century kings of Wessex recovered strength and conquered the 'Danelaw' it became a question whether they would advance far enough and fast enough to keep the frontier of 'Angleland' at the Forth, or whether the kings of Alba would obtain by force or agreement some part of Northumbria.

As early as 937 King Athelstan had fought and won a mighty battle at Brunanburh against Constantine II, king of Alba, Owen, king of Strathclyde, and Olaf Godfrey's son, leader of the Norse in Dublin, who, fearing Athelstan's growing power, had combined against him. Yet the cost of such a victory was probably heavy, and Edmund, Athelstan's successor, thought it better to detach Alba from his enemies by an agreement.

In 945 Edmund of England, according to the Anglo-Saxon Chronicle, 'allowed' all Cumbria to Malcolm[18] on condition that Malcolm would be 'his helper on sea and land'. Of course Cumbria (Strathclyde) was not his to give, and to let its king become a client of Malcolm I of Alba was a small price to pay for making Alba an ally of England and not of the Danes.

This new policy may also have been continued in a similar arrangement for Lothian. We may trust an account contained in the *De Regibus Saxonicis* (written early in the twelfth century) that Edgar, king of England, gave Lothian to Kenneth II, king of Scots,[19] 'and with great honour sent him back to his own' for a glance at the map shows that if, after 945, the Scots had control of Cumbria or Strathclyde, Lothian was heavily outflanked and virtually untenable by England. Edinburgh was abandoned by Northumbria to Alba not long after 950. True this may not have been the final acquisition of Lothian; moreover 'Lothian' in 975 may have meant the land between the Forth and Lammermuir Hills only. And it is possible that all was lost to Alba if Malcolm II was soundly defeated at Durham in 1006, as our obscure and difficult sources suggest. But it is generally agreed that the battle of Carham (in 1018), when Malcolm II defeated a Northumbrian army, confirmed the Scottish hold on the land between the Forth and the Tweed.[20]

Note what has happened: the kings of England have abandoned to the Scots the most northerly part of Northumbria to maintain their hold on the rest. The ruler of a Celtic kingdom has brought under his sway a people of Anglo-Saxon speech and has abandoned the frontier which nature provided, the broad and stormy Firth of Forth and the impassable marshes of the River Forth, for a line which has no natural strength, no ethnic significance, but represents a balance of power only. If that balance tilted one way or the other, might not the frontier be shifted too?

About the same time as the battle of Carham, moreover, Owen king of Strathclyde died, and Malcolm II's grandson, Duncan, succeeded to Strathclyde (possibly through a dynastic connection) and became 'king of the Cumbrians'. We can be fairly sure that by this time the Solway was the southernmost limit of his kingdom and that Cumberland ('land of the Cumbrians') was no longer Cumbrian, but English, and loosely controlled by the earl of Northumbria. The memory, however, of a Cumbria stretching from the Clyde to the border of Westmorland remained, and even in the thirteenth century the bishop of Glasgow claimed all this for his diocese. When Duncan succeeded Malcolm II in 1034 and reigned as Duncan I, his kingdom included Pict-land, Scotland, Lothian, and Cumbria or Strathclyde—roughly the land of modern Scotland, though large tracts in the north, as well as Orkney, Shetland, and the Western Isles, were still held by the Scandinavians, and the boundary between Scotland and England, already drawn, had still to be confirmed by long usage and political stability.

Above all, these old kingdoms and peoples had yet to be fused together to form one kingdom and one people, under one law and one king. In the twelfth century the Scottish kings were addressing their charters to their faithful subjects, French, English, Scots, Welsh, and Galwegians—and even the order of address is important: for these different groups represent Anglo-Norman incomers, the Angles of Lothian, the (Picts and) Scots of Scotia (the old Alba), the British (Welsh) of Strathclyde, and the Galwegians[21] of the south-west. In 1305, for an English administration, the kingdom was divided into four regions, and while a little later we find the simple administrative division 'north of the Forth' and 'south of the Forth', in the south-west Galloway was for long a 'difficult' part. But steadily a strong central government, and more especially the feudal administration of the twelfth and thirteenth centuries, began to weld the different parts together; the organization and work of the church also helped towards unification. So the balance of power in Britain remained unaltered, habits of obedience to one king were accepted almost everywhere north and south of Forth, and a strong sense of community spread among the landowning class and even downwards among townsmen and peasantry. When the English sought to conquer Scotland, sense of community became a strong patriotic spirit.

NOTES

1. That is, the 'Pettaland', or 'Pictland Firth'.

2. Roman patrol-vessels in the fourth century were called *Pictae* presumably because they were camouflaged by being painted sea-green.

3. It is not correct to state that Bede calls Nechtan 'King of the Picts'. Bede writes in Latin, without a definite article and the title need be only 'King of Picts'.

4. This is stated by Bede.

5. The Pictish 'symbols' are also to be found occasionally on the walls of caves, and on small objects of stone, bone, and metal.

6. Above, p. 19. The first mention of Scots (*Scotti*) seems to be by Ammianus in the fourth century.

7. According to Bede, Columba came to preach to the northern Picts and received the island of Iona from their king, Brude, son of Maelchon.

8. A name which possibly goes back as far as the voyage of Himilco the Carthaginian (*c.* 500 B.C.) is used by Ptolemy (*c.* 150) and referred to by Bede.

9. So Drum Alban is the ridge or spine of Alba, the high mountains running north and south from Ben Hope in Sutherland to Ben Lomond. Breadalbane is the upland of Alba.

10. Even in the twelfth century the Britons of the north were still called the 'Welsh'—a word given to the Britons by the invading Anglo-Saxons and apparently meaning 'strangers'.

11. Above, p. 33.

12. Sutherland was so named because it was the land to the south of their first settlements in Caithness.

13. Apparently as far south as the Beauly Firth. Dingwall is an interesting place-name, derived from Thing-vollr, the field or meeting-place of the thing (the assembly of the people). Fortunately such relics as place-names cannot readily be transported from the place with which they are associated.

14. Such a secular treasure was found in recent years buried at the little chapel on St. Ninian's Isle, Shetland. It may be seen in Edinburgh.

15. For the office and dignity of mormaer, see below, pp. 52-3.

16. See above, p. 3.

17. See below, p. 309.

18. Great-grandson of Kenneth MacAlpin.

19. The 'gift' was therefore made between 971 and 975.

20. In Symeon of Durham's account of Carham, the Northumbrian army is said to have been composed of the people from the Tees to the Tweed, which suggests that Lothian was already held by the Scottish king.

21. The Gall-gháidhil, that is a mixed people drawn from Norse and Gael in the Western Isles or Ireland.

CHAPTER 4

Early Saints and the Early Church

IN the 1860s a visiting antiquary noticed that two stones serving as gate-posts at the graveyard of Kirkmadrine, Wigtownshire, bore at their heads, and within a circle, an equal-armed cross of which, in each case, one of the arms was also used to form the Greek letter ρ—a combination of chi and rho, the first two letters of *Christos*. Further examination revealed Latin inscriptions—on the one stone 'Here lie holy and worthy bishops, that is Viventius and Mavorius'; on the other, and unfortunately broken, '......s and Florentius'. At the very top of one stone were also cut the Greek letters α ET [ω]; while a third stone discovered in the same neighbourhood in 1916 also bore the chi-rho monogram and the words INITIUM ET FINIS, with the same meaning as α ET ω: the beginning and the end. The chi-rho monogram in various forms was widely used by the early Christians, and the design of the monogram cut on these Wigtownshire stones is found in use from the end of the fourth century to the middle of the sixth century.

The names of three of these bishops or priests, Viventius, Mavorius, and Florentius, have survived only on their gravestones; but Bede writes cautiously of another, Ninian, of the race of the Britons, 'a most reverend bishop . . . who had been regularly trained at Rome', whose church was named in honour of St. Martin, who converted the southern Picts, 'as they say', and built a church of stone, which was unusual among the Britons, at a place commonly called Candida Casa. The name of St. Martin takes us back again to the fifth century when the example of that great bishop of Tours in leaving the affluence of his city to take Christianity to the country-dwellers (*pagani*) had a profound influence among the Romanized Britons. So two bishops, Palladius and Patrick, went in turn to convert Ireland, and, founding on Bede's 'church of St. Martin', we may conjecture that a similar mission by an unknown bishop had gone to the furthest end of Galloway, perhaps to Kirkmadrine, to convert the Irish–Scots settled (as they surely must have) there.

In the same way there is evidence in Christian stones of an early mission in the Southern Uplands, with its church perhaps at Peebles; it would seek to convert the invading Angles, and a measure of its success may be the existence of a seventh-century Anglian bishopric at Abercorn and monastery at Melrose—places whose Celtic names may indicate continuity of the Christian church there.

Ninian still remains a shadowy figure; Bede's account of him may have been influenced by the acceptance by Nechtan, king of Picts, of the Roman calculation for Easter, and the wish to further the tradition of an early saint who had been 'regularly' trained 'at Rome', that is, perhaps, in Roman, not 'Celtic' usages. Ninian's work among the Southern Picts may have spread far or been limited to the shores of Forth and Tay estuaries where early Christian burials in stone coffins ('long-cist') are recorded. His church may have been St. Ninian's at Bannockburn, he may have worked about A.D. 500—these are conjectures; more certainly he returned to Galloway, built a stone church for his see in a formerly pagan cemetery at Whithorn (Candida Casa), and here in due course the conquering Northumbrian Angles maintained an episcopal see.

After Ninian we have traditions of other early Christian missionaries of whom we know little more than their names and possibly the areas of their work. St. Serf, a shadowy figure, associated with Culross and Lochleven, is linked in an untrustworthy twelfth-century Life with St. Kentigern or Cuno-tigern; a bishop of that name attended a synod at Paris about 565. The name Cuno-tigern,[1] meaning 'hound lord', betokens not only strength and fleetness but also aristocratic origins, and we can be fairly sure that Kentigern came from a distinguished Welsh or Cumbrian family. He may have been a bishop elsewhere before he came to the lower Clyde, probably to the British kingdom of Dumbarton, whose presumably Christian king and war-band had been upbraided by St. Patrick in the late fifth century for unchristian acts. The establishment of an episcopal see at Glasgow was doubtless Kentigern's work; he died in all likelihood about 612, and so was a contemporary of Columba.

The history of Christianity in Scotland does not begin with Columba, but with him our knowledge of it attains a new breadth and depth. For Columba came from Ireland, where the tribal structure of society had encouraged the development of monasteries, sometimes independent of each other, sometimes linked by having a common founder or by foundation of one from another and so forming a group or *paruchia*. Each had an abbot as its head, an office often filled from within the royal house of a tribe—and Columba was such a one. It is often said that the bishop was under the abbot's authority, but the bishop had sacramental functions— he had authority to ordain—and at Lindisfarne, of which we shall speak later, he delegated headship of the monastery to an abbot, a headship which he could well have retained. None the less in Ireland the diocesan episcopate was gradually subordinated to the spreading monastic organization. This Irish church thus differed from the Continental church in several ways. There was no central organization; indeed, there were many individual 'saints' who went out to preach or on pilgrimage—and a special secular and religious significance attached to pilgrimage overseas. If there was organization by dioceses it was rudimentary when compared with that of the Continental church; and there was no effective hierarchy, no organization similar to that which developed in the wider church under bishop, metropolitan, provincial council, pope, and general council. Moreover, the Irish church, like the Spanish and Gaulish churches, observed its own reckoning for the date of Easter; and its monks had their own form of tonsure. Yet all were within one Church, and the differences between them were far less than the common inheritance in orders, sacraments (including mass), and liturgies.

It was as a pilgrim overseas that Columba left political difficulties in Ireland about 563 to cross to Dalriada and there to found a monastery at Iona, which together with Derry and Durrow (we do not know if they were founded before or after Iona)[2] formed Columba's *paruchia*. Apart from what Bede tells us—and Bede was a master of the 'date of Easter' problem, who undoubtedly gave it far too much prominence in his version of events—we are fortunate in possessing a life of Columba written by Adomnan, himself an abbot of Iona, who appears to have used an earlier Life, and who died in 704. Although Adomnan's Life is an account of prophecies, miracles, and visions (all such works were similarly generous for they were written for the edification of the people and not as histories) the Life of Columba written within three generations of the saint is remarkable for the way it reflects the secular society of the seventh century as well as the splendid library available at Iona by 700. There is inevitably the danger that, because we know more of Columba through Adomnan's Life, he has been given a larger place than others in the history of the early church. Yet undoubtedly his work was great, and his labours gave to Christianity in Scotland a firm and lasting foundation; the importance of his achievement is shown, if by nothing else, by the earliest 'Irish' annals, which are now thought to have been first written down at Iona, beginning in Columba's lifetime, and continued there until the middle of the eighth century.

About the year 559 these annals record a flight of the Scots before Brude, Maelchon's son, king of Picts, and, according to Bede, after converting Brude, Columba received the island of Iona from him. According to Adomnan, however, some time after establishing his monastery in Iona Columba journeyed to Brude, by whom, after certain miracles in the name of God, he was honoured and revered. And it is noteworthy that after that visit there is little evidence of hostility between the Picts and the Scots until the early part of the eighth century though only Bede claims that Columba converted the northern Picts and Adomnan is almost careful not to say that Brude was baptized, whether by Columba or another. Again, in 574, when Conall, king of the Scots, died, Columba, claiming divine guidance, reluctantly ordained Aidan as king rather than Eoganan, Aidan's brother; and Aidan, as we have seen, apparently halted the advance of the Angles into the land of the Scots. Finally, in 575 Aidan crossed to Ireland with Columba where, in a 'conference of kings' he met Aed, king of the northern part of Ireland, in an endeavour to secure agreement on the relationship of the men of Irish Dalriada to the king of Ulster on the one hand and the king of Scottish Dalriada on the other. All the accounts of the meeting are late and obscure, but it would appear that friendly agreement was reached whereby the right to military hosting went to Aed who abandoned taxes and tributes (and with them effective government) to Aidan.

In these important political achievements, Columba's part may have been exaggerated. But Adomnan's Life tells us of his miracles in Skye and in the Great Glen as well as of the small monastic communities in the Isles which were added by him to the *paruchia* of Iona. Adomnan describes the life of Columba's monastery on Iona, within the broad delineation of the ditch and rampart or *vallum*. Columba's wooden-floored hut was his place of writing, of receiving a visitor, of teaching a novice—but its door was guarded by two servants, for Columba was a prince as well as an abbot. In the wooden church were said at least six of the daily 'hours' or services of the church. Although private mass is not mentioned, the Eucharist on Sundays and at Easter with communion were clearly celebrated. For their daily life the monks had a 'common house' also built of wood, doubtless a refectory, but also a place of teaching by the abbot. Little is said of the balance between work in the field and study, but it may be that the novitiate involved domestic and rural service of which the monk who had taken his vow (and the vow echoes that of the Benedictine monk) was free.

When Columba died in 597, the year of the arrival of Augustine (the missionary sent by Pope Gregory I) in Kent, Iona had become perhaps the most famous and most important monastery in the Irish church north of the Boyne. But its *paruchia* was to be yet more strikingly extended. In brief, under Oswald, king of Northumbria (635-43) who during the reign of Edwin had taken refuge in Iona,[3] and had there caught the fervour of the monks, Northumbria was regained for Christianity, and the monk Aidan, sent from Iona at Oswald's request as bishop, established his monastery at Lindisfarne. After the death of Oswald, Oswiu, his brother (who had also lived in exile at Iona), likewise furthered the work of the church. Indeed, missionaries sent out from Lindisfarne by Aidan and his successor, Finan (who also came from Iona), spread the truth through all the provinces of the Angles and from the Thames to the Forth, for the movement was both northwards and southwards. A monastery (a 'double monastery' with separate communities of men and women) was founded at Coldingham about 640 and placed under the superintendence of King Oswald's sister, Ebba; and from a monastery at Melrose (later called Old Melrose to distinguish it from the Cistercian Abbey built nearby), founded before 650, Cuthbert went on his missionary tours through the modern Lothian, the Border country, and even it seems to Fife.

And so the Irish-Northumbrian church contributed vitally to the extension of a Christian organization (which meant bishops) in southern England. The conflict over the date of observance of Easter, which was settled at Whitby in 664, arose because the southern English church followed one method of computation, that of Rome, which had been accepted by the southern Irish church in 631 and by the Spanish church in 634, while the northern Irish church and the *paruchia* of Iona-Lindisfarne, like some of the

Frankish church,[4] retained other computations. With the victory of the Roman party at Whitby in 664, Bishop Colman of Lindisfarne retired to Iona with some monks and thence to Ireland, the whole of which accepted the Roman Easter in the 680s. Thus, although Irish influence in the English and Frankish churches remained strong, the *paruchia* of Iona had again contracted and when Abbot Adomnan accepted the Roman usage (*c.* 680–700) he was unable to persuade his conservative monks, respectful of their elders' wisdom, to follow suit; the final conformity of Iona in 716 has probably been over-simplified.

It is necessary to consider briefly some curious features of the 'Irish', that is Iona, annals for the seventh century. For they tell us that Columba was not the only Irish saint who undertook a pilgrimage to the Isles. His contemporary, Moluag, established an abbey on Lismore which flourished in succeeding decades, while another later saint Maelrubha established his community at Applecross, with a cell (for his personal retreat) on an island in the loch now named after him, Maree. On Eigg St. Donan established what seems to have been a more individualistic or cenobitic group, which may have been the victim of a great massacre. Archaeology has revealed another monastic site in Kingarth on Bute. None of these was of Columba's *paruchia*, but they show the strength of the Irish-Dalriadic monastic movement at the period; and all were recorded at Iona.

Similarly recorded were some of the battles and sieges of Dalriada and Pictland, including the deaths of Pictish kings, and not a little about Northumbria, its kings, Bishop Aidan, and the withdrawal of Bishop Colman in 664. Yet among these many entries there is no word of a monastery or 'saint' in Pictland,[5] and it is reasonable to conclude that the *paruchia* of Iona did not include abbeys in Pictland. This is not to deny that Columba and his followers achieved many conversions and the establishment of churches among the Picts. It is indeed striking that the Picts were clearly provided with a strong caste of pagan seers or priests, and that in the area where Columba is known to have worked occur the earliest and best examples of the committal of Pictish symbols (inherited from the pagan past) to the Christian medium of an incised memorial stone. Near some may have stood the simple wooden churches of which we have many Irish or Ionan depictions. Nor is it to deny that others followed Columba, and that during the seventh century most of

Pictland was converted to Christianity, so that about 710 Nechtan, king of Picts, sent to Ceolfrith of Jarrow for 'exhortatory letters' by which he could confute 'those who presumed to observe Easter not at its proper time' and for builders who might make among his people a church of stone in the Roman manner.

But it is to question the generally accepted view that several or many Columban monasteries existed in Pictland, and that the monks were expelled by Nechtan in 717; that may have happened, although it surely mars the claim that churches later dedicated to Columba (for example Dunkeld, Deer) were Columban foundations. As an alternative we may accept the word of the annals and of Bede that in 716 Iona adopted the Roman Easter, and that the annal for 717 recording, after the death of Abbot Duncan who had led the acceptance, 'the expulsion of the *familia* of Iona across Drumalban by King Nechtan', referred not to an expulsion from Pictland but to an expulsion of some of the community under another abbot, Faelchu (elected in 716), *from Iona into Pictland*; Iona, it seems, suffered a schism. In 718 when 'the tonsure-crown was put upon the *familia* of Iona' this was the imposition of a final mark of conformity by the Romanizing Nechtan. A new abbot was chosen at Iona in 722, but when Faelchu died in 723 he too had a successor, so schism evidently continued. These were years of war among the rival tribes of Dalriada, in which, and at Iona, Nechtan could well have meddled; and his having done so would explain why his contemporary, Bede, chose to think (surely wrongly) that Columba had converted King Brude and been rewarded with a Pictish gift of Iona.

Amid the seeming aridity of the Easter dispute we should recall Bede's words, written in appreciation of Lindisfarne and the Irish-inspired monks—'The whole care of those teachers was to serve God, not the world; to feed the soul, and not the belly . . . If any priest happened to come into a village, the inhabitants flocked together to hear from him the word of life; for the priests and clergy went to the villages only to preach, to baptize, and to visit the sick: in brief, to care for souls.'

Finally, no account of the church of this period could be complete without paying tribute to the beauty of many of the manuscript books written by its monks. In these books, mainly copies of the four Gospels, in Latin, individual scribes devoted themselves to the joy of multiplying in loveliness the Word of God. One of the most beautiful of all those which have survived is the 'Book of Kells', which, despite some argument for a Pictish origin, was probably written in Iona. In the twelfth century Giraldus Cambrensis thought it so beautiful that it seemed to be 'rather the result of angelic than of human skill', and in the nineteenth century an archaeologist wrote that he had examined its ornamentation for hours together under a magnifying glass 'without ever detecting a false line or an irregular interlacement'.

The Book of Deer, a much later work of the eleventh century (and consisting only of parts of the Gospels of St. Matthew, St. Mark and St. Luke, the whole of the Gospel of St. John, a fragment of an Office for the Visitation of the Sick, and the Apostles' Creed), is poor and crude when compared with the Book of Kells in its ornamentation and workmanship: but the Book of Deer is important in another way. In its margins and blank spaces, and written in Gaelic, some time late in the eleventh century or early in the twelfth century, is the story of Columba's supposed foundation of the monastery at Deer in Aberdeenshire, followed by a number of entries noting various grants of lands and rights that were subsequently made to the monastery. These *notitiae*, or entries made 'for remembrance', are exceedingly valuable because of their references to early Celtic officers (like the *mormaer* and the *toiseach*) and to lay society.

We know that the beautiful manuscript books of the church were frequently kept in gold and silver shrines, rich in filigree work, and often set with precious stones. Unfortunately no such shrine has survived in Scotland.[6]

Other shrines, equally beautiful, were used to house sacred relics and, of these, one or two have fortunately been preserved. The most famous is the jewelled and enamelled Monymusk Reliquary[7] which, enshrining a relic of St. Columba, was known as the *Brecbennoch*. When borne by its keeper into battle, it was held to bring victory provided the cause was just, and it appears to have been so borne on the field of Bannockburn.[8] The only relic to survive today is the pastoral staff of St. Moluag of Lismore; it is shorn of all its medieval adornments, a plain wooden walking-stick.

In the middle of the eighth century we hear for the first time of an abbey, undoubtedly Pictish, at Kinrymond, 'the chief mound of the king', later called St. Andrews since a Pictish king had obtained for it relics of the saint, possibly from Northumbrian Hexham.

Other monasteries, notably Abernethy, claimed an origin in these centuries, doubtless with justification. At the same time we hear occasionally of bishops, at Abernethy (early eighth century), Dunkeld (865), Iona (712, and in the tenth century), Kingarth, St. Andrews (tenth century), and there were doubtless others in the Celtic north, as there were at Anglian Whithorn. During the Viking period the bishops of Glasgow may have moved their see to Hoddom in Dumfriesshire; other bishops doubtless fled hither and thither with their relics, as did the successors of St. Cuthbert from Lindisfarne, so that the bishops' sees of the twelfth century are found at other clerical centres—Brechin, Dunblane-Muthil, Mortlach, but not at Iona, Abernethy, or Kingarth. The emergence of dioceses is thus very obscure, but it is clear that these bishops, like those of Ireland and Wales, remained free from subjection one to another, save that Whithorn (and perhaps for a time Glasgow as well) owed obedience to the archbishop of York. Otherwise the Scottish Church was made up of bishoprics owning the authority of the pope in matters of faith and discipline—but doubtless controlled in effect by the Scottish king.

Early in the tenth century Columba was apparently regarded as the 'apostle' of the Scots, and his name was invoked in battle. Some verses which seem to belong to the time of Alexander I (1107-24) ask him to be 'sword and defence of the Scots'.[9] But by the twelfth century, and with the growth in importance of St. Andrews—with its priory and cathedral, and with its legend that St. Regulus (St. Rule) had brought thither certain relics of St. Andrew—and possibly also of the stronger influence of the church of Rome, the patron saint of the church at St. Andrews had become the patron saint of Scotland. Then, too, a white cross placed diagonally on a blue field (for St. Andrew was said to have been crucified on a *crux decussata*, X, known heraldically as a saltire) became the national flag.

NOTES

1. The diminutive of Cuno-tigern was Munghu (Mungo), 'my hound'.
2. Bede places the foundation of Durrow before Columba came to Dalriada; Adomnan seems to place it after that event.
3. Edwin had defeated and slain Ethelfrith, king of Northumbria, in 617. Ethelfrith's sons, including Oswald and Oswiu, had fled into exile, and Edwin

had ruled as king of Northumbria until 633, when he was killed in battle against Cadwallon and Penda. In 634, however, Oswald had slain Cadwallon and had become king of the whole of Northumbria, both Deira and Bernicia. In 642 Oswald was defeated and slain by Penda; but in 655 Penda was in turn defeated and slain by Oswiu, Oswald's brother, and Oswiu ruled over an again united Northumbria.

4. Until the 740s Iona was conservative; it was not 'cut-off'. There were 'Celtic' observances in Brittany in the early ninth century.

5. An exception may be Ithernan or Ethernan (associated with the Isle of May) and Corindu, who died among the Picts in 669.

6. A shrine containing a copy of the Gospels at one time lay on the high altar at St. Andrews. A number of Irish shrines are to be seen in the National Museum in Dublin.

7. Now in the National Museum of Antiquities of Scotland in Edinburgh.

8. Likewise beautiful, in their silver and gold, set with precious stones, were the casings made for the heads of pastoral staffs—that of St. Fillan, also in the National Museum of Antiquities of Scotland, being a lovely example.

9. *Ensis Scottorum et munimen eorum.*

CHAPTER 5

Early Society

IN the *History of the Men of Alba*, which seems to preserve in a tenth-century version fragments of a seventh-century account of Dalriada, we read of the three ruling kindreds (the *cenéla* of Oengus, Lorn, and Gabrán) to whom were attributed descent from the ruling house of Scottish Dalriada, and of the 'houses' from which they drew tribute. The *cenél* of Oengus 'divided land' in Islay, land which is listed in some eight districts of 20, 30, 60, or 120 houses; the *cenél* of Lorn had become three *cenéla*, the descendants of three of his sons, each named descendant having between 5 and 30 houses. Their districts are not named, but one of them, Baotan, seems to have had Morvern as his twenty houses, and to have 'divided land' there among his sons and their sons, for the medieval name for Morvern was Kinalbadon—the *cenél* of Baotan. Perhaps dependent upon Gabrán was his brother Comgall but by the early eighth century the latter's descendants or *cenél*, occupying the territory named from him Cowal, had thrown off this clientage, for the name 'Kethromecongal', the 'quarter of Comgal' shows that their land was now regarded as one of the *four* divisions of Dalriada. Thus a *cenél* was not only a kindred but also sometimes, perhaps always, a territorial division, a district or group of lands owned by men of common ancestry.

The *cenéla* of whom this text tells us were undoubtedly the aristocratic level of a society in which descent and kinship counted for much, but it was not a genteel eighteenth-century aristocracy of patronage. To belong to a *cenél* brought a share in the landed wealth of that kindred, but often only after struggle against others, even brothers, who sought the dependants, land, and stock of the kin. Success in these struggles doubtless explains the greater 'house' assessments of some descendants of Lorn—and from their number would probably come the head of the kindred, *ceann cineil*, certainly not by definition the eldest son of the eldest son and not necessarily the senior member of the *cenél*, but probably *a* senior member who was conspicuously able to maintain the interests of the kin in peace and war. We might imagine him a rough, tough ale-drinker, sword-girt, his woollen cloak fastened by an enamelled brooch fashioned by an expert jeweller from silver looted in distant raids with the kindred and their followers. His home in Dalriada would be a hill-top dun, a stone-built citadel perhaps some twenty metres in diameter; small rock-girt plateaux on the hillside might have their natural defences completed by walling to create subordinate fortifications for his clients and pounds for his wealth in cattle.

The *annals* of both Ireland and Northumbria show us how the kings and chiefs of those lands and of Dalriada and Pictland raided far and wide in their search for the moveable wealth of the late Roman and post-Roman world. It is in this context that we should see such expeditions as those ending in famous events like the battles of Degsastan and Nechtansmere, or the 'restitution' or 'buying-off' of 'Iudeu' (probably Stirling)—they were raids for weapons, coins, and other silver objects, and for cattle. It may be that sometimes there was also an intention to enforce political subjection: perhaps as the authority of kings over lesser chiefs became more effective by and in the eighth century this motive for expeditions became more important—a search not merely for booty now, but for continuing annual tribute, payable for the most part in livestock and other produce, but in precious metals also on occasion. The duns of Dalriada are not found in the same form in Pictland or Northumbria, but other forms of hill-forts are the equivalent, with ditch and rampart sometimes multiplied to enclose quite large areas with recognizable remains of huts for the dependants of the lord. Each of the peoples of later Scotland used defences appropriate to the geology of their region and patronized art-styles traditional to their origins in the personal ornaments whereby each man proclaimed his standing. But the peoples had in common a way of life in which warlike acquisitiveness was elevated into a code of behaviour with heroic virtues of bravery, loyalty, and generosity. The genesis of this way of life was the enormous wealth of the civilized Roman world, which in the fifth and sixth centuries lay ready for the taking by the stronger from the weaker. But as the weaker doubtless combined or submitted, the unit which would prey successfully must needs grow larger too—and so perhaps the development of kingships which enjoyed wider authority. They mastered the lesser *cenéla* in the seventh and eighth centuries, but to tame was not to abolish but to co-operate and to use.

For, if we return to the *History of the Men of Alba*, we find that it is concerned not only with kindreds and their descent but with the 'houses' which they owned and the number of men who might be produced for the army and the fleet from each group of houses. In other words, these are assessments for the rights of lordship (including kingship) and duties of clientage—rights and duties in war. They explain how the great raid of King Aidan to Degsastan was mounted, the king deriving a contingent of predictable size from each *cenél* or district according to the number of 'houses', the *cenél* making itself responsible, doubtless at the command of its chief, for the provision of the required men of military capacity, fitly armed and perhaps horsed—for swords, spears, and defensive armour were precious objects much repaired during their long lives.

The 'house' of the *History* was a notional rather than an actual settlement, for the *History* treats not of single, but of groups of five, twenty, thirty (and multiples thereof), 'houses'. Doubtless it was based upon what a real noble 'house' (perhaps dun) might command by way of men, arable, grazing, and stock, but it is probably a mistake to identify the twenty-house unit of the *History* with the later township (*baile*) of the Western seaboard, assessed at twenty houses, or the ounceland of twenty pennylands, for if there is an equivalence it is more likely to be of 'house' with township and ounceland. We should rather compare the 'house' with contemporary equivalents such as the Anglo-Saxon hide, a word which has the same ambiguity as 'house'—it is a family of parents and children and also its possessions. So Bede could describe Iona as having 'the land of five families' that is five hides. But the hide which would be used in Anglian Lothian was superseded by other units of assessment which took account of the continuous extension and rise in importance of arable cultivation (acre, oxgang, ploughgate) and then in the thirteenth century and later of money valuations (merkland, poundland). These changes were of far greater significance than the will-o'-the-wisp of equivalence between units of different periods—arguably the only continuity which is demonstrable from these assessments is that of counting in twenties or of dividing into twentieths.

It is certain that those of noble standing enjoyed the tribute and service of clients, but we have no Scottish evidence to set beside the Irish law books with their elaborate social hierarchies, placing men according to grade and status. Perhaps it is as well, for the division of clients into free and unfree commoners on the Irish model is fraught with difficulties, and any similar scheme would doubtless obscure the facts of economic life in which no two men, of whatever status, are exactly alike. There may have been free commoner clients. It is more likely that all who were free chose to regard themselves as noble members of a *cenél*, and that commoners were clients to whom a noble had given seed and stock in return for proportional tribute, service, and obedience enforced by the judgement of the noble. There would also be poorer men more heavily burdened, and slaves both domestic and agricultural.

The society of medieval Argyll was strongly pastoral, with limited areas of ploughed land; the same must have been true of earlier Dalriada and of the upland parts of neighbouring Lennox, and in both these areas the tribute of commoner or peasant to landlord continued to reflect this fact—tribute based upon the township (the men of which could divide the liability up according to cattle grazed) or upon the dwelling-house, each house yielding a penny or cheeses (a pastoral rent). For hill-grazing of varying quality cannot be assessed like ploughed land in a standard unit, and so the commoners' township or even the commoner's house was treated by the noble as the unit of payment of tribute, just as the king assessed his noble clients in round numbers of (noble) 'houses' —each 'house' being what a noble might be expected to own.

We have already indicated that the warring aspect of early society was widespread in the fifth–sixth centuries. It is faithfully reflected in an old Welsh poem about the heroes of the Gododdin in a great and disastrous expedition of 300 warriors against the Angles of Northumbria at some date not long before 600—warriors who fought bravely for their lord after feeding and drinking in his hall at Edinburgh, receiving generous gifts of bracelets from him, and thinking nothing more shameful for a man than to turn his back to the enemy. We may look at the Pictish symbol stones of a later age and see the warrior class depicted there too, though significantly now more often engaged in the hunt than in the fellowship of the war-band. But the Picts too must have known that fellowship for no people has left more striking examples of the personal ornaments —bracelets and great silver chains to mark wealth and lordship— of the heroic age. What can we say about other aspects of early society outside Dalriada?

Although we have no early sources to put beside the Dalriadic

History of the Men of Alba, much can be learned from the record of later times. Thus in Pictland a medieval unit of land assessment was the 'davach', that is 'tub' or 'vat', each—and sometimes fractions of a davach—having a name. It was a large area akin to the hide or later ploughgate but seems (from having a name) not to have been a measure of arable; it was perhaps a unit of pastoral production from which tribute in cheese was due. And food-tribute, it is now recognized, has left common traces in Wales, northern and western England (less distinctly in other parts of England), and Scotland, surviving into much-better-documented times, traces which can only be explained by a common early social organization. The regional names are different, but the institutions all take us back to a time of territorial lords or chiefs relying for their sustenance upon hospitality owed them by client landholders. This hospitality, known as 'wayting' from Humber to Forth, as *coinnmedh* or *conveth* north of Forth, was payable in produce of various kinds, probably with an increasing grain content, though even in the twelfth century Scone abbey took from each ploughgate 1 cow, 2 pigs, 10 hens, 200 eggs, 12 sheep, 10 bundles of candles, soap, and 20 half-measures[1] of cheese, as against 4 sacks of meal and 10 thraves of oats.[2] This was payable at All Saints, the end of the fruitful season, and at least on the royal estates the large quantities of produce rendered were accounted the hospitality of one night (from Fettercairn), two nights (from Forfar), and four nights (from Kinross). At one township in the Mearns we are first told how this ancient burden was distributed equally on each house (despite inequalities in the status of the occupants), which must produce 3 cheeses and 3 man-days' work at harvest along with service when required in the king's army. There was certainly arable here, but the relics of a predominantly pastoral economy are evident especially when the record goes on to explain how about 1200 a new lord expelled the peasantry, put plough to the land, and swept away the old order. When we see this due in the twelfth century, expansion of arable is in rapid progress; five centuries earlier a more exclusively pastoral character would be evident.

It is clear that many landlords lived in hall or house on the produce of the labour of unfree men dwelling in townships and subject to their lord's discipline, the hospitality dues from each township supporting a lord in his status. Throughout eastern Scotland it is possible to discern estates each of which was the share, *scir*, or shire

of a great man. These shires consisted of perhaps ten or more townships whose wayting or *conveth* was paid to one township (from
which the shire was named) to be consumed by the lord there.[3] In
many cases the names of shires are taken from places with early
names (e.g. *Aber-*) and sometimes a shire contains a church-name
in *Eccles-*, a form which seems to belong to the fifth-seventh
centuries. Here we have the territorial unit of exploitation which
sustained the king and the noble class throughout the dark centuries
from Roman times to the twelfth century. But there must have been
many more instances where a smaller landowner was sustained by
the *conveth* of one township or even of a part thereof, and had an
incentive to create new *conveth*-rendering settlements on pieces
of cleared land. Such new pieces seem to have given us the place-
names of Pictland beginning with Pit- (a word cognate with English
'bit', 'piece') but often ending with a Gaelic suffix and so belonging
to the ninth century or later.

Associated with the shire is the thane, like 'shire' a word of
Anglo-Saxon origin and unlikely to have entered Scotland as the
name for the king's or lord's manager of the shire until the ninth
century. From such humble beginnings the thane throve until in
the eleventh century he was often in effect the tenant of the shire,
responsible to the great lord for agreed *conveth*, but probably
collecting more from the shire's townships. A law code which seems
to belong to this period and said to be in use among 'the Brets and
Scots'—the Britons and Scots—is little more than a valuation roll
of society, each grade having appropriate *cro*, or blood money
payable in compensation for killing a person in that grade. Much
of it is unreal, but it is significant that the thane is by implication
a lord, with a *cro* of a hundred cows, while other grades have
multiples or fractions of that figure. His is the basic grade of noble
society—and probably the name of thane was now applied to many
who had no connection with the management of other men's shires.

It may be that in once Pictish Alba an alternative name for the
Anglian 'thane' was the Celtic *toiseach*. In the tantalizingly brief
and allusive notes (*notitiae*) of benefactions in the Book of Deer
we read of the *toiseach* of kindred (*clann*) of Cano and the *toiseach*
of the kindred of Morgann. This head of the kindred is surely a
synonym for the *ceann cineil*, head of kindred of western areas—
and the privileges of certain kindreds, notably those of Macduff,
persisted until the fourteenth century. In other societies the

kindred might be responsible for helping a man pursue someone
who had done him wrong, while the kindred of the wrongdoer
should compel him to make amends (according to a tariff such as
the Laws of Brets and Scots) or abandon him to the vengeance of the
victim's kin. Presumably the kin-groupings of early Scottish society
also fulfilled these functions. Moreover, when in 1256 the earldom
of Carrick passed to Earl Neil's daughter, Marjory, the office of
Earl was separated from headship of the kin ('kenkynnol', *ceann
cineil*) and the latter conferred on the countess's cousin, among
whose duties was leading the men of Carrick in war. As late as 1451
a royal charter confirmed to Gilbert Kennedy of Dunure the right
of being head of his kin (*caput progeniei* meaning the same as the
Gaelic *ceann cineil*), *together with the right of leading his kin in war
and judging in all matters touching his kin.* To these latter rights we
will return.

There is some evidence (albeit slight) from Galloway to suggest
that these chieftainships went from brother to brother and perhaps
even cousin before descending to sons; the reputation for fierceness
of medieval Galloway and of the Highlands till even later was perhaps as much due to feuds within a kindred for the headship (for
peaceful choice would probably be rare) as to feuds between
kindreds. More certainly we might surmise that every few generations a lineage would become so large that it would break, perhaps
not into fragments, but at least losing the remoter cousins who
would become a new *clann* in right of a more recent common
ancestor.

The *clann* of Cano or Morgan like the *cenél* of Baotan were clearly
kindreds of propertied men,[4] owning townships and having beneath
them free followers, serfs, and perhaps even slaves, over all of
whom the chief had rights of discipline. We might guess that the
free followers would claim (often unjustified) relationship with the
kindred but this guess would be based on the analogy of similar
societies elsewhere. Certainly the free followers would pay rent in
kind, *conveth*, to their lord, and similarly the members of the kindred
are likely to have paid *conveth* as tribute to the chief as a sign of his
lordship, for the land which they held would presumably be part
of the patrimony of their common ancestor.

In the *notitiae* of the Book of Deer we read too of the *mormaer* of
Buchan and the *mormaer* of Mar; now according to an early legend,
the Kingdom of Alba was divided into seven provinces—Angus,

Atholl, Strathearn, Fife, Mar, Moray, and Caithness—but there were undoubtedly provinces other than these (e.g. Menteith, Gowrie, Buchan, Ross) and 'seven' is only a conventional figure. Moreover, the evidence suggests that the *mormaer* was the head or governor of a province. The word means a 'great mair' or 'great steward', and the office may have arisen from arrangements made to meet the Norse attacks for it is not heard of before the ninth century. In the east we find *mormaers* of Moray, Buchan, Mar, and Angus; the Mearns means 'the Stewardship'; in the west we find a *mormaer* of Lennox; and Morvern is said to mean '*mormaer*'s land'. The office apparently became hereditary; and it is almost certain that, in some cases at least, there was a renaming in the twelfth century from *mormaer* and province to Celtic earl and Celtic earldom. Both *mormaer* and *toiseach* had dues from lands, as the Book of Deer makes clear, and the clergy of Deer were clearly anxious to escape from the dues of *mormaer* and *toiseach* alike: 'let them be exempt from all office of laymen and undue exaction' said David I's charter, clearly referring to the same burdens.

Fortunately, we can be fairly sure that the earl and before him the *mormaer* were responsible for calling out and leading the host within the earldom or province—that all propertied men owed military service with their followers in defence of the province and of the kingdom, led by the *mormaer*. It appears that under the *mormaer* each propertied man and his following gathered with his kindred, the lineage (*clann*, children) of a common ancestor (though at how many generations removed we do not know), under their *toiseach* or *ceann cineil* to make up a contingent in the provincial host.

This obligation of the followers of a noble kindred to army service was often linked in documents with *conveth* and indeed both were proportional to the amount of land held; it persisted throughout the history of medieval Scotland under names such as 'forinsec service' and '*feachd* and *sluagh*' and made possible not only the wars of Malcolm III, of 1136-8, 1173-4, and 1215-17 but also the long struggle for independence. But like *conveth* and the shire it was not unique to Scotland, but was well known elsewhere, for example as the fyrd of Anglo-Saxon England.

With this second widespread institution of army service we may perhaps link a third, known in Scotland simply as a 'due' *cain* or *can* payable in cattle and swine to the king from Galloway, Ayrshire, Renfrewshire, and Argyll; we should pause to consider why it does not appear in the heart of Strathclyde[5] nor in Lothian. These are exactly the provinces where we find in feudal times a widespread obligation to do castleguard duty, a form of knight service, while across the Border we have clear evidence that *cornage*, the equivalent of *can*, was a peasant obligation not imposed on those holding by knight service. Castleguard was probably introduced in the twelfth century in eastern lowland areas to replace the ancient British–Celtic due known as *commorth* in Wales, *cornage* or *noutgeld* in England, and *can* in parts of Scotland. Only the former Pictland (where the name *can* is found but apparently as a more general term for *conveth*) then stands outside this common obligation, which was enforced by fierce penalties, a fine of 100 cows, and was collected by royal agents called *mairs*, a title also found in Pictland and Wales, and undoubtedly an ancient borrowing from Latin. This tax was not wholly distinct from a hospitality due—the king might on occasion visit Ayrshire and consume his *can*—and it was not payable in every year from Galloway and Argyll which unlike Ayrshire had their own princes. Its origins are lost in the remote past: it may have been a due for rights of grazing; but it may be more closely connected with military service than we have suspected, for in Pictland the *mormaer* led the army from each province and would then enjoy this due to feed the army, while in Strathclyde David I, before becoming king, Fergus of Galloway, and Somerled of Argyll, each held a similar position, by which he would acquire a title to this levy.[6] Perhaps the link is most clearly provided in Lennox where there was a *mormaer* and where each house must pay cheeses —an attenuated form of *can* or *cornage*—as its service in the army. If we look back to early Dalriada we may surmise that the noble kindreds and free commoners warred and the unfree provided the food for their hosting.

Moreover, and fourthly, we find in these same regions of Britain that the *mair* (under various names) was responsible for policing the countryside by arresting suspects, making indictments, and executing on his own 'say-so' the thief and murderer caught in the act. To exercise these remarkably wide powers the *mair* was also entitled to hospitality from the townships when he made his rounds—and neither his duties nor his rights were popular. In former Pictland and even outside it the *toiseach dereth* (*dereth* has never been explained satisfactorily) is equated with the *mair* and clearly represents a relic of the same system of law enforcement which, although it is found in Northumberland, cannot be traced in Lothian. Whether we should link the rights of the *mair* (or serjeant or *toiseach dereth*) with the rights of the head of the kin is uncertain, but it is very likely that within the greater estates, the shires, the thane enjoyed those rights exercised elsewhere for the king by the *mair*, and so disciplined the churls and slaves of the townships.

Although we have stressed some elements which under different names were common to the societies of Scotland, northern England, and Wales, it must also be said that custom varied from district to district with many local laws. Law was not a written law; it was known to its hereditary holder and preserver, the *brehon* of the province, by memory and tradition. The *brehon* held the law 'in his breast', and he handed down to his 'pupil' his knowledge of what the law was. When a dispute was decided by a legal assembly (and not, as was probably often the case, by force of arms) the *brehon* 'declared' the law. He was thus the judgement-finder (*iudex*) in those disputes which were brought before him by the parties or the *mair*—and there is evidence that the court which he served employed ancient methods of proof to aid him in finding a just judgement: the testimony of witnesses, the oaths of compurgators,[7] the ordeal, and perhaps armed combat.

NOTES

1. Recalling the fact that half davachs were relatively common.

2. The passage is paralleled in remarkable fashion in a clause of the laws of Ine King of Wessex (688–726), and in the Welsh laws.

3. The shire is to be distinguished from the sheriffdom or county. There might be several or even many shires in a sheriffdom. But in a few cases, notably Kinross and Clackmannan, the modern sheriffdom does represent an early shire.

4. As were the Kennedys of Dunure.

5. Lanarkshire and Dumfriesshire.

6. Cf. the earl's third penny in England.

7. What we might call 'witnesses as to character' of the parties.

CHAPTER 6

The Consolidation of the Kingdom

UNTIL the eleventh century the boundary between Scotland and England was fluid and subject to change. There were 'English' settlements in 'Scottish' lands, and vice versa;[1] and changing allegiances might well result in changing spheres of influence. But the border line spoken of in the Treaty of Canterbury in 1189 had probably been already long recognized. A century and a half later, England was holding most of Scotland south of the Forth; and as a relic of that situation today the town of Berwick, although on the north bank of the Tweed, is still part of England, and Berwickshire was deprived of its ancient and natural 'head burgh'. From 1018 until the fourteenth century, however, it has been generally agreed that the eastern border held firm on the line of the Tweed and the Redden Burn. On the west matters are not so clear, as we shall shortly see.

Clearly if the new 'Kingdom of Scotland', which had been formed under Duncan I from the union of Pictland, Scotland, Lothian, and Strathclyde, was to expand, expansion could only be southwards; but although Malcolm III (1058-93, son of Duncan I), who succeeded to the throne after killing Macbeth and Lulach, made five invasions of northern England, he failed to extend the lands of his kingdom.

Malcolm's first wife, Ingibjorg, was a daughter of Thorfinn, earl of Orkney,[2] and a granddaughter of Earl Sigurd the Stout who had married a daughter of Malcolm II; his second wife, whom he married about 1070, was the Saxon Margaret, sister of Edgar the Atheling who had fled north after the Norman Conquest of England —an alliance with the legitimate royal house of England.[3] Both marriages were important. Malcolm may well have hoped that through his first marriage, and through his royal descent, his invasions of northern England would not be accompanied in his absence by trouble in any part of what was still a loosely knit 'Scotland'. In the north he was assured of the friendship of the Norse earls by his marriage to Ingibjorg; in the heart of Scotland, in Atholl, his grandfather, Crinan, had been abbot of Dunkeld; in the south-west his father, Duncan, had been 'king of the Cumbrians' before he became king of Scots, and Malcolm himself was known as 'the son of the king of the Cumbrians'. Through his second marriage into the English royal house, he doubtless counted upon some support in northern England from those who still opposed the Norman conqueror. Moreover, if Scotland was still a loose-knit kingdom, so was England. While William was still busy consolidating his hold on the south, could not Malcolm seize part of the north?

Even before the landing of William, however, and before Malcolm's marriage to Margaret, the Scottish king had invaded Northumbria in 1061: the Northumbria which had sheltered him during the reign of Macbeth, and whose earl, Siward (died 1055), had invaded Scotland on his behalf in 1054, and had fought for him against Macbeth, in a battle near Scone.[4] Tostig, Siward's successor in the earldom, and Malcolm's sworn brother, was absent on a pilgrimage to Rome, and Malcolm seized this opportunity to harry Northumbria far and wide; but he made no territorial gains. Again in 1070 Malcolm invaded northern England, this time on the west; but again there is no record of any territorial success, though an English chronicler writes mournfully that Malcolm drove away so many captives 'that even to this day there cannot be found a hamlet or even a hut [in Scotland] without slaves and handmaids of the English race'.

And now, probably in this same year, Malcolm married the Saxon Margaret, the sister of the Atheling, and his court became a refuge for all those who were at enmity with William. Moreover, in 1068 and 1069 William had had to face a series of risings in northern England (with at least one of which the Atheling was associated), and had finally harried and wasted Yorkshire so terribly that further revolt by the people there was well-nigh impossible. But the Atheling was still at Malcolm's court, and Malcolm was still a danger to stability in the north. Hence, in 1072, with a land army supported by a fleet, William invaded Scotland itself. According to the *Anglo-Saxon Chronicle*, Malcolm retreated before him until at last the two kings met at Abernethy, where they 'came to peace', and Malcolm became William's 'man', handing over his son Duncan as a hostage[5] —a clear indication that Duncan was accepted as Malcolm's legitimate first-born son.[6]

The peace thus secured at Abernethy lasted until 1079. Then, when William was absent in Normandy, fighting against his own son, Robert Curthose, Malcolm, 'unmindful of the treaty made between him and King William', broke their relationship and again invaded Northumbria, harrying the land as far as the Tyne. Moreover, in the spring of the following year a sudden revolt of the Northumbrians against the Norman administration of the earldom led to the massacre, at Gateshead, of the Bishop of Durham, his clerks, and all the knights and men who were with him—a massacre which William avenged, in the usual fashion, by the harrying and burning of the lands of those who had been involved.[7] Thus large tracts of northern England now lay waste and open to further invasion, and perhaps occupation, by the Scottish king. To prevent such a move, and also as an answer to Malcolm's raid, William, in the autumn of the same year (1080), sent an army under his son Robert Curthose (with whom he was now reconciled) against Scotland. But in the words of the chronicler Symeon of Durham, when Robert 'had come to Falkirk he returned without accomplishing anything, and founded a New Castle upon the river Tyne'. This New Castle, built upon the northern bank of the Tyne, was designed to strengthen the English defences in the north, for the land between the Tweed and the Tyne was still perhaps 'debatable land' or 'no-man's land'; certainly it was still a land coveted by the Scots.

In 1091 Malcolm III had again invaded Northumbria, at a time when William II (Rufus) was absent in Normandy, and had spoiled and harried as before. When Rufus heard of this he returned to England and marched north into Lothian where Malcolm was glad to make peace with him, becoming his 'man' as earlier he had become the 'man' of the Conqueror, while Rufus in turn promised that Malcolm should be received honourably in coming to the English court and especially should hold again all the manors in England he had held before, apparently as residences for his journeys.

And now we must face the problem of the Border on the west. Historians are agreed that the Northumbrian rule over Cumberland, Dumfriesshire, and Galloway apparent in Bede's day vanished in the tenth century under Norse–Irish attacks. By 1000 Strathclyde had pushed southward to the Solway and perhaps for a brief time even beyond it to Cumberland, but the evidence is uncertain. The title 'King of the Cumbrians' used of Duncan I in the eleventh century has been thought to refer to Cumberland. But the men of

Strathclyde were also called Cumbrians and our one piece of documentary evidence shows that the earls of English Northumbria had rule over the native lords of Cumberland in Duncan I's time. When Malcolm III ravaged Cumberland in 1070 it was certainly English, and the suggestions that Earl Siward took Cumberland from Macbeth, or that Malcolm III took it from Earl Tostig are alike lacking in authority. Cumberland was an appendage of the Northumbrian earldom during the eleventh century, and the Solway border was as old as the Tweed one, or almost so.

Historians have searched for a Scottish occupation because in 1092 the year after his treaty with Malcolm III Rufus, in the words of the *Anglo-Saxon Chronicle*, 'went north with a great army to Carlisle, and restored the town and built the castle . . . And he garrisoned the castle with his vassals', and thereafter sent many people there, with women and cattle, to dwell there and to till the land. But the *Chronicle* does not suggest that this was an anti-Scottish move; he seized Cumberland from its native lords and not from Malcolm III as is usually suggested. And when in the following year (1093) Rufus fell ill, 'in his sickness vowed many vows to God', and Malcolm sent to him, peaceably, to ask for the fulfilment of their 'late agreement', Malcolm was surely asking for the manors promised in 1091; for the 'late agreement' in no way refers to a supposed expulsion of Scots from Cumberland. Rufus summoned him to Gloucester, but when Malcolm arrived there Rufus had recovered from his illness and had revoked his vows. The English king would neither hold speech with Malcolm nor grant a fulfilment of their agreement. 'Therefore they parted in great enmity, and King Malcolm went home to Scotland', where 'he gathered his army and advanced into England', harrying with great wantonness, but only to be trapped, treacherously, by the river Alne and there killed with his eldest son.[8] And when, three days later, the news was brought to Margaret, Malcolm's queen, she 'was distressed even to death . . . and gave up her spirit'. Intermittently Malcolm had been the 'man' of the English king, his vassal, bound to serve and honour him, as the English king was bound to support and honour Malcolm. If we like to say so, the relationship was personal and not territorial, but the men of the eleventh century would understand us with difficulty.

By his marriage to Ingibjorg, Malcolm III had a son, Duncan; and by his second marriage six sons, whose names illustrate the influence which Queen Margaret had over him—Edward, the name of Margaret's father; Edmund, the name of her grandfather; Ethelred (her great-grandfather); Edgar (her great-great-grandfather); Alexander, perhaps named in honour of Pope Alexander II; and David, possibly named after David, the youngest son of Jesse.

Although Malcolm III had a long reign, when he was killed in England in 1093 the *Anglo-Saxon Chronicle* records that 'the Scots chose as king Donald, Malcolm's brother,[9] and drove out all the English who were with King Malcolm before'. Perhaps this was a preference for the old system of succession, though as we have seen it was rare for a king to be succeeded by his brother; more certainly it revealed a Celtic opposition to the English members of, and English influences in, the court of Malcolm and Margaret— and those influences may have included the concept of primogeniture, though succession in England before 1066 can hardly be said to show much regard for primogeniture. But although the Celtic opposition had chosen Donald to be king, Duncan, the son of Malcolm III and of Ingibjorg, marched north in 1094 with Anglo-Norman aid (he had been at the court of Rufus), claiming the throne as his by inheritance, that is, as Malcolm III's eldest son.[10] For a few months he was able to oust Donald and to reign as Duncan II, though the *Anglo-Saxon Chronicle* states that the Scots slew most of his followers and that he reigned 'on the condition that he should never again introduce English or French into the land'; and when there was again a Celtic reaction, Duncan was slain and Donald once more became king. In 1097, however, Edgar, the oldest surviving son of Malcolm and Margaret,[11] again with Anglo-Norman aid, marched north and, overthrowing Donald, ruled as king from 1097 to 1107, though William, son of Duncan II, undoubtedly had the better claim to the throne under a system of primogeniture.[12]

It has been suggested that Rufus gave support to Duncan II and to Edgar in an attempt to make royal amends to Malcolm III's sons for the killing of their father by Morel—'a deed so base and cruel that the king [Rufus] and his nobles were greatly aggrieved and utterly ashamed that it had been done by Normans'. Edgar, like Duncan II, had lived at the English court and, in anticipation and in hope of English aid, had accepted Rufus as his feudal superior for the kingdom of Scotland; and it seems to be clear that both Duncan II and Edgar were vassal kings.

Alexander I (1107-24), Edgar's brother and successor, had likewise frequented the English court and had married Sybilla, a natural daughter of Henry I. His feudal relationship to Henry I (who in 1100 had married Matilda, sister of Edgar and Alexander) is less clear, but it may be that as a feudal vassal he led a Scottish army to serve with Henry I in the Welsh campaign of 1114. Certainly Anglo-Norman influences, intermarriages between Anglo-Norman houses, and a feudal relationship between the kings of the two kingdoms were drawing Scotland and England closer together though still with uncertainty whether the days of raids and ravaging were over. In 1121 the bishop of Durham built a castle at Norham on the south bank of the Tweed as a weak spot for incursions 'upon the boundary of the kingdoms of the English and the Scots'. In 1133 Henry I procured the creation of a new diocese at Carlisle probably to end the claims to ecclesiastical authority there of the bishop of Glasgow—a relic of the distant days of Strathclyde rule. In such ways the Tweed-Solway border was consolidated and confirmed by the new feudal and ecclesiastical order.

It remains to be noted how the northern parts of the mainland, the Western Isles, and Orkney and Shetland were brought in to become parts of the kingdom of Scotland.

By an expedition in 1098 Magnus Barefoot, king of Norway, had strengthened the hold of the Norwegian king over Shetland, Orkney, the Western Isles, Anglesey, and Man. Entering into treaty with Edgar, king of Scots (1097-1107), Magnus secured formal acknowledgement of the Norse possession of the Isles, but apparently made no claim to Norse possession of Ross and Caithness (including Sutherland), though those parts still remained in Norse hands. Moreover the difficulties of communication and the ease with which the Norsemen could retire to Orkney and then return again for long precluded any effective Scottish control in the far north. By campaigns of 1179, 1196-7, and 1202, William the Lion strove to secure his authority there and built royal castles to maintain it, including Dunskaith and Redcastle to dominate the Cromarty and Beauly Firths. But not until the reign of James IV were these northern parts brought into something approaching control by the Scottish king.

Yet if the Scottish king had difficulty in maintaining his authority over the northern mainland, equally the king of Norway had difficulty in maintaining his authority over the distant Western

Isles, and the 'kings' there, although paying, when necessary, allegiance to the king of Norway, were virtually independent rulers. Then, in 1156, Somerled,[13] a 'kinglet' in Argyll, defeated Godfrey, the Irish-Norse king of the Western Isles and Man, in a bitterly contested sea-fight and thereby gained the whole of the Islands south of Ardnamurchan. Shortly afterwards he invaded the Isle of Man and routed Godfrey who fled to Norway. Somerled was now all-powerful in the West. Feeling himself strong enough to challenge the Scottish king (though we do not know the background), he led an army of men from Argyll, Kintyre, the Isles, and Ireland against Malcolm IV in 1164, but was defeated and slain near Renfrew.

The West, nevertheless, was still outside the control and sovereignty of the Scottish king. By a campaign in 1221 or 1222, Alexander II subjugated part of Argyll, probably Cowal and Kintyre, and secured the allegiance of the mainland chiefs, but in 1249, when he had assembled a fleet for an attempt to subdue the Isles, and had arrived at Kerrera, he was taken ill and died there. His successor, Alexander III, sent an embassy to Hakon, king of Norway, to negotiate for the cession of the Isles by purchase but the mission was unsuccessful. In 1262 the Scots invaded Skye, and Hakon was forced to a show of strength. In 1263 he assembled a large fleet[14] and sailed round the north of Scotland and down the west coast, to meet the challenge of the Scots. Anchoring off Arran (for he had a claim to Arran and Bute) he was drawn into negotiations by Alexander III—who was probably 'driving time' until he could assemble the Scottish host. Hakon had drawn up his fleet between the Cumbraes and Cunningham, by Largs, and was already short of supplies when struck by a storm on 1 and 2 October. A merchant ship driven ashore attracted a Norwegian foraging party which was attacked by the local men. Each side brought in reinforcements and in the end the Norse withdrew, and the Scots were glad to let them do so. Short of food, the battered expedition withdrew as best it could; and its leader, King Hakon, died in Orkney on the return voyage to Norway. Magnus, king of Man, threatened with invasion, now submitted to Alexander; a number of the Isles were invaded by the Scots and hostages taken; and Hakon's son and successor, Magnus IV of Norway, was able to persuade the Norwegian assembly that the Western Isles were of little value to Norway, that they were difficult to hold because of their remoteness, and that, if held, they were likely to be a constant cause of war. As a result, by the Treaty of Perth of 1266, the Western Isles and the Isle of Man[15] were ceded to Scotland in return for a payment of 4,000 merks[16] and an annual rent of 100 merks.[17] But, although the Western Isles had now become part of the kingdom of Scotland,[18] the chiefs of the Clan Dougall or MacDougall, in direct descent from Somerled, were powerful there until driven out by Bruce; while later the chiefs of Clan Donald, the Lords of Islay and then of the Isles, also in direct descent from Somerled, long enjoyed there a virtually independent authority. The Lordship of the Isles was brought to an end in the reign of James IV, but it was not until the Statutes and Band of Iona of the early years of the seventeenth century that the government began to have any effective control in those remote and almost inaccessible parts.

Finally Orkney and Shetland, of which Norway retained her sovereignty by the Treaty of Perth, became part of Scotland in an unusual way. By a treaty of 1468, which arranged for the marriage of James III to Margaret, daughter of Christian I, king of Denmark, Sweden, and Norway, not only was the annual 100 merks from the Western Isles finally extinguished but also Christian pledged and mortgaged the royal lands and rights in Orkney for payment of the greater part of Margaret's dowry; and in 1469 he further pledged Shetland for the greater part of the remainder.[19] The balance of the dowry was never paid, and the pledges were never redeemed. Then, in 1470, the earl of Orkney (William St. Clair) resigned the earl's lands and rights to James III in exchange for lands in Fife, and in 1472 the Scottish parliament annexed and united the earldom of Orkney and the lordship of Shetland to the Scottish crown. It is possible that Christian, like Magnus IV in 1266, realized the difficulties of holding Orkney and Shetland in view of a steady Scottish infiltration; and he may have had no intention of redeeming the pledge. Later, however, Denmark made several attempts to raise the question of redemption and the return of the islands—even as late as the middle of the eighteenth century—but always unsuccessfully. Today, the long Scottish occupancy and administration of Orkney and Shetland are held in international law to have created a British sovereignty *de jure* as well as *de facto*— a matter of some significance when the sea-bed and the riches thereunder are rouped to the highest bidder.

NOTES

1. The population of Cumbria in the eleventh century included Britons, Angles, Norse, and Scots; in Lothian there were Britons and Scots as well as Angles.

2. This marriage may have been contracted in an attempt to secure the friendship of the Norsemen in the northern parts of the mainland, possibly even to recover some of the territory which the Scottish crown is said to have lost to Thorfinn during the reign of Duncan I. Thorfinn and Duncan I, it should be noted, were both grandsons of Malcolm II.

3. It is true that the Atheling had been passed by on the death of Edward the Confessor—possibly because he was felt to be too weak, or too young—but upon the death of Harold at Hastings the Londoners at once chose the Atheling to be king; he was the direct descendant (grandson) of Edmund Ironside.

4. After this battle, moreover, Malcolm apparently ruled southern Scotland in independence of Macbeth.

5. Probably, too, under the terms there agreed, the Atheling had to leave Malcolm's court, for later he appears on record in Flanders.

6. Although Duncan was released, as a hostage, upon the death of William in 1087, he apparently remained at the English court until 1094 when he marched north to claim the Scottish throne following the death of his father in November 1093. (See p. 60.)

7. Here it is worthy of note that, had Malcolm III in 1079 wooed and not wasted Northumbria, an alliance between Malcolm and the north of England might have been too much for the resources of the Conqueror.

8. He was apparently killed by Morel of Bamburgh (a nephew of Robert de Mowbray, who was also present), an act which horrified contemporaries for Morel was Malcolm's 'gossip' or 'sworn brother'.

9. Shakespeare's Donaldbane.

10. In a charter granted by him to the monks of St. Cuthbert at Durham, when on his way north, he calls himself 'Dunecanus filius regis Malcolumb, constans hereditarie rex Scotie', that is, 'Duncan, son of King Malcolm, agreed to be the king of Scotland by inheritance'.

11. The eldest son Edward, who was with his father at Alnwick, was wounded there and died of his wounds; the second son Edmund appears to have ruled part of Scotland, south of the Forth and Clyde, jointly with his uncle Donald, 1094–7, an action of which he apparently repented for he 'entered religion' and died a monk; another son, Ethelred, became abbot of Dunkeld, an office his great-grandfather, Crinan, had held.

12. He was, however, a minor and was possibly regarded as the descendant of an illegal marriage. The near-contemporary William of Malmesbury, probably expressing the current ecclesiastical opinion, calls Duncan II 'base-born', i.e. illegitimate. Malcolm III and Ingibjorg were within the forbidden degrees of consanguinity and probably no dispensation to marry had been obtained from the pope.

13. The name Somerled appears to be a form of *sumarlidi*, 'summer rover', a name given to the Vikings who came over the North Sea in the early summer when the prevailing wind is usually from the east and who returned when the

prevailing wind had changed and blew from the south-west. But this Somerled belonged to a family settled for several generations in the Western Isles.

14. The Norwegian account, which is probably exaggerated, states that he had some 160 ships and 20,000 men, and that the king's own ship held 300 men—240 warriors and 60 oarsmen.

15. In the treaty the Western Isles and Isle of Man are called the Sudreys (that is, the Southern islands). The Nordreys, Orkney and Shetland, were still reserved to Norway. The old name, Sudreys, still survives in the title of the Bishop of Sodor and Man.

16. A merk was not a coin but a reckoning of value. It was two-thirds of a pound, that is, 13s. 4d. or 66p.

17. Which was often in arrears.

18. During the War of Independence the Isle of Man changed hands several times. In the period of Edward Balliol's attempt to wrest the crown from David II it fell once more into English hands, and thereafter the Scottish kings were apparently content to allow it to remain an English possession.

19. Margaret's dowry was to be 60,000 gold florins, and at first Christian agreed to pay 10,000 florins and pledged his lands and rights in Orkney for the remaining 50,000. Then, finding it impossible to pay the promised 10,000 florins, he agreed to pay 2,000 florins and pledged Shetland for the remaining 8,000.

CHAPTER 7

Kingship and the Kings of England

KING Edgar died, so far as we know unmarried, in 1107, and was succeeded by his brother, Alexander I. Alexander I died without lawful issue in 1124, and was succeeded by his brother, David I. These successions enabled the royal house to avoid conflict between the conflicting claims of a senior adult relation of the deceased king and his eldest son; both were successions of adult brothers; but in both cases the king had died without heirs of his body and thus, even under a system of primogeniture, the eldest surviving brother would succeed.

David I (1124–53), who, like his brothers, had spent much of his youth in England, by marriage became an English earl and so vassal of Henry I. In his reign the feudal subjection of the Scottish kings lapsed, and, for a time, the initiative passed to Scotland; for, with the death of Henry I in 1135, when Stephen was crowned as king of England, David seized the opportunity of conflict between Stephen and the Empress Matilda to press territorial claims. David had sworn to Henry I that he would support the Empress as the rightful successor to the English throne; but if the Empress Matilda, claimant to the English throne, was David's niece, so also was the other Matilda, Stephen's queen.

Yet in 1136, and before civil war broke out in England, David invaded the north and seized Carlisle and Newcastle—the two strategic strongholds on the west and the east. It is clear that in this move David was in no wise concerned with the position of either of his two nieces; his sole concern was to acquire the northern English counties, to which he had acquired a right through his queen (another Matilda) who was the daughter and eldest co-heiress of Waltheof (son of Earl Siward) at one time earl of Huntingdon and Northampton, at another earl of Northumbria; David had been given the midland earldom when he married Matilda, but now he pursued also his wife's claim to Northumbria.

Thus, when Stephen marched north against him, and the two kings met at Durham, their discussions appear to have been solely

Table 3. INTERMARRIAGE OF THE SCOTTISH AND ENGLISH ROYAL HOUSES

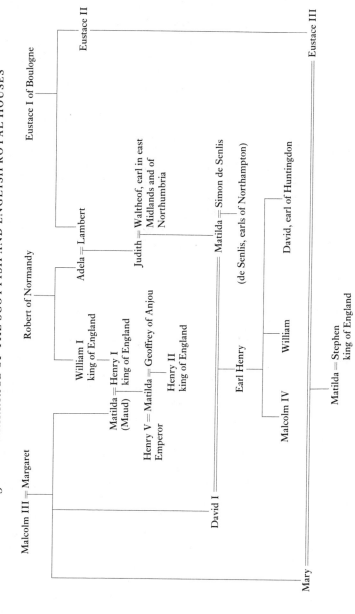

territorial. By their treaty at Durham (1136), David's son Henry was to hold Carlisle and the midland earldom (thereby David did not have to do homage to Stephen and so break his oath to support the Empress) and Henry's claim to Northumbria was to be taken into consideration by Stephen.

In 1137 Stephen's memory was jogged by another Scottish incursion and when that failed there was yet another in 1138, pressing southwards into Yorkshire. There, on Cowton Moor (near Northallerton), in a battle known as the 'Battle of the Standard',[1] David was decisively beaten by an army gathered together by Thurstan, archbishop of York. But Stephen was now preoccupied with civil war in southern England and in 1139, by a second treaty at Durham, David was able to secure terms of peace from Stephen which could hardly have been more favourable had he been victorious in the battle. By this new treaty Stephen granted to Henry, David's son (in addition to the midland earldom) the whole of Northumbria (except Newcastle and Bamburgh). He held it as an earldom of King Stephen whom he helped against the Empress. That David was as unscrupulous as other men of his time is made amply clear by his failure to give the Empress a jot of help until in 1141 she seemed to be winning. David hastened to her aid, and narrowly escaping from her débâcle at Winchester returned to Scotland with his son. They now had possession of Newcastle and Bamburgh but Henry had lost the midland earldom to Stephen; according to the near-contemporary chronicler, William of Newburgh, the whole of the north of England, as far as the river Tees, remained in peace and in the power of David, king of Scots. But while Henry ruled as Earl in Northumbria in the east, David kept Carlisle in his own hands, perhaps intending to annex it to Scotland.

Eight years later, in 1149, the whole question of the status of these northern lands was raised again, this time in a new agreement entered into between David and Henry of Anjou, the Empress Matilda's son. Henry took an oath that, 'if he became king of England, he would give to David Newcastle, and all Northumbria and would permit him and his heirs to possess in peace for ever and without counter-claim the whole land which lies between the rivers Tweed and Tyne'. In return for Scottish help, Henry of Anjou gave to the Scottish king rights over the modern county of Northumberland, apparently (though not certainly) to be held as an earldom in England. Our source says nothing of Cumberland and Westmorland which David also controlled; perhaps it understood these counties also to be part of the Northumbrian earldom.

Henry, son of David I and earl of Northumbria, is often said in charters to 'agree' to his father's grants; and in certain charters, of about the year 1145, Henry is styled 'designated king' (*rex designatus*). That style suggests that not only was the king's eldest son heir apparent according to primogeniture, but also that during the king's lifetime he had been formally recognized as such. Henry, however, died in 1152, predeceasing his father. And at once, according to the chroniclers, David took steps to ensure that Henry's eldest son—who was the heir apparent according to the law of primogeniture—should be accepted as his successor, perhaps in the same way as Henry had become 'designated' king. We read that David 'took forthwith his son's first-born, Malcolm, and giving to him as guardian Duncan, earl [of Fife], with a numerous army, commanded that this boy should be conducted round the provinces of Scotland, and proclaimed to be the heir to the kingdom'. And upon the death of his grandfather, in the following year (1153), this eleven-year-old boy, Malcolm, succeeded to the throne as Malcolm IV. It was no longer impossible to have a minor as king; and in the part played by Earl Duncan we may perhaps see the nomination of a 'guardian' or, as we would put it, a regent.

But in 1152 Earl Henry's second son, William, had become earl of Northumbria similarly at the instigation of David I. In 1154, Henry of Anjou, aged twenty-one, became king of England as Henry II; and he was to prove one of the most efficient of English kings, who was not slow to perceive that the power of Scotland under her boy-king Malcolm IV was vastly different from her power under David I. In 1157, by a treaty at Chester, Malcolm IV was induced (or perhaps compelled would be the better word) to resign the three counties of William's northern earldom in return for the grant to Malcolm of the midland earldom (of Huntingdon). This treaty of 1157 was a clear breach of Henry's oath taken in 1149, but then neither had King David fulfilled his part of that 1149 bargain, to help Henry against Stephen. Yet even the English chronicler, William of Newburgh, when recording the treaty, distinguishes between Malcolm's 'right' and Henry's 'might'.

King William, who succeeded his brother Malcolm IV in 1165, never forgot his lost birthright. In 1173, when Henry II's sons (urged on by Louis VII of France) rose in rebellion against their father, he entered into alliance with them (receiving in return from the young Henry, son of Henry II, a new grant of his earldom of Northumbria as far as the Tyne), and thereafter invaded the north as of old. While most of his army was plundering and harrying widely, both east and west, William, with part of his force, laid siege to Alnwick. No general, he was taken prisoner by an English force which, moving northwards in a thick mist, found the Scottish king in the open with only a few attendant knights (July 1174). Brought to Henry II at Northampton, 'with his feet shackled beneath the belly of his horse', William was taken to Normandy and imprisoned at Falaise; and, at Falaise, William concluded a treaty with Henry (December 1174) by which he secured his release only in return for an acknowledgement of Henry's feudal superiority over himself and his kingdom.

The terms of the treaty of Falaise were clear and unambiguous. William became the liege man of Henry II 'for Scotland and for all his other lands' (though he had lost the earldom of Huntingdon). More than that, the castles of Edinburgh, Stirling, Roxburgh, Jedburgh, and Berwick were to be placed at the disposal of England, to be held by England with English garrisons at Scottish expense, 'for the sure observance' of the treaty; only Edinburgh, Roxburgh, and Berwick were so occupied.

That complete feudal subjection lasted for fifteen years. Henry II died in July 1189; his son, Richard I, was crowned in September 1189; and Richard left England to join the third crusade in December 1189. For his crusade, however, Richard needed money. Accordingly, at Canterbury, a week before his departure, and in return for a promise of 10,000 merks of silver, Richard freed William from 'all compacts' which Henry had 'extorted by new charters and by his capture', and restored to him his castles of Berwick and Roxburgh.[2] This release, which is in the form of a feudal charter of quit-claim (that is, a charter whereby an overlord renounces some right previously held by him), definitely cancelled the humiliation of the treaty of Falaise. Scotland was once more a free and independent country.

One clause in the charter of quit-claim granted at Canterbury ran, 'And whatever our father [Henry II] has granted to King William aforesaid, we [Richard I] wish to support and confirm it'. Possibly relying upon this clause, William constantly strove to secure the return of the earldom of Northumbria—demanding the three northern counties as his earldom from both Richard I and John. But his demands even when accompanied by an offer of 15,000 merks were as constantly refused.

Richard's charter of 1189 was a statesmanlike move. He secured a friendly north during his long absence from England; indeed, friendly relations between Scotland and England continued throughout the whole of Richard's reign. William contributed 2,000 merks towards Richard's ransom, and he carried a sword of state before Richard at his second coronation in 1194.[3]

On the death of Richard in 1199 William might have supported the claim to the English throne of his great-nephew, Arthur of Brittany—but held his hand when John, Richard I's brother, promised to look into his claim to Northumbria. John became king, Arthur was murdered, yet John consistently refused William's claim to the northern counties though negotiations continued year by year. Finally in 1209, in despair, William seems to have turned again to an alliance with France; in a characteristic burst of energy, John advanced with a strong force to Norham to settle with William, including satisfaction for the destruction of his new castle at Tweedmouth which the Scots, regarding it as a threat to Berwick, had thrown down. At Norham the ageing William (who was now sixty-six), 'wishing to have peace rather than war', agreed to pay John 15,000 merks and to hand over two of his daughters, Margaret and Isabella, to be married to John's sons, Henry (later Henry III) and Richard;[4] the erection of a castle at Tweedmouth was to be abandoned. William also handed over some thirteen baronial hostages.

In 1212, 'for the knitting of a stronger bond of love', William's son Alexander was promised in marriage to the daughter, Joanna, born to John in 1210 and the two kings agreed to support the rightful succession in the other's realm—a promise which was surely aimed at the succession to the aged William.

There is no doubt that in all these terms William had humiliated himself and the reason seems to have been a written promise by John that the English lands of the Scottish king would always in future be held as a lordship by the heir to the Scottish throne, and a verbal promise to include the Northern counties in this lordship. But John had no intention of keeping this promise, and all William's sacrifices were in vain. Alexander II (1214-49), finding John still obdurate and unwilling to implement the agreements of 1209 and 1212, supported the English barons in their struggle against their king; in Magna Carta (1215) John agreed to do him 'right' in relation to his sisters and his other claims, and the barons tried to put this into effect by 'awarding' him the northern counties (as an earldom in England). But the pope released John from all his promises in Magna Carta and John harried and burned in Lothian to cow the Scottish king. Later, when Louis of France landed at Dover, Alexander marched south to join him, taking and holding Carlisle on his way; but, in the general settlement of 1217, he surrendered this, his only gain.

In 1221 Alexander II married Joanna, sister of Henry III, and friendly relations between Scotland and England were renewed by finding husbands for Alexander's two sisters, and promising a third sister, more of Henry III's age, as wife for him. But when in the 1230s Henry broke that undertaking and married elsewhere, Alexander II regarded the 1209 treaty as of no force. He demanded the northern earldom of three counties and the return of the 15,000 merks paid under the 1209 treaty. In the following year (1235) Alexander's third sister, Marjorie, was married to Gilbert, earl of Pembroke, the earl marshal of England, and a leader of the baronial opposition to Henry; and at one time it appeared as though Henry would have to face an alliance between Alexander, Llewelyn of North Wales, and a strong group of discontented lords. War, however, was avoided. Alexander and Henry met at York in September 1236, with apparently friendly results, and in 1237, again at York (and with the good offices of a papal legate, Otto, sent by Gregory IX to reconcile the differences of the two kings), a final peace was concluded between Scotland and England. By the treaty of York of 1237 Alexander II abandoned his claim to the counties of Northumberland, Cumberland, and Westmorland and to the return of the 15,000 merks and, in return, accepted from Henry 200 librates of land in the northern English counties,[5] to be held of the English king. Also, by the treaty, the two kingdoms returned to the relationship existing between them before the agreement of 1209.

The treaty of York, it is generally said, recognized the Tweed–Solway line as the line of the Border. It makes no mention of Tweed, Solway, or Border; the treaty of Falaise in 1174 (the earliest treaty between the countries of which a text survives) implies a recognized and established Border which is explicitly mentioned in grants by

Richard I to William the Lion in 1189 and 1194. It was almost two centuries old then, save that in the hills a few doubtful points remained; perambulations by mixed juries, under officials of the two countries, were held on rare occasions to determine the exact line of the boundary (though even in the sixteenth century, partly as a consequence of the Wars of Independence, there were still parts that were 'debatable'); and the administration of the Border was henceforth conducted by the sheriffs, and from the early fourteenth century by specially appointed Wardens of the two countries, under 'Border law and custom' which had many archaic features, and with special meetings ('Days of Trew' or 'Days of Truce') to hear and determine, by mixed juries, complaints of raiding, cattle-thieving, and so forth made by the borderers of either side. In contrast with the Welsh March, the Border was never defined by a series of systematic fortifications; but its line was recognized long before the treaty of York.

When Malcolm IV died, without issue, in 1165, and was succeeded by his brother William, there was no other who might challenge his accession save the distant descendants of Duncan II. When William died in 1214 he was succeeded by his only son, Alexander II who had been recognized as heir in 1201, and again by King William's deathbed; and when Alexander II died in 1249 he was succeeded by his only son Alexander III (although he was not yet eight years old). And now the custom of primogeniture had become so well established that in February 1284, when the king's only surviving son had died,[6] the magnates of the kingdom, perhaps reluctantly, acknowledged an infant girl, Margaret, the child of a daughter of Alexander III, to be heir to the kingdom if the king had no further issue. So firmly established was *male* primogeniture as the rule of the throne that the possibility of a king's daughter carrying kingship to her husband was cast aside by the Scots in 1195 when King William (at that time with daughters but no son) proposed it. And although it was apparently accepted in 1284, when the king died in 1286 other claims were quickly raised.

Opposition to the royal house was partly dynastic, in favour of the 'house of Moray' and the descendants of Ingibjorg, and directed against the sons of Malcolm and Margaret; and partly it was a Celtic opposition to the Anglo-Norman families, laws, and customs which the sons of Malcolm and Margaret were steadily introducing into Scotland, with 'a new nobility and a new social order', and with 'the charter instead of the pedigree, the feudal superior in place of the head of the kin'—all of which will be examined later.

There were risings against the house of Malcolm and Margaret in 1124, 1130, 1134, 1151, 1153, and 1156. Galloway rose against the king and against 'the English and French' in 1160 and 1174. And from 1181 to 1187 Donald MacWilliam, grandson of Duncan II, was a thorn in the side of William. According to Fordun, Donald MacWilliam 'aimed at the whole kingdom'; and, indeed, he could claim to have a better title to the throne as being descended from Malcolm III's first marriage, whereas William the Lion was descended only from the second marriage, with Margaret.

At last William, seeing 'that he must either lose the kingdom of Scotland or slay MacWilliam, or else drive him from the bounds of his kingdom', made a supreme effort, and Donald MacWilliam was eventually overthrown and slain near Inverness in 1187 at the hands of the lord of another Celtic province, Roland of Galloway. Again in 1211–12 there was trouble in the north, this time stirred up by Guthred, son of Donald MacWilliam, and apparently once more with support from some of the magnates; but Guthred was captured and 'hanged by the feet, after his head had been cut off', and, following royal practice, King William built further castles in the north in his attempt to hold it secure.

On the death of William, and the accession of Alexander II, there was further trouble in the north, this time led by Donald bán, another son of Donald MacWilliam, 'with a numerous band of malignants', but, according to the *Chronicle of Melrose*, 'Machen-tagar [Farquhar Maccintsacairt] attacked them, and mightily overthrew the king's enemies; and he cut off their heads, and presented them as new gifts to the new king. And because of this, the lord king appointed him a new knight'.[7] This is doubly interesting. It shows a Celtic leader in the north now on the side of the royal house descended from Malcolm and Margaret; and, because of his services, the Celtic leader is made a feudal knight. Thereafter, despite a rising in Badenoch–Lochaber in about 1228, there were no further serious internal challenges to the established royal line until 1286.

Moreover, after the treaty of York in 1237 peace and friendly relations between Scotland and England continued until the eve of the War of Independence, though crises and periods of strain were not unknown. In 1244 Alexander (thought to be in league with France) and Henry III faced one another, in arms, at the Border. But at Newcastle Alexander promised to make no alliance with Henry's foes and Henry agreed to give his daughter, Margaret, in marriage to Alexander's son, later Alexander III.

The marriage of Alexander III (1249–86) to Margaret took place in 1251 when Alexander was ten years old and Margaret eleven. For two years an ambitious baron, Alan Durward, had monopolized power; Henry III helped the Scottish barons to oust him and to set up a new council. Half-heartedly Henry claimed homage for Scotland from Alexander III and was strongly refused. But this time one family, the Comyns, gradually monopolized power and in 1255, on the argument that the queen, his daughter, was being treated dishonourably, Henry led an army to the Borders where, at Roxburgh, he was met by the lords of a moderate party of Scottish magnates who had seized and brought with them the king and queen. A council of regency, drawn from the moderate party, all too easily thought of as an 'English' party, was appointed by Henry himself; Alexander was given Henry's 'protection'; and it was announced by Henry, though not by Alexander, that any who opposed these arrangements would be regarded by Henry as rebels against his authority. Two years later, however, the Comyns and other lords who had been removed from office in 1255, and who, in the words of an English chronicler, formed a 'native and natural' party, fearing 'the dishonour of the king and of the kingdom', themselves seized the king, assembled their forces in arms to oppose Henry and his supporters in Scotland, and, in 1258, concluded an alliance with the Welsh (then in revolt against Henry) for mutual support and defence. But Henry III at this very juncture lost all power in England to *his* barons, while in Scotland Alexander III was now old enough to put an end to factious quarrels among his magnates. A compromise was reached, and a new council was appointed which contained representatives of all parties and which ruled until the king came of age at some date between 1259 and 1262.

The crises of 1251–8 have a special interest in that they show each group among the Scottish barons in turn seeking help from Henry III, whose behaviour, if sometimes ill-advised, was never malicious or unfair. If we survey the tensions between England and Scotland, which on three occasions (1136–9, 1173–4, and 1215–17) bred open war, it is surely apparent that the ambitions of the Scottish kings for territory or an earldom in northern England were the major cause of friction and of the humiliations of 1174 and 1209. It is also clear that Scotland, too weak in resources to compel the English king to yield, found a ready ally in the French king. The one threat which roused the English king to action against Scotland was a Franco-Scottish alliance, and among the anti-Scottish weapons in the English armoury was a claim to homage for Scotland. So long as the Scottish king remained benevolently neutral, the claim to homage lay dormant; when he moved in hostile fashion to secure 'his' northern English earldom, the claim to homage was brought out, and in 1174, was enforced. But these were moments of tension; for the most part the two kingdoms flourished together in the arts of peace during the twelfth and thirteenth centuries.

NOTES

1. The English army had in its midst a ship's mast upon which were hung a silver pyx and the banners of St. Peter of York, St. John of Beverley, and St. Wilfrid of Ripon.

2. These are the only two castles mentioned in the release. Edinburgh had been restored earlier, upon William's marriage to Ermengarde de Beaumont.

3. In 1194 the rights of the Scottish king to hospitality in coming to, and going from, the English court were defined by a charter of Richard I—a matter left over from the quit-claim of 1189. This charter mentions the Anglo-Scottish Border.

4. The 15,000 merks could thus be regarded as *maritagium*: a gift, usually of lands, made by a father to a daughter at the time of her marriage in order to help to support her in her new married estate. Henry was two years old, Richard a few months, in 1209.

5. That is, lands valued at £200 a year.

6. Alexander, who died in January 1284, aged twenty.

7. He was later created earl of Ross, and greatly assisted Alexander II in suppressing a rising in Galloway. His name means 'son of the priest' and he is thought to have been lord of the secularized Celtic monastery of Applecross.

CHAPTER 8

Feudal Scotland—I

D AV I D I, the youngest son of Malcolm III and Margaret, succeeded to the Scottish throne in 1124 when he was about forty-four years old. Much of his youth had been spent at the English court, and in 1113 he had been given in marriage Matilda, the widow of Simon de Senlis, and with her the midland earldom of Northampton-Huntingdon. Thus he had seen much of the central government of England under Henry I, and he had had experience of local government on his wife's vast estates. This new king at once strove to 'improve' his kingdom by establishing and developing the Anglo-Norman institutions and the Anglo-Norman system of central and local government which he had learned in England and had come to admire.

Before long, Anglo-French whom he had brought with him to Scotland (many of them from his Northamptonshire estates), or subsequently attracted north, were holding most of the important offices in church and state. To them, and to other Anglo-French, the king gave large extents of Scottish lands, with accompanying rights and duties. With a grant of land there went authority over every aspect of the lives of those living on the land. So, gradually, starting in Scotland south of Forth under David I, and spreading northwards under his grandsons, many free men in the south, in the Midland Valley, and in the eastern coastal plain, found themselves bound to serve new lords, their relationship with whom was bound up with the tenure of land. Indeed, under David I and his immediate successors, something very like a peaceful 'Norman conquest' of Scotland took place. A French-speaking aristocracy was established, which administered a new, precise, and orderly rule, and the greater part of Scotland was gradually knit together by a well-organized system of government similar to that of England under Henry II.

The essentials of Anglo-Norman feudalism were the 'fief' and 'vassalage'—the 'fief', a holding of land by a 'tenant' of a 'lord'; and 'vassalage', the rendering of 'fealty' or fidelity and appropriate services by the tenant to the lord in return for the enjoyment of his holding and also in return for his lord's protection. Moreover, because the tenant held his land 'of' his lord, he was subject to his lord's jurisdiction: his lord's court would hear actions touching the tenant or his holding.

The tenant, or vassal, however, might himself dispose of or 'subinfeudate'[1] part of his holding to a sub-tenant who would then acknowledge him as his lord; and that new tenant, in turn, might subinfeudate part of his holding. So a large fief might contain within it a number of smaller fiefs, some or all of which might contain smaller fiefs still. And at the same time a concept emerged that the king was lord of all the land and fountain of all justice. So, in the fief of Mow, we find Helen de Lindsay holding of her father, Simon de Lindsay, who held of Robert de Pollock, who held of Simon de Mauleverer, who held of the abbot and convent of Melrose, who held of the king. The lord who holds of the king is the king's tenant-in-chief, he holds 'direct'; the lord who holds of a tenant-in-chief is called a mesne (or intermediate) lord.

Going a stage further we may say that the king, in granting a fief to a great lord and making him one of his tenants-in-chief, has delegated, with the fief, part of his royal authority; the tenant-in-chief, in turn, in subinfeudating part of his fief, has likewise delegated part of his authority to a mesne lord. Behind such delegations lay the concept, 'I grant to you this part of *my* land to hold *of* me. You will keep it secure, and maintain law and order there, *for* me. In all this I will support you; and you can develop and improve the land and enjoy its fruits. But, as the holder of this part of *my* land, you must help *me* in battle, in my court, and with aid and counsel, whenever I call upon you to do so.' Moreover, in this relationship between 'lord' and 'man', so much depended upon the keeping of faith that often the tenant, in a solemn act on bended knees, with his hands placed between the hands of his lord, bound himself to be his lord's 'man' and to bear faith with him against all others—though, if his lord was not the king, with the saving clause, 'except the faith that I owe to the king'. This ceremony was known as homage. Less solemn was the oath of fealty (*fidelitas*). It might be taken at the time of homage, or taken alone. Here the tenant stood, with his hand on the gospels or on some sacred relic, and swore to bear faith to his lord, again with a saving clause if his lord was not the king. Fealty was considered to be less binding than homage;

in the oath of fealty the tenant did not bind himself to be his lord's 'man'.

Such a system of government and administration by delegation to local lords was an admirable one for holding down outlying (and possibly unruly) parts of the king's land, and for maintaining law and order there; and particularly so when there were no roads and when communications were slow and difficult. So we find it introduced to Badenoch and Ross in the thirteenth century. Moreover, for pacifying the land, the Normans had not only developed this new method of government by delegation, they had also evolved new methods of warfare[2] and a new art of castle-building—not the stone castle, which was still exceptional, but the *motte-and-bailey* castle: a wooden castle built on a raised mound and protected by a palisade and ditch—so that the lord with his castle could dominate his land.

Thus, at the very beginning of his reign, David I granted Annandale to Robert Bruce to be held with its castle (the motte of Annan) and with those customs which Ranulf Meschin had in Carlisle (i.e. in his lands in Cumberland). So, gradually, motte-and-bailey castles were built here and there over the land. Some were the king's castles, into which he put his own officers; some were the castles of his Anglo-Norman followers and friends to whom he had granted lands in those parts; but every castle was a strong-point for governing an area of land.

A grant of lands, moreover, was sometimes confirmed by a charter—a written document, on parchment, stating that the lands had been granted, with particular rights and for certain services therefrom, listing those who were witnesses to the charter confirming the grant, and authenticated with the grantor's seal. David I's charters are simpler than, for example, those of King William; but the charter soon takes a definite form, which with variations and extensions runs roughly, 'Know that I have given and granted, and by this charter confirmed, the land of X to A, to be held by him and his heirs, of me and my heirs, in return for the service of Y. These are the witnesses.'

Some charters grant land for the service which the historian regards as particularly characteristic of feudalism—the provision of one knight, an armoured horseman. For smaller holdings, the service might be the provision of half a knight or even one-twentieth part of a knight;[3] and sometimes we find the provision of a 'sergeant' on a horse, or an archer with a horse, or simply one archer. On the western coast-line we find feudal grants involving the service of a galley with rowers. Such service is called military service. A rule arose by about 1200 that the service should be rendered for only forty days in any one year: though in later medieval Scotland there are also frequent references to twenty days' service. In addition, land held on military service must pay feudal 'casualties' or 'incidents'—money payments which *may* arise. As a relic of the days in the history of feudal relationships (before they came to Scotland) when a fief was given to one man for his lifetime only, when the holder of the land dies, the land returns 'into the hands of the lord of whom the land is held', and the heir, if of age, must pay a 'relief' (usually a sum equal to one year's issues of the land) when he 'takes up the land again' (*re-levat*) out of the hands of his lord. If the heir is a minor, he becomes a 'ward' of the lord; the lord holds the land in 'wardship', providing a reasonable sustentation for the minor who, when he comes of age, takes up his land again. The lord has also a right of 'marriage'—a male heir who is still a minor, or an heiress of any age, can be disposed of by the lord in marriage to someone of his own choice, and he may make a profit thereby. If there is no heir at all, the lands 'escheat' into the hands of the lord, who again holds that which he or his ancestor had formerly given away.[4] Again, the fief held upon military service may be called upon to pay an 'aid' (*auxilium*)—a money payment to help the lord in his necessity; and this right was used in particular by the king to pay off the English after the 1189 and 1209 treaties. Finally, military service may include the provision of men to garrison the lord's castles, a service known as 'castle-guard'.

So far we have seen two closely associated movements: a migration of Anglo-French, and the adoption of that association of land tenure with military service which we call feudalism. Perhaps we should pause to point out that the families of native (Celtic) earls were not ousted by these newcomers but that gradually by intermarriage and in other ways they and some other families adopted Anglo-Norman ways and manners. At the same time we should put this 'feudalism' in its context. As we have seen there had long existed in Scotland a general duty upon all landed men to military service when required; but although it provided foot soldiers (the Scots at the battle of Largs were called the 'infantry of the countryside') some of whom were mounted to travel and even to fight, it did not provide the specially armed and mounted knight who was to warfare of the twelfth century what perhaps the tank was to that of the earlier twentieth century.

In short the twelfth century was a period of rising prosperity and population throughout Europe, and it was this economic expansion which sustained, among other things, advances in techniques of warfare and the arts of peace. An example of the first of these was the knight, his service, and his castle, an example of the second was the charter, and the growth of 'feudal' theory which, put into practice, was a system of protecting property-owning by peaceful means. The doctrine that *all* land was held as a fief created new feudal tenures; and since each lord must guarantee his tenants in the fiefs held of him, the doctrine that *all* land was held ultimately of the king demanded royal courts and royal justice for all disputes over land. And so the new prosperity also sustained a great increase in the scope of government.

The new tenures were for the most part old obligations given French or Latin names and written down in charters. Prayers became the usual service for lands that were granted to endow a church or a religious house. Sometimes the saying of certain masses was stipulated in the grant, but usually the lands were simply stated to be given to the church in free alms (in *frankalmoign*, or *in liberam elemosinam*), that is, for the return of no secular service at all. Lands once given to the church were given for ever for the church does not die (no relief is ever payable, and there is no possibility of escheat through lack of heirs); the church is never a minor (the lord can never enjoy the rights of wardship or marriage); the church does not break faith, or commit treason, whereby the lands can return to the lord through forfeiture. Because of all this, later kings, pressed for finance, regretted the pious generosity of their predecessors. The church held vast extents of land which rendered no tangible return and which could never be recovered. While the intangible returns were greatly valued, James I is said to have called David I a 'sair sanct for the croun'.

Again, lands might be held for service in some office: for acting, for example, as the king's high constable, or his cup-bearer; or, on a lord's estate, for acting as his bailie, or his smith. Or—and this was the most common obligation to survive from Celtic times— lands might be held for a render of food; commuted into a money-payment the land is said to be held in feu-ferme (it pays a *firma*, or rent, for the feu, or fief), which is a perpetual heritable holding,[5] as opposed to the tack, or lease, which is for a number of years only, probably also common but about which little is known since leases were rarely committed to parchment.

Lastly, and particularly after the later years of the reign of William, lands might be held of the king or of a lord for a token service only—such as 'rendering a rose in the season of roses', or 'paying one penny if it is asked for'. This is known as 'blenche-ferme' (*alba firma*) tenure. The token render, however small, still acknowledged the lord's superiority and hence his obligation to guarantee the tenant in his holding.

Thus we now recognize in feudal Scotland not just the men of French origin who were new, and knight service which was also new, but many other things which were a development of ancient and native institutions, albeit tricked out in new French or Latin names.

Thus tenants owed service to the lord's court. Known as 'suit of court', this entailed personal presence, or the provision of a fully qualified and accepted 'suitor', at the sittings of the court. The Latin word used for such suit clearly indicates the relationship of the lands to the court—suit is *secta*, from the verb *sequor*: the lands *follow* the court of the lord of whom they are held. Not only must actions relating to the lands, or to their holder, be heard in the lord's court, there to give his lord 'aid and counsel' both in judicial causes and in general matters of administration—for all feudal courts were both judicial and administrative. In the court itself it was the free tenants of the lord, the suitors of his court, who made judgement or gave decision. The judgement, or decision, was said to be that of the 'body of the court'; so judgement by the tenants in any action relating to a tenant is the judgement of his peers (*judicium parium*), the judgement of his equals in rank. But such functions and the attendance of such suitors were concentrated at three specially solemn meetings or 'head courts' in the year. At other (probably monthly) meetings the lord or his bailie settled disputes among his peasants (whose holdings would not be regarded as feudal), punished them for not using his mill or brew-house (where the lord took a profit), and enforced his right to a multitude of exactions from them, as well as dealing out heavy penalties for actual crimes. There is good reason to see in these latter functions something which would have been familiar to an eleventh-century Celtic landlord; on to this court the functions of a court of free-tenant suitors have newly been grafted.

The change-over from the Celtic organization to the new Norman feudalism was not only slow and gradual, but was essentially a compromise of new and old. Moreover the Celtic risings in the north and west in the twelfth and early thirteenth centuries[6] were, as we have seen, not solely dynastic; partly they were directed against the 'foreigners' who were displacing the Gael, and partly they were an endeavour to uphold the old order against the new. But as, one after another, the risings were defeated, motte-and-bailey castles were built,[7] and another part of the country was brought to the king's peace. In the south Anglo-Normans settled peacefully, but in the north and west they penetrated only with difficulty or against active resistance. Admittedly in the reign of William we find Celtic earls, the sons of Celtic earls, and native landholders in the north-east parts of 'Scotia' receiving from the king charters of infeftment of lands to be held for feudal services; but in the western highlands the new feudalism remained alien and largely unknown.

The importance of the Anglo-Normans whom David I introduced as administrators, officials, military leaders, and local governors is to be read in the royal charters themselves. In the lists of witnesses, French names, and often the same names, either appear alone or heavily predominate: that is to say, Anglo-Normans predominate among those who are around the king. Regularly we find as witnesses Gervase Ridel, Hugh de Moreville, Robert Corbet, Hugh Bret, Berengar Engaine—all from David's Northamptonshire estates. The Bruces, with vast estates in Yorkshire, were given Annandale; FitzAlans (of Breton origin) became Stewards (an honorific court office) and eventually established a royal line; and, somewhat later, the Balliols, with many manors in Durham, settled by intermarriage in Galloway.

Walter of Coventry, writing at the end of the thirteenth century and describing the overthrow in 1212 of Guthred, son of Donald MacWilliam, 'of the ancient line of Scottish kings',[8] tells us that 'the more recent kings of Scots profess themselves to be rather Frenchmen, both in race and in manners, language, and culture; and, after reducing the Scots to utter servitude, they admit only Frenchmen to their friendship and service'.[9] Here, 'utter servitude' may be an exaggeration, though with the many grants made to Anglo-Normans by David I, Malcolm IV, and William there must have been many dispossessions, of both lands and rights, about which the records are silent; and although Scots, like Duncan earl of Fife, and Malise earl of Strathearn, may have been 'admitted to friendship and service', the men who were around the king and gave him their 'aid and counsel' were mainly Anglo-French until, over the generations, the Scottish earls and lords themselves became as Normanized as the newcomers. About the middle of William's reign we find Fergus, Celtic earl of Buchan, granting three davochs of land, by charter, for the render of one archer and suit to the earl's head courts at Ellon, 'as any earl may freely infeft a vassal in Scotia'. His daughter married and took the earldom of Buchan to William Comyn (a family ultimately from one of the several French places called *Commines*).

But some compromise is still there. The Celtic earls for long remained the only 'earls'. Even the greatest and most important of the new Anglo-Normans were not given that dignity; and at first they acquired it only by intermarriage—as when the Comyns gained also the earldom of Menteith and the Bruces the earldom of Carrick.

Again turning to the evidence of the charters, we find in the reign of Robert I (1306–29), when feudal tenures become more regularly categorized, that a fief can be held of the king *in liberam baroniam*, or 'in free barony'. There was nothing new about this except the regularity and precision with which the phrase was used to denote certain rights and privileges enjoyed by a lord or now conferred upon him. A century earlier these rights were covered by the phrase 'with sake and soke, gallows and pit, and *infangandthef*'.[10] The lord whose fief has been 'erected' by the king into a 'free barony' (and only the king could create a barony) now definitely enjoyed *haute justice* ('top-quality judicial rights'), with 'pit and gallows'. His court could hear not merely the disputes which might arise between the lord and his tenants, or between the tenants themselves, relating to their holdings, to their services, and to their labouring of the lands; in its general maintenance of law and order, it could decide more than simple actions of assault with bloodshed (*bloodwite*) and of 'strife and trublance'. The court of a barony enjoyed a jurisdiction of 'life and limb'. The thief, the man-slayer, and often simply the 'unwanted general nuisance' could, by its sentence, be hanged or drowned; and no question would be asked, for it was the court of a barony.[11] Indeed, the king sometimes says in his charter that he has erected the lands into a barony 'for the maintenance of peace and to put down robbers'. In it the social and economic aspects of a feudal holding became more clearly defined. The lord had his mill, his brewery, his smithy—to all of which his tenants were 'thirled'. Just as they had to attend the lord's court, so they had to grind their corn at his mill (and pay 'multures' for the miller's work), so had they to take their iron-work to his smithy (and pay for the services of the smith). The lord might build a church, endow it with a holding of land, and appoint a priest; to it his tenants would pay their teinds and oblations; and barony and parish would tend to become identical. Later, when our records become fuller, we even find some lords exercising through their courts a paternal authority over their people: this young man (who has got into monetary difficulties) is ordered to cease playing at cards and dice; because of certain disorderly scenes, ale must not be sold to women unless they are in the company of their husbands.

More important, however, the greater lords soon obtained further rights and privileges from the king. Again in the reign of Robert I we have references to 'regalities'; and the regality, a holding *in liberam regalitatem*, or *in liberam regaliam*, was simply a barony with more extensive rights—regal rights, as its name implies. The lord of regality was virtually king in his own lands. The king's writ did not run in the regality; the king's officers had no right to enter its lands. The court of the regality had a jurisdiction virtually equal to that of the king himself: usually it could hear 'the pleas of the crown'; and only treason (a crime against the king and his rule) was excluded from its cognizance.

The complete independence and power of a lord of regality are aptly illustrated in 1320 when an official return recorded that 'de Vesci held Sprouston in Roxburghshire *regaliter*, by the same liberties and customs with which King Alexander III had held the lands of his kingdom; that de Vesci had the right to his own justiciary, his own chamberlain, his chancellor, his coroner, his sergeants, and also his standard measures in the manner of the said King Alexander'.[12] Such extensive rights, often held over extensive lands, descended heritably, with the lands, from father to son; whether they were effectively exercised is another matter: unfortunately our earliest record of the proceedings of such courts comes from about 1500 and shows that its business was over comparatively trifling matters. We may believe that there had been

D

shrinkage since the thirteenth century but it would be valuable to have evidence to confirm that belief.

Much of feudal Scottish society was but ancient institutions under new names. What was new about feudal Scotland? Anglo-French settlers, not very numerous but with a strong cultural tradition. Aspects of this tradition such as the emphasis upon tenure were, however, accepted because accompanied by a gradual transformation of the old hospitality dues into money rents; that transformation was brought about not by royal edict nor by the strength or superiority of a 'feudal *system*' which was largely invented by later lawyers and historians. It was brought about in the twelfth century by a rapid increase in population, in the demand for food, in the amount of land ploughed—in short, in the level of economic activity.

In the fertile land between the Forth and the Tweed we see most clearly the increased stress upon arable measured by the 'acre', an extent of land related to ploughing and the ploughteam, which originally may have been equivalent to 'one day's ploughing'.[13] Gradually, from Lothian, this new superficial measurement of land spread over those parts of Scotland where the land was fertile and where arable farming, as opposed to the raising of cattle and sheep, could be developed. Other land-measurements based upon the acre were all related to the plough and the ploughteam, and they indicate a system of agriculture, with related land-measurements, that was Anglo-Danish in origin and was common in northern and eastern England. That system eventually prevailed throughout Lowland Scotland until the middle of the eighteenth century.

So, in those parts of Scotland where arable prevailed, we find references to the ploughgate (Latin *carrucata*)—generally, though not necessarily, 104 acres[14]—an area of arable land which one ploughteam was supposed to be able to cope with each year. Probably, however, with the primitive ploughs then in use, a ploughteam would be able to work only about half that extent of land in any one year; and even in the middle of the eighteenth century, with better drained land and better tillage, but before the invention of Small's 'swing-plough', one plough could cope with only about 50 acres in one year. Thus, from the first, there may have been something like a 'two-field' system, each 'field', or half the ploughgate, being worked in alternate years; or there may have been an 'infield' and 'outfield' (or waste), with periodic intakes from the outfield as the infield became exhausted; but the evidence is insufficient to enable us to reach any definite conclusion, and there must have been many variations. Also the 'baulks' (or sometimes the ditches) and the 'head-dykes' (which, respectively, separated individual holdings and protected the ploughed land from invasion by the cattle) would considerably lessen the area actually ploughed and sown with crops.

The ploughgate, in turn, was divided into oxgangs (or oxgates, Latin *bovata*) and, in the south-east, into husbandlands. Some 8 oxgangs, of approximately 13 acres each,[15] formed 1 ploughgate; and 2 oxgangs formed 1 husbandland. Thus, if each oxgang provided an ox for the common plough, a ploughteam of 8 oxen[16] could be formed to work the plough, so also a team of men might be required to work it—1 man to hold the plough, 1 man to drive the oxen (usually walking backward in front of them), at least 1 man to walk beside the plough to help to guide it and to adjust the plough-beam, and probably even 1 man to ride upon the plough to help to keep it steady in the soil; though in easily worked soil we might find only 2 men—the 'halder' of the plough and the 'gadman', or goader of the oxen.

The arable was divided into strips, which were separated from each other by 'baulks' (or sometimes by ditches): to use a purely Scottish term, the arable was divided into 'rigs'. Apparently in early times these rigs were allocated among the different families or households of the village in such a way that no one household held two or more contiguous rigs. It may be that the rigs were allocated to the members of the ploughteams as the work proceeded from rood to rood; certainly, whatever the method of allocation, the good land appears to have been roughly apportioned among all the families in what were later called in Scotland 'runrig' holdings; but there is no evidence that an annual reallotment of the rigs was customary. Many rigs were assigned to particular tenements so that an oxgang or husbandland might consist of many scattered rigs, or, where a name was given to it, it might be one compact unit of adjacent rigs.

But although the stress was upon arable, the other land was not forgotten. So we find holdings like 'one ploughgate together with common pasture for twenty-four cattle and one hundred sheep'; or again, 'two oxgangs with sufficient pasture for four hundred sheep, sixteen cattle, two draught-horses, and twelve swine'. In the phraseology of the later charters, the arable was held with its 'pertinents'—that is, with wood and plain, pastures and hayfields, moor and marsh, fishings and peat-bogs—all necessary for the community: providing grazing and pasture for their sheep, horses, milk-cows, and plough-cattle, hay for winter feed, peat and dead wood for burning, thatch and green wood for building, pannage for their pigs, and so forth. The plough-oxen, indeed, consumed great quantities of fodder, so that one of the chief problems facing every community was that of trying to raise sufficient hay to feed the plough-cattle throughout the winter.

While it should be constantly borne in mind that ploughgates, husbandlands, and oxgangs were not definite measurements like those of our modern exact surveying, this stress upon arable, and the provision of ploughteams according to land-holding, meant that the men who provided the oxen for the common plough tended to live in compact groups of houses or villages. The village, with the arable surrounding it, was the heart of the settlement in Lothian. This emphasis upon extensive arable, as opposed to the emphasis upon grazing, distinguished the village from the early township; but, as arable farming, with the ploughgate, spread to the south-west, into the Midland Valley, and up the eastern coastal plain, the villages of Lothian became the later Scottish 'ferm touns'—farm townships of the Lowlands and elsewhere; and for long in Scotland a group of farm-steadings was called a 'toun'. With the introduction of feudalism, the barony might have many such 'ferm touns' for its many farms or ploughgates,[17] including a 'Milton' (where the mill was), a 'Kirkton' (where the church was), and the 'Mains' (the 'ferm toun' of the lord's demesne or domain).

In the Highlands, where grazing still predominated, such 'ferm touns' were less common, and the houses of a township were usually more scattered; but again, with the introduction of feudalism we find that the new feudal services might be based upon the old Celtic units, or might run side by side with old renders from houses and townships. So we find a davach[18] of land to be held for the service of one-tenth part of a knight; we find a render of 'the service which pertains to ten townships'; and there are continuing renders of 'two cheeses from each house in which cheese is made', and the payment of a silver penny 'from each house from which smoke comes', or 'from each fire-house'.[19]

In the Lowlands as in the Highlands, however, grazing was still for long reckoned according to the number of sheep or cattle it could support; usually only arable was measured and defined. Thus we frequently find such definitions as 'a ploughgate of land, measured and arable with common grazing'. When, in the reign of King William, Elena de Moreville gave to the abbey of Melrose part of the lands of the *villa* (or 'toun') of Gillebeccokestun,[20] she gave it with sufficient of the common pasture, pertaining to the same toun, for 700 sheep with their lambs up to 2 years old, 40 cows with their calves up to 2 years old, and 1 bull, 49 oxen, 8 horses, and 4 pigs with their young up to 3 years old. In the charter recording this gift we also see that, when boundaries were given, they were defined by natural features and that, when there were no suitable natural features, ditches were dug (*fossae factae ad divisas*) or boundary stones ('meith stones' or 'march stones'), often incised with a simple cross to stress their sanctity, were erected.

We have seen how the shires of Lowland Scotland were exploited by the great landlords (of whom the king was the greatest) as the men of each township or village paid their produce-rents to one place where the thane was responsible for its collection and supervision. At some of the centres of these estates the king had a larger-than-usual residence and so we hear of his 'festivities', his 'palaces', his 'killings', and of the waste products of his 'kitchen' at such places as Roxburgh, Edinburgh, Dunfermline, Stirling, and we can guess that there may have been similar residences at Scone or Perth, at Invergowrie or Longforgan, at Haddington and Linlithgow. In the thirteenth century the thane begins to *hold* his thanage and to pay a money rent for it instead of administering it on behalf of the king. He tends to be equated with the feudal tenant, and in the reign of David II the king converted many thanages into baronies.

In the thirteenth century, too, the unfreemen and perhaps the lesser freemen appear under various designations, such as *husbandi, bondi, cottarii, rustici*, and *nativi*. Of these, the *nativi* ('native' or 'born' unfree) could not leave their lord or their land. They were not slaves as we understand that term today; some of them undoubtedly had substance of their own, but they inherited unfree blood, 'went with the land' and could be sold with it, or given away with it. If a *nativus* fled he could be seized and brought back again to the land to which he belonged. When, in the records, we read of 'fugitives', these are not runaways, but *nativi* whose ownership was in dispute just as land could be in dispute. And so land could be granted with 'meadows, *men*, and pastures'. The 'men' undoubtedly worked the lord's land for him (in addition to paying rent for their own holdings) though we know little of the scale of such services until, in the later thirteenth century, we hear less of *nativi*, more of *husbandi* (with a house) and *cottars* with a humbler dwelling (or 'cot') both comprehended in the term *bondi* meaning 'peasants'. Like their predecessors the *nativi*, they held by no written title but only by right of paying rent in produce and work and by their lord's good will.

A rental of the abbey of Kelso describes the holding and working of the abbey's lands about the year 1300. There we find *husbandi* who pay a yearly rent of 6s. 8d., but who also render certain services to the abbey, such as five days' reaping in harvest-time, one day's carting of peats, the service of a man and a horse to bring corn, salt, or coal from Berwick once a week, and other tasks at the sheep-shearing and so forth. Sometimes, with his land, the husbandman received from the abbey the cattle and seed necessary for its cultivation. Certain husbandmen, for example, at one time received from Kelso with their land two oxen, a horse, three chalders[21] of oats, six bolls[22] of barley, and three bolls of wheat, and these, or their equivalent, would have to be returned to the abbey when the husbandman ceased to work that land; and such a system, including the provision of implements, can be traced at work as late as the second half of the eighteenth century, when it is known as 'steelbow tenure'. At least one tenant, moreover, no longer held at the will of his lord: he held half a ploughgate heritably and in perpetuity, paying an annual rent of 8s. but also still rendering services in plough-time and harvest. The *cottarii*, we find, held varying extents of land from one to nine acres, paying a varying money rent of 1–6s. a year, and rendering services which might amount to nine days' labour in the year. Whether or not these men were free to leave their holdings and their lord at this time (1300) is by no means certain but without doubt it was becoming easier for them to do so. One factor which made it easier was the lord's need for cash which he could raise by taking rents in place of services (and even produce-rents could be sold to feed the hungry towns) and by leasing out his own land, which he no longer had labour services to cultivate. When this has happened there is little left to be a mark of unfreedom, and by 1400 we hear no more of unfree men.

We know from the records in general that the chief crops were oats, and barley, and, south of Forth, wheat; peas and beans gave necessary protein and were much imported as well as grown. Ale was the common drink of the people, and the bishop or lord was already importing wine from France. Cheese was a staple food; meat and fish were plentiful; and there are many references to hens. But the dearth of hay and the absence of root crops (which did not appear until the agricultural improvements of the eighteenth century) meant that, if the plough-cattle were to be fed throughout the winter, most of the milk-cows would have to starve. Thus, with the approach of winter, cows would be killed and their carcases salted for winter food; this was usually done about Martinmas (11 November) and such salted carcases were known as 'marts'.[23] There was an abundance of wood and peat for fuel, and in the second half of the twelfth century the monks of Newbattle were already working the coal-seams near Dalkeith. Building was mainly of wood and, for humbler dwellings, of earth and turves. In one of the earliest Exchequer accounts there is a reference in 1287 to stone-masons at work 'building' the castle of Stirling, and, in another account, their work is spoken of as 'the new stone work'. But this was exceptional. When, for example, a 'new hall' was built for Alexander III at Kettins it was built of boards, and, for the same king, a Scottish house (*domus Scoticana*), built in the castle of Inverness, was likewise built of wood. On the other hand the royal castles of Kincardine, Kinclaven, and Tarbert were undoubtedly built in stone between 1200 and 1240.

With the multiplication of charters and other records we are no longer dependent upon stray references from which to draw tenuous conclusions. It is not simply the case that for the Celtic period record has perished while for the feudal period it has survived. Record, in the form of charters confirming the holding of lands, or in rolls for financial and judicial proceedings, was itself a part of the history of feudalism. And with the reign of David I, when the history of feudal Scotland begins, we come to know much more, not only about the organization of society and the lives of the people, but also about the working of local and central government.

NOTES

1. But he should not sell, give away, or otherwise alienate so much of his fief as to endanger the rendering of the services due from the whole fief to his lord.

2. They had developed the use of cavalry, of the sword and the lance, and of armour. Protected by a shirt of mail, wearing a conical iron helmet, and carrying a kite-shaped shield and a sword (a far more efficient weapon than the cumbrous two-handed battle-axe of the foot soldier), the Norman 'knight' (or armoured horseman) was vastly superior to his contemporary English or Scottish adversary. At Hastings the English fyrd fought mainly on foot and without any protective body-armour; at the battle of the Standard, the Galwegians charged 'naked'.

3. Which suggests a proportional money-payment towards the cost of one knight.

4. This applies even today, when estates for which no heir is known or can be found escheat to the crown. The national newspapers frequently carry advertisements running in the name of the Queen's and Lord Treasurer's Remembrancer and announcing that an estate left by a named deceased will escheat to the crown unless heirs come forward to claim it.

5. See below, pp. 254-5. So until 1974 practically all land in Scotland was held in feu, on a perpetual heritable tenure, in return for the payment of a feu-duty to the superior.

6. See above, pp. 73-4.

7. We have already noted how King William, after the defeat of Guthred, son of Donald MacWilliam, built castles in the north (*firmari fecit castella sua in Ros*) to hold it secure (above, pp. 61, 74).

8. Above, p. 30.

9. Walter of Coventry was writing of Malcolm IV and William, and it is to be noted that Jordan of Fantosme also wrote of William that he held only foreigners dear, and would never love his own people.

10. Meaning, in effect, a right to hold a court for his lands and, in his court, to try thieves caught with stolen goods in their possession which had been taken either inside or outside the lord's lands. This seems to have been the jurisdiction of the thane in the eleventh century.

11. Admittedly, as we shall see later, the king's sheriff was supposed to ensure that baronial jurisdiction was not abused; but, although a right of 'appeal' in civil causes from baron court to sheriff court long continued, in criminal causes the sheriff's supervision over the baron courts within his sheriffdom was apparently little exercised and soon ceased altogether (see below, p. 95).

12. The de Vesci family had led the opposition to King John of England. William de Vesci was married to an illegitimate daughter of William the Lion.

13. It is important to bear in mind that there was no exactness in early measurements. So-called acres were often smaller, and sometimes larger than the exact acre of modern surveying. 'A man's foot was still a foot, even though it might be only ten inches.'

14. We find ploughgates as small as 64 acres and as large as 160 acres. But a ploughgate of 104 acres is described in one of David I's charters; that was its 'official' extent; and that extent was finally laid down by the Scottish exchequer in 1585.

15. Again the size of the oxgang varied. In the rental of the priory of Colding-ham (1301) we find oxgangs of differing sizes between eight acres and fourteen acres.

16. Oxen were preferred to horses for the drawing of the plough (as, later, they were preferred for drawing the early guns) because of their steady plodding gait. But it should be noted that some ploughteams consisted of more than eight oxen, and that eight was merely a notional figure. The five 'ploughs' of Redden, belong-ing to the abbey of Kelso, had among them sixty oxen.

17. In the Strathmore rentals of the mid eighteenth century the separate farms were still called 'ploughgates', and individually they were from 80 to 85 acres in extent.

18. The davach is found north of Tay, as a measure of land sometimes equiva-lent to two ploughgates, sometimes to one ploughgate.

19. That is from each *inhabited* house. Later there are similar renders of 'reek [smoke] hens': 'from ilk fyir hous ane reick hen'.

20. This was the toun (an Anglian word) belonging to the 'devotee of St. Bethoc' whose name has a Celtic form. The place was in Peeblesshire, evidence of the various racial influences there. It has since disappeared in later (?sixteenth-eighteenth century) agricultural reorganization.

21. The chalder contained sixteen bolls (see the next note).

22. The boll, which contained four firlots, was a measure of capacity at one time equal to twelve gallons. In the reign of James I its capacity was fixed at eight and a half gallons; but local variations persisted—in 1649, for example, the boll in Dumfriesshire and Annandale was two and a half times the size of the Lin-lithgow boll.

23. *Mart* and *Martinmas* are etymologically unconnected, but the coincidence appears to have led to a kind of folk-etymology.

CHAPTER 9

Feudal Scotland—II

IN their endeavours to hold down the outlying parts of their kingdom, or, perhaps we should say, in their endeavours to weld the outlying parts to the king's authority, David I and his immediate successors did not rely upon grants of lands and powers to feudal lords. The king, too, had his halls and built his castles here and there throughout his kingdom; and into these he put his own officers to exploit his rights and revenues within their 'castle-areas' in his name. So, in the reign of David I we hear for the first time of a new royal officer, the sheriff (*vicecomes*), and, under his control and administered from a royal castle held by him, a castle-area which is called a sheriffdom (*vicecomitatus*) and which eventually became the county or shire, surviving with only slightly modified bounds until the reform of local government in 1975.

From the records it would appear that these new units of government, these sheriffdoms, were first established in Lothian, the midland valley, and the eastern coastal plain; those beyond the Don are not found until after 1200, those in the south-west after 1235; and as late as 1293 Skye, Lorne, and Kintyre were erected into sheriffdoms 'for the peace and stability of the kingdom'.[1] The reach of the sheriffdoms marked the reach of the new royal power. The king's castles, with sheriffdoms attached to them, held and administered by the king's sheriffs, were planted here and there throughout the kingdom just as trees are planted to hold firm a shifting soil. The sheriffdoms were new units for the government of the kingdom of Scotland; the estates of the king and the fiefs held of him were the units of the sheriffdoms.

The sheriff was the strong hand of the king in the localities; and his duties were all-embracing—financial and administrative, judicial and military. The sites of early sheriffs and their castles—Perth, Dunfermline, Stirling, Crail, Edinburgh, Roxburgh, and Berwick—are also the main royal residences, and we have seen that the king dwelt where he had estates rendering produce to feed his household. Sometimes we can see in Celtic Scotland that the very earliest sheriff was a thane of a royal estate under the new name. Even our earliest financial records, which are more than a century later than David I's time, show that in the 1260s while many thanages were leased for money, near to each royal castle there was often a thanage . paying food rents for which the sheriff was responsible, presumably to victual a royal visit to the castle.

The same accounts show that as a financial officer the sheriff collected all money and victual due to the king from the lands of sheriffdom—as rents, as feudal casualties, as escheats, and so forth—and, upon the king's instructions, he made out-payments. For all his ingatherings (his *charge*) and for all his outgoings (his *discharge*) he was expected to make account once a year in the king's exchequer. When special taxes were imposed,[2] the sheriff was usually made responsible for their collection.

From the evidence of charters of the thirteenth century, we know that he held a court in the name of the king for the whole area of the sheriffdom,[3] a court which had both a civil and a criminal jurisdiction. Suit was paid to his court by those who held their lands direct of the king within the sheriffdom and decisions made by lower courts within the sheriffdom could be reviewed, upon what we should now call appeal, by the court of the sheriff. In effect, the dissatisfied litigant could 'gainsay' or 'false' the doom of the baron court. In a later formula, he could denounce the doom as 'false, stinking, and rotten'; he could refuse to accept it, and thereby his case would come before the sheriff court, and the sheriff court, in its decision, would state whether the doom in the baron court had been 'well said' (the appeal failed) or had been 'evil given' (the appeal succeeded). The sheriff, or his sergeant, was also at first required to supervise baronial justice, and although this safeguard apparently soon lapsed, it does suggest to us how the sheriff's court may have had its origin in the twelfth century: the king remitted to this officer (whom he conceived of primarily as a manager of his estates and revenues) occasional cases, then frequent cases, arising from the inadequacy of baronial courts—for example, cases between the vassals of different lords (which obviously could not be heard in the court of either).

The king's castle, held by the sheriff, was the king's strong-point for that locality. At the time of Hakon's expedition of 1263, the records show that the sheriff of Inverness strengthened his castle with additional outworks, the sheriff of Dumfries put his castle in repair, additional watchmen were enlisted at Stirling Castle, and the sheriff of Ayr increased both his military stores and his garrison. When the host was called out, the sheriff was the leader of the men of the sheriffdom, a duty which he shared with the earl in Celtic Scotland and in parts of southern Scotland.

In his administrative capacity the sheriff executed every order sent to him by the king, and in due course many and varied duties were placed upon him by the king's council or parliament. By the end of the fifteenth century we find that he had to hunt 'the wolfe and the whelps', to destroy illegal fish-traps, to inspect weights and measures, to enforce sumptuary laws, to license beggars, and so forth. In addition he acted as the executive officer to the justiciar and the chamberlain when those royal officials visited his sheriffdom.

Counties existing till 1974, like Peebles, Selkirk, Roxburgh, Stirling, Aberdeen, Banff, Inverness, and so forth represent the old sheriffdoms; their names come from the royal castles (and from the burghs which, as we shall see, grew up beside them) which were the sheriffs' seats and from which the sheriffs exercised their authority. A few counties, like Sutherland, Ross, and Fife, are real counties, in the true sense of the word, taking their names from territories once held by an earl (*comes*). Kirkcudbright, exceptionally, was called a stewartry, a designation going back to 1369 when David II granted it to Archibald, later third earl of Douglas, and his heirs, who put in a 'steward' to administer the lands and to collect the revenues on his behalf.[4]

These many changes in the local government of Scotland accompanied many changes in the central government and in the administration of the law. In the early twelfth century, for the first time, we hear of the Chancellor, the Chamberlain, the Constable, the justice or (later) Justiciar, and so forth—with offices and duties adopted from the administration of England.

The Chancellor was the most responsible counsellor of the king and the keeper of the king's seal. At first one of his main duties was to examine every document carefully before it received the king's assent and validation—that is, before the king's seal was attached to it. Later, with the growth of government and an increased bureaucracy, the king's seal was called the 'Great Seal', to distinguish it from the 'Privy Seal' which appears on record late in the thirteenth century. In the middle of the fourteenth century we hear of the 'Signet', the king's 'ring seal', and, by the middle of the fifteenth century, there had emerged a whole system of warrants, and payments at each step, whereby, for example, a royal grant of lands had to 'pass' the Signet, and then the Privy Seal, before it could finally receive the appending of the Great Seal.

The Chamberlain was the chief financial officer of the king. He took his name from his duty to finance the king's 'chamber' which was the financial aspect of the itinerating household. It was also his duty to supervise the king's burghs (which were on the king's lands and which paid money rents to the king),[5] and, to carry out that duty, he went on circuit (he held an *ayre*, Latin *iter*) visiting the king's burghs to ensure that justice was being rightly administered, that each burgh's affairs were being well managed,[6] and, above all, that the king's revenue from his burghs was not suffering through fraud or maladministration. Theoretically the chamberlain went on this ayre round the king's burghs once a year, but practice often fell short of theory.

The Constable was responsible for maintaining peace in a wide area (called the 'verge') around the king's presence, and for guarding the door of the king's chamber. He had under him twenty-four 'doorwards' who took their stations at the king's door, and who rode before the king on his progress through his realm. The Marischal, on the other hand, maintained due order on the other side of the door—inside the king's hall and chamber. And the king, the constable, and the marischal might hold a 'court of chivalry': before them, a knight might defend his honour with his own hand by battle in the lists.

Again, by the mid thirteenth century, our fuller records show that the justiciars were itinerant officers providing, like the chamberlain, a close link between the centre and the localities. They travelled on ayre throughout the kingdom, moving from sheriffdom to sheriffdom, ensuring that each sheriff was efficiently carrying out his many duties and, in each sheriffdom, holding a court to hear appeals from the sheriff's court and also to hear those pleas, 'the pleas of the crown', which were regarded as so serious that they were reserved for them. These early records refer to several justiciars—for *Scotia*, for Lothian, for Galloway; but early in the fourteenth century there was a simple administrative arrangement of one justiciar for the sheriffdoms south of the Forth[7] and one justiciar for those north of the Forth. Theoretically, the justiciars went on ayre twice a year (in spring and autumn); but again intention was often better than practice, and in troublous times (and, following the outbreak of the War of Independence, the times were often troublous) the ayres tended to be few and infrequent. Nevertheless it cannot be too strongly stressed that the ayres of the chamberlain and the justiciars were of supreme importance: they ensured not only that the authority delegated by the king to his officers in the different parts of the realm was being rightly exercised, but also that the final authority was still the king's.

The king, however, like any other feudal lord, could call upon his tenants to render suit and service to his court. And the tenants-in-chief whom the king called to give him 'aid and counsel', together with the officers whom we have named,[8] formed the king's court (*curia regis*). This court of the king, like any other feudal court, was both judicial and administrative. The court of a feudal lord was concerned not only with justice but also with the well-being and orderly government of the people on his lands; and, in the case of the king, the lands were the kingdom.

As we have seen, this new administration brings in its train the concept that the king is lord of all the land and fountain of all justice. So, should there be a failure of heirs, the lands will return to the king; should there be a failure of justice, the plea will be heard by the king. Not only does the king reserve his own royal justice should there be a lack of justice in the court of the feudal lord, but by the thirteenth century we find there is a pyramid of appeal which rises from the baron court to the sheriff court, from the sheriff court to the court of the justiciar on his ayre, and from the court of the justiciar to the court of the king. Finally, in addition to hearing these appeals, the king's court will also hear important causes or the causes of important men.

At first the king would sit in his court with the officers of his household and with those great men who happened to be with him at the time. In 1230 we have reference to such a sitting with one bishop, two earls, one prior, three barons, and 'many others' (a resounding phrase which probably means little or nothing); in 1245 an ordinance was made with the counsel, advice, and consent of two bishops, three abbots, seven earls, eight barons, and 'many other earls, barons, and worthy men of the kingdom' (which again may mean very little).

Naturally the king called only those whom he thought fit or necessary for the occasion; and attendance was always a burden.

Nevertheless there were some upon whose advice the king regularly relied, and who were regularly asked for their counsel; these men, who were so often asked to give him counsel, became the king's council (and the Latin word *concilium* means both 'counsel' and 'council'); but our records make it difficult to distinguish between the king's council and fuller meetings in the king's court.

The council might sit in various capacities and various ways; and at first there was apparently no distinction between its sittings for the various aspects of its work. It might sit as a court of justice or as a court of inquiry; it might sit for financial matters, or to give counsel in matters of state, including the general administration and government of the kingdom. Gradually, however, with increasing affairs of state, distinctions began to creep in. Thus, by the beginning of the thirteenth century (if not earlier),[9] when the council, or a group of its members, sat for financial matters it was said to be sitting 'in exchequer' (*in scaccario*).[10] About the same time, for important affairs of state the council might sit in discussion (*in colloquio*). Finally, in 1293, we read of certain pleas which have been heard 'in the presence of the king [John Balliol] and his council in his first parliament' (*in parliamento suo primo*).

At first, a *colloquium* or a *parliamentum* was probably a full and formal meeting of the council for a discussion, a 'talking', about a matter that was regarded as being of particular importance, but, by the end of the thirteenth century, the surviving records show that a Scottish 'parliament' had become primarily a sitting of the council in its capacity as the supreme court of law—the 'King's Court in Parliament'. Moreover, and the point is important, this court of parliament declared the law. Feudal law was the law declared by the king's court. A case was heard by parliament—either a case of first instance, or a case which had risen on appeal from court to court until, finally, it had come to the highest court, the king's court of parliament; parliament gave its decision; and that decision became the law for all similar cases in time to come. By its decision parliament had laid down the law: indeed the dempster (doomster) of parliament, when declaring parliament's decision, used the phrase, 'This court of parliament shows for law.' Parliament might reaffirm the old law, or declare a change in the law to meet some changing need. Thus, the king alone might be the fountain of justice, but he was the fountain of the law in his court. But new laws, as opposed to the law that was determined by adjudication, tended to be concerned only with the details of government and administration, and with the maintenance of order in the realm.

Parliament was a court of law; a meeting of parliament had to be publicly proclaimed in advance; and those who were summoned to attend had to be given at least forty days' notice. Although parliament might do work other than that of a court of law, a sitting of parliament was always a much-advertised-in-advance occasion for all men to come to seek the king's justice in the king's own court, and to bring to him their petitions and complaints. In 1399 a general council (one in which all three estates were represented) even suggested that a parliament should be held each year for the next three years so that the king's subjects could be 'servit of the law'—that is, could obtain justice.

In all affairs of state, however, the king was still supreme. He was *dominus supremus dominus noster Rex*. He might, or might not, take the 'counsel' offered to him. Not until the second half of the fourteenth century do we find a parliament opposing his wishes. Frequently, in the exchequer accounts, we find a marginal note, *consulendus rex*—the king must be asked about this: does he agree? Everything was still dependent upon the king's decision and the king's writ. The king was a 'personal' king; his actions were 'personal'. If David I had issued a charter confirming his gift of certain lands, it was as well to have that charter confirmed by Malcolm IV when he succeeded to the throne, and, when Malcolm IV died, to have the gift again confirmed by William. Even at the beginning of the fifteenth century a writ issued in the king's name, could be called in question if, in the meantime, the king had died. The concept of an 'impersonal crown'—that is, 'the government', as we call it today—only slowly developed. Thus, and the point is important, homage was also personal; and, as we shall see, even a king's ransom might be regarded as a personal payment too.

Again, this new feudal administration, developed by David I and his immediate successors, was also accompanied by equally important changes in legal procedure. Already, in David's reign, we hear of the 'jury', a body of local men who are sworn (*jurati*) to ascertain the truth which they must declare in a 'verdict', a 'true-saying' (*veredictum*). The jury might sit in judgement (assize, *assisa*, a sitting), or they might form an 'inquest' (*inquisicio*) to inquire (*inquirere*) into certain facts—as, for example, what was the boundary between these two holdings of land?[11] Who was the rightful heir to the lands of Scrogges of which the holder has just died? Was John taking so much water from the stream to work his mill-wheel that there was insufficient water to work the mill-wheel of Henry?

Moreover, in the king's courts (such as the courts of his sheriffs and his justiciars), all these inquiries made by local juries, and also all civil actions, were initiated by the purchase of a 'brieve' (a letter, a writ) from the king. The man worried about some infringement of his boundaries, or a lack of water for his mill-wheel, the prospective heir to lands, or the raiser of a civil action, purchased from the king's 'central office' (his chancery) a brieve directed to the local sheriff, charging him to look into the matter by means of an inquest. In certain cases the brieve also charged the sheriff to report back to chancery. In those cases the finding of the jury was 'returned' to chancery; the jury made a *retour*. This was done, for example, when the jury decided who was the lawful heir to lands of which the holder had just died—and naturally so, for the king was interested. If the rightful heir were a minor, the king would enjoy wardship of the lands; and in all cases the king would want to know from whom was to come the payment of 'relief'. And, for any such payment to the king, the king's local officer, the sheriff, was responsible.

These brieves, with their standard wording and their standard directions, sent out to the king's officers in the different districts from a central office in the king's chancery, helped to ensure that the law should be uniform throughout the kingdom. Local and customary laws tended to disappear; and there was a steady approach through the government of one king to the ideal of one land, one community, one people, one law.

All these many changes and developments, however, were not achieved in a day and a night. Only slowly and gradually did the king's law and the king's authority reach the more distant parts of the realm. The king might build his castles at Inverness and Dumbarton and place his sheriffs there, but, west of the 'Highland line', feudal tenures and feudal incidents, baronies and regalities, sheriffs and justiciars were largely unknown. Even in the sixteenth century, when Campbells and Gordons held the flanks of this line, the sentries on the castle of Stirling saw the tops of distant peaks in a land that was known to few and where even fewer knew the way. In the Western Highlands and Islands the king's writ hardly ran until the beginning of the seventeenth century; until then the Highlanders obeyed the king only if they so chose. In the extreme south-west the Galwegians for long refused to accept the new Norman jury system, preferring a system of 'compurgation' in which 'oath-helpers' swore with a litigant that his cause was good and true. In the reign of Alexander II, in 1245, an order to the justiciar to 'enquire into the misdoers in the land' added 'except in Galloway which has special laws within it'. In 1324 Robert I partially extended the jury system there, though still allowing some continuance of the 'laws of Galloway'; and as late as 1384 it was noted in a meeting of the king's council that Galloway still had special laws of its own.

Nevertheless, the sources for the history of Scotland in the twelfth and thirteenth centuries reveal, in general, and apart from the 'heart of Gaeldom' in the far north-west, a country which was being gradually welded together, a country under law and order, with a strong central government ably served by an efficient local administration. Then came a sudden and disastrous change. Ten years after the death of Alexander III in 1286 came the War of Independence and the beginning of long centuries of resistance to English claims. In those years of war and disorder men looked back to the good government and to the peace and plenty of the thirteenth century as a 'golden age'. The earliest known piece of Scottish poetry, preserved for us by Andrew of Wyntoun, a chronicler writing in the opening years of the fifteenth century, records the change in a sad lament:

Quhen Alysandyr oure Kyng was dede	When Alexander our King was dead
That Scotland led in luve and le,	That Scotland led in love and peace
Away wes sons off ale and brede,	Away was choice of ale and bread
Off wyne and wax, off gamyn and gle;	Of wine and wax, of games and glee;
Oure gold wes changyd in to lede;	Our gold was changéd into lead.
Chryst, borne in to Vyrgynyté,	Christ, born in Virginity
Succoure Scotland, and remede	Succour and nourish Scotland
That stad is in perplexyté.	That stayed is in perplexity.

NOTES

1. Though these erections did not last, Robert I created the sheriffdom of Argyll, but a later attempt by James IV to establish sheriffs-depute for the Isles, both north and south, failed.

2. For example the 'tenth penny' granted to Bruce in 1326 and the 'contribution for peace' to raise the £20,000 due under the treaty of 1328 (below, pp. 171, 187). Presumably the same was true in 1189–90 and 1209–12.

3. Though later the regalities were outside its jurisdiction (see above, pp. 84–5). When there were regalities within the sheriffdom the lands of the sheriffdom were differentiated as 'royalty' and 'regality'.

4. It should perhaps be noted that the names of certain districts, like Mar, Buchan, and the Lennox, come from old earldoms; others, like Kyle and Cunningham, come from extinct bailiaries (lands administered by a bailie).

5. Below, chap. 10.

6. In a document of the latter part of the reign of Robert I, outlining the 'points' to be inquired into by the chamberlain, he is to ascertain, among many other points, whether justice is done equally to rich and to poor, whether good weights and measures are used, whether the burgh's market privileges are maintained, and whether the rents and issues pertaining to the king are reaching the king. In a somewhat later document of a similar character the chamberlain is to inquire, *inter alia*, whether the miller is using two measures, 'ane to tak with and ane uther to deliver with', and whether the souters are using 'fals and rotten threid throu the quhilk the schone [shoes] ar tynt or [worn out before] thai be half worn'.

7. That is, south of the narrow neck of the Forth–Clyde isthmus.

8. They are called the officers of the king's 'household'; and the king's household of medieval times was the Whitehall, or perhaps Downing Street, of today.

9. Unfortunately the earlier records have been lost.

10. The word *scaccarium* means a chess-board, or a reckoning-board, chequered in squares. Until the introduction of the Arabic system of numbers such a reckoning-board, with counters, was the only way of carrying out addition and subtraction. The reader need only try to subtract xxv from ccli, or to add xxix to xli, without recourse to the Arabic system, to realize the difficulties.

11. Called a 'perambulation', for the jury walked round the boundary to define its line.

CHAPTER 10

The Early Burghs

In the twelfth century we also begin to read of 'burghs'—the earliest burghs known to us being those of Berwick and Roxburgh which are referred to in a charter granted by David I a few years before he became king.

Undoubtedly there were *towns* in Scotland before the twelfth century. Berwick, Dunfermline, St. Andrews, and Perth, for example, at once spring to mind; and other settlements specializing in manufactures and exchange must have arisen at places which were important because of their geographical situations—for example, Stirling, with its crossing of the Forth—or places with good harbours at the mouths of rivers or a basin, such as Montrose. It is no coincidence that the king's hall, palace, or castle of David I was sited where also the earliest burghs are found, for the king had surplus produce from his rents to sell, and the king had need to buy cloth, wine, arms, and armour. The market place which was at the heart of the town met the secular needs of society, as the altar met its spiritual needs.

But the burgh was not simply an earlier town or village which had grown larger or more important. By royal grant a town was given a new status—the status of a burgh. It might be an old settlement or it might occasionally be a new settlement which had grown up by the new castle. Or the king might even 'plan' an entirely new burgh, to be built at the time of the building of his castle and inducements might be offered to businessmen to settle there. The town would grow up because favoured by geography or (very occasionally) because planned by a ruler; the burgh was made. A town or village settlement became a burgh only when the king had made it one, only when he had 'erected' it into a burgh, only when he had conferred that status upon it. Then it was the king's burgh: it was on the king's land, its burgesses were the king's men, its rents were the king's rents, it was subject to the supervision of the king's officers. This new status of being a burgh was, therefore, largely a legal concept—for the burgesses of a burgh enjoyed special laws and privileges; the 'laws' of the burghs were different from the law of the land.

The burgh was a natural and necessary part of a mercantile revolution which had swept through western Europe and had come belatedly to Scotland. It was the concomitant of a change in economic life, a change from a self-supporting and rural economy (whether of pasture or arable) to one in which there were organized manufactures (notably of cloth) and in which organized trading began—surplus of agricultural products, wool, skins,[1] and hides, for example, being exchanged in overseas commerce for manufactured goods, for luxuries (such as wine and spices), or for raw materials in which Scotland was deficient (such as iron). And this trading was in the hands of the burgesses of the new burghs. Significantly, too, we now have, in David I's reign, our earliest known Scottish coinage—silver pennies, minted at Berwick and Roxburgh—for exchange is the basis of the rapid development of urban life.

The fact that each of these early king's burghs (or 'royal burghs' as they came to be called from 1400) was usually adjacent to one of the king's castles ensured the king's peace and provided protection. Merchants and craftsmen clustered beside it and formed a supply-centre for the castle's needs[2] and a market-centre for the castle's area, the sheriffdom. But because the sheriff at this early period was primarily a manager of the king's demesne estates and so was best placed in a castle near a burgh market-place, it was usually not in the king's interests to have more than one burgh in each sheriffdom. Each burgh also soon appreciated the advantages of such a monopoly and, in the reigns of William and Alexander II, we find the king granting to a number of his burghs a monopoly of trade for the whole area of their respective sheriffdoms.[3]

At the end of the reign of David I at least fifteen of these new burghs had been erected in Scotland, and steadily their number increased thereafter. Moreover kings, from David I onwards, gave leave to a number of abbeys, cathedrals, and great lay lords to have burghs of their own. David I, for example, gave leave to the abbey of Holyrood to have its own burgh (Canongate) adjacent to the king's burgh (Edinburgh); he gave leave to the bishop of St. Andrews to found a burgh there. Thus, in addition to the king's burghs there were soon episcopal burghs, abbatial burghs, and baronial burghs—of which three groups typical examples are St. Andrews and Glasgow, Arbroath and Kelso, Kirkintilloch and Dunbar.

Both castle and burgh were new: the burghs were settlements of men with a new status, of new men, or of men who had broken away from the servile ties of lord and land.[4] William of Newburgh, writing in the closing years of the twelfth century, says that 'the towns and burghs of the Scottish realm are known to be inhabited by English'; but, from the records themselves, including lists of the names of burgesses, we know that these new burghs were inhabited also by Flemings, Normans, Anglo-Danes, and Scots. And, like the castle, the burgh was a place of security—its very name, derived from *burh*, *burg*, meant a fortified enclosure.[5] As a settlement of men of business, traders, and artisans, its wealth lay in movable goods which could be easily looted and carried away. Like the castle it was probably 'timbered' with its palisade, and it had a fosse or an earthen wall with gates ('ports' or 'bows') which could be securely closed at night or when danger threatened. These features are found most clearly where there was danger of trouble either internally as in Moray, or from England, as at Berwick. So King William agreed with his burgesses of Inverness that, when he had made a fosse around the burgh, the burgesses would erect thereon a stout palisade which they would keep in sound repair to enclose their burgh. There are many other references to burgh enclosure and 'watch and ward' was a duty always imposed upon every burgess. Both castle and burgh were units in a new royal administration intended to colonize and to make prosperous the land.[6]

Because the burgh was an enclosed strong-point, it was what we should call today a 'built-up area'. It was the duty of the new burgess to build his 'tenement' within a stated period of time (usually one year), and the 'back' of his 'land' (his 'burgage holding') had also to be well secured so that it formed, with the 'backs' of his neighbours, a further line of defence. Outside the burgh, however, there were cultivated lands (worked in run-rig) and common grazings—often later referred to in such phrases as 'the town's acres', the 'burgh muir', 'the burgess acres', and so forth—and many a burgh, like Aberdeen, had 'burgh fishings'. These lands and fishings were granted to the burgesses and the burgh by the king. Often they are said to have been granted 'for the support of the burgh'; and it is amply evident that the early burgess was a farmer as well as a man of business. And naturally so, for a group of people concentrated together in a settlement could not rely solely upon the victuals which might be brought to their market from the surrounding countryside.

In some situations, for a burgh to grow, or to grow rapidly, inducements were necessary. Partly the protection afforded by the neighbouring castle, together with the enjoyment of the king's peace, was in itself an attraction; in addition, the newcomer was offered a 'period of peaceful sitting' (sometimes called *kirset*), usually one year,[7] which was allowed for the building of his tenement and during which he paid no rent. But more than this was necessary, particularly if the burgh were to attract men from the landward areas as well as 'new men' of foreign origin. Above all, the burgh's trading activities (in sale and delivery of goods, settlement of debt, contracts and agreements, and so forth) required a law and a procedure far different from the law of the countryside. So, because of their particular needs, the burghs were quickly given particular rights and special privileges; they were given their own 'customs' which formed a burgh law. And in this Scotland borrowed much from England and the continent.[8]

In the burghs if, perchance, a man had lived there unchallenged for a year and a day, he could henceforth live there freely; no lord could claim him as his 'man'. In the burghs the burgess held his toft and tenement as freely as he held his goods. The only burden upon his land was the payment of his rent. A year-and-a-day's possession of a toft and tenement (a 'land') without challenge gave him full right thereto. He could divide his holding. He could marry, and give his children in marriage, without seeking the leave of any lord or paying any feudal render. His heir paid no relief; if he died leaving his children minors, wardship was governed by the burgh customs and not by feudal law. He was free in his person and could come and go as he wished. Above all, he enjoyed and could claim the jurisdiction of his own burgh court which had special procedures and special laws to meet his own particular needs, and which imposed fixed monetary penalties to which he knew he was subject. The travelling merchant, for example, would want his action to be settled quickly so that he could move on to the next burgh he wished to visit. So the action of the travelling merchant had to be settled 'within three tides' (or thirty-six hours). Again, in the burgh court there was greater reliance upon the *witnesses* to a transaction: two witnesses were sufficient to prove the payment or receipt of any sum.

The possession of a court, with its own special laws and procedures (to which all the burgesses of the burgh were subject, and in which all, as suitors, at first took part), all bound the burgh together as a 'community'. By the early thirteenth century the burgesses refer to themselves as a 'community of burgesses'. The new burgess, upon his admission, takes an oath to be 'leel and feel' to the king and to the community of the burgh. At the time of his oath he must possess a house (or find a pledge that he will build a house within a year); and his house becomes a 'gage' for his performance of common duties and for his observance of 'good neighbourhood' (*vicinitas*) towards his fellow burgesses. If he fails therein, his house may be destroyed, thus making it impossible for him to remain within the community.

To begin with, in the time of David I, the king had secured his rents from each burgh holding through his own officer, the sheriff; from each 'land' there was due to the king a rent of fivepence from every rood, and the king also drew the tolls (later called 'petty cutoms') levied on the produce brought for sale at the burgh market. It seems likely that at a very early date, even perhaps from the establishment of each burgh, the king and his chamberlain rounded up or struck a notional figure for the sum due from it, and charged the sheriff this lump sum (fixed, *firma*, hence ferme or farm), while the sheriff's agents, *prepositi*, collected the individual amounts for him. During the later twelfth century the sheriff was removed from this mediating position, and his agents became responsible for the ferme directly to the chamberlain with whom they negotiated its amount yearly or from time to time. How this came about, and whether for each burgh individually or for several at a time, we do not know, but we can be sure that the burghs paid well for the change.

It happened in the same period (from about 1160) as the recording of royal grants to the burgesses of a burgh, in charters. Such things had been unknown under David I when each individual was the king's burgess and there was no communal organization or officer to receive a charter. By 1200, however, it seems the burgesses were a community not only in the geographical but in the political sense. They have an organization to negotiate with the chamberlain to collect fermes, to pay the king, to hold lands outside the burgh for common grazing, and so on.

At the beginning of the thirteenth century we begin to read of burgh seals. The burgh seal was affixed to a document in the name of the community; the burgh seal could bind the community to take certain action, or to pay a given sum. In 1296, when the treaty of alliance between Scotland and France was ratified, the seals of the communities of six burghs (Aberdeen, Perth, Stirling, Edinburgh, Roxburgh, and Berwick) were affixed to the ratification, binding those burghs (and possibly, through them, all the king's burghs) to maintain and implement the treaty's terms. The seal represents the burgh as a self-governing community. As early as the reign of King William in some burghs the *prepositi* (some three or four in number) were burgesses and in the thirteenth century they were clearly elected annually by the burgesses from among their own number; the election took place at the 'head court' held at Michaelmas, when all the burgesses were expected to be present; and at that 'head court' the burgh's 'acts' (its by-laws as we should call them today) were also confirmed by the community, and any new 'acts' were approved. In the fourteenth century the elected officers of the burgh usually came to include a provost, bailies, sergeants, liners, tasters of wine and ale, and apprisers of flesh. The liners were responsible for defining the boundaries of burgage holdings within the burgh (and in a burgh a 'land' was always defined and referred to by the street in which it lay and by the names of the owners of the 'lands' on either side of it); the tasters of wine and ale and the apprisers of flesh were appointed to ensure that the quality was maintained and that fair prices were charged. The provost (or alderman) was the head of the community; the bailies presided over the burgh court (having the sergeants to help them in making summons and in ensuring that the court's decisions were carried out) and were also responsible to the king for the burgh's finances.

But this self-government had nothing to do with democracy. If in the time of David I all inhabitants of a burgh were burgesses, the rapid economic expansion of western Europe in the twelfth century soon differentiated the wealthy, the property-owners, the employers, the investors, from the poor, the rootless, the artisans, the labourers, and confined the effective voice in burgh government to the former, the men of business. They alone could pay for burgh privileges (such as the right to choose the *prepositi*) from the king, and could produce the silver to guarantee his ferme, and their money spoke more loudly to the king than any abstract notion of community. To him and to themselves they were *the* community, the 'good folk', and their meetings for conviviality soon acquired serious business purposes. This gild of business or 'gild merchant'[9] may have existed in the larger burghs from David I's time; it first appears in documented history at Perth in telling fashion. King William having promised at Norham in August 1209 to pay 15,000 merks to King John, summoned a council to Perth on 29 September 1209 to raise the money; equinoctial rains and tides flooded the town and the council hastily disbanded to meet again at Stirling where the king was granted his money. But at this very same council the burgesses of Perth were granted a long royal charter. Overseas merchants might not trade directly with the men of the county but only in the burgh—the Perth merchants were entrenched middlemen; they might not sell cloth even in the burgh except during June and July—the Perth cloth manufacturers wanted no 'unfair' competition; no one living in the county might make quality cloth to sell in competition with that made in Perth; all those non-burgesses living in Perth and trading in its market must contribute to the king's aid along with burgesses even though excluded from burgess-ship. And the burgesses are to have their gild merchant from which the toiling artisans of the cloth industry, the weavers and fullers, are excluded; the only persons who may make quality cloth in Perthshire are the burgesses in the gild merchant who pay the king's aid along with the other burgesses.

There were grain merchants, wine merchants, and wool merchants in Perth, as well as masters of all kinds of trades and crafts, such as the masons, wrights, skinners, bonnet-makers, tailors, bakers, and fleshers.[10] All these were admitted burgesses and to the gild, which was essentially an employer's organization, but at this juncture a particularly important group were the burgh cloth masters, buying wool in the county, selling some to visiting English and Flemish merchants for export, and putting some out to domestic spinners and weavers (on piece rates probably) in order to have it fulled, dyed, and finished in their own sheds by their own wage-labourers. These men helped to meet the king's pressing needs, and in return received recognition for their gild and economic privileges which we can be sure were accompanied by a consolidation of their hold on the government of the burgh. Thus the gild in effect pre-elected the *prepositi* of the burgh and regularly included the president of the gild, the alderman, among their number. So pre-eminent was he that gradually the title of *prepositus*, provost, was reserved for him and the others were called *balliui*, bailies, once meaning 'agents of the king' but now meaning 'agents of the provost'.

In the latter half of the thirteenth century, however, the manufacture and trade in cloth declined; and early in the fourteenth century the merchants were claiming a monopoly in buying and selling only wool, skins, and hides. But the overseas trade of the merchants increased the revenues of the king and the bullion of the kingdom—through the customs dues on their exports and the profits of their trade. These 'great customs' (to distinguish them from burgh tolls or 'petty customs') were introduced in the 1270s and 1280s, payable upon exports of wool skins and hides and became a major source of royal income. In the king's and the merchants' eyes the craftsmen, who worked with their hands and merely served local needs, came to be regarded as men of lesser standing in the burghs and men of lesser importance in national affairs; and because of that, the merchants gradually gained more and more control in the affairs of the burghs and were granted more and more power in burghal administration—particularly when, in the middle of the fourteenth century, large sums of money had to be found for the ransom of David II. Then money could be raised from the burghs only through the activities of the merchants; because of that, only the merchants mattered; and so the merchants became the real rulers in the burghs and the craftsmen soon had little or no voice in burgh affairs.

When the burgh escaped from the control of the sheriff, the king's financial interest was maintained by the chamberlain who, in theory if not always in practice, passed on his ayre from burgh to burgh ascertaining that justice had been done in the burgh court 'alike to the poor and the rich', hearing appeals from the decisions of the burgh court, and, above all, ensuring that an appropriate revenue duly reached the royal coffers. In the early fourteenth century we find him still fixing a definite sum to be paid annually by the burgh for a stated number of years in place of all the individual rents and other issues except the great customs, separately accounted for,[11] leaving the burgesses to make their own arrangements for the raising of the annual amount. But under Robert I the king began to grant charters to his burghs whereby in future, and *in perpetuity*, this or that burgh would pay an annual fixed sum in lieu of all its issues. Under such a charter the burgh acquired 'feu-ferme' status; it paid a 'ferme' annually and in perpetuity for its 'feu' from the king. The precedent was set by Alexander II who in or about 1235 granted feu-ferme status, in imitation of English models, to Berwick, the most important of the Scottish burghs; the ferme was fixed at 500 merks (£333·33). Aberdeen was the first to receive this privilege from Robert I, in 1319, for a ferme of £213·33. Berwick received a confirmation in 1320 and Edinburgh a grant in 1329 (for a ferme of £34·66); by the end of the fourteenth century most of the important burghs had been granted a like privilege. Sometimes, though not always, the fixed sum laid down in the charter was higher than the previous total of the separate issues,[12] for the king was allowing for growth and development; but, as we shall see, there was to be a rapid decrease in the value of money, mainly through debasement of the coinage,[13] and, with the fall in the value of money, the burghs that were fortunate enough to hold a charter of feu-ferme benefited enormously, with a correspondingly enormous loss to the royal treasury.

Finally, because the 'law' of the burghs was different from the law of the land, the burghs had their own court which, in hearing and deciding cases that came before it, declared the law of the burghs, just as the king's court in parliament declared the law of the land. Before this 'parliament' of the burghs, known as the Court of the Four Burghs, and presided over by the chamberlain, went disputes between the burghs as well as appeals from the burgh courts and the chamberlain's ayre. The earliest record evidence for the Court of the Four Burghs is to be found in 1292[14] when a question relating to the interpretation of the 'law' of the burghs with regard to debt was referred to 'the four burghs'; and in 1296 the burgesses of Berwick, Edinburgh, Roxburgh, and Stirling made a declaration with regard to the law of 'heirship goods'.[15]

The 'Four Burghs' were thus Berwick, Edinburgh, Roxburgh, and Stirling; but in 1369, because of continued English occupation of Berwick and Roxburgh, those two burghs were replaced by Lanark and Linlithgow. Later, the Court of the Four Burghs was enlarged to include representatives of more than the Four Burghs, and, probably in emulation of it, there emerged the Convention of

Royal Burghs. But, whatever the constitution of the Court, it served to stress and to maintain the position of the burghs as communities which were somehow different and which were outside the common law and the administration of the rest of the king's land.[16]

NOTES

1. The sheep's skin with the wool still on it.

2. Many of the early plans of the burghs show the main street running direct to the castle, that is, to the centre which the burgh first served. This can be seen in the early 'lay-out' of, for example, Edinburgh, Banff, Berwick, Elgin, Forres, and Inverness. In a like way the three main streets of St. Andrews converge on the cathedral and priory.

3. Possibly also to other burghs whose records have been lost. It may well be that all the 'head burghs' of sheriffdoms received such a privilege.

4. The man who has lived in a burgh unchallenged for a year and a day cannot thereafter be claimed by a lord.

5. Possibly the importance soon attached to 'The Four Burghs'—Berwick, Roxburgh, Edinburgh, and Stirling (above, p. 112)—may reflect an importance that had formerly belonged to them as [Anglian] *burhs* built and fortified at an earlier time. All four stood at points of the highest strategic importance; two of them carry the word *burh* in their names; and two of them (Berwick and Roxburgh) are, as we have seen, the earliest Scottish burghs on record.

6. The idea of the burgh as a colony to help to civilize a difficult part long continued. As late as 1597, for example, parliament ordered three burghs to be erected and built in Kintyre, Lochaber, and Lewis for 'civility and policy' in those parts. And 'policy' here means what we would now call 'improvement'.

7. Though in remote or dangerous parts a longer period of 'rent-free sitting' might be offered: in Dumbarton, five years was offered, and, in Dingwall, ten years.

8. Trading contacts not only provided knowledge of the laws and privileges of the burghs in other lands, but also necessitated some uniformity in a 'mercantile' law. The travelling merchant, to be encouraged, must not be subject to arbitrary laws; he must be reasonably aware of the laws which govern his activities. Trade will be encouraged if the laws of trade are more or less the same in all burghs in all lands. Moreover, because the burghs had direct contacts with one another, when one burgh enjoyed a particular privilege other burghs would be quick to claim a like privilege for themselves.

9. The word 'merchant' here is an adjective; this was not a 'gild of merchants'.

10. It is interesting to note how many modern surnames are derived from the exercise of a craft—Webster, a weaver; Cordiner, a shoemaker; Lorimer, a maker of horse-trappings; and Walker [= Fuller], Mason, Wright, Skinner, Taylor, Baxter, Potter, Glover. It is also strange to note how the old Scottish term *Flesher* is giving way to the English *Family Butcher*—surely a murderous occupation.

11. The great customs on the export of wool, woolfells, and hides were always kept separate and distinct from the issues of the burgh and were accounted for

in exchequer by special officers, for each seaport burgh, known as custumars (*custumarii*).

12. Thus the amounts fixed in the charters of feu-ferme do not necessarily reflect the relative importance of the burghs concerned.

13. Cf. below, p. 246.

14. That it was then functioning almost certainly indicates an earlier origin, and there is indeed non-record evidence of its existence about 1270.

15. That is, the goods to which the heir was entitled to succeed as of right.

16. The various returns to the Exchequer at the end of the reign of Robert I show that at that time there were five important and relatively wealthy burghs—Berwick, Aberdeen, Edinburgh, Perth, and Dundee—while all the others were a long way behind, much smaller and less prosperous.

The amount gathered in from the burghs towards the three annual payments of £6,666·66 due under the treaty of 1328 (below, p. 171) also provides an indication of the place of the burghs at that time in the national economy. The burghs as a whole compounded with the chamberlain for three annual payments of £333·33; and this small sum (although a bargain for the burghs) is in striking contrast to, roughly, £5,000 annually from the lay holders of land and, roughly, £2,000 from the Church.

Thus the early Scottish burghs must have been small in size. We have few figures upon which to work, but it would appear that the population of Berwick in 1296, when it was sacked by Edward I, was only about 1,500. Edinburgh seems to have had about 400 houses in the reign of David II; and Stirling had only about 1,500 inhabitants in 1550. In most of the medieval burghs the population would probably number only a few hundreds.

CHAPTER 11

The Medieval Church—I
The Regulars

FOLLOWING the decision at the Synod of Whitby[1] the church in northern Britain rapidly accepted obedience to Roman usage. They were adopted by Nechtan, king of the Picts; Iona conformed; before 731 Candida Casa was a bishopric subject to York; and in 735 Egbert, archbishop of York, received the *pallium*[2] from the pope. Then came the Danish-Norwegian invasions. In the north, Orkney and Shetland, the Western Isles, and the modern counties of Caithness, Sutherland, and Ross were seized and held by the Norse; to the south, a great pagan wedge soon stretched across northern England from sea to sea; to the west, in Ireland, a Norse kingdom, with its centre in Dublin, was established and consolidated. To a large extent Scotland was isolated. She was separated from southern England, and a pagan sea-power could cut her communications with Ireland and the continent. Towards the end of the ninth century we have a lone reference to the *Ecclesia Scoticana*, but it was a church deprived of further contact with Western Christendom and Rome.

When we have fuller evidence of this 'Scottish church' we find at St. Andrews a community of clergy, maintained by family succession, whose members could hold personal property, and whose life was said to be shaped 'in accordance with their own ideas' rather than with the 'precepts of the holy fathers'. The clergy serving this church were called Célidé;[3] there were also known Culdee communities at Lochleven, Monifieth, Brechin, Muthill, Monymusk, Abernethy, and Iona; and it was some of the 'traditions' of the Culdees that Margaret, the Saxon queen of Malcolm III, strove to correct.

The Célidé were the descendants of an eighth-century anchorite movement, in the Celtic (Irish) church, which was a movement for revival and reform, and led to the drawing up of 'rules' defining the true monastic way of life. Thus the Célidé exercised a disciplined life (with the possibility of greater seclusion by the withdrawal of individual members into solitary places and the living of an eremitic life), and their monasteries became more properly communities or colleges of secular priests, similar to the minsters in England and of southern Ireland. There were certainly other clergy in the Celtic church, individual priests and parishes each with a 'mother church' or (where served by two or three priests) a 'minster'; these were not Célidé (Culdees), and in the time of Margaret's sons the whole corporate framework of the Culdees began to collapse.

By contrast the founding of the monasteries of Subiaco and Monte Cassino by St. Benedict early in the sixth century marked the beginning of a monastic movement which rapidly spread throughout western Europe. When civilized life was in decay from external attacks by barbarians and internal rivalries, the monasteries were 'retreats' into which men could go to lead a Christian life away from the ills and evils of the world.

The Benedictine monks, having taken the vows of poverty, chastity, and obedience, and living a corporate life within their own community, followed a 'rule' laid down by St. Benedict.[4] Their house was 'a school for the service of God'; their first duty was worship, which was 'the work of God'; thereafter their hours were to be employed in manual labour or study, and in manual labour they became ardent agriculturalists. The monk and the community were bound together; a monk, once admitted to a monastery, lived and died there. In this the Benedictines differed from the Irish monks who went out from their monasteries as missionaries or to lead hermit lives. Individual Benedictine abbeys had no constitutional links one with another—the Benedictine 'order' was a uniformity of aims and methods, we might say.

Later, when Europe had become more settled, monasteries were still founded as houses of God—a very profusion of foundations took place in the eleventh and twelfth centuries—and they still attracted men with the same idea of a retreat from the world.

Yet Scotland remained so isolated from the civilization of continental Europe that the revival of Benedictine monasticism in the tenth century which led to the foundation or re-establishment of some forty abbeys in England found no patron among the Scottish kings. Not until the late eleventh century, when Lanfranc archbishop of Canterbury was bringing a new canonical order to the religious life of his province, did the Benedictines come to Scotland

—and it was Queen Margaret who besought a colony from Canterbury to establish a house at the place where she had married—Dunfermline. Yet this promising and important beginning does not seem to have borne much immediate fruit. It is possible that Margaret founded another Benedictine abbey on Iona, and certainly King Edgar was generous to the Benedictines of Durham, giving to them a whole royal estate at Coldingham because of his devotion to St. Cuthbert; but Coldingham became a priory only in the 1140s and Edgar founded no monastery in Scotland.

Meanwhile in France the time of Margaret and her sons saw a great monastic revival which took men to new, sometimes remote, places to follow the rule of St. Benedict with purer devotion and stricter discipline. Such a new beginning was the abbey of St. Bernard at Tiron, near Chartres, to visit which came David brother of Alexander I. What he saw so moved his spirit that he persuaded the Tironensians to send a colony to found a new abbey at Selkirk in his Cumbrian principality, the first abbey of any of the reformed Benedictine observances to be established in Britain (1113); and although there are reasons to think that David was influenced by his chaplain John, who had some link with Tiron and was soon made bishop of the revived see of Glasgow, the master and not the servant bore the main responsibility.

Meanwhile, King Alexander I responded differently to the spiritual influences upon his generation. For just as Benedictine monasticism was revived in stricter forms, so the many communities of non-monastic clergy in Europe were moved to seek a stricter and more spiritual life. For these communities of canons a rule was evolved in the early twelfth century, strongly influenced by St. Benedict's rule, but ascribed to St. Augustine, and differing from the Benedictine rule for monks in that Augustinian canons, while living a monastic life in the convent, were also allowed to minister to the laity, for example in parishes, outside the convent. At some date between 1115 and 1120 King Alexander brought a community of Augustinians from Yorkshire to the ancient (pagan perhaps) cult-centre of the kings of Scotland at Scone, to found a new priory. At the end of his reign the prior was appointed bishop of St. Andrews in furtherance of the king's efforts to establish the Augustinian rule there. Since he also tried to have the endowments of the ancient Celtic abbey of Dunkeld made over to Augustinian canons, and was unsuccessful at both places, it may be that Scone was founded

E

as a step towards introducing the Augustinian rule at the two chief episcopal churches under Alexander's control: St. Andrews and Dunkeld.

In 1124 Scotland had three monasteries: Scone, Dunfermline, and Selkirk. In the following thirty years David I wrought a transformation which can too easily read like a catalogue only. If we first follow the Augustinians we find a new abbey of the Holy Rood established below the king's castle and residence of Edinburgh. Its first abbot, formerly a canon of Merton in Surrey, was later David's chaplain, a clear indication that the order was suited to ministering to the royal court. To Jedburgh, another royal centre, Bishop John of Glasgow and King David brought Augustinians probably from Beauvais in Normandy, and to Stirling the king attracted canons from Arrouaise in Picardy which had become famous through the adoption of constitutions for the strict Augustinian life; thus below the castle and palace of Stirling arose the abbey of Cambuskenneth. At St. Andrews the attempt begun by Alexander I to introduce Augustinians was successfully completed in 1144, so fulfilling the order's function of bringing a more canonical life to an existing community, for in 1147 the pope granted to the canons the right to elect the bishops of St. Andrews while at the same time decreeing that upon the death of any Culdee his place was to be taken by an Austin canon. But this provision was a dead letter, so strong was the force of vested interest.[5] To the Culdees of Lochleven David offered the choice either of accepting the Augustinian rule and becoming canons, or of being expelled from the island, and in this case his efforts seem to have been successful.[6] Dunkeld never received an Augustinian convent, and eventually, under Malcolm IV, its bishop settled for an Austin priory in a detached portion of the diocese, the island of Inchcolm in the Forth.

We have seen that under David I the Benedictines of Durham established a priory at Coldingham. But it was neither to these nor to his early Tironensian friends that David I poured out the fullest measure of his generosity. In the 1130s he came into contact through his friends and family with the most radical and appealing of the twelfth-century attempts to recover the spirituality of Benedictine monasticism—that named Cistercian after one of its earliest houses, Cîteaux. The Cistercian order was an organization in the sense that each abbey was visited and disciplined by the abbot of the house from which it was founded, and all abbots foregathered each year (soon, for the Scots however, every third year) at Cîteaux. These things however were unimportant compared with the Cistercian attempt to free its monks from the secular concerns which might make them business-minded rather than servants of God, fit to receive the divine love shown in Christ's life and especially in the love of Mary for her son.

Thus the Cistercians rejected many of the forms of income upon which other monasteries depended: mills, bakehouses, the revenues of appropriated kirks, and most important, the labour of servile peasants. They sought out places remote from lay settlement, even on occasion had a village moved far away from the monastic site. The monks divided their time between the church and labour in the fields, but with far more time devoted to the latter than in a Benedictine or Tironensian house. Yet as we shall see, the worship of God demanded their first care, and so the Cistercians admitted to each monastery lay brothers (*conversi*) who took vows of celibacy, lived in quarters alongside, but separate from, those of the monks, attended at least one of the 'hours' or services daily, but devoted most of their time to labour in the fields or amid the sheep on the grazings. The Cistercians rejected not merely the elaborate if beautiful architecture and furnishings of a Benedictine monastic church, and the complex liturgies allowed there, but insisted upon dress in a simple habit of unbleached wool (hence the 'White monks') and an austere diet with no relaxations. There could be no doubt of the calling ('vocation') of any man who professed himself a Cistercian monk.

Kings were not the most usual patrons of men of such spirituality but David I was in no doubt that the welfare of his kingdom—its spiritual welfare—would be impoverished without their prayers and example. His first foundation, at Melrose (1136), seems to have involved him in elaborate transactions to recover their land (associated with St. Cuthbert) which had been given to Selkirk abbey; the Tironensians of Selkirk were moved to Kelso, and (perhaps an added compensation) were encouraged to establish a dependent priory at Lesmahagow. And not long after the foundation of Melrose abbey monks from it established an abbey at Newbattle in thanksgiving for the recovery from illness of the king's son, Earl Henry, while David also established abbeys at Dundrennan in Galloway, Kinloss in Moray, and Holm Cultram in Cumberland, and planned yet another, carried out by Malcolm IV, at Coupar Angus. This last was an exception to the decision (made before David died) by the Cistercian order, alarmed at its too rapid expansion, to permit no new foundations.

So remarkable was David I's achievement as patron of the monastic orders that three hundred years later two men commented upon it in contrary senses. To Wyntoun (*c.* 1420)

> He illumynyd in his dayis
> His landys with kyrkys and wyth abbayis

while to James I (1424-37) he was 'ane sair sanct to the croun'. But David was remarkable among and to men of his own age; even in Scotland few followed his example though those who did were, as we might expect, his faithful Anglo-Norman barons. Walter fitz Alan, the Steward, brought another variant of Benedictine observances, the Cluniac, to a priory at Renfrew, later Paisley abbey, while Hugh de Moreville established regular canons at Dryburgh about 1150. These last illustrate the spiritual vitality of the twelfth-century church, for they came from Alnwick where the customs followed were those of Prémontré (Premonstratensian), the rule of St. Augustine purified and made stricter for canons by the influence of Cistercian monastic observances. Thus Scotland had black (from the colour of their habit) monks (Benedictine, Cluniac, and Tironensian) and white monks (Cistercian), black canons (Augustinian) and white canons (Premonstratensian)—and together these made up the regular clergy, those who followed a rule.

The Cistercian embargo on new foundations was relaxed occasionally as when the lords of Galloway founded Glenluce abbey. Early in the thirteenth century three modest houses were founded by the aristocracy at Culross, Balmerino (by Queen Ermengarde), and Deer, but Sweetheart abbey near Dumfries founded in the 1270s is late and virtually isolated from the earlier devotion to Cistercian ideals.

During the later twelfth century, when Cistercian foundations were scarcely allowed, the Tironensians enjoyed an important revival in their appeal. Following the murder of Thomas Becket (1170) his canonization (1172), and the defeat of King William (1174) in which the saint was thought to have taken a hand, the King sought a better fortune, a more powerful interceder, a more abundant grace, by founding at Arbroath the wealthy and splendid abbey dedicated to St. Thomas the Martyr (1178). Its convent came from Kelso, and the Tironensians went also to Lindores and Kilwinning abbeys, founded in the late twelfth century.

Nor should we forget the spread of the canons regular. The Premonstratensians established a cathedral priory at Whithorn in 1177 and other houses in the south-west. The Augustinians had houses there, and, later in the thirteenth century, former Culdee houses at Abernethy and Monymusk, long secularized, were revived as Augustinian priories.

What was the life led by a Cistercian monk?

In the first place, the monks were cloistered, they were shut in.[7] Their monastery was surrounded by a precinct wall which cut them off from the world. They were 'out of the world' and all its evil; and within their wall they prayed in their church that their own sins and the sins of the world might be forgiven. These prayers ('choir services') were their daily task and their chief duty; and the church and the precinct wall were two outward signs and visible tokens of a monastic house.

The Cistercians (observing the rule of St. Benedict as well as their own 'Charter of Love') praised and prayed seven times a day and had also a service at midnight—so fulfilling two verses of the 119th Psalm, 'At midnight I will rise to give thanks unto thee because of thy righteous judgments', and 'Seven times a day do I praise thee because of thy righteous judgments.'[8] And because of the midnight service there was a staircase (the 'night-stair') leading from the long dormitory (the 'dorter'), in which the monks slept, down to the church, into one of the transepts by the choir. Also because of this midnight service the monks slept clad and girdled.

The plan of one monastery might vary slightly from that of another but, in general, the plan of every Cistercian house was the same. Within the precinct wall was the church, the monks' dorter and the lay-brothers' dorter (both with their night-stairs, leading into the choir and the nave (the eastern and western arms of the church) respectively), the monks' frater and the lay-brothers' frater (the refectories where they ate together), the infirmary, the kitchens, the bakehouse, the malthouse and brewery, the vegetable gardens (mainly peas, beans, and herbs) and the orchards. In addition, the monks had a cloister (an enclosed open space with a sheltered walk around it, usually on the south, or sunny side, of the church),[9] a chapter-house for the discussion of business (and so called because every day they met there to hear a chapter of their rule read to them), a parlour where they could talk to one another (for elsewhere, and even at meals, the monks were expected to be sparing in their conversation), and a warming-room, the only room in the monastery where there was a fire—save for the necessary fires in kitchens and bakehouse, and save for a fire in the guest-house and possibly also one in the abbot's chamber.[10]

At 2 a.m., then, the monk rose for a service in the church called Matins, or Lauds; and thereafter there were services at dawn, the first hour (Prime, 6 a.m.), and at roughly three-hour intervals, at the third hour (Terce, 9 a.m.), at Sext (12 o'clock), at None (3 p.m.), at Vespers (6 p.m.), and Compline just before bedtime. The hours, however, might vary at particular seasons or on particular days; and, in general, they were gradually anticipated so that the service of None eventually moved back towards midday and thus gave us our modern word 'noon'. In all, these services might take up some six hours of the monks' day.[11]

After Prime, there was an early mass. After Terce, the monks assembled in the chapter-house where first of all there was a reading, from the Martyrology, of the account of the saint and martyr commemorated on that particular day, then the reading of a chapter of the rule, then, if there were one, the hearing of some case of discipline, some instance of a brother who had broken the rule, and finally, if necessary, a discussion of some business matter that required decision. Thereafter, about 10 a.m., High mass was celebrated, and, after mass, the monks sat down to dinner in their frater—though during the autumn and winter the strict Cistercians fasted by omitting dinner and taking only the one other meal of the day, namely supper, which came immediately after Vespers.[12] After supper came Collation, a reading from a work by Johannes Cassianus called *Collationes Patrum*;[13] and thereafter came the last service (Compline) and then bed.

During their free time the monks were expected to work in their gardens or orchards, or at building or woodwork, or perhaps in their scriptorium writing music for their services, or otherwise making a copy of some manuscript book. Partly they had to be self-supporting; partly the founder of their order believed in a balance of work and prayer: to him 'idleness was the enemy of the soul'. So the early Cistercians became expert farmers and agricultural improvers and the different houses exchanged notes with one another, as well as exchanging seeds and cuttings. They were also good craftsmen. Gradually, however, the work within the monastic precinct, as well as the work of the outlying granges (the management of the sheep runs and of the farms on lands conferred upon the monks by the generosity of kings and nobles), was left wholly to the lay-brothers. Thereby the monks lost the balance of prayer and work, and tended to become remiss in matters of the spirit, though always attentive to the business well-being of the monastery.

Cut off from the world and living a cloistered life behind his precinct wall, the monk sought the salvation of his own and other men's souls through the fitting worship of the Lord, through contemplation, and through obedience—if he had a vocation for these things. Yet only years rather than decades after their foundation the Cistercian (and indeed other) monasteries had acquired more wealth and ease of living than was consistent with the rule, and were recruiting many who had little or no vocation. Monastic life in the thirteenth century was well-fed, comfortable, and in many ways complacent; a lofty choir and nave, vaulted and adorned was doubtless pleasing to the eye of God and his saints, and carried to heaven most fittingly the chant from the stalls below. But it was paid for by unremitting attention to every business opportunity in estate management and often by plunging the monastic business into debt and even bankruptcy. As yet there was only lack of fervour and some relaxation of the rule. And perhaps we should wonder not that corruption and evil eventually set in in the sixteenth century, but that they were delayed for so long. They were delayed because the monastic life met a spiritual need of those outside as well as those inside the precinct wall—the assurance that a watchful Lord heard the intercessions and measured the life of those who laboured and those who fought as well as those who prayed. The monastery was a necessary part of a stable and essentially rural society.

Yet by the late twelfth century the ribald life of towns, far removed from the ethos of feudal and monastic society, seemed to pursue only money and have no ears for the real meaning of Christ's gospel. Early in the thirteenth century the popes blessed the new orders of *Friars* who did not cut themselves off from the world, who lived among the people and with the people, who embraced poverty, who preached in the streets and markets, who tended the sick and heard confession, and who gave both spiritual and temporal help to the ordinary folk. In addition, although the orders of friars had their 'houses' in the burghs, the individual friar could always be sent here, there, and everywhere to carry out his work. As opposed to the monk, the friar had 'the whole world for his cloister'.

At first the friars, embracing poverty, held no possessions either individually or as an order. Unlike the monastic houses, they had at first no corporate endowments. They were entirely dependent upon alms, and so were often called *Mendicants*.[14] The most important of these new mendicant orders were the Franciscans (or Grey Friars, or Friars Minor), founded in 1209; the Dominicans (or Black Friars, or Friars Preachers), founded in 1215; and the Carmelites (or White Friars) who, at first hermits, became in the middle of the thirteenth century an order analogous to the Franciscans and Dominicans.[15] The Trinitarians (often called Red Friars), founded in 1198, were more properly canons regular who devoted themselves to the raising of money for ransoming Christians who had been taken captive by the Moors and Saracens—sometimes even offering themselves as captives in exchange.

These orders of friars reached Scotland in the reign of Alexander II,[16] and soon both the Franciscans and Dominicans had houses in many Scottish burghs. Because the Trinitarians devoted themselves to the release of Christian captives (and also to meeting the needs of pilgrims) their houses were often in important seaport burghs like Aberdeen, Berwick, and Dunbar.

If the wealthy lord could grant an endowment of lands to this or that monastery and thereby secure masses for his soul, now even the humblest dweller in the towns could receive the ministrations of a friar. The work of both the monks and the friars was supplementary to that of the secular clergy in parish and diocese.[17]

NOTES

1. Above, p. 41.
2. A band of white lamb's wool (from lambs presented by the nuns of the Convent of St. Agnes at Rome) adorned with purple crosses, and consecrated at St. Peter's. At first granted by the popes as a mark of honour, it was in due course conferred upon all metropolitans, primates, and archbishops as a symbol of the jurisdiction delegated to them by the Holy See, and an archbishop was not allowed to exercise the functions pertaining to his office until he had applied for, and received, the *pallium*.
3. Servants of God.

4. In the ranks of the clergy, the 'regulars' were those who were members of an order observing a 'rule' (as, for example, the Augustinians, or 'canons regular', and the cloistered monks) while the 'secular clergy' were those 'living in the world' (as, for example, the bishops and the parish priests).

5. About 1200, the Culdees of St. Andrews were transformed into the collegiate church of St. Mary of the Rock and, as such, claimed some share in episcopal elections until the middle of the thirteenth century.

6. The Augustinian (Austin) canons were probably the nearest parallel to the Culdees for, although living according to a rule, they could go outside their cloister to serve neighbouring churches.

7. The word *cloister* comes from the Latin *claustra* from *claudere* to enclose, to shut in, to cut off.

8. Verses 62, 164. The Psalm is no. 118 in the Vulgate.

9. At Melrose, owing to the configuration of the ground, the cloister is on the north side of the church. The cloister walk was to be used for study—but the Scottish climate may have modified that aim!

10. Though later, fireplaces are sometimes to be found in the monks' dorters.

11. The services were in the choir of the church; mass was celebrated in the presbytery. The lay-brothers had their own shorter services in the nave— usually little more than a repetition of the *Pater Noster* and later the *Ave Maria*. In most Scottish houses the laity of the neighbourhood were admitted to the nave, which served as a parish church, and one of the monks, or a secular priest, con- ducted the parish services there. The nave was separated from the choir by the *pulpitum* and rood-screen.

12. A practice grew up, however, of taking an early 'breakfast' of bread and ale—which was probably necessary for reasons of health.

13. A series of dialogues showing the way in which the dangers of monastic life (gluttony, unchastity, pride, avarice, apathy, etc.) might be avoided or over- come. Because it later became common for ale and bread to be taken during this reading, the word 'collation' took its modern meaning of a light meal at an odd hour.

14. Later, however, they accepted worldly wealth.

15. Likewise the Augustinian Friars, at first eremitical, later moved into the towns and became one of the mendicant orders.

16. The Black Friars were established in Edinburgh in 1230, and the Grey Friars in Berwick in 1231. The first Scottish house of Carmelites, however, was not founded until the reign of Alexander III—at Tullilum, near Perth, 1262— and there was one house of Augustinian Friars, at Berwick, founded before 1299.

17. It should perhaps be added that the nuns, like the monks, lived in a closed community and took vows of observance but, being debarred from exercising any priestly office, devoted themselves to a life of contemplation. The Scottish nunneries were small, and most of them were of the Cistercian Order.

CHAPTER 12

The Medieval Church—II
The Seculars

WE have remarked that the Viking invasions which isolated the Scottish church from that on the Continent left intact something of the tradition of anchorites in the communities of Culdees. But, probably more important, it left intact a number of episcopal sees from which the future disciplined growth of the church might spring, even though diocesan boundaries were vague or fluctuated with the authority of this or that local magnate or king. It used to be thought that David I founded the medieval Scottish bishoprics, but more modern scholarship has shown that they certainly existed in the eleventh century, although inadequately endowed and wholly at the disposal of the king—hence the long vacancies while he drew the revenues. So it is not surprising that no bishop from Scotland was present at a church council at Windsor, in 1072, when it was agreed between Lanfranc, archbishop of Canterbury, and Thomas, archbishop of York, that all churches from the shores of the Humber to the furthermost limits of Scotland should be within the province of York and their bishops subject to the archbishop of York as their metropolitan.[1]

Yet 1072 was only a year or two after the marriage of Queen Margaret to Malcolm III, a queen who earned canonization for the sanctity of her life and whose concern for the life of the church is shown by her correspondence with Lanfranc and the establishment of Dunfermline priory. But there is no indication that she called for reforms such as clerical celibacy or the dispossession of the lay holders of church property.[2] Indeed, one of Margaret's own sons, Ethelred, became abbot of Dunkeld while possibly still a layman; and both Margaret and Malcolm gave benefactions to the Culdee community of Lochleven. If we are to trust the contemporary account of her confessor, Turgot, Margaret concerned herself mainly with certain points of observance, such as the date of the beginning of Lent, the use of certain 'barbarous rites' in the celebration of mass, and the scruples of the Scottish clergy who regarded themselves as 'unworthy' to take the sacrament on Easter day—all observances in which the Scottish church differed from Rome (and indeed, England or France), and every difference probably arising only from the long severance of contact with Rome.

But Margaret's 'reforms' were important in that they marked the beginning of a change—a change to be continued and expedited by her sons, and notably by David I, whereby in every way, in organization, in administration, and in observances, the church in Scotland was brought into line with the churches of England and the continent. And, under David, the reformed, reorganized church was used to further and to support the royal reorganization of the state. The key to that administrative reform was the revival of bishoprics, the foundation (perhaps) of new ones, and the appointment as bishops of men intent upon ensuring that their flocks, lay and ecclesiastical, followed the ways to the means of grace made open by the church—the sacraments and lives of good works.

The line of Celtic bishops of St. Andrews came to an end in 1093 with the death of Fothad, who, York was to claim much later and probably falsely, had professed obedience to Archbishop Thomas of York. For nearly fifteen years and, for reasons unknown, the see remained vacant until, soon after his accession, Alexander I invited Turgot, prior of Durham, and formerly Queen Margaret's confessor, to be bishop of St. Andrews. But who was to consecrate the new bishop?—for canon law (hitherto probably ignored in this matter by the remote Scottish church) required the consecration of a bishop either by his metropolitan or by a papal legate. According to the contemporary chronicler, Symeon of Durham, 'dissensions' at once arose 'between the Church of York and the Church of St. Andrew of Scotland; for the former demands for herself as by a certain right the ordination and subjection of the primate of the Scots, but the latter on the contrary asserts that she owes nothing by any right of antiquity or custom'. Then, in 1109, a new archbishop of York, Thomas, was consecrated. He at once claimed a right to consecrate Turgot, and, in the same year, Turgot was consecrated by him, though with agreement that the consecration should be without 'subjection, saving the authority of both churches, so that later a just conclusion should decide the controversy'. With Turgot now consecrated bishop of St. Andrews, and now in Scotland, however, 'quarrels' soon arose between the bishop and the king. We do not know what these quarrels were—possibly they arose out of the relationship of the church to the king—but apparently they were irreconcilable, and Turgot finally left Scotland, retiring to Durham where he died in 1115.

At this time the see of York was again vacant,[3] and Alexander I at once wrote to Archbishop Ralph of Canterbury asking for his advice and assistance. In this letter, the king declared that 'the bishops of the church of St. Andrews in ancient times used not to be consecrated save by the Roman pontiff himself or by the archbishop of Canterbury. This we have adhered to, and have established by authority', though Archbishop Lanfranc, 'by what agreement we know not, and in the absence of us and ours', placed the church in obedience to York; 'but we permit that by no means to continue any longer, being supported, if it please you, by your authority'. Finally, in 1120, at Alexander I's request, and despite a letter addressed to the bishops of Scotland in 1119 by Pope Calixtus II ordering them to give canonical obedience to the archbishop of York and commanding that 'no one henceforth be consecrated as bishop in your churches save by your metropolitan the archbishop of York, or by his permission', Archbishop Ralph of Canterbury, with the agreement of King Henry I, sent Eadmer, a monk of Canterbury, to Scotland, where he was elected as bishop of St. Andrews. But again difficulties arose over the bishop's consecration. Eadmer wished to be consecrated by (and hence to promise obedience to) the archbishop of Canterbury; the archbishop of York insisted upon his right; while Alexander I was determined to be king in all things in his kingdom and would not agree to any other authority having any power therein.[4] And within a year Eadmer had returned unconsecrated to Canterbury.

Upon Eadmer's death in 1124, Alexander I promptly chose as his successor Robert, who, although a Yorkshireman, was prior of the Augustinian house at Scone. This was clearly a choice of a Scottish churchman, and Robert was duly elected. But again, who was to consecrate the new bishop? Alexander I died a few months after Robert's election, and his successor David I was equally determined that the Scottish church should be independent and free. Robert, too, refused to acknowledge the archbishop of York as his metropolitan. There were four years of argument and when, finally, Robert was consecrated by Thurstan, archbishop of York, the consecration was 'without profession of obedience, saving the just right of the church of St. Andrew'.

Meantime, in 1126, David I had endeavoured to solve the whole problem with a request to the pope that St. Andrews should be erected into a metropolitan see with Scotland as its province; owing to English opposition, the request was refused. From these discussions, including the bulls of Pope Calixtus, it is abundantly clear that the Scottish church was provided with a number of bishoprics and that most of them had incumbent bishops. At old ecclesiastical centres like Dunkeld and Brechin (which also may have had Culdee communities) or Whithorn, there may never have been a break in the episcopal succession. Strathearn or Dunblane was probably vacant but David either continued or restored the succession of bishops at Aberdeen, Moray, and Ross (Rosemarkie), while Caithness may have been a new see to whose church at Dornoch the king sent a convent of monks from Dunfermline abbey. By 1153 the kingdom of Scotland had ten dioceses.[5]

In the dispute between Scottish kings and the archbishops of York and (sometimes) the pope, the issues were far deeper than the obedience of the Scottish church to York. Alexander I, David I, and their immediate successors were insistent upon the independence of the Scottish church because church and state were closely interrelated. The cathedral churches and the monastic houses held vast extents of lands; they had jurisdiction over the tenants on their lands. No king could allow a lord, lay or spiritual, holding many lands within his realm, to be too greatly subject to an overlord in another realm. More than that, the church, through its spiritual work, had a great influence over the lives and thoughts of the people; while its bishops, abbots, and priors, by virtue of their office, had voice in the king's council and, as learned men, frequently filled high offices in the state. How then could the Scottish king allow the Scottish church to be subject to the directions of an English metropolitan, its bishops traipsing to York at every command of the archbishop? Even if Scotland and England enjoyed friendly relations, it would be intolerable that the king's choice of a bishop should be frustrated by the refusal of a mere archbishop (over whom he had no hold) to carry out the consecration; if Scotland and England were in opposition, it was vital that the church should support the state.

Under Alexander I this struggle for the independence of the

Scottish church had taken place in relation to St. Andrews; under David I there was a long and similar struggle with regard to Glasgow. There the bishop, John, who had been consecrated by Pope Paschal II, consistently refused to acknowledge the claims of York despite all papal commands and admonitions; and, upon his death in 1174, the claims of York were still evaded when his successor, Herbert, was consecrated by Pope Eugenius III.

In the reign of Malcolm IV, however, we find what appears to be a change in papal policy. Early in Malcolm's reign, in 1155, the English pope, Adrian IV, had written to the bishops of Scotland enjoining them 'to love and honour' the archbishop of York as their metropolitan and to 'offer him the obedience and reverence due to him by metropolitan right'; but in 1159 Pope Alexander III, while regretting his inability to grant a petition from St. Andrews (almost certainly a petition of freedom from the claims of York and for the erection of St. Andrews into an archbishopric and metropolitan see—for St. Andrews was then vacant), nevertheless appointed William, bishop of Moray, to be legate of the apostolic see in Scotland, and it was by William, acting as papal legate, that the new bishop of St. Andrews was consecrated in 1160. Then, in 1164, Engelram, bishop of Glasgow, was consecrated by Pope Alexander III himself, 'although the messengers of Roger, archbishop of York, very greatly opposed it'; and in 1165 Richard, who succeeded Arnold in St. Andrews, is said to have been consecrated by the other bishops of Scotland by special papal authority.

This change in papal policy was undoubtedly influenced by Henry II's attack on the jurisdiction of the church courts in England and his estrangement from Thomas Becket, archbishop of Canterbury from 1164; the pope supported Becket in vain until Henry's great mistake, the murder of Becket in 1170. After the capture of King William and the treaty of Falaise in 1174 the bishops and abbots of Scotland swore fealty to Henry II; the treaty required also that they should make to the church of England 'the same subjection as their predecessors were wont to make and which they ought to make', conceding that the church of England was to have 'that right in the church of Scotland which by right she ought to have'. This was Henry's second bad mistake in his dealings with Pope Alexander III, whose functions were usurped when two kings tried to settle the relationship between their two churches. The pope was not fooled by the attempt to disguise this new arrangement as though it were a restoration of old custom. In 1175 the new bishop of Glasgow not only secured confirmation by the pope and consecration by his legate but also a bull making the see of Glasgow the 'special daughter' of the pope 'no-one in between', thereby excluding all the English ecclesiastical claims from Glasgow.[6] When, at a council held at Northampton in January 1176 and attended by King William and many of the Scottish bishops, abbots, and priors, Henry II demanded the subjection which the Scottish church 'ought to make', he was met with the Glasgow claim of direct dependence on the pope, and the blunt reply from the Scottish bishops that 'their predecessors never made any subjection to the church of England, neither ought they to make any subjection to her'. Then an unseemly dispute arose between the archbishop of York and the archbishop of Canterbury, each claiming the subjection of the Scottish church, 'and thus ended that conference'.

King Henry's audacity was counterproductive: despite lobbying at Rome by agents of York flourishing forged letters from King William admitting their claims, Pope Alexander III in July 1176 wrote to the bishops of Scotland condemning the oath to obey the English church which Henry had exacted from them,[7] informing them that he had enjoined the archbishop of York not to exercise any metropolitan right over them, and commanding them to obey only the pope himself until the claims of York were proved. If York had had a good case, it would have seen the light of day long before, and this bull, known by its Latin title, *Super anxietatibus*, gave the Scottish church that freedom from a foreign metropolitan which it had sought for three-quarters of a century. All was imperilled, however, when, in 1178, King William entered into a violent quarrel with the papacy over an election to the see of St. Andrews.

We know little about the formalities of episcopal appointment in early times. Turgot, we are told, was appointed 'by the king and by the clergy and people'; Eadmer was 'elected by the clergy and the people, the king consenting'; and, in the case of Robert, Alexander I 'caused Robert to be elected bishop of St. Andrews', and this doubtless represents the facts of the situation: the king chose the new bishop and although formal election by cathedral chapters followed and was now becoming the rule, the king's prior consent to an election was regarded as necessary.[8]

As we have already seen, Pope Eugenius III, in 1147, had given to the chapter of St. Andrews the right of electing its bishop; it had twice dutifully elected the king's nominee until in 1178, on the death of Bishop Richard, the chapter unanimously but without King William's knowledge elected John, called 'the Scot', who was a relative of the former bishop, Robert, to succeed him. William refused to recognize the election. But then the king went beyond all his rights. He intruded his own chaplain, Hugh, secured his consecration, and expelled John from the kingdom. At once John took his appeal to Rome. The pope wrote a stern letter to the king and sent a legate to Scotland who, following a church council at Holyrood (by the treaty of Falaise, the English garrisoned Edinburgh), deposed Hugh, confirmed the election of John, and caused John to be consecrated by four bishops. But William was still obdurate and so there were two bishops of St. Andrews. In the resultant struggle, John was again banished by the king and then Roger archbishop of York made legate in Scotland by the pope, who thus openly threatened to take away that freedom which he had given to the Scottish church. Hugh was excommunicated by the legate and Scotland laid under an interdict; and finally, when the king had banished those of the clergy who supported John, the king himself was excommunicated.[9]

At this stage Pope Alexander III died (1181), the powers of his legate lapsed, and the new pope, Lucius III, at once made gestures of reconciliation. He released King William from his excommunication and Scotland from its interdict; he also sent to William, as a mark of grace, the Golden Rose.[10] But the situation was not finally resolved until 1188 when, Hugh having died and John the Scot having been elected bishop of Dunkeld (an election to which William agreed), representatives of the chapter of St. Andrews, sitting at Perth, elected as bishop Roger of Leicester, the king's cousin and chancellor.

The election of Roger[11] at Perth, and not at St. Andrews, is significant. Perth was a royal residence, and royal influence could be exercised there more easily. Moreover in England, by the Constitutions of Clarendon (1164), Henry II had claimed that elections to bishoprics and abbacies had to take place in the royal chapel and were to be subject to the approval of the king and his council. The king's interests had to be secured, and those interests were now recognized. In 1239 in a papal mandate relating to the election of David de Bernham as bishop of St. Andrews, we read that the chapter had first sought from the king leave to elect (*eligendi licentia*), according to custom (*iuxta morem*), and that the king had subsequently given his assent to the election of David, whose name he had surely suggested. And it may be that, while the king wanted bishops who were acceptable to him, the cathedral chapters were not unwilling to see eye to eye with the king. After all, a bishop who enjoyed the royal favour would be able to further the interests of his cathedral at the royal court, perhaps even to secure for its benefit further gifts of lands and privileges.

Neither Pope Alexander III nor his successors took away that freedom which had been granted to the Scottish church in 1176; in 1189 the quit-claim of Canterbury made Scotland once more a free and independent kingdom. In 1191 after a long vacancy a new archbishop of York was appointed and the Scots hastened to tie up the loose ends of recent controversies. In 1192 Pope Celestine III made the Scottish church a 'special daughter' of Rome (as the bishop of Glasgow already was), an acknowledgement that York could never have any right to metropolitan authority in Scotland. By this bull, *Cum universi*, the Scottish church[12] was to be subject only to Rome 'with no intermediary' (such as Canterbury or York); further, to rule out the danger that York might come in again, as in the 1180s, as papal legate, it was granted that henceforth no one save the pope, or a legate *a latere*,[13] could publish a sentence of interdict or of excommunication within the kingdom of Scotland; and no one who was not 'of the kingdom of Scotland' could exercise the office of papal legate in Scotland unless he were sent for that purpose direct from the apostolic see. This, the definitive bull of the liberties of the Scottish church, was confirmed by subsequent popes, and the church was never again in serious danger of subordination to a foreign archbishop—though York never gave up hope![14]

In the whole Western Church the Scottish church was unique in having several bishops and no archbishop. Now at the great reforming fourth Lateran Council,[15] convened by Innocent III in 1215, and at which four bishops, an abbot,[16] and representatives of the other prelates of Scotland were present, it was decreed that metropolitans should hold annual provincial councils or synods of their clergy to review the state of the church within their provinces, to ensure that papal decrees were being observed, and to pass provincial statutes. But Scotland had no metropolitan, only nine or ten independent bishops, each directly subject to the pope.

Scotland was not even a province of the church. Moreover, according to canon law, no body of clergy could hold a council among themselves without the consent of their metropolitan. How, then, could the church in Scotland observe and obey this decree? Nor can it be taken for granted that there was still a desire for St. Andrews to be erected into a metropolitan see. So far as the Scottish king was concerned he had seen, in England, that an archbishop could oppose the king and the king's council; so far as the Scottish bishops were concerned, probably not one of them was anxious to see the bishop of St. Andrews raised in authority over them all.

Some representations (of which we have no record) must have been made to Rome. They resulted, in 1225, in the bull *Quidam vestrum*,[17] granted by Pope Honorius III, whereby the Scottish church was commanded to hold a provincial council by authority of the apostolic see. But, again, who was to preside over the council when no one bishop had authority over the rest, and when doubtless each bishop was jealous of his independence? Here the expedient was adopted during the thirteenth century of choosing a 'Conservator' for each council—at first called the 'Conservator of the Statutes of the Council'; later called 'Conservator of the Privileges of the Scottish Church'. The Conservator was chosen from among the whole body of bishops; he presided over the council; it was his duty to enforce its statutes and decrees; but he held office only from the one council to the next. In this way parity was still secured.

It would be quite wrong to see the bishops only as agents of royal authority. Their functions as priests of higher order who alone could consecrate priests and churches, as teachers responsible for Christian doctrine in all the parishes in their dioceses, and as judges in matters spiritual, these functions were held up to them by the popes as the ideal to which they must constantly strive. And whatever their failings, the indications are that thirteenth-century bishops on the whole strove harder than those of the twelfth, and that despite inevitable compromises with secular politics, there was no significant falling away from duty in the fourteenth and fifteenth centuries. The bishops equipped themselves with agents, first the archdeacon (who, by the thirteenth century had often defined his administrative and judicial functions so carefully that the bishop could not meddle in them) and then an 'official' and (occasionally) a 'vicar-general' with judicial and administrative functions respectively. The bishops and their subordinate functionaries knew the rules of the church, and strove to put them into effect fairly. They were not lacking in courage, and if Christ had commanded, 'Go ye therefore and teach all nations, administering them with the checks and balances of canon law', then the church would indeed have matched the word of its Master.

Within the dioceses the smaller divisions of parishes, each under a parish priest, had gradually taken shape, many in the twelfth and thirteenth centuries. As churches were built, so they served areas round them, and in due course those areas became parishes—that is, the district served by a 'baptismal church', a church with a priest who could administer the sacraments of baptism and marriage and perform the rites of burial, and who was subject to the 'visitation' of the bishop of the diocese within which the parish lay. Often the baron or laird would build a church on his lands, would endow it, and, acting as its patron, would himself appoint the priest. In the spirit of the times he would do this almost automatically—for the weal of his soul and the souls of his ancestors and his family. He himself would be buried there, and masses for his soul would be said there. His wife, his son, his son's son, and so forth would also be buried there and masses said for their souls. In due course that particular church would acquire the standing of a parish church; and later we often find that barony and parish are indentical. But although the dioceses had taken definite shape by the reign of David I, the building of churches, the growth of the parish system, the subdivision of the many large parishes, and the provision of parochial clergy were piecemeal and sporadic; parishes emerged and became defined more rapidly in Lothian and the eastern coastal plain than elsewhere.

The exaction of 'teinds' (or, in England, tithes) from a particular area for a particular church (enforced by David I and his successors) undoubtedly helped to define the early parishes. For, in addition to any endowment of lands that a church might enjoy, together with the offerings of the faithful, it was also supported by payment of teinds, a payment of one-tenth of all 'increase', for while man planted it was God who gave the increase. So payment was made (and could be enforced) of a tithe of all crops, a tithe of the offspring of animals (calculated according to a monetary scale), a tithe of milk, butter, cheese, and eggs, and, with the growth of trade, a tithe of the profits of merchandise and craftsmanship. And the area of exaction for the support of a church was the area of its parish.

Yet, just when the new parochial system was settling down, and the church was becoming organized in dioceses and parishes, there arose the need to support the monasteries and other religious houses and, as it happened, they were supported at the expense of the parishes. Lands, rights (fishing rights, hunting rights, trading rights), exemptions (from tolls, from customs, and so forth), and monetary grants (from the king's treasury, from the rents of burghs, and from the profits of justice) were showered upon the monasteries; the great nobles followed the example of the kings; and these grants to abbeys and priories included also many grants of parish churches which allowed the religious houses to draw the teinds.

David I's charter to Holyrood abbey, given between 1128 and 1136, included, in its grants to the abbey, lands in Broughton, Inverleith, Pittendreich, and Whitekirk; tofts in the burghs of Stirling, Edinburgh, Berwick, and Renfrew; £2 a year from the burgh fermes of Edinburgh, £5 a year from the customs of Perth, and £10 a year from the royal treasury; fishing rights at Stirling, Berwick, and Renfrew; freedom from toll and custom in trading throughout the realm; a right to have its own burgh (Canongate); and *also certain churches*, the church of the castle of Edinburgh, the church of St. Cuthbert with its chapels at Corstorphine and Liberton (which would later 'hive off' and become parishes on their own), and the church of Airth. In the reign of William, the new abbey of Arbroath was given no fewer than thirty-four churches; and by 1265 the abbeys of Kelso, Paisley, Holyrood, and Arbroath held among them 126 churches. Or again, we find Gilbert, earl of Strathearn, granting to the abbey of Inchaffray (which he had then founded) the parish church of Aberuthven (Perthshire) with its tithes, oblations, and other income, and with the land with which it had been endowed by the earl's father and mother—and the church of Aberuthven was only one of five churches given at that time (*c.* 1200) by Earl Gilbert to Inchaffray for its support.

In assigning a church, a lay patron may have been moved not only by an endeavour to secure the weal of his soul, but also by a feeling that the priest could more appropriately be appointed by the religious house; and in a number of early instances only the right of patronage was assigned. But the practice of 'assigning' or 'appropriating' churches to abbeys and priories quickly developed into an assignment to the religious house for its benefit (*ad proprios usus*). All this was not peculiar to Scotland, but in Scotland it became so common that a system of independent parish churches was everywhere modified. A monastery might now hold parish churches in far distant parts; Holyrood, for example, held churches in Galloway, and Inchaffray held churches in Argyll. Also, and in a like way, parish churches were frequently assigned to the bishops' seats—perhaps to support a canonry, or for the general support of the cathedral chapter—and, later, to collegiate churches and academic colleges. So what might have been a simple administrative system of church government through dioceses and parishes was rendered complex. More than that, the parish churches soon began to suffer.

Admittedly an 'appropriated' parish church was still served by a priest, but the teinds and endowments all went to the cathedral, abbey, priory, or college to which it had been assigned, and out of them the priest was paid a stipend, so becoming a vicar,[18] or deputy. Moreover, while the assignment of a parish church had to receive the consent of the bishop of the diocese within which it lay, and while it was the duty of the bishop to ensure that 'a decent maintenance' (in the thirteenth century fixed at the insistence of reforming popes and bishops at a decent minimum of ten merks a year)[19] was provided for the priest, the records reveal that this minimum payment was not provided, even when the revenues of the church were amply sufficient. And in the fourteenth and later centuries the process was, as it were, doubled. The appropriated church now had a fixed stipend for a vicar; that too could be appropriated and a modicum only used to maintain a chaplain. By the eve of the Reformation, in the middle of the sixteenth century, nearly nine-tenths of the parish churches in Scotland had been assigned to religious houses, to bishops' seats, and to collegiate churches and academic colleges.

Wherever there was wealth in the church there were churchmen eager to divert it to new uses, forgetful that it was a permanent income tax of 10 per cent upon peasants as well as lairds, intended to provide not only a decent living for the parish priest but also alms for the poor. The cathedral, abbey, or priory was tempted to enrich itself at the expense of the parish; it underpaid priests who, all too often, were men of small ability.[20] So, while the parishes were neglected or ill-served, the cathedrals, abbeys, and priories, with their many endowments and their enjoyment of many assigned churches, became possessed of enormous wealth.

NOTES

1. In the organization of the church an archbishop who was metropolitan of a province had jurisdiction over all the bishops within his province.

2. Indeed, the Celtic church in Scotland had now become so largely laicized that probably those of the clergy who still continued the services of the church in the various monasteries were now called Culdees, and the name may even have been applied to groups of clergy who had never been true Célidé.

3. Archbishop Thomas had died in 1114 and Archbishop Thurstan was not consecrated until 1119.

4. This is a paraphrase of the attitude of the King of Scots as explained to Eadmer by John, bishop of Glasgow.

5. About 1180-90 the number became eleven, when Lismore (Argyll) was separated from Dunkeld. In 1472, when St. Andrews was erected into an archbishopric, Whithorn (Galloway) was transferred from the province of York to that of St. Andrews, and the bishopric of Orkney and the bishopric of the Isles were also transferred from the province of Nidaros (Trondheim, Norway) to St. Andrews. Thereby the Scottish dioceses, numbering thirteen, all came within the obedience of St. Andrews. See below, pp. 276-8. The convent at Dornoch was short-lived.

6. Jocelyn, bishop of Glasgow, could now claim that his church (dedicated to St. Kentigern who lived about 600) was a special daughter of Rome, exempt from all subjection of bishops to archbishops; and, in a *Life of Kentigern* probably written about this time, the author is careful to state (quite anachronistically) that after the pope had confirmed in person Kentigern's election and consecration, and had sent him back to Scotland, the pope later conferred upon him a special privilege to the effect that he was to be subject to no other bishop but was to be the pope's own vicar and chaplain.

7. Again an attempt to protect the church in general against the invasion of its liberties by Henry II for, as the pope's letter maintained, 'it is not for any king or prince to exercise control over churches or ecclesiastics'.

8. Cathedral chapters were, moreover, slow in taking shape. The chapter of Glasgow was in rudimentary existence by the end of the reign of David I, but, in other cases, the 'chapter' may at first have consisted of the clergy of the see. In the dioceses of Dunkeld and Dunblane the 'chapter' consisted of the archdeacon and certain parish clergy, especially the rural deans, until early in the thirteenth century; and the local clergy, headed by the archdeacon, preserved a claim to some say in episcopal elections at Sodor, Lismore, Whithorn, and Aberdeen. This was in accord with canon law, and was not necessarily a legacy from 'Celtic' practices.

9. An *interdict* was a 'forbidding'. It forbade, as a punishment (i) the celebration of divine service (though particular dispensations might be granted for the celebration of mass behind closed doors); (ii) the administration of certain of the sacraments—baptism and confirmation were usually permitted, but neither marriage nor extreme unction; (iii) holy burial. It was directed against a community of people rather than against an individual.

Excommunication was a 'cutting off from all communication with other Christians'. The excommunicated was outside the church and all Christian society. He was excluded from the sacraments and the prayers of the faithful. He was denied holy burial. He could not plead in a civil or ecclesiastical court—though actions could be brought against him. No one could have business or social relationships with him. The punishment was usually directed against an individual though it could also be directed against a whole community.

10. 'On the Sunday which falls in the middle of Lent, the Pope is wont to bear in his hand a rose of gold, enamelled red, and perfumed. This he may bestow as a mark of grace, sometimes on the most favoured of his attendants, at other times on a foreign prince. By the rose, Christ is figured; by the gold, His kingly office; by the colour red, His passion and death; and by the perfume, His resurrection.'

11. According to one chronicler, Roger was not even in holy orders at the time of his election. Certainly he was not consecrated until some nine or ten years later.

12. In the bull, only the episcopal sees of St. Andrews, Glasgow, Dunkeld, Dunblane, Brechin, Aberdeen, Moray, Ross, and Caithness are mentioned. Argyll (Lismore) is strangely omitted; so too is Whithorn which, until 1472, gave obedience to York.

13. A legate *a latere* is one sent by the pope from the Holy See (originally from the pope's own 'household') and possessing full papal authority.

14. York tried to revive its claims in the 1290s.

15. When a General Council of the Church met in Rome itself, the council was called a 'Lateran Council' because it was customary for it to meet in the cathedral church of St. John in Laterano (as it now would meet in the Vatican). The fourth Lateran Council was the twelfth General Council.

16. The bishops of St. Andrews, Glasgow, Caithness, and Moray, and the abbot of Kelso.

17. *Quidam vestrum nuper auribus nostris intimaverunt quod cum non haberetis archiepiscopum cujus auctoritate possitis concilium provinciale celebrare* . . .

18. In some cases vicars received the 'lesser tithes' or 'vicarage tithes' in place of a stipend; always they received the oblations—and hence, to some extent, the later rapacity in their demands.

19. Ten merks, or £6·66, was probably a sufficient maintenance at that time, for the exchequer accounts show that then a cow could be bought for 4s. (20 p), a pig for 2s. (10 p), and a hen for 1d. ($\frac{1}{2}$ p).

20. In 1549 the minimum stipend was raised to twenty merks, and in 1559 to twenty-four merks; but these belated increases were far from sufficient to meet the greatly increased cost of living. Moreover, on the eve of the Reformation some vicarages still had less than the old minimum of ten merks.

CHAPTER 13

The Succession and the Great Cause

ALEXANDER III's first wife, Margaret, sister of Edward I of England, died in February 1275, and in October 1285 Alexander married, as his second wife, Yolande, daughter of the comte de Dreux. Less than six months later, on the night of 18/19 March 1286, in a storm of wind and rain, the king, riding from Edinburgh to join his wife at Kinghorn, apparently lost touch with his guides and, near Kinghorn, was thrown from his horse and killed. Of Alexander's children, the younger son, David, had died in 1281 when he was eight years old; the king's daughter, Margaret, who had married Eric II, king of Norway, had died in 1283 leaving an infant daughter, Margaret. In February 1284, a week after the death of Alexander, the king's elder and only surviving son (at the age of twenty), the magnates of the realm, called together at Scone, had acknowledged the king's granddaughter, Margaret, as heiress to the kingdom of Scotland should the king have no other issue.

It seems that the magnates concurred in this settlement reluctantly, and none more so than Robert Bruce who in 1291 was to claim that when Alexander II, still childless, was about to make an expedition to the Isles, the magnates of the realm, at the request of the king, had named Bruce as heir to the throne.[1] In this decision the magnates are said to have preferred Bruce, as the son of the second daughter of the king's uncle, David, earl of Huntingdon, rather than Dervorguilla, the daughter of the eldest daughter, for of course it was unthinkable that a woman should succeed as ruling queen. So in April 1284 Alexander III wrote to Edward I that 'much good may yet come to pass through your kinswoman our heir apparent' which was a plain suggestion that Margaret, the Maid of Norway, should marry an English prince, for her husband would become ruling king of Scots if she inherited the kingdom.

In March 1286 Bruce immediately made it known that he considered his claim to the throne better than all others save that of a son of Alexander III—and in April it was known that Queen Yolande was indeed pregnant. Gathering together, the Scottish prelates and magnates took a new oath (which replaced that of 1284) pledging loyalty to the (unspecified) rightful heir to the late king (by blood), and appointed an interim government of six guardians—two bishops, William Fraser, bishop of St. Andrews, Robert Wishart, bishop of Glasgow; two earls, Duncan, earl of Fife, Alexander Comyn, earl of Buchan; and two barons, James the Steward and John Comyn of Badenoch.[2] The supposed distribution into three northern and three southern magnates, if true, was probably accidental;[3] much more noteworthy is the absence from this collective leadership of any 'middling' landowners or of even the wealthiest burgesses. The community of the realm of Scotland, a phrase sometimes used of themselves by those who took communal decisions after March 1286, were its 'good folk', the well-born, wide-landed, and rich; they alone had political responsibility in this feudal society.

As the time for the queen's delivery drew near, Bruce insured against the outcome by entering into a bond or pact with his adherents at Turnberry in September, so that when the child was still-born in October or November, he was prepared and in the winter of 1286-7 raised war in the south-west against those who opposed his claim to the throne. Evidently he was in the weaker position for his rising failed and the guardians who suppressed it continued to govern in the name of an unknown future king for a further two years. We should sympathize with them in their terrible dilemma, for there was no book of rules to tell them who should succeed; such matters were the concern of the king acting with the advice and consent of his barons, for the grace of God, under whom alone kings rule, was conferred upon kings and no others to rule. Barons alone, no matter how responsible, could not set themselves up as judges in this matter; this was only the first of their difficulties since, even if they had tried to judge, it was already clear that they included partisan groups supporting John Balliol, son of the widowed Dervorguilla, and Robert Bruce. The danger of renewed civil war among these partisans pushed all parties back into acceptance of the 1284 settlement and the Maid seemed likely after all to inherit her kingdom.

In May 1289 Eric of Norway sent ambassadors to Edward I to discuss the position of Margaret, and the guardians appointed representatives to join in discussions with the Norwegian ambassadors and with Edward's own representatives, 'saving in all things the liberty and honour of Scotland'; and in November 1289 the discussions concluded with the treaty of Salisbury. By that treaty the Norwegian envoys promised to send Margaret to England before 1 November 1290 'free and quit of all contract of marriage'; Edward promised that, if Margaret came to England, and if the kingdom of Scotland were then 'fully settled in quietness and peace' so that she could safely stay there, he would, when requested by the Scots, send her to Scotland 'as free and quit of all contract of marriage as when he received her'; and the Scots representatives promised to establish quietness in their land before Margaret came there, and, further, that they would not contract her in marriage save with 'the ordinance, will, and council of king Edward', and save with the assent of the king of Norway, her father.

Much stress was here laid upon the freedom of the Maid from marriage contract; but Edward, in anticipation, and probably with the knowledge of the guardians and other influential men, had already sent messengers to Pope Nicholas IV applying for a dispensation for the marriage of Margaret to his son Edward (later Edward II) since they were within the forbidden degrees of the canon law.

Table 4

EDWARD I AND THE MAID OF NORWAY

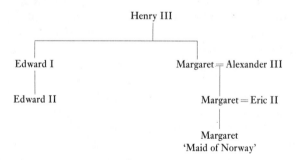

The dispensation was granted ten days after the conclusion of the treaty; and the Scots, when later they heard of its granting, accepted it as joyful news and agreed wholeheartedly to the proposed marriage. In what must have been a well-nigh unanimous letter sent from Birgham in March 1290, the four surviving guardians (the bishops of St. Andrews and Glasgow, John Comyn, and James the Steward),[4] the eight other bishops of Scotland (and also the bishops of Galloway and the Isles), twelve earls, twenty-three abbots, eleven priors, and forty-eight barons spoke of the joyous news of the dispensation and cordially agreed to the marriage, 'subject to such reasonable conditions as they might put forward'; and another letter, sent by the Scots to Eric, urged him to send his daughter to England.

In the following July a new treaty, the treaty of Birgham,[5] was concluded between Scotland and England—a marriage treaty, but one in which the 'rights, laws, liberties, and customs of Scotland' were for all time to be 'wholly and inviolably preserved'. The kingdom of Scotland was to remain 'separate and divided from the kingdom of England' and to be 'free in itself and without subjection'; failing heirs to Edward and Margaret, or either of them, the kingdom of Scotland was to return to the nearest heirs 'wholly, freely, absolutely, and without any subjection' so that the king of England, his heirs, or any others should neither gain nor lose thereby; while other clauses preserved the separate character of the Scottish parliament, the independence of the Scottish courts, and the freedom of Scottish chapter elections.

All these were reasonable conditions and, on the face of it, the treaty of Birgham was both fair and statesmanlike, though it is relevant to speculate on how this union of crowns might have worked, for in many ways the treaty protected the Scottish magnates from government demands, without giving thought to how the government was to work in practice. Moreover, in each of the two clauses guaranteeing the rights, laws, liberties, and customs of Scotland, and the separateness of the kingdom, there was an added sentence: 'Saving always the right of our lord king [of England] and of any other whomsoever, that has pertained to him, or to any other, on the marches, or elsewhere, before the time of the present agreement, or which in any just way ought to pertain to him in the future'.[6] Undoubtedly Edward I had not abandoned English claims —claims which he was later to advance and extend—but, for the present, they might rest. And when, immediately upon the conclusion of the treaty, he demanded that all the castles and places of strength in Scotland should be delivered up to him 'on account of a rumour of some dangers and suspicions of which he had heard', was that with a desire to secure internal order in Scotland on behalf of Margaret and her chosen husband, his son, in the light of Bruce's previous rebellion? Or was Edward I intending to be a masterful ruler of the kingdom of Scots in their name? The demand was refused; and Edward bided his time.

Margaret sailed from Norway in September 1290, but never reached her kingdom. Somewhere in the islands of Orkney she died 'between the hands of Bishop Narve of Bergen and in the presence of the best men who accompanied her from Norway'— possibly of excessive sea-sickness, or possibly because the ship was wrecked: both likely events on such a voyage at the time of the autumnal equinox. Her corpse was taken to Bergen where she was buried, beside her mother, in the choir of Christ's Kirk.

All plans and agreements were now waste parchment, the decision of February 1284 with regard to the succession to the Scottish kingdom had looked no further than the Maid. Who now was the rightful heir to the throne? And perhaps more important: who should decide who was the rightful heir? A letter from William Fraser, bishop of St. Andrews, addressed to Edward I on 7 October, reported that, upon a 'sorrowful rumour' of the death of the queen reaching the people, the kingdom of Scotland had become disturbed; Robert Bruce had come with a great following to Perth; his supporters, the earls of Mar and Atholl, were collecting their forces; parties were beginning to form, and there was fear of general war which could be averted only by Edward's good services. The bishop's letter, however, did not end there. 'If', he continued, 'Sir John Balliol should come to your presence we advise you to take care so to treat with him that in any event your honour and your advantage may be preserved'; and, if indeed the Maid be dead, then let Edward come to the Border to console the people, to save the shedding of blood, and to set up 'for king the man who ought to have the succession, provided he will follow your counsel'.

Here was a single charge and a double hint—a charge to make the rightful heir king and a hint that Balliol ought to succeed to the kingdom, and that Balliol would follow Edward's counsel to Edward's own honour and advantage. And as early as 16 November Balliol had declared himself to be 'heir of the kingdom of Scotland'. At the same time Bruce's supporters were appealing to Edward I against the way in which Balliol's allies were usurping the function of the 'seven earls of Scotland' to choose the king. Modelled without doubt upon the seven electors of the Holy Roman Empire, these seven (they were never named) were historical fiction invented by the Bruce party to encourage the Bruce case that the throne descended by 'imperial' laws.

Perhaps the most telling document of all to come forth from Scotland late in 1290 is one which, though long in print, seems never to be quoted, though it balances, indeed outdoes, Bishop Fraser's letter on Balliol's behalf. Although anonymous there is no doubt that it comes from Robert Bruce the Competitor and is intended for Edward I. It describes first a peace (the treaty of Falaise, 1174), as providing:

that if the king of Scotland ever turned against the king of England the seven earls of Scotland were bound by oath to the king of England . . . Then came Richard I who sold the homage of the king of Scotland . . . but we do not think that this sale is of any validity because the English king and council are so wise that they shall soon be advised whether one can dismember the crown of such a limb. And since the crown must be held undivided, (I) let him [King Edward] know by Elias de Hautville [the messenger] that, when he wants to make his claim in legal form, I shall obey him, and help him with all my friends and my kin . . . And I beseech your grace for my right and my truth which I want to demonstrate before you . . .[7]

The message from Bruce is plain: King Edward must claim to be overlord of Scotland; Bruce will help him and in return expects to be made king of Scots. Fordun, writing in the second half of the fourteenth century that the magnates, not knowing how to decide the succession, asked for Edward's help, was not entirely inaccurate, but Fordun, writing under a Bruce king, failed to name his magnates: Robert Bruce.

But Edward who had just lost his beloved wife, chose this critical juncture to retire into deep mourning, and for three months or more the affairs of Scotland hung fire. Since 1291 we have been in ignorance of the next move and whence it came. Yet in the 1970s new light has been thrown on the matter by the discovery of historical arguments prepared by the Scots in 1321 including the statement that (in 1291) Edward wrote to the Scots urging them not to proceed in debating the right of succession (which could only give rise to discords among them) until he came to the Border. Perhaps we should beware of this *ex parte* statement, but the coyness of Edward I's own record on the point (it would surely have included any invitation from the Scots to intervene as judge) suggests that the Scots were telling most of the truth: Edward came at his own invitation, and not that of the guardians or the community. He invited Scottish clergy and nobility to meet him at an English parliament at Norham on 6 May 1291 (in fact the proceedings began on 10 May), and he also summoned the northern levies of England to be at Norham on 3 June 1291, and hired a band of archers and footmen, possibly as a sign of strength, possibly to accompany his peaceful progress into Scotland.

Assembled at Norham, the Scots were at once informed that Edward had come to do justice to all 'as the superior and lord paramount of the kingdom of Scotland', and that before he could act as judge in the cause of the succession his position and competence as lord superior must first be recognized. But whatever may have been the earlier relationships between English and Scottish kings in the reigns of William the Conqueror, Rufus, and Henry I, it is clear that ever since the quit-claim of Canterbury in 1189 the Scottish kings had regarded their homage paid to English kings as homage solely for the lands which they held in England; and though in 1251 and 1278 English kings pressed for homage for Scotland, Alexander III refused, in 1278 'speaking openly': 'To homage for my kingdom of Scotland, no one has right, save God alone, nor do I hold it, save of God alone.' The Scottish position was clear and it was the guardians' duty to maintain it. On the other hand it was also Edward I's duty to press his right, denying the relevance of the quit-claim of Canterbury for (as Bruce's letter had pointed out) Richard I could not alienate the inheritance (including homage for Scotland) passed on by Henry II to *all* his descendants on the English throne. And if that homage had lapsed into disuse, it was no matter, for 'time does not run against the king'. There was no deep-laid intention to subvert Scottish independence, merely a blinkered determination to insist upon every jot and tittle of the English king's rights.

Clearly the demand which he had made took the Scots by surprise; and the 1321 text recently discovered gives the courteous but courageous rebuttal of Robert Wishart, bishop of Glasgow. Edward graciously granted an adjournment for consideration for three weeks to 2 June. The answer given there by the 'good men' of the community of the realm (who had consulted others in the interval given to them) if partly astute, was certainly to the point. Edward's claim, they declared, was new to them; they had no knowledge of any previous claim by Edward or by any of his predecessors, for recognition as 'superior lord of the realm'. Moreover, how could they admit Edward's claim when they had no king, to whom alone such a claim should be made and who alone could answer it? And did they not put themselves in jeopardy were they so to commit in advance their future king?

Was this a courageous stand, a noble and dignified answer? Perhaps—but if it was not a 'yes' to Edward's claim, neither was it a 'no', for the Scots, it seems, wanted to avoid confrontation and war. Already Edward was uttering threats to take over Scotland; when on 3 June he spoke of his hereditary right to the kingdom of Scotland there was perhaps a threat that Scotland might be held to be a male fief, which, since there were no male heirs, would return into the hands of the superior (and the three principal claimants, as we shall see, all claimed through females). And, at a later date, Edward protested that, although of grace he had consented to judge the cause of the succession, he had never intended thereby to prejudice his own rights, that is to 'escheat' the kingdom.

But it was not necessary; for if only a king could answer Edward's claim, then he would ask it of all those who claimed the throne, among whom *one* was bound to become king. And so on 5 and 6 June 1291 Bruce, Balliol, and seven other 'competitors' for the crown set their seals to documents acknowledging Edward's right to the 'sovereign lordship' of the kingdom of Scotland (and, thereby, his right of determining the cause), agreeing to stand by his award, and also granting that sasine of the land and castles of Scotland should be given to him so that, when judgement was given, they could be delivered by him to the man adjudged to have the right to the throne. All the competitors, it would appear, were prepared to accept Edward as overlord to whom the realm should pass during a vacancy in the throne. With Balliol and Bruce falling over each other in leading this betrayal, did the other competitors recognize this direct lordship, each in the hope that his lord would award him the crown and support him thereafter in wearing it? Or, to put the most generous interpretation upon it, did they feel that Bruce and Balliol were the real contenders and that only by such a recognition could the competing claims of those two be decided and civil war (or an assertion of the English claims by force) be avoided? A mysterious week elapsed. What happened we do not know but by the end of it the guardians and prelates and barons put their seals to similar documents. Edward misdated events in documents in order to put the best face on what happened, but he never got what he really wanted—an unequivocal acknowledgement by the whole community of the realm sealed by the great seal of the realm.[8]

One promise he gave in return—to respect the laws of the kingdom; so long as the succession was under judgement, he would not hear appeals from Scottish courts in England; that promise was honoured when Edward heard such cases at Berwick.

So, the kingdom of Scotland was now in Edward's hands as supreme lord. He reappointed the four surviving guardians (possibly in the hope of governing Scotland by Scots) with an English colleague; a number of English officials were appointed to act in co-operation with Scottish colleagues; certain administrative rearrangements were carried out; an oath of fealty was taken from the bishops, earls, magnates, and others, including towns, and, in turn, Edward swore to govern the realm in accordance with its laws and customs.

The nine competitors now grew in number to thirteen—some claiming through illegitimate children of William the Lion or Alexander II. Most claims were put in to be on the record, for one day the throne might again fall vacant. The constitution of the court, forty each nominated by Bruce and Balliol, twenty-four by Edward I, shows who the serious claimants were. Florence, count of Holland, claimed that David, earl of Huntingdon, had resigned all claim he might have to the Scottish throne which now passed to his sister, Ada, and her descendant, Florence: a claim like this was so strong (ruling out Balliol and Bruce alike) that it led to a postponement of the hearing of the cause so that the resignation could be found and produced. After nearly a year's delay, the resignation was not forthcoming and Florence appears to have abandoned his claim which in any case he had traded to Bruce, agreeing to pass the Scottish throne to him (if he won it) in return for Scottish lands—evidence of Bruce's determination to succeed. The abandonment of Florence's claim meant a return once more to the claims of Balliol and Bruce.

Balliol claimed that the law to be applied was feudal custom in Britain, so far as it related to a dignity such as an earldom. If an earl died leaving three daughters then the dignity of earl went to the eldest and her husband (as in this case) and their heirs. Balliol claimed the kingship as such a direct heir of line, senior descendant of Earl David's eldest daughter. Unfortunately, as John Hastings eagerly pointed out, in English law the lands of an earldom would be partitioned among all three daughters and if the Scottish kingship were adjudged to Balliol in this way, then he and Bruce should have one-third each of all the royal lands and revenues.

To Robert Bruce these arguments were irrelevant. Scotland was a kingdom, and a part of the great lordship of King Edward which included Ireland and Wales. The appropriate law for the rules of such an empire to apply to a subordinate kingdom was 'imperial', that is, Roman, law, according to which the rightful heir was the senior male descendant by degree (that is, of the generation nearest to Earl David) who was David's grandson, Bruce. Already Bruce had used the fiction of seven electors (as in the empire), and if Edward modelled the court, with 105 members, upon the Roman tribunal of *centumviri* he seemed to accept the argument.[9] And when he put the issue to lawyers in Paris for counsel's opinion their views were on the whole in favour of Bruce.

From Edward's point of view each legal tradition had a flaw: in 'imperial' law there could be no escheat in future for failure of heirs to the overlord—a right he was determined to preserve for the English crown. And if, following feudal law, the kingdom of Scotland was partitioned, then what would happen in England if Edward's only surviving son should die leaving several daughters to inherit? For in April 1290 Edward I had defined by ordinance the succession to the kingdom of England: first to his son Edward and his heirs; if Edward died without heirs, to any son who might yet be born to the king; failing such heirs and such son, to Eleanor, the king's eldest daughter and her heirs; whom failing to Joan and her heirs; whom failing to the king's younger daughters and their heirs in strict order. Here, failing male heirs, was succession according to the heir of line. Here it was clearly shown that the kingdom was impartible, and that there was to be no division of its lands among the king's daughters as equal co-heiresses. And when, immediately afterwards, Edward married his daughter Joan to the powerful earl of Gloucester, he bound the earl by solemn oath to maintain the order of the ordinance and therewith to maintain the order of Eleanor before Joan.

In 1292 King Edward asked the eighty Scottish members of the court for guidance on the law of succession in Scotland; it was not

F

his fault that they could not agree an answer, and that the English councillors had to take the lead in answering the question: who has the better right, Balliol or Bruce? The twenty-four followed by the eighty gave the answer 'Balliol'. Bruce immediately changed his ground, arguing now with Hastings for partibility, but the final judgement (on 19 November 1292), much to the court's credit, was for impartibility, and for John Balliol as king. On 20 November he swore fealty to Edward I; on St. Andrew's day (30 November), the only feast day in the otherwise 'closed' period of Advent, he was inaugurated on the stone at Scone, and on 26 December he did homage at Newcastle to the English king.

It is sometimes said that Balliol was chosen because he was a complaisant man; this ascribes to the aged Bruce and his spineless son far more principle than they ever showed, and is a great injustice to Edward I and his court. But the English king now showed that his strength as a stickler for due process of law was not tempered by political wisdom.

Seizing on one point on which he knew the Scots felt strongly, he chose to adjourn an appeal being heard by his court at Berwick in Scotland to Newcastle upon Tyne, and to a protest from King John himself that this infringed the promises made at Norham in 1291 and the Treaty of Birgham (1290) he returned the answer that the Norham promises were for the duration of the succession case only (which was true) and were no longer in force. The Scots did not deny that the right to hear Scottish appeals pertained to him as sovereign lord of the kingdom of Scotland; but they were appalled to discover that under that right he could if necessary summon the king of Scotland himself to appear before his justices, and that each and any of them who had won a case in Scotland might have to answer at Westminster at the instance of the loser.

Edward's claim to be 'superior lord' of the kingdom had brought the response from the community in 1291 that only a king could answer so fundamental a claim; now the community was hoist by the logic of its own answer, for in January 1293 King John accepted Edward's demands, and formally released him from all agreements, promises, and obligations undertaken by him during the time (1291–2) that the kingdom was in his hands—and annulled the Treaty of Birgham (1290). The document suggests why King John relinquished so much: he did so for himself, his heirs, and *any other future king of Scotland*. This phrase is extraordinary, unprecedented, because it shows that a future Scottish king might not be King John's heir. Evidently King Edward pointed out that having adjudged Balliol to be king, he might undo that judgement in favour of another. The Bruce wolf was always outside the door, and so John Balliol might never be master inside the house.

A little later, indeed, Balliol made some endeavour to resist Edward's unprecedented demands. Summoned to London to maintain there a judgement that had been given in the parliament of Scotland against Macduff (a younger son of a former earl of Fife), he ignored the summons. Summoned a second time, he appeared before the judges and, asked to defend his proceedings in parliament, is reported to have replied: 'I am the King of Scotland. To the complaint of Macduff, or to aught else respecting my kingdom, I dare not make answer without the advice of my people.' Under threats to seize three Scottish Border castles, however, he caved in, recognized the court's jurisdiction, and was given time to prepare his case. Meanwhile other cases against him, cases which have the suspicious appearance of being raised by friends of Bruce, were multiplied at the English court. The Macduff case was postponed again without a hearing in the early summer of 1294, when Edward was threatened with the loss of Gascony; for a general muster he demanded from Scotland the military service of her king, and of a number of her earls and barons. But since the whole muster was apparently cancelled, the demand from Scotland did not provoke a confrontation. Whether because of this demand, or because of King John's weakness over appeals to Westminster, early in July 1295 a special council consisting of four bishops, four earls, and four barons was set up by the Scottish community to be responsible for all public affairs—probably an indication of a patriotic baronial move in defence of the realm rather than the appointment of a representative council to strengthen the hand of the king. Through this council an alliance was concluded with France, Edward's enemy (October 1295).

Later Edward was to claim that this alliance provoked his invasion of Scotland. It did nothing of the kind, for he was then in ignorance of it. The slow processes of English justice had eventually run their full course. King John had not lodged his defences against Macduff; the court had given him until 13 October 1295 to do so and when nothing happened, it then required delivery of three Scottish castles as security that he would respond. When they were not delivered, Edward I prepared an army and on 26 March 1296 crossed the Tweed to take sasine of them. He was enforcing an interim judgement of his court. He had no inkling that Scotland's struggle for independence had begun.

NOTES

1. See the genealogical tree below, p. 153.

2. Often and wrongly called the Black Comyn. He and his son were of the Badenoch branch of the family, the 'Red' Comyns. The 'Black' Comyns were the earls of Buchan. A similar distinction was later made between the Red and Black Douglases.

3. Both Comyns were powerful in Galloway; the earl of Fife and the bishop of St. Andrews had wealth on both sides of the Forth. The 'north-south balance' is not very convincing. And it distracts attention from the truly remarkable fact that with all the Scottish families to choose from, two Comyns were elected.

4. Duncan, earl of Fife, had been murdered in 1289; and Alexander Comyn, earl of Buchan, had died in 1289.

5. Confirmed at Northampton in August 1290.

6. Too much of a sinister intent has been read into these clauses which represented possible *territorial* claims by the English king—as the phrase *on the marches or elsewhere* indicates. Edward I was undoubtedly anxious to claim the Isle of Man which the Scots had annexed in 1264-6 though it had earlier been a dependency of England. These clauses probably refer to an intention to claim Man.

7. F. Palgrave, *Documents and Records illustrating the History of Scotland . . .*, i (1837), 21-2. Many important documents relating to 1286-1306 are printed in this volume and in J. Stevenson, *Documents illustrative of the History of Scotland* (2 vols., 1870) and E. L. G. Stones, *Anglo-Scottish Relations, 1174-1329* (1965). Translations will be found in Dickinson, Donaldson, and Milne, *Source Book of Scottish History*, i (2nd edn., 1958). But the story of these years, and particularly of the Great Cause of 1291, cannot be considered as satisfactorily dealt with until many more English records have been examined, and in some cases re-edited. The many documents (sometimes with conflicting testimony) relating to the Great Cause are to be published in a major new edition by E. L. G. Stones and G. G. Simpson. In the revision of this chapter A. A. M. Duncan has benefited from many discussions with Professor Stones, whose generous help he gratefully acknowledges.

8. Crucial documents which seem certainly to have been misdated were those from the keepers of the various Scottish royal castles surrendering them to Edward; dated 7 June, they must surely have been sealed after 12 June.

9. Professor Stones thinks that the model of the *Centumviri* was a much later (*c.* 1340) interpretation of the court. It is certainly not mentioned in 1291. And to the eighty Bruce-Balliol assessors, Edward was allowed to name as many auditors as he wished.

Table 5. THE THIRTEEN CLAIMANTS FOR THE THRONE

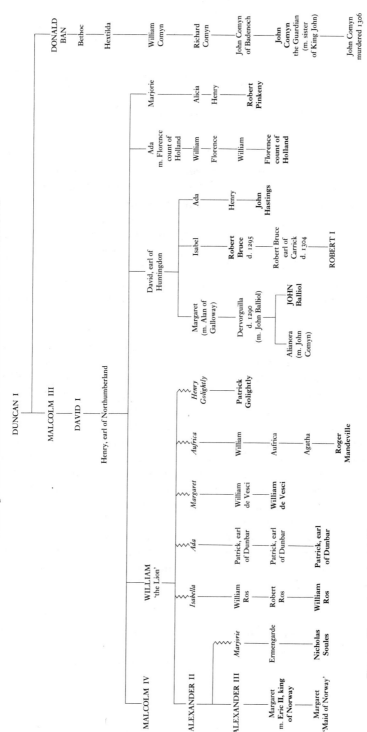

The names of the competitors are given in **bold type**.

followed by a name in italics signifies an illegitimate child. It is noteworthy that the descendant of an illegitimate son of David, earl of Huntingdon, did not put forward a claim; also the claims of Patrick

〰 Golightly and Robert Pinkeny probably misrepresent their true descent.

CHAPTER 14

The War of Independence—I

I T was the Scots who made the aims of the war broader, when the formal denunciation of King John's homage and fealty (*diffidatio*) on the grounds of the English invasion was delivered from Jedburgh to Edward I. When Berwick, garrisoned by the men of Fife, was taken by storm on 30 March 1296, many of its inhabitants, men, women, and children were mercilessly killed; on 27 April the Scottish army was overwhelmed at Dunbar; Edward turned south-west and then north in his search for the fugitive Scottish king, who had no stomach for a fight; on 10 July, at Brechin, the spineless Balliol formally repeated to Edward the surrender of his realm, his people, and his kingship, which he had made shortly before at Kincardine.[1] Making a triumphal progress northwards, Edward reached Elgin on 26 July and then turned southwards again by a slightly different route. From Scone he took the stone said to be that on which the Scottish kings were enthroned (wrongly called the 'Coronation Stone'), and from Edinburgh he took the Black Rood of St. Margaret. Returning to Berwick (which was to be replanned and rebuilt) he held a parliament there; and there he began to take homages and fealty from Scottish bishops, earls and barons, and priests, freeholders and burgesses.[2] English officials were installed, the castles were 'stuffit' with English garrisons, and the government of the forfeited kingdom of Scotland was entrusted to John de Warenne, earl of Surrey, and Hugh Cressingham. To all appearances Edward had secured his fief. Many of the Scots' leaders who had been captured at Dunbar obtained their freedom on the promise of military service for Edward in Flanders and in time departed thither; most of the important castles were in English hands; and homage and fealty had been exacted from lords and commons alike. But 'not all the substantial free tenants of Scotland went to Berwick to do homage; some never did homage; one of these was biding his time near Paisley; and there were others in Moray'.

It may be that the English officials were too exacting in the discharge of their duties, or too overbearing in their office; undoubtedly they were foreigners and unwelcome, as likewise were the soldiers who gave them armed support. Certainly when opposition arose to the English administration, it arose in the localities, and the opposition came mainly from the 'middle folk' and the people; one of their fears was of an English demand for military service in Flanders as Edward had extended forgiveness to the Scottish nobles on condition that they served him there. Of these middle folk, William Wallace soon stood out; but it is well to remember that before Wallace slew the English sheriff of Lanark (May 1297) there had already been trouble in other parts, in Ross, Argyll, Moray, and Aberdeen. In the west, too, certain lords were making some show of resistance. The young Robert Bruce, earl of Carrick (whose grandfather, the Competitor, had died in 1295), James the Steward, William, lord of Douglas, and Bishop Robert Wishart of Glasgow had assembled in arms apparently to press Edward to acknowledge Robert Bruce (the competitor's son, the earl's father) as vassal king of Scots; but, when faced by an English force under the command of Percy and Clifford, and unable to agree among themselves, they capitulated on terms at Irvine in July 1297; it seems that Edward I did not confirm the terms and Earl Robert did not carry out his capitulation. Thus in that same month (July 1297) Cressingham was reporting to Edward that the whole land was in turmoil, that in many shires the Scots had set up officials of their own, and that proper order existed only in the shires of Berwick and Roxburgh.

William Wallace, a younger brother of Sir Malcolm Wallace of Elderslie, had suddenly 'lifted up his head' (in the words of Fordun) when he had killed the sheriff of Lanark, and now, under him, the scattered risings against the English domination gradually took the shape of a national resistance. At Perth, Edward's justiciar, William de Ormesby, barely escaped a surprise attack by Wallace; in July 1297 Cressingham reported him as 'lying with a large company in the Forest of Selkirk'; and in August he was apparently besieging the castle of Dundee. Moreover, he was 'bestriding' the land 'not in secret, as before, but openly'.

Meanwhile, in the north, the castles of Aberdeen, Urquhart, and Inverness had fallen to Scottish forces led by Andrew de Moray (the son of Sir Andrew de Moray of Petty), and the fall of Montrose, Brechin, and Forfar quickly followed. Wallace and de Moray joined forces; they became, in their own words, 'leaders of the army of

Scotland'; and the greater part of the land to the north of the Forth was now under their control. Those few of the great magnates who were not in Flanders looked on in silent sympathy.

Edward, however, intent upon a campaign against France, and refusing to believe the alarming reports of Cressingham, sailed for Flanders on 22 August 1297. But both Warenne and Cressingham, despite the capitulation of some Scottish lords at Irvine, were under no illusions. The threat from the north was too serious. Realizing that Wallace, de Moray, and their 'band' had to be crushed without delay the English leaders advanced northwards with a strong force of heavy cavalry, some northern English levies, and a contingent of Welsh archers. They reached the Forth at Stirling, intending to cross there; instead they found the Scots under Wallace and de Moray barring the way, with their forces drawn up on the foothills of the Ochils, to the north of the bridge,[3] and with the swampy carse protecting their front.[4] Despite the strength of the Scottish position, Cressingham is said to have succeeded in bringing about an immediate attack—'Why,' he is reported to have asked, 'should the king's treasure be wasted in prolonging the war?' But the bridge was narrow, and the English mounted knights, the spearmen, and the Welsh archers could cross only slowly and two or three abreast. And when 'as many of the enemy as he believed he could overcome' had crossed, Wallace gave the order to attack. His men cut off those who had crossed and then seized and held the northern bridge-head. All was at once confusion. Those who had crossed were attacked on both flanks; those who had not crossed were unable to move to the support of their fellows; the cavalry were unable to manœuvre on the swampy ground; the Welsh foot fled; Cressingham was killed; and Warenne barely escaped to Berwick. The Scottish triumph was complete (11 September 1297). The castle of Stirling surrendered; and soon the only important castles holding out for England were those of Edinburgh, Dunbar, Roxburgh, and Berwick. In October the Scots were over the Border, raiding Northumberland and Cumberland.

For ten months the government of Scotland was in Wallace's hands. On 11 October 1297 Wallace and de Moray wrote triumphantly to Lübeck and Hamburg that trade with Scotland could now be resumed, 'because the kingdom of Scotland, thanks be to God, has been recovered by war from the power of the English'. And they wrote from Haddington, south of the Forth. De Moray, however, who was probably wounded in the battle of Stirling bridge, died soon after this letter, leaving Wallace to lead alone.

But Wallace was fighting in the cause of King John: the Bruces and their supporters could hardly fight in such a cause; and some of the great men still stood aloof in uncertainty. Finally, on 31 January 1298, Philip of France made truce with Edward and deserted his Scottish allies.

Edward returned to England and having moved the seat of government from London to York, on 3 July crossed the Tweed at Coldstream with a strong force. By mid July he was approaching Edinburgh. Prudence would have dictated a retreat before him and the use of guerrilla tactics. On the other hand it was known that Edward's army was suffering from lack of supplies and that the Welsh, who formed a large part of his footmen, were on the verge of mutiny; moreover there was the danger that as harvest-time approached many of those in the Scots army might slip away. Wallace decided to stand and meet the English threat forthwith. He awaited Edward's force near Falkirk—only to suffer a disastrous defeat (22 July 1298).

Wallace's tactics at Falkirk were perfectly sound. The spearmen, his main strength, were drawn up, like bristling hedgehogs, in four rounded compact groups, each probably three-deep, called *schiltrons*;[5] his few archers were ranged in the intervals between these schiltrons; and his cavalry, few in number and of doubtful quality, were in the rear. But, despite the gallantry of the thick-grouped spearmen, who broke the first English charge, the English archers soon took a heavy toll; the close formations were broken up; and then the English knights rode in. Wallace, alas, possessed no heavy 'covered horse' to meet those of England, nor even sufficient light horse to disperse the English archers; as it was, most of his small force of mounted men had fled the field at the beginning of the fight.

Falkirk was never a rout—the spearmen stood their ground to the last; but it was a heavy and grievous defeat, and it marked the end of Wallace's brief but glorious career as leader and 'Guardian of the Realm of Scotland'. His subsequent moves are not easy to trace, though there is evidence that he went to France in an endeavour to secure French support, and that he received letters from King Philip, recommending him to the pope and to Hakon of Norway.

But Falkirk, seemingly decisive, was not decisive. Edward had won a battle, but his subsequent campaign was ineffective. Scotland was still in revolt and still unconquered. Wallace had shown that something could be done, and as early as December 1298 his place as guardian of the realm had been taken by two magnates—Robert Bruce, earl of Carrick (and later to be King Robert I), and John Comyn the younger, lord of Badenoch.[6] The Bruces had always thought of a crown; but Comyn was the son of Balliol's sister, Alianora, and his cause was bound to be that of Balliol. In the appointment of these two guardians by the community of the realm there may have been some hope of uniting forces and of sinking all differences in the face of a common foe, but, as was soon to be proved, old antipathies and old jealousies were too hard in dying. At a council of war at Peebles, in August 1229, accusations of treason were made, and Comyn seized Bruce by the throat. The quarrel was patched up, and William de Lamberton, bishop of St. Andrews, was appointed as principal guardian—possibly in an endeavour to hold the opposition together; but the conflict of interests was still too strong, and the feud between Bruce and Comyn became irreconcilable. Bruce resigned his guardianship in 1300 and, later, fearing the possible return of King John, submitted to Edward I in return for an undertaking to examine the Bruce 'right', apparently to the throne of Scotland. Like his grandfather, this Bruce was determined to become king, either as Edward's enemy or as his vassal. His place as guardian was first taken by Ingram de Umfraville, while, later, we find John de Soules acting as sole guardian in the name of Balliol.

Nevertheless, the English control, such as it was, was virtually limited to Lothian and the Borders; all the land to the north of the Forth was held by the guardians. A campaign by Edward in the summer of 1300 was a fiasco, achieving nothing save the capture of the castle of Carlaverock. A second campaign in the summer of 1301 achieved little more—though another castle, Bothwell, was captured; and although Edward wintered at Linlithgow from 1301 to 1302 his efforts were proving fruitless. Even without a king (and the person of a king was of supreme importance in times such as these) the Scots, under guardians, or a guardian, were more than holding their own. Soon there were to be setbacks; but also, soon thereafter, the Scots were to be fighting under a king.

The year 1303 opened with the rout at Roslin of an English light cavalry force; but that proved to be a solitary Scottish success. Philip of France again deserted the Scots,[7] and in May 1303 Edward invaded Scotland once more—but for the last time. As in 1296 he again made an armed progress through the realm, as far as Kinloss, and returned to winter at Dunfermline. In March 1304 he held a Scottish parliament at St. Andrews, when most of the nobility and men of note once more came into his allegiance; in July 1304, after a siege of three months, Stirling castle (which alone was holding out and which had been in Scottish hands since November 1299) surrendered; and in August 1305 Wallace (who had been captured), great of heart to the end, was 'tried' in London and suffered an agonizing death as a traitor to a king whom he had never acknowledged and to whom he had never sworn fealty and allegiance.

Edward might well think that his troubles in Scotland were now over. He had once again dealt not unfairly, even generously, with his erstwhile baronial enemies: some paid fines, a few heavy fines, and a very few were exiled; only Wallace died. If the Scottish nobility remained true to the allegiance they had newly sworn, peace and quiet might yet be assured. After functioning for seven years at York, the royal administration returned to Westminster; in September 1305 Edward approved an Ordinance for the government of Scotland, a statesmanlike document according to which, while the principal offices were to be held by Englishmen, authority was to be largely shared between Scottish and English officials— though its whole framework of government still stressed that Scotland was subject to the English king.[8]

Given time, surely all would now be well. But time was not given. On 10 February 1306 Bruce attacked, and his companions slew, John Comyn in the Franciscan church at Dumfries. Certainly the murder was unpremeditated—for no one would choose a consecrated place for the murder of an enemy, thereby committing sacrilege of the deepest kind. Equally certainly the murder hastened whatever plans may have been taking shape. Although one of the romantic stories of Scottish history,[9] the murder of John Comyn decided Bruce to assert his right to the throne. The claim made by his grandfather in 1291–2 was now to be advanced by force of arms. Whatever Bruce's previous vacillations may have been—and despite the opposition of Comyn, and the possibility of the return of Balliol, which led him to desert the Scots and return to Edward I's allegiance early in 1302, he had never abandoned hope of the throne—now it was essential for his success that he should lead the Scottish revolt as a Scottish king. Moreover, would not Scottish support rally to a king at last? On the first available feast day in Lent, 25 March 1306, wearing a golden circlet on his head, Bruce was enthroned on a stone in traditional manner at Scone by Isabella, countess of Buchan, the sister of the late Duncan, earl of Fife.[10] Few were present: no bishop (the bishop of St. Andrews was forced by threats to join the new king two days later to say mass for him), only one or two abbots (Scone and Inchaffray), and at most two earls (Atholl and perhaps Menteith). It was an inauspicious beginning, even though Robert Wishart, bishop of Glasgow, courageous as ever, had come out in enthusiastic support, and was waiting in the west, probably for Irish mercenary help.

King Robert's following had still to be built up, and he had to face not only Edward of England but also the feud of the Comyns and those of kin or alliance with them—notably John Comyn, earl of Buchan, Alexander of Argyll and his son, John of Lorn, and the MacDowells of Galloway. And on 18 May 1306 sentence of excommunication for sacrilege was passed upon him by Pope Clement V.

After a respite during which he seems to have recruited as far north as Aberdeen or Banff, Robert I was defeated with great loss at Methven, near Perth (19 June 1306), by the earl of Pembroke, Edward's commander in Scotland. Pursued to Atholl, he was defeated by an English detachment at Loch Tay, and later to the west he was perhaps again defeated, this time at Dalry (near Tyndrum), by the lord of Lorn (July or August 1306).[11] Fleeing through Breadalbane and Lennox, he found refuge for a brief space in Dunaverty; but when the castle was taken in September, King Robert had gone—no one knew where. Blown first by equinoctial storms to Rathlin off the north coast of Ireland, he evidently sailed north and forced his unwelcome company upon the Macdonalds, probably at Dunyveg in Islay.

Meantime Edward, whose dream of a settled Scotland had been so rudely shattered, and whose recent trust in the Scottish lords had been so ill rewarded, showed little mercy. Upon his orders, William de Lamberton, bishop of St. Andrews, and Robert Wishart, bishop of Glasgow, were imprisoned in irons; he petitioned the pope to have Scone abbey thrown down stone by stone. Others of Bruce's supporters (including his brother Nigel and the earl of Atholl) who were unlucky enough to be captured were hanged; and Bruce's wife, who had been taken from Kildrummy by Atholl upon the approach of an English siege-force, was dragged from the sanctuary of St. Duthac, at Tain, and, like the countess of Buchan, imprisoned.[12] Nor did Edward propose to leave the new troubles in Scotland solely to the care of his lieutenants. Old and ill, and unable to ride, he was already being carried slowly northwards in a litter until, reaching the priory of Lanercost, near Carlisle, in September 1306, he was compelled by illness to stay there for a period of nearly six months.

Yet, despite these seemingly overwhelming reverses, Bruce returned to Scotland in January 1307, landing in Arran, and then crossing over to his own lands in Carrick; and about the same time his brothers, Thomas and Alexander, landed in Loch Ryan with a small Irish force. Again disaster ensued. His brothers, defeated by Dougal MacDowell, were taken prisoner and a week later executed at Carlisle. Deprived of their support, the new king, with only a small company, was again compelled to take to the hills; he escaped from an English force in Glentrool, and later (10 May 1307), at Loudoun Hill, he tried to defeat another force under the earl of Pembroke himself, but inconclusively.[13] As 'King Hob' still eluded his agents Edward determined to lead his army in person. He had moved from Lanercost to Carlisle, and now, abandoning his litter, he rode on horseback towards the Solway; but he was so weak that in four or five days he had advanced only some six miles. Grim, determined, striving to force his body to obey his will, he died at Burgh-on-Sands on 7 July 1307.

From that moment the tide turned in Bruce's favour. Edward II, weak and intemperate, neither soldier nor statesman, was an unworthy son and successor to Edward I, and apparently none knew it better than the Scots.

NOTES

1. Balliol had been previously promised an English earldom for his surrender but by 10 July Edward I knew the full terms of the Franco-Scottish alliance which were so treasonable that he took a much harder line with Balliol. The nickname 'Toom Tabard', *Empty Jacket*, later given to Balliol, apparently comes from his surrender when the heraldic insignia on his tabard were ripped off indicating that he was not worthy even of knighthood.

Balliol was sent to England where he remained until 1299 when he was allowed to retire to his estate at Bailleul in France. He died at Bailleul in 1313.

2. The record is known as the 'Ragman Rolls'. It is likely that many homages were collected subsequently in the sheriff courts.

3. A wooden bridge situated about sixty metres upstream from the present fifteenth-century stone bridge.

4. It is probable that a firm but narrow causeway led northwards from the bridge across the carse.

5. An interesting use of this word in medieval anatomy, to indicate the *rounded three-deep* joints in the hand and the foot, is noted in *The Scottish Antiquary*, xiv. 185–8.

6. Son of John Comyn the guardian of 1286.

7. The treaty of Paris (May 1303) was probably inevitable after the French defeat at Courtrai, but it left Edward free to concentrate all his forces against Scotland.

8. Scotland was to be governed by a lieutenant, with a chancellor, a chamberlain, and a comptroller. The lieutenant was to have a council consisting of the officers of the crown together with four bishops, four abbots, five earls, and nine magnates of Scotland. Two justiciars (one an Englishman, and one a Scot) were to be appointed for each of four regions (Lothian, Galloway, 'Scotland' south of the Mounth, and 'Scotland' north of the Mounth); sheriffs were to be appointed who were 'fittest for the maintenance of good order' irrespective of whether they were Scots or Englishmen, and, indeed, many of those named were Scots. Finally the laws of David I were to be revised in an assembly of the people and thereafter proclaimed and observed.

All this was a distinct and statesmanlike advance on the *ad hoc* arrangements that had prevailed since 1296; to be at once defeated by the march of events early in 1306.

9. The story of Bruce's words, 'I doubt I've slain the Red Comyn', and Kirkpatrick's answer, 'Doubt ye? I'll mak siccar', is of late date.

10. The earl of Fife enjoyed the right of placing the new king upon the inaugurating stone at Scone; but in 1306 Duncan of Fife, son of the earl who was guardian (d. 1289) and nephew of the countess of Buchan, was in ward in Edward's hands.

11. There is documentary evidence for the battle with the English at Loch Tay. The battle of Dalry narrated by Barbour may be a confusion with events in 1308 when Bruce defeated John of Lorn thereabouts.

12. Possibly the queen had hoped to reach Norway via Orkney. Bruce's sister, Isobel, had married Eric, king of Norway. She was Eric's second wife; his first wife was Margaret, daughter of Alexander III and mother of the Maid of Norway.

13. The account given on pp. 160–1 differs slightly from that usually given. It is based upon unpublished material in the records of the English wardrobe.

CHAPTER 15

The War of Independence—II

TURNING south with Edward I's body the new king entrusted it to the care of the archbishop of York at Richmond; then, marching northwards again, he made a futile advance through Upper Niths-dale to Cumnock, and after a week returned to England, leading back the great army that had been assembled to crush the rebellious Scots—but which had been quite unable to find the enemy. Edward II's inglorious retreat was an immediate encouragement to the king. Moreover, it left him free to fight his personal enemies in Scotland (mainly those who had embraced the blood-feud of the murdered Comyn) and it deprived his enemies of English support.

So after a campaign of fast-moving strikes by Robert between Ross and the Don valley in Aberdeenshire over the winter of 1307-8 (including inconclusive skirmishes at Slioch between Christmas and New Year), John Comyn, earl of Buchan, was finally routed at Inverurie (23 May 1308); his lands were wasted with fire and sword (the 'Herschip of Buchan'); and the power of the Comyns was completely destroyed. Turning now to the west and south-west, Bruce defeated and made a truce with John of Lorn in 1308 and in the autumn of 1309, with the help of Sir James Douglas, defeated him in the battle of the Pass of Brander; John, his father, and the bishop of Argyll, joined the Comyns in exile in England. Edward Bruce ravaged Galloway, though not until 1313 was the south-west finally subdued with the surrender of the castle of Dumfries.

Having secured himself against attack from his personal enemies, Robert I was now able to attempt the greater task of winning back his kingdom from the power of the English. But already much had been done. Following the overthrow of the earl of Buchan, Bruce himself had helped the burgesses of Aberdeen to take the castle that dominated their burgh; and thereafter most of the other castles in the north were quickly captured. Men in every part of the lands north of Forth now began to range themselves openly on the side of Bruce, and with every success his following grew. By March 1309 the king had so established himself that during a truce with his enemies he was able to hold a parliament at St. Andrews, and a letter, sent from that parliament to the king of France, and sealed by a large number of lords and barons, affirmed that Robert was recognized by them as their 'leader and prince'. By the autumn of 1309, in all Scotland north of the Tay, only Dundee and Banff were still held by England; while between the Tay and the Firths of Forth and Clyde the only important fortifications still in English hands were those of Stirling and Perth. Even those strengths, moreover, were probably able to hold out only because they could receive occasional supplies by sea: for all the land-routes north of the Forth were now commanded by the Scots.[1]

Meantime Edward II, in constant financial difficulties and in strife with his magnates, was unable to give any attention to Scotland. Undermanned and under-supplied castles fell to the Scots one by one; and each, as it was captured, was slighted, its palisades razed to the ground—a deliberate policy to prevent the English forces from re-establishing themselves in fortified positions. So, in Barbour's epic poem, we may read that at this castle or that

> And syne gert brek doune the wall
> And fordid well and castell all   [destroyed

or

> Tour and wall rycht to the ground
> War tumlyt in ane litill stound   [a moment

And when in the autumn of 1310 Edward II led an unhappy English army through the southern counties of Scotland, achieving nothing, and suffering hardship from the weather and inadequate supplies, Robert retaliated in 1311 with devastating raids into northern England on both east and west.

Then in June 1312 Piers Gaveston, Edward II's hated favourite, was seized and hanged, without trial, by a number of the Lords Ordainers,[2] and for nearly a year there was danger of civil war in England. Neither party had time or thought for Scotland. The *Chronicle of Lanercost* regretfully records, 'Now, while the aforesaid things were being done with Piers, the march of England had no defender against the Scots, and therefore they rendered tribute to Robert in order to have peace for a while.' And the chronicler then tells of an invasion by Bruce as far as Durham when the men of that county paid £2,000 for a ten months' truce, at the same time agreeing to give the Scots unopposed passage through their lands whenever they wished to raid in England; whereupon the Northumbrians, fearing that the Scots would visit them, 'gave them other two thousand pounds', and the people of Westmorland and Cumberland 'redeemed themselves in a similar way'. Truces, indeed, continued to be bought for a number of years; they were bought for lands as far north as Lothian within his own kingdom and as far south as Ripon and Richmond; and it has been calculated that Bruce must have collected some £20,000 in various payments exacted from the northern counties of England.

Yet Bruce did not allow the harrying of northern England (or the welcome payments 'to have peace' (*pro pace habenda*), or 'for tribute to Robert Bruce' (*ad tributum Roberto Brus*), or for *souffrance de guerre*) to take precedence over the important work still to be done in Scotland. The town of Perth, and castles of Dumfries, Roxburgh, and Edinburgh were all recaptured in 1313 and the early months of 1314—all tributes to the daring and inventiveness of the besiegers for, throughout his campaigns, Bruce never possessed the massive siege engines which were almost essential for the reduction of any strongly built medieval stone castle. Bothwell, Stirling, and Berwick were now the only important castles still held by England, and at the siege of Stirling in September or October 1313 King Robert entered into an agreement[3] with its constable, De Mowbray, whereby De Mowbray too would surrender unless he were relieved by Midsummer Day (24 June) 1314. The agreement was undoubtedly made in the expectation that no such effort by England was likely—and perhaps, when that calculation proved mistaken, there began the tales which blamed Edward Bruce for the agreement.

With the fall of Stirling now expected, the time had come to bring pressure to bear upon those who still hesitated over their duty. Late in October 1313 at Dundee it seems that a council or a parliament was held which decided that one more year's grace would be given to those recent opponents of King Robert, so that they might submit and keep their Scottish lands; thereafter their lands would be forfeited.[4] The decision, it was said, was widely and often proclaimed, but we have no means of knowing how effective it was, and the knowledge of English preparations may have neutralized it. It was clear in the spring of 1314 that an English relieving army was in preparation and the Scots must choose whether to resist relief by the English force, committing themselves to a pitched battle in which they would be confronted by England's superiority in knights and archers, or to allow Edward to march up and march away again —as in 1310-11, 1319, and 1322. After all, Stirling could wait till another day.

Edward II led into Scotland a large army perhaps 20,000 strong and including some 3,000 heavy cavalry. He reached Edinburgh on 21 June 1314, with only three days to spare. The Scots, about one-third in number to the English, were already assembled in the Torwood, to the south of Stirling, though Bruce was not yet committed to a battle.

Any reconstruction of the subsequent movements of the English army and of the battle itself is far from easy. Advancing from Edinburgh, Edward's army apparently reached the Bannock burn towards the evening of 23 June. A body of horse, under Clifford, made a dash to reach Stirling castle but, challenged by Randolph's spearmen, was severely handled and compelled to withdraw. Nearer to the Scottish lines, De Bohun was killed in single combat with Bruce. It was these successes, perhaps, which determined the vastly outnumbered Scots to stand their ground. Probably the whole English army (but not its baggage train) now crossed the Bannock burn and took up its position for the night somewhere in the angle formed by the burn and the loops of the Forth. They were within easy distance of the castle for its relief next day; and, although their position was wet and uncomfortable, they were well protected by the nature of the ground. The Bannock burn and marshy ground guarded their left; bog and marsh guarded their right; the Forth guarded their rear.

But, so far as we can reconstruct events, on the morning of the next day—St. John's Day, 24 June 1314—the English commanders, greatly to their surprise, saw the Scots boldly advancing to the attack. Great general that he was, Bruce had noted the cramped position of the English host and its inability to deploy and to manœuvre; if it could be contained in the position where it had passed the night, with marshy and impassable ground on both its flanks, and with only a narrow front[5] on which to fight, its very numbers would be a hindrance rather than a help. His well-trained spearmen, in their schiltrons, stopped, and then pushed back, the first challenge of the English knights under the earl of Gloucester; the English archers could not fan out to harass the Scottish schiltrons from the flanks (and those who strove to do so were dispersed by Bruce's light cavalry under Sir Robert Keith); the English knights, discomfited, were slowly and inexorably driven back into the ranks of those behind them, thus masking the footmen, and, finally, throwing them into disorder. The battle became one between the Scots in ordered formation and the English crowded together in complete confusion and disarray; its end, after a hard day's struggle, was the total rout of the impressive might of England. Many of those who strove to escape were drowned in the Forth; the Bannock burn was 'so filled with horses and men' that others passed over them as over a bridge; wandering small groups of fugitives were at the mercy of the countryside; and Edward II, accompanied by a few horsemen, was lucky to escape to Dunbar. Nor should we forget that the spoil, which was enormous, and the ransoms of those English barons who were taken prisoner, helped to fill many an empty Scottish purse. 'Scotland', it was said, 'became rich in one day.' That was the kind of exaggeration by which war engendered more war.

The victory of Bannockburn secured all Scotland except Berwick and on 6 November 1314, a year after the suggested Dundee parliament of 1313, a parliament, sitting at the abbey of Cambuskenneth (near the field of the recent battle), passed judgement of forfeiture on all those who had not declared their loyalty to King Robert. The king, now secure from England, was to be assured of the faith of all men in his own kingdom—but this was used by Robert as an 'enabling' measure, for only the Balliols, Comyns, and the earl of Atholl (who deserted Bruce on the eve of Bannockburn), were treated as irrevocably forfeited and in 1315-16 the earls of Fife and Dunbar, and as late as 1327 the earl of Mar, on return to Scotland, were reconciled and restored to their lands. The rule of Bruce was the rule of reconciliation.

Nor was that all. In the following year (1315) a further important question was decided—that of the succession to the throne. Bruce had as yet no son and the recent long struggle with England discouraged any thought of the succession of Bruce's daughter, Marjorie. Accordingly, in an assembly at Ayr and with the consent of Marjorie Bruce, it was agreed that Edward Bruce, the king's brother (then on the point of departure to fight the English in Ireland), and Edward Bruce's male heirs should succeed to the throne should King Robert leave no son. Failing male heirs to the king and to Edward Bruce, then the succession was to revert to Marjorie and her heirs; and failing all heirs to the king, to Edward, and to Marjorie, the prelates, earls, barons, and others of the community of the kingdom were to assemble to decide upon the succession to the throne. The lesson of 1291–2 was not to be forgotten; the decision of 1284 had not looked beyond the infant Margaret; and her premature death, with no declared successor, lay in the background of all the ills that had followed. Here, too, was a reversion to something like the old law of succession: the king-to-be was the king's brother, and he was named as successor because of his suitability to reign—Edward Bruce was chosen 'as a man above all strong and expert in the arts of war for the defence of the right and liberty of the realm of Scotland'.

Edward Bruce, however, was killed in Ireland in 1318, fighting against the English; he left no lawful son; and accordingly the succession to the throne had again to be defined. In December 1318, in a parliament held at Scone, Robert, the infant son of the deceased Marjorie Bruce and Walter the Steward, was declared to be the heir to the throne should Robert I leave no son; if Robert, or a son born to the king, was of minor age at the time of the king's death, then Randolph was to be guardian of the young king and the realm, and if, perchance, Randolph was dead, James, lord of Douglas, was to be the guardian. In 1324, however, the king had a son, David (who succeeded as David II) and, in 1326, again to define the succession, the entail of 1318 was extended to cover the possibility that David might leave no lawful heir of his body.

With England heavily defeated and in no position to renew the conflict, with Robert the acknowledged king of Scots, with those who had previously opposed him either forfeited or now on his side, and with the succession settled, the next step was to secure the recognition of Bruce's kingship by both England and the pope.

While the English church had supported Edward's policy (although resisting his financial demands), many important Scottish churchmen (and notably the bishops of Glasgow and Moray) had consistently supported Bruce, even in defiance of the pope who equally consistently had refused to recognize Bruce's kingship. Only a few days after the killing of the Red Comyn, Robert Wishart bishop of Glasgow had absolved Bruce. In 1309 a number of the clergy (doubtless after prompting) issued a declaration (which was accompanied by a declaration, possibly in identical terms, by the nobles and community) in which they proclaimed that Robert I had been 'solemnly made king of Scots' and that 'with him the faithful people of the kingdom will live and die as with one who, possessing the right of blood, and endowed with the other cardinal virtues, is fitted to rule, and worthy of the name of king and the honour of the kingdom, since, by the grace of the Saviour . . . he has by the sword restored the realm'.

In 1317 the pope had tried to impose a truce upon the Scots and English, and took it ill that Robert captured Berwick by a surprise attack in 1318. Papal–Scottish relations deteriorated as the English gleefully told tales at the papal court of Scottish war-making and obstinacy. In 1320 when, at the instance of Edward II, Pope John XXII cited four of the Scottish bishops to answer at the papal court, and sent two legates to publish a further sentence of excommunication against Bruce (for so the pope persisted in calling the king), the letter of defences sent by the barons to the pope (the 'Declaration of Arbroath'), was almost certainly drafted by Bernard de Linton, abbot of Arbroath, chancellor of Scotland. There the position of Robert Bruce, and what he meant to his people, were made abundantly clear. There it was boldly affirmed that all were bound to him 'both of right and by the service he has rendered'; there it was declared that never would there be submission to the yoke of England; there, in noble words, the Scottish barons proclaimed that they fought 'not for glory, or riches or honours, but only for liberty, which no true man would yield save with his life'.[6]

But papal opposition to Bruce still persisted; the pope refused to recognize his kingship, and in 1324 he was still insisting upon a prerequisite to lifting the ban of excommunication and recognizing Robert as king of Scots. All these fulminations were in vain. An English siege of Berwick in 1319 was a failure while the Scots, invading Yorkshire, nearly caught Edward's queen at York and routed an English force at Myton-on-Swale. After a two-year truce, from December 1319, Edward II again invaded Scotland; he marched up to Edinburgh and he marched down again. And on all his march he found only empty fields, empty houses, empty byres, empty barns.

And in May 1323 a truce for thirteen years was concluded between Scotland and England, and with renewed tension between England and France over the question of Gascony (1324), and with the conclusion of the treaty of Corbeil (1326) between Robert I and Charles IV of France—a treaty under which neither country was to make peace or truce with England if the other country were still at war with England—the pope, anxious for an end of the war, became more favourable to the Scots. Yet after striking victories year after year, Robert I was still denied a peace settlement. For he could not strike at the heart of England in the wealthy south; and the English with enormous resources of men and money were not yet brought to admit that the war was lost. It was the troubles in England after the fall of Edward II which led to the full recognition of Robert I by both England and the papacy.

In January 1327 Edward II was compelled to abdicate to be succeeded by his fourteen-year-old son, Edward III. For a time the government of England was in the hands of Queen Isabella and her lover Mortimer; it was a bankrupt and very unpopular government and it simply could not afford the expense of renewed war.

The Scots simply broke the truce of 1323. In the summer of 1327 they were ravaging over the Border and King Robert was even making grants of lands in Northumberland, perhaps planning its annexation from a restored and grateful Edward II. After a disastrous campaign against seasoned Scots troops led by Randolph and Douglas (who nearly captured the young Edward III in his tent), Isabella and Mortimer, their treasury empty, decided to sue for peace. Ambassadors with full power were sent to Newcastle, where terms were negotiated. To conclude matters an embassy came to Scotland; the terms of a treaty were concluded with King Robert (now suffering from a grave disease which may have been paralytic leprosy) in his chamber at Holyrood Abbey (March 1328); and, exceptionally, and more binding, the treaty was confirmed in an English parliament at Northampton (May 1328).

It is important to note that the final documents were preceded by a renunciation by England of all claims to superiority over Scotland, and by a recognition by England of Robert Bruce as king of Scotland. Thus the treaty itself was concluded between two kings of two independent kingdoms. By the treaty, Robert was again recognized as king of Scotland; there was to be 'good peace, final and perpetual' between the two kingdoms, 'saving on the part of the king of Scotland the alliance made between him and the king of France' (an important exception, dictated by virtue of the treaty of Corbeil, continuing the alliance of 1295, and, at times, to lead Scotland into disaster); all documents that could be found in England touching the subjection of the people or land of Scotland to the king of England, or touching the freedom of Scotland, were to be returned to Scotland;[7] Scotland was to pay (and did pay) to England the sum of £20,000 by three annual instalments;[8] for assuring the peace David, the king's son, was to marry Joan, the sister of Edward III; and finally, the English were to use their endeavours to secure the removal of the papal censures against Robert and any other Scots. The treaty did not include any mention of the return of the Stone of Scone nor any mention of the restoration to their lands of those who had been forfeited by Bruce, and who, with others, were later to cause trouble in the reign of David II.

The marriage of David and Joan took place at Berwick on 12 July 1328. We have record of the arrangements for the wedding and of the food provided for the guests; and that the wall of the churchyard 'was broken down to the ground at the time of the marriage' may be some indication of the throng of people who crowded to see the event. King Robert was not present—possibly through his illness: more likely because Edward III refused to be there. But the Queen Mother, Isabella, attended her daughter's wedding, and the evidence of the English records suggests that there she promised to return the Stone of Scone to Scotland, while the Scottish magnates agreed to restore Percy and perhaps Wake and Beaumont to their lost Scottish lands, to which, in fact, their claim rested mainly on recent English grants. Although Robert was strongly opposed to the restoration of the 'disinherited', he seems to have been willing to listen to Percy's claim to the Bruce earldom of Carrick; but, in the result, neither the Stone nor the lands were restored.

With this treaty of 'final and perpetual peace', Pope John XXII released Bruce from the ban of excommunication (October 1328) and addressed him as 'Our dearest son, Robert, illustrious King of Scotland'. More than that, less than a year later on 13 June 1329 he issued a bull authorizing Robert I and his successors to be crowned and anointed as kings of Scotland—a clear recognition of their independent status as rulers of an independent kingdom.[9] But the great king who, in the words of the Declaration of Arbroath, had 'cheerfully endured all manner of toil, fatigue, hardship and hazard' that 'he might deliver his people and his heritage from the hands of enemies', had died at Cardross[10] a week earlier and never knew of this final recognition of his kingship and, with it, the independence of his kingdom.

Nor had he striven for that alone. The legislation of one of his parliaments (that of 1318) has been preserved; it is not just an *ad hoc* ordinance upon this or that pressing issue but a systematic and determined effort to restore law and order within the realm and to strengthen the executive and the judiciary, as well as to provide for future defence. There we find enactments relating to the land law, to the criminal law, and to the arming of the lieges; we even find an act proscribing the sale or transfer of arms to 'our enemies of England'. The king and his men had turned their minds to the reconstruction of orderly government in a new and thoughtful way. It is not surprising that within the following decade some Scottish clerk began the work of describing in writing the law and custom of Scotland by adapting the English treatise by Glanville to Scottish conditions. This adaptation, *Regiam Maiestatem*, was a lawyer's standby for three more centuries.

Something more than independence had been gained. The long struggle with England had completed the task that both the state and the church, working hand-in-hand, had earlier striven to achieve. A country had been moulded into a nation. Men from all corners of the land fought side by side at Bannockburn. The bitterness of long and destructive war, however, and, shortly after upon Bruce's death, its renewal by England and therewith Scotland's continuing struggle to maintain her independence, turned a new patriotism into a hostility to England too easily aroused. England became the 'auld enemy'. In these succeeding years of warfare with England, invasion and counter-invasion, raiding and harrying became accepted as part of the Scot's inheritance, but also that inheritance now included a fierce spirit of independence which, in this and in other ways, became part and parcel of the Scottish character.

Why had the first two Edwards failed in the 'Scots War'—for undoubtedly England had a number of factors in her favour? Some of the Scottish magnates, including both Bruce and Balliol, were of Anglo-Norman descent, holding lands equally in England and Scotland, and many had small parcels of English land. Few continued to fight on the English side during the whole of the struggle. Some who had at first supported the English king gradually came over to the side of Bruce and, even after the forfeiture of 1314, Bruce was generous to those who were willing to come into his peace.

Again, at first, Edward I could play upon disunity. The Bruces would not fight for Balliol—nor would some others who regarded him as not worth fighting for. Later, when Bruce became king, the Comyns and their allies fought for the English king. In general, Scotland, a much smaller country, could raise no fighting force comparable with that of England. She was particularly weak in knights and 'covered' horse; and the bows of her archers were not equal to the English 'long bow'. She could not afford to hire mercenaries nor find ways to import them and, despite the alliance with Philip IV, she received no real help from France. On the contrary, France twice deserted the Scots by making truces with Edward in 1297 and 1301.

On the other hand England suffered from a number of disadvantages. With simultaneous wars in Scotland and France (until 1303), Edward I could not concentrate his forces on one front only; and his frequent demands for fighting service to be rendered by his barons in continual campaigns outside England led to trouble between them and the king. Because of this, and because of protracted military operations in Scotland, mercenaries had to be paid. But the English treasury was empty; and Edward's use of highhanded methods to secure the necessary finance led to further opposition from the clergy and the merchants, and to borrowing instead of taxing. Edward II's difficulties accordingly arose from the enormous burden of debt which he had inherited from his father, as well as from baronial opposition—at first directed against his favourite, Piers Gaveston, later fomented by the king's cousin, Thomas earl of Lancaster. Domestic strife in England enabled Bruce to consolidate his position in Scotland.

In the actual warfare itself, the physical geography of Scotland made conquest difficult and guerrilla warfare easy; and Bruce's policy of destroying the castles prevented the English from holding strongpoints. All this, in turn, faced the English with constant difficulties in supply. When lines of communication could be cut, it was impossible to maintain a large army inland for any length of time, and the outlying castles were difficult to supply. Moreover there were no roads worthy of the name. Thus, in the end, only those castles which could be supplied by sea were able to continue to resist; and supplies by sea were dependent upon favourable winds. Feeding an army, moreover, meant feeding horses as well as men— notably the 'covered' horses of the knights and the sumpter horses of the baggage train—and there was always a dearth of fodder in Scotland. This meant that real campaigning could be carried on only during the summer months; and the cessation of movement during the winter months gave the Scots opportunities for recovery. Even when Edward wintered at Linlithgow, in fertile Lothian, in 1301-2, he lost many horses through lack of feed.

But the English effort failed principally because Edward I failed to appreciate the determination of Scottish opposition to English rule—a determination revealed in one sentence in the 'Declaration of Arbroath': 'so long as but one hundred of us shall remain alive, we shall never consent to bow beneath the yoke of English domination.' And that fervent spirit was fostered by the leading churchmen who had a strong hold over the lives and thoughts of ordinary people.

NOTES

1. Also, we should remember that Edward I, beset by financial difficulties, had never been able to build in Scotland strong castles like those which he had built in Wales. Nor was he able to do much to strengthen the Scottish castles which he captured.

2. In effect a group of barons, appointed by the Council, to reform Edward II's ineffective government.

3. This account follows English sources rather than the usually accepted Barbour, whose year's grace is too long to be accurate, and was a confusion with the year given to Scots to submit.

4. This account is based upon the forfeiture at Cambuskenneth in November 1314 and Barbour's account of the year's warning given which he misplaces after Bannockburn. A group of charters indicates a council at Dundee in October 1313.

5. Barbour speaks of 'the gret stratnes of the plas' (*The Bruce*, book XII, line 430).

6. Though the propagandist aspect of these Declarations must be kept in mind.

7. It is to be noted that not *all* the Scottish records removed by Edward I were to be restored; but, so far as we know, not even those records touching the freedom of Scotland were returned. In August 1937, 600 years after the treaty, nine solitary Scottish documents, out of the vast mass of record removed by Edward I, were solemnly transferred from the Record Office in London to the Record Office in Edinburgh, and later a number of other Scottish documents were similarly handed over. All the many rolls of financial, judicial, and executive affairs which Edward had carried away were lost in English keeping, and we possess only lists of the records that have been lost and that would have enabled a fuller history of Scotland to be written.

8. This seems an 'Alice through the Looking Glass' arrangement, whereby those who came to sue for peace were paid reparations by the victors. But it was

sensible for the Scots to bolster up the bankrupt English government which had given them what they wanted.

9. By virtue of the bull of 1329, David II was the first king of Scots to be anointed and crowned, in 1331.

10. This is not the Cardross on the modern map; it lay on the right bank of the river Leven, across from, and now part of, the burgh of Dumbarton.

CHAPTER 16

'Dark and Drublie Days'

ALTHOUGH the treaty of 1328 was accompanied by the marriage of David and Joan—a marriage 'for the assurance and confirming' of peace between Scotland and England—the treaty was unstable. It was unpopular in England, where it was ascribed to treachery and cowardice on the part of Isabella and Mortimer who, it was argued, had sold to Scotland her independence for the paltry sum of £20,000 and, moreover, at a time when Bruce was dying. Above all, once Edward III had established himself as personal ruler (1330), he soon found an agent willing to help him to imitate the Scottish designs of his grandfather, Edward I. So the reign of Robert I's son, David II, was to be one of much misery and distress: unfortunate or incompetent regents were succeeded by a devious king; internal dissensions accompanied a renewed struggle with England, at a time of great economic distress; for, in the midst of it all, the plague of the Black Death afflicted Scotland in 1349 and 1350, recurring with equal violence in 1361 and 1362.

David II, the son of King Robert I, was just over five years old when he became king. In accordance with the act of 1318 settling the succession to the crown, Thomas Randolph, earl of Moray, assumed the regency; and, in accordance with the papal bull of 1329, David was anointed and crowned at Scone on 24 November 1331. But within a year thereafter Scotland was again fighting for her independence against a new threat from England.

Randolph, 'a man to be remembered while integrity, prudence, and valour are held in esteem', died on 20 July 1332. According to the act of 1318 he should have been succeeded in the regency by Sir James Douglas, but Douglas, taking the heart of Bruce to the Holy Land, had been killed in Spain when fighting against the Moors (August 1330). The new regent, chosen by the magnates (2 August 1332), was Donald, earl of Mar, a nephew of King Robert I but a friend of Edward II who had stayed in England until 1327! Within the next few days, on 6 August 1332, Edward Balliol, son of King John, landed with a small force at Kinghorn in Fife. On

12 August 1332 the new regent was defeated and slain at Dupplin, near Perth.[1] The struggle had begun anew.

It is customary to refer to those who had landed with Edward Balliol as 'the disinherited'. Certainly his followers included a number of those (e.g. the earl of Atholl) who, because of their adherence to the side of England,[2] had been deprived of their lands in Scotland; but there were others in Balliol's following—some English who hoped to gain Scottish lands and, ere long, some Scots who sided with him through various motives of their own—fear for their lands, greed for other men's. Moreover there can be little doubt that from the very outset Balliol received the support and encouragement of Edward III, who had already secretly received Balliol's homage and fealty as king of Scotland.

Following his victory at Dupplin, Balliol was crowned at Scone (24 September 1332). There are indications that the defeat of Mar's army—the defeat of a large Scots force by a mere handful under Balliol—was regarded by some as a judgement of God and a vindication of Balliol's right to the crown. This might account for the presence, at the coronation, of former loyalists including William Sinclair, Bruce's 'fighting bishop' of Dunkeld, though, according to one chronicler, all who were there 'were armed save for their helmets, since people and nobles inclined to Balliol more from fear than from love'. Within three months, indeed, Balliol was surprised at Annan by the earl of Moray (a son of Thomas Randolph) and by Archibald Douglas (a younger brother of the 'good Sir James'), and was compelled to seek refuge over the Border, fleeing, it was said, 'with one leg booted, and the other naked'.

Hitherto Edward III had preserved an outward peace with, and recognition of, David II; but now a few minor Scottish raids over the Border enabled the English king to denounce the treaty of 1328. Balliol, with English support, once more entered Scotland and made his way towards Berwick; in May 1333 Edward III and Balliol began a combined siege of Berwick; and in July 1333 the Scots, under Archibald Douglas as regent, attempting to raise the siege, were massacred in trying to come to grips with the English army which was posted behind a marsh and on the rising ground of Halidon Hill. Although it was vital to prevent Berwick from falling into English hands and so becoming an English base on the Scottish side of the Tweed, the regent's strategy and tactics were both at fault. The English archers 'won the battle at a distance' with the use of the long bow that was soon to decide the field of Crécy.

'It was the general opinion', writes an English chronicler, 'that the Scottish wars were over; for no man remained of that nation who had either the influence to assemble or the skill to lead an army.' In two disastrous defeats—at Dupplin and at Halidon Hill—Scotland had suffered enormous casualties and the loss of most of her important men. In February 1334 Balliol and his supporters, Scots and English, held a parliament at Edinburgh in which, acknowledging the help he had received from Edward III as lord paramount of Scotland, Balliol surrendered the castle, town, and county of Berwick to be forever annexed to the kingdom of England—and this was only the first instalment of a promised concession of lands worth £2,000 annually. The record of that parliament, moreover, shows how the 'disinherited' had been restored to their lands and how others who had come north from England had received their rewards from Balliol. There we read of Henry de Beaumont, earl of Buchan; David of Strathbogie, earl of Atholl; Richard Talbot, lord of Mar; while elsewhere we read that John de Warenne had been granted the earldom of Strathearn, that Percy claimed Annandale, and that Wake held Liddesdale. In the following June, at Newcastle, Balliol, again acknowledging the 'great assistance' he had received from his 'dearest lord', granted to Edward III the southern counties of Scotland from Haddington in the east to Dumfries in the west, to be annexed and united 'to the royal dignity, crown, and kingdom of England in all times to come'. Into these southern counties, although treated separately from England, Edward III promptly put his own sheriffs; in their castles he placed English garrisons; over them he appointed an English chamberlain and an English justiciar.

By these surrenders, in return for Edward's help, Balliol committed Scotland to more than 100 years of warfare in the recovery of her southern lands. Not until 1460 was Roxburgh castle finally regained from the English hold (in a siege which cost the life of James II); and not until 1461 was the castle of Berwick regained— only to be lost again, for ever, in 1482. But also by these surrenders, Balliol, emphasizing the position of Edward as his overlord, stiffened a national resistance that had suffered but had not yielded. And, to complete the story of Edward Balliol's 'gratitude' to Edward III, six days after granting away so rich a part of the realm, he did homage to his liege lord for his kingdom of Scotland—that is, for what was left of it.

The situation seemed so black that already the young King David II and his queen had been sent for safety to France (May 1334). Yet in the following summer the regents overran much of southern Scotland, and Balliol once more apparently found it advisable to retire into northern England. In the autumn of 1334, and again in the summer of 1335, Edward III led large English forces into southern Scotland and (in 1335) to Perth, in support of his puppet king, when, according to Wyntoun, so many Scottish lords submitted to him that only the children dared to own that they were on the side of David. Even David's heir, the Steward, submitted. It was the nearest Edward III came to subduing Scotland, and he confidently expected the submission of the regent Sir Andrew Moray (son of Wallace's colleague in 1297).

But too many houses had been burned, too many kye butchered, and too many fields left unsown. Balliol's restored 'disinherited' began to evict the tenants of former patriotic landowners and no one could feel safe in his inheritance. And so men rallied to the regent and in the winter of 1335, with Patrick, earl of Dunbar, and William Douglas of Liddesdale, he defeated and slew Balliol's lieutenant, David earl of Atholl, in the forest of Culblean in Mar. Once more Edward III intervened to do his work all over again. In the summer of 1336 he made a 'progress in strength' as far north as Lochindorb[3] where he relieved Catherine de Beaumont (the widow of the earl of Atholl) who was holding the castle against an attack by loyal Scots. Forres, Elgin, and Aberdeen were burned, and expensive new defences were made at Bothwell, Stirling, Edinburgh, Perth (where Balliol skulked in the winter of 1336–7), and other places. But Sir Andrew Moray, wiser than his predecessors, refused to be drawn into battle and, as soon as Edward had returned to England, he reduced one by one the castles that were held for Balliol. A vast English expenditure (£16,000 in 1336 alone) was wasted upon a land whose revenues were a fraction of that figure in peace time—and in time of war had sunk to almost nothing. By 1337 Sir Andrew Moray was confidently raiding northern England again.

For a short time in the summer of 1337 Edward was back in Scotland, compelling Moray to abandon his siege of Stirling castle; and then, in 1338, he sailed to the Low Countries to advance his claim to the throne of France. So began the French wars—'happily for Scotland', Bower records, 'for if the king of England had continued his warfare in Scotland, he would have gained possession of the whole land, without difficulty, as far as it is humanly possible to judge.' A modern historian might dissent from that judgement.

Certainly, with Edward III's new commitments in France, the whole picture in Scotland began to change. In the west Sir William Douglas, the 'Knight of Liddesdale', was driving out the English forces. Before long the castles of Perth and Edinburgh were recaptured from their English garrisons; in the summer of 1341 it was deemed safe for David II and his queen to return from France; and in 1342 Stirling castle was starved into surrender. Balliol had again retired to England.

The years 1332-7 were the most sustained English attempt to conquer Scotland, which, at enormous cost, was a total failure. But the seeds of distrust sowed at this time were bound to bear fruit; almost every Lowland landowner had made some token submission to Edward at some time and some had not scrupled to steal their neighbour's lands. David II came back to a difficult time; he had to make concessions here and turn a blind eye there in order to woo his realm back to peace and order.

But he also owed something to France which had given him refuge and some—a little—help. In 1346 after the great defeat of the French at Crécy, while Edward was investing Calais, and in fulfilment of the treaty of Corbeil of 1326, the young David II (he was then twenty-two) invaded England as far south as Durham, wasting as he went. At Neville's Cross, near Durham, he was met by an army that had been assembled by the northern lords still in England and was defeated and taken prisoner while his nephew, Robert Stewart, disgracefully deserted the field. The king, as befitted the son of Bruce, had fought bravely and, when at last overpowered, had been twice wounded. Robert Stewart[4] now became regent of the realm. David II was to be a closely guarded prisoner in England, and the Steward was to be regent in Scotland, for almost exactly eleven years.

As early as 1348 negotiations were begun for the release of David, the payment of his ransom, and the settlement of a treaty of peace. In 1352 David came home on parole with a draft peace which involved recognition of Edward III as his heir if David should die childless—but the Scots indignantly rejected the scheme and David returned to the Tower of London. In 1354 by a ransom treaty concluded at Newcastle, 'David de Bruce' was to be ransomed for 90,000 merks to be paid in nine annual instalments of 10,000 merks each, and during that time there was to be a truce between the two realms. But the Scots influenced by France would not confirm the agreement. The French sent to Scotland a small force of knights and men-at-arms and, with them, a sum of money[5] to be distributed among the nobility to persuade them to renew the war. Whereupon the Scots ravaged the Border and, with the help of French troops, seized Berwick. This was promptly followed by the 'Burnt Candlemas' of 1356 when Edward III, who had returned from France, regained Berwick and thereafter ravaged and burned the whole countryside between Roxburgh and Edinburgh. Late in the same year the French were heavily defeated at Poitiers, their king joining David in the Tower. It was high time for the Scots to cut their losses and bring back their king with the best deal they could obtain. Negotiations were begun in January 1357.

By a treaty concluded at Berwick (October 1357) David II was released from his eleven years' captivity for a ransom of 100,000 merks to be paid in ten annual instalments of 10,000 merks each during a ten-year truce—terms that were virtually identical with those of the treaty of Newcastle in 1354 save that now the Scots had to pay 10,000 merks more. But, from the exchequer accounts that have been preserved, it would appear that at this period the royal receipts and the royal expenditure barely balanced; and now Scotland should find, somehow, for the next ten years, an additional £6,666 a year (an additional annual sum which seems to have been about equal to the total of the gross annual revenue of the crown), as well as supporting the costs of twenty noble hostages who were to be maintained in England as security for the ransom payments.

During the many negotiations, from 1348 to 1357, which preceded the treaty of Berwick, it is twice reported by the chroniclers that David had been willing to barter the independence of his kingdom in return for his release. As early as 1350, in a petition to the pope, David had declared that the king of England would grant him his freedom if he would do homage to him, would be willing to be cited as a vassal to the parliaments and councils of England, and would be ready to concur in an agreement under which, if he died without a lawful heir, the king of England or one of his sons

G

should succeed him on the Scottish throne. These were reported as Edward's terms and were clearly represented as outrageous.

The office of king of Scotland had (in English eyes) belonged to Edward Balliol until in January 1356 he resigned the kingdom which he had so nearly destroyed into the grasping hands of Edward III. Why then did the Treaty of Berwick accord to David the title of 'King of Scotland', and why did Edward forgo the hostages for the ransom to whom he was entitled—for they were never delivered? It almost seems that while he had no clear plan, Edward III conceived that by allowing the ransom to fall hopelessly into arrears, he might build up a claim to receive the kingdom from a king (David) whose title he had again recognized. Certainly he had not abandoned his ambitions in Scotland.

David II was still childless. His successor, according to the settlement of 1326, would be the Steward—Robert, the son of Marjorie Bruce; and David had little cause to like or respect Robert Stewart. But for five years after his return David ruled circumspectly but efficiently. He paid only two instalments of the ransom, evidently because he hoped to escape the remainder. In 1362 his queen, Joan, died and David was free to remarry; the prospect of an heir cannot have pleased the Steward. And finally the magnates who had done what they pleased with the kingdom and its revenues for eleven years, took no pleasure in the king's reliance upon the advice of efficient 'civil service' clerics and knights. And so in 1363 the earl of Douglas, with Robert Stewart and the earl of March, rose in revolt on a cry that the king, ransomed at great cost to his people, was squandering the monies collected for the ransom payments to England. The king dealt vigorously with the rising and immediately after it had collapsed and stringent oaths of fealty had been exacted from the rebels, he married the widow, Margaret Drummond. Hopeful now of an heir, David II proceeded to London where, in November 1363, his councillors and those of Edward III drafted out a plan for peace. In return for a final peace, the cancellation of all the arrears of the ransom, the release of the Scottish hostages, the restoration of occupied Scotland and even of the English lands held by Alexander III, the preservation of the name, title, laws, and customs of the kingdom, and the recognition of David II, for all this the Scots must accept that if David were to die childless the king of England should succeed to the kingdom of Scotland.

According to this agreement, David was to 'sound the inclinations' of his people, upon his return to Scotland, and to report back to Edward before 7 April 1364. We do not know what the king said to his parliament; but we know what parliament said to the king. 'It was there expressly replied by the three estates that they were in no way willing to comply with, nor in any wise willing to assent to those points' which had been put before them: and the Latin of the record even more than an English translation has the ring of finality —the people of Scotland preferred the burden of the ransom, with all the heavy taxation which that implied, to the possibility of rule by an English king.

In 1365 the Scots prevailed upon the English to reduce the annual instalments (6,000 merks) but only at the cost of greatly increasing the total sum due. Then in 1369, when, after nine years of peace, the French wars broke out again, Edward III, completely without allies, and anxious to have a quiet Scotland at his back, agreed that, since 44,000 merks had now been paid, the balance of the ransom should be paid off by reduced annual instalments of 4,000 merks over a period of truce lasting fourteen years. Under that arrangement Scotland regularly paid her 4,000 merks a year from 1369 until the death of Edward III in 1377,[6] when she ceased to pay,[7] possibly on the grounds that the ransom was a personal payment to Edward III. The latter's interest in Scotland had none of his grandfather's legalism. To him war was a means to glory and chivalric renown and kingdoms were prizes to be handed round his family like dynastic sweetmeats. But what of David II's record?

There is no evidence that David II welcomed Edward III's proposals for an English succession but considerable evidence that he resented the waste of royal revenue in paying off the ransom. David II wanted peace with England to end the drain upon his resources which, he knew, should be applied to the better governing of Scotland. He was not unable to pay ransom instalments after 1360; on the contrary he had ample funds with which he paid men to put down the 1363 rising led by the Steward. If he was insensitive to the strength of Scottish feelings about English kings, he was also probably confident that he could leave behind a child who would render those fears superfluous. And so he tolerated too readily Edward III's proposals.

In 1371 David II died still childless, and estranged from his second wife, but expecting to marry for a third time. He was only forty-six years old. The records prove that he strove to strengthen the authority of the crown and the administration of the law which had languished under the Steward; to Wyntoun, his chief characteristic was his 'radure'—his rigour, or severity. It is perhaps easy to forget his long imprisonment and its effect upon him; equally easy to underrate his difficulties. He is reputed unworthy of his great father—whose career before 1306 was marred by several compromises with expediency. Rather he should be reckoned a very different man but one no less determined that, whoever lost his patrimony, it should not be the Bruce.

David II tried to improve the efficiency of parliament, and there is evidence that he strove to combat the cumbrous and slow machinery of the courts of law. On the other hand it is clear that, apart from its forthright reply in 1364, the king's council in parliament was beginning to make demands of the king. In 1357, for example, immediately upon the conclusion of the treaty of Berwick, it was enacted that the king must not alienate the crown lands and rents, but that they must be retained with the crown to provide the crown with its essential revenues, so that 'the community of the kingdom, already burdened with the payment of the king's ransom, may not be further burdened with his expenses'.[8] But the difficulty of raising the ransom payments gave a new prominence to parliament and especially brought the burghs (which could contribute through their overseas trade) definite and regular representation there. In the reign of David II we read, for the first time, of 'the three communities', or as they are called from the early fifteenth century, 'the three estates'.

NOTES

1. It is said that Balliol's force was guided to a ford over the river Earn by a Murray of Tullibardine, and was thus able to make a surprise attack on the sleeping Scots in the hours of darkness. But the defeat of the Scottish army by a much smaller English force was due partly to Mar's military incompetence, partly to distrust and jealousy of his leadership, and partly to the English archers who, spread out on the flanks, poured a murderous rain of arrows on to the massed Scots.

2. This was the de Strathbogie, earl of Atholl. A new line of earls had been created by Robert I.

3. On the border of the counties of Elgin and Nairn. The castle, on an island in the loch, was protected by very deep water and was regarded as being well-nigh impregnable.

4. It is perhaps important to remember that the Steward, although David II's nephew (he was the son of David's sister, Marjorie), was older than the king. In 1346 the Steward was thirty years of age.

5. Variously stated to be 10,000 merks or as much as 17,000 merks.

6. The treaty of 1357 had provided for the payment of the whole ransom even if David died before complete payment had been made. David had died in 1371, and that part of the treaty was thus observed.

7. The outstanding balance of 24,000 merks was never paid.

8. But much the same thing was said again with greater emphasis in the parliament of 1366, which suggests that the earlier enactment had not been effective. Parliament might pass good laws but, unless the executive chose to enforce them, they remained little more than expressions of good intent.

CHAPTER 17

The Burgesses come to Parliament

WE have already seen the burghs as privileged towns. We have seen them as strongpoints encouraging trade and the arts of peace: for trade is dependent upon peace. We have seen the kings granting charters to their burghs (the king's burghs, later known as 'royal burghs'), by which the burgh adjacent to the sheriff's castle was given a monopoly of trade over the area of the sheriffdom. And we have noted that the burgh was essentially a community for trade and manufacture.

We have seen, too, that because trade requires special laws of its own, different from the feudal law which is largely a land law, the burghs, in consequence, had a separate central court, the 'Court of the Four Burghs', which, sitting under the chamberlain, heard appeals and determined burgh law. Indeed, as we shall see, this court was sometimes called the 'Parliament' of the Four Burghs; and naturally so, for at first it was essentially a court of law: it declared the law of the burghs just as the other and better known parliament declared the law of the land.

But how did the burghs become one of the 'estates' in parliament?

There is no reference to the burghs in the early negotiations with Edward I, nor in the letter sent from Birgham in 1290, agreeing to the marriage of the Maid of Norway with Edward I's son. Yet in 1296 the seals of six leading burghs (Edinburgh, Berwick, Roxburgh, Stirling, Perth, and Aberdeen) were appended to the ratification of the alliance with France 'in token of their consent and approval'. This was something new. Six of the leading burghs were associated with an important step in national affairs, though we do not know whether they were participators in the deliberations which preceded that step.

At a parliament at Inchture in the Carse of Gowrie in April 1312 the king and his council ordained that the burghs were to treat about taxes and army service only through the chamberlain; clearly burgesses were present if only as petitioners. In the parliament which we have suggested was held at Dundee in October 1313, the king gave pensions to the Black Friars of Inverness and Elgin from the burgh fermes of Inverness and a thanage respectively, and granted the forest of Stocket to the burgh of Aberdeen: at that council or parliament burgesses were also surely present in some capacity. And the same argument from coincidence with the grant of privileges to this or that burgh can be made for the parliament at Scone in December 1318 and for an important council or parliament at Berwick late in March 1320. Whether they were summoned to attend, or came a-begging for favours, burgesses certainly knew about parliaments by the 1320s.

The next stage was reached in 1326 when we find the 'burgesses' agreeing that they, with the earls, barons, and freeholders, would pay one-tenth (a 'tenth penny') of their annual revenues to King Robert I to enable him to maintain his royal state—the crown lands and rents having been sadly diminished by war. This agreement was made at Cambuskenneth when the king was holding his parliament there, and it was in the form of an indenture—a duplicate agreement, of which one part, sealed by the king, was to be held by the earls, barons, freeholders, and burgesses, and the other part, sealed by the earls, barons, freeholders, and burghs, was to be held by the king. It was a bargain as well as an agreement. The king was granted a tenth penny; he, in turn, giving up the practice of feeding his army by requisitioning, promised, among other things, to pay, in ready cash, the market price for anything requisitioned by his officers for his own personal needs when on his journeyings through his kingdom.

All the evidence indicates that burgesses, equally with the prelates and barons, had been called to a parliament to agree there to a financial burden that was to be imposed upon all of them; the presence of burgesses of the king's burghs at the king's court was compatible with feudal theory: though how far the king was influenced by feudal theory when finance was required is another matter. Again, in 1328, when the treaty of 'perpetual peace' was drawn up at Edinburgh and when again the burghs would have to contribute towards the payment of £20,000 to England, the records show that the burgesses were called to the parliament which agreed the treaty, and that they had 'full power' to bind their constituents to pay whatever they agreed to. This was in itself an advance in acceptance of the theory of representation: for it was a comparatively simple matter to send a man to the king to give the opinion of the burgesses of a burgh, but a far more sophisticated one to give him full power in a written commission to agree to something—a tax—about which those who were to pay had heard nothing. The king was perhaps able to command the burgesses to take this step because each burgh had long been accustomed to negotiate its ferme with the chamberlain: presumably it had delegated one or two burgesses to do this in its name.

But while, in 1326 and 1328, and again in 1340 and 1341, burgesses were called to parliament when the burghs were involved in parliament's financial decisions, there is no evidence that they were called to other parliaments at which no such financial decisions were made. The necessity of finding large sums of money for the payment of David II's ransom not only again brought the burgesses into parliament, but also led to the regular attendance of burgh representatives at all subsequent parliaments where they sat as a community or an 'estate' of the realm. That is to say, out of the endeavours to meet David II's ransom the Scottish parliament became a body of 'three estates'—prelates, nobles, burgesses.

Here it is essential to bear in mind the characteristics that by now distinguished a meeting of parliament from other meetings of the king's council. A parliament was now publicly proclaimed; it was summoned by precept; and both the proclamation and the precepts had to give at least forty days' notice in advance. And those characteristics were now emphasized in the confirmation of the treaty for the release of David II and the payment of his ransom.

In September 1357 the Steward as lieutenant of the king, the clergy, the magnates, and seventeen named royal burghs, had empowered plenipotentiaries to negotiate for the ransoming of the king. The treaty of release and ransom was finally concluded at Berwick on 3 October, and was ratified there on 5 October by the king and the Scottish plenipotentiaries, but confirmation by David II under the great seal had to reach Berwick on 11 November, or within eight days thereafter. Such a short interval, however, made it impossible to summon a parliament: there was not sufficient time to prepare all the summonses and to give the requisite forty days' notice. Accordingly David confirmed the treaty in a council held at Scone on 6 November 1357. And in the proceedings of that council (as recorded in a near-contemporary transcript called 'The

Black Book': for unfortunately the original record has not survived) we find the phrase 'the three estates' (*tres communitates*) used for the first time. Apart from the use of this phrase, the proceedings, as they have come down to us, provide no clear indication of the attendance of burgh representatives; but confirmation of the treaty meant finding the money for the ransom payments. In the account of the proceedings of the council at Scone it is significant that the trading privileges of the burghs are expressly confirmed and it is laid down that foreign merchants are to be allowed to enter peacefully to buy and to sell—which suggests not only the presence of burgesses but even some representations by the burghs that if they were to contribute to heavy ransom payments they could do so only if their trade was protected by the crown. That is, the evidence indicates that some representatives of the burghs were present at the council at Scone in November 1357; and the use of the phrase 'the three estates' may mean that the burgh representatives took a full part, with the prelates and the nobility, in the council's deliberations.

Then on 11 November parliament met, a parliament of whose composition we have no description. But obviously the prelates and barons were the same as those present at the council on 6 November, and it is so likely as to be almost a certainty that the burgesses also stayed on for parliament for not only were the great customs doubled at once and ordered to be trebled in six months, but a tax, *contribucio*, similar to those of 1326 and 1328, was granted in parliament. And as parliaments were held almost annually in succeeding years to raise finance, the continued presence of burgesses is highly likely, though from the absence of record it cannot be proved.

The earliest record of a parliament's proceedings is that copied into the 'Black Book' for the parliament of March 1364, to which David II presented the draft proposals agreed with Edward III. Although those present are said to be the prelates and the nobility (*proceres*), the rejection of the agreement is stated to have been made 'by the three estates'. Possibly the prelates and the nobility thought that they, and they alone, were concerned in such a high matter as the succession to the throne; but the rejection of David's scheme meant continuing to pay the ransom—a matter in which the burghs also had a lively concern.

But we may take the argument further, for the proceedings of the parliament of March 1364 are interesting in another way. As we have seen, the burden of the ransom was preferred to an English

king on the Scottish throne, but, nevertheless, it was decided to
send an embassy to England to try to negotiate easier ransom payments. We then read that the prelates and the nobles (again there
is no mention of the burghs) undertook to meet again immediately
upon the return of the ambassadors; more than that, they agreed
that they would meet in response to royal letters under whatsoever
seal, that they would come together 'as if they were lawfully summoned upon forty days as to a parliament', and that they would
raise no objection to a shorter summons: a clear proof that parliament was summoned upon forty days' notice and that the precepts
summoning the prelates and nobles to parliament were issued under
a particular seal. But when they did meet again, in January 1365,
the names of those present, five bishops, six abbots, two earls,
eighteen barons, eight burgesses, and those others unnamed
(probably civil servants) 'accustomed to be called to a council of
this kind' show clearly that the parliament of 1364 had included
burgesses, and that councils of three estates were now an accustomed
feature of Scottish government. Moreover, the record tells us the
name of such reconvened meetings of the members of a previous
parliament: 'general council'.

For the rest of the 1360s our evidence is fuller. Held mainly to
devise ways and means of paying the king's ransom, those summoned
to the parliament of July 1366 'in the due and accustomed way'
were the bishops, abbots, priors, earls, barons, and tenants-in-chief
of the king, and from each burgh certain burgesses summoned 'for
the purpose and cause then on hand' (*qui ad hoc fuerunt ex causa
summoniti*). The 'purpose and cause then on hand' was simply the
raising of money for the ransom. Finance, as in 1326, 1328, 1357,
and 1364, was the controlling factor whereby the burghs could
claim, and were given, a right to take part in the discussions. And in
1367 burgh representatives were again in parliament, and we read
'It is enacted by the three estates in parliament' (*Statutum est per
tres communitates in parliamento*).

Admittedly the burgesses were in parliament only for a special
purpose; they were present *ad hoc* and *ex causa*. But, from now
onwards, they stayed in. The limiting phrases *ad hoc* and *ex causa*
disappeared in the 1420s,[1] and in the fifteenth century we find that
from every burgh 'three or four of the more sufficient burgesses,
holding sufficient commission', were to be summoned to each parliament. That is, the burgess-representatives were to come with

authenticated documents (their commissions) showing that they had been duly appointed by their fellow burgesses and were capable of speaking and acting for them so that the decisions of the parliament were binding upon the burghs.

At the same time we should note that not every royal burgh accepted the new privilege with its attendant expenses, and, until the second half of the sixteenth century, the presence of representatives from this or that burgh tended to be somewhat haphazard. The burghs might wish to have a say in matters that affected them, but attendance could be burdensome and was always expensive. During the fifteenth century we can trace irregular attendance from various burghs numbering some thirty-four in all, but in the second half of the sixteenth century there was fairly regular attendance from about fifty burghs. By then, too, the burghs had come to an agreement among themselves that Edinburgh should send two representatives to parliament while the remaining burghs should send one each. But until the second half of the sixteenth century, the new 'third estate' was never strong. Moreover, the burgh representatives came into parliament to give their consent to a policy that entailed taxation—and, to the very end, burgh representation in parliament was closely associated with the burghs' contributions to national taxations. As a result, there was a tendency for the burgh representatives to think mainly of the protection of their purses and the maintenance of their trading rights.

This attitude was aggravated in other ways. For example, the burghs had their own assembly to discuss their own affairs, and in the fifteenth century the practice grew up of holding a convention of burghs immediately before a sitting of parliament, so that it might 'instruct' the burgess representatives. The aim was probably to increase effectiveness by speaking with unanimity. Naturally this accentuated a concern with matters touching 'the common weal' of the burghs, rather than a concern with matters touching the welfare of the whole realm. In due course the convention of royal burghs even endeavoured to ensure that no individual burgh representative should raise any matter in parliament without the previous consent of the convention. Again, when the burgh representatives came into parliament they were a lone group and, isolated from the prelates and the nobles but sitting in the same chamber with them (for the Scottish parliament was always unicameral), they would be apt to suffer from their inferior social position. Until the very end of the sixteenth century there were no representatives of the shires, as there were in England; and thus the medieval Scottish parliament, unlike that of England, had no third estate composed of burgesses with the more vocal knights of the shire. In the Scottish parliament influence and power still lay with the great lords, spiritual and temporal. Some burgesses there might be, but they were there to help with the finding of money, and they were expected not to interfere too much in important matters of state.

Again, with the financial burdens falling upon the realm to meet the ransom of the king, it was vital that burgh privileges (the source of much money) should be protected, and also that law and order should be maintained, so that trade could flourish. As we have seen, when the first arrangements for raising the ransom money were made in 1357, it was enacted that the burghs and burgesses were freely to enjoy all their wonted rights, liberties, and privileges. Then, in 1364, when the agreement entered into between David II and Edward III was rejected, and there was a continuing need to find money for the ransom payments, the king issued a general charter to all his burghs granting that trade with foreign merchants was to be limited to the king's burghs, and that the buying and selling of wool, skins, hides, and other merchandise was to be conducted only through the burgh merchants.[2] At this time, too, each succeeding parliament and general council emphasized the necessity for maintaining peace throughout the realm; the king's officers were to be men capable of giving 'justice to every man' with 'one common justice' which was to be done 'without exception of person'. Yet the constant re-enactment that law and order must be maintained is in itself proof that enactment was not enough; and although there was some attempt to secure better justice with more efficient judges in the local courts, it was clear that the executive relied always upon the unpaid services as judges of those who might be party (or allied to a party) in the disputes before the courts.

Finally a word on the subsequent history of 'general council', which under David II was a reconvening of some of those at parliament to complete unfinished business. Between 1406 and 1424 the term came to be used of any great council at which the three estates were present (such as those councils of 1357); such general councils were summoned with informality and without public proclamations, but in addition to advising the king they were sufficiently 'strong' (that is a sufficiency of those who mattered were present) to approve ordinances enacting measures for better government. But they were not formally summoned and constituted as the king's court, and could not act as such. And (despite many modern statements to the contrary) they could not grant taxation, a function which was limited to parliament. Moreover, about the middle of the fifteenth century, as legislation became accepted as an important means of changing the law, that function too was reserved to parliament. One of the consequences is the disappearance of records of subsequent general councils which occasional references show to have been held in the late fifteenth century—and even in the early sixteenth century.

The long years of warfare before 1357 left many problems of law and order, of claims and counter-claims to lands and goods. For fear of the lack of impartial justice in the local courts, men sought justice more and more in the king's own court of parliament— sometimes on appeal to the highest court, sometimes on petition for the remedy of some wrong or the enforcement of some right. But parliaments, to which all the great lords, spiritual and temporal, were summoned, could be neither frequent nor of long duration, and, when sitting, had increasingly important matters of state to demand their attention. To ease this situation we find, in the reign of David II, that parliament had begun to appoint two small com- mittees for judicial work: one committee for falsed dooms (*ad judicia contradicta*), and one committee for causes, complaints, and petitions (*ad causas et querelas* or *supplicationes*). This development enabled parliament to get on with the work of government while the committees reported their findings to parliament for parlia- ment's confirmation. Later, as we shall see, James I set up a new court to try to secure better justice for his lieges (and again to relieve parliament of the burden of appeals and complaints); but a final solution to the problem of a central court for civil justice was not found until the establishment of the College of Justice in the reign of James V.

Early in the sixteenth century, too, we hear of meetings called congregations or conventions of prelates and nobles, some unofficial faction-meetings and some summoned by the crown; the function of the latter was simply to give advice, and they may be regarded as parallel to the convention of burghs which was developing simultaneously. During the reign of Mary and the minority of James VI it became convenient to summon burgesses to these informal meetings which were thus named general convention or convention of estates.

NOTES

1. See below, p. 220 n. 7.
2. That is, confirming the trading monopolies granted by earlier charters.

CHAPTER 18

The Early Stewarts

A FULL month elapsed between the death of David II and the coronation of his uncle Robert Stewart as Robert II. Apparently a claim to the throne was advanced by the earl of Douglas; it attracted little support but probably explains why, on the day after his coronation at Scone in March 1371, the king secured a declaration of his own right to succeed by virtue of heredity and of the 'Acts of Settlement' of 1318 and 1326.[1] But, once more, there was also need to define the succession to the throne. Not only was Robert II nearly fifty-five years old, but also, it has been argued, there was some dubiety about the legitimacy of his children by his first wife, Elizabeth Mure, daughter of Sir Adam Mure of Rowallan. The Steward had been granted a papal dispensation in 1347 for his marriage to Elizabeth Mure, but, on the other hand, his eldest son John, earl of Carrick (and later Robert III), had been born some ten years before the dispensation was granted. Admittedly the canon law laid down that children who were born out of wedlock were made legitimate by the subsequent marriage of their parents; but could subsequent marriage under a papal dispensation make legitimate the children already born to parents who were within the forbidden degrees? If the parents were not ignorant of their relationship, were not such children born in incest? Were they not debarred from every legal right? Was John, earl of Carrick, made legitimate by the dispensation for the marriage of his parents? Could he, indeed, claim to be the lawful and legitimate heir to the Scottish throne? And, if all the children of Elizabeth Mure who were born before the granting of the dispensation were not legitimate, was not the rightful heir to the throne David, earl of Strathearn, the eldest son of Robert II by his second wife, Euphemia, daughter of Hugh, earl of Ross? We do not know whether such arguments were canvassed in 1371, but there is no doubt that they could be advanced by the children of Euphemia, David (later earl of Strathearn) and Walter (later earl of Atholl). And they were advanced by others to explain the murder of James I in 1437.

Table 6. THE EARLY STEWARTS

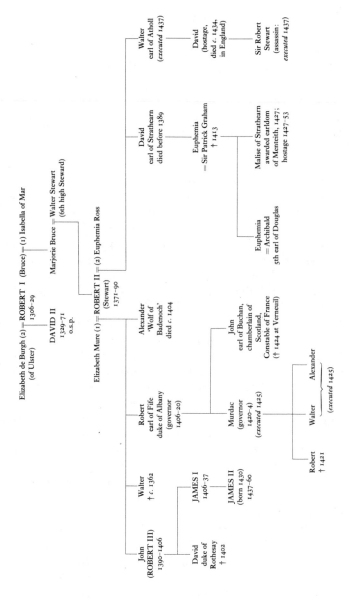

Certainly it was essential, in view of the king's advanced age, that the succession to the throne should be put beyond question. Accordingly the king's declaration of right went on to declare 'for greater certainty' that John, earl of Carrick, the eldest son of Robert II and Elizabeth Mure, was the rightful heir to the throne[2] — a declaration to which the prelates and nobles assented and which they swore, individually, to maintain, and to which, when written on parchment, they affixed their seals; and the whole nature of this declaration which, with its many seals, has fortunately survived, indicates the serious nature of the decision that had to be made. Again, two years later, in 1373, and to avoid 'the uncertainty of the succession', parliament, perhaps to deal with the question of the legitimacy of the king's sons, more probably to restrict the rights of his female descendants (as Edward I had done in 1290 for England), defined the order of succession. In the event of the failure of the line of John, earl of Carrick, and his heirs male, the crown was to pass to Robert, earl of Fife, and his heirs male; whom failing, to Alexander, lord of Badenoch, and his heirs male—all these being the three surviving sons of Robert II by Elizabeth Mure. Only if all those lines were to fail was the crown to pass to David, earl of Strathearn, and his heirs male; whom failing, to Walter, his brother, and his heirs male—these being the two sons of Robert II by Euphemia Ross. Only after all these lines had died out might the inheritance pass through a female.

Of Robert II's own right to the throne there should have been no doubt; but his ability to rule was another matter. Throughout his reign his rule was weak and inefficient, and that of his son, John, who succeeded as Robert III,[3] was even weaker still. And the weakness of the royal rule was revealed in the growing strength of the nobility. Perhaps to the more powerful among the nobility these Stewarts were merely a noble house raised to kingship by a marriage in the heroic past,[4] and lacking the 'divinity that doth hedge a king'? It is possible to see the fifteenth-century history of Scotland as a grim struggle between the Scottish kings and their over-mighty subjects: a struggle that was prolonged partly because of the feudal power enjoyed by the great lords in their own localities, and partly because of an unhappy sequence of minorities in the Stewart line.[5] Now, when the king was weak, the strong magnate assumed in his locality powers which were subject to no royal control; in the locality of this or that great feudatory, smaller men found it necessary to submit to the lord's authority in order to obtain a protection that the king was impotent to give, and thereby the lord became more powerful still with further followers.

When the king was a minor, there had perforce to be a regent.[6] Then there were lords who were jealous of the regent's power; there were lords who supported him and lords who put him to defiance. Factions arose; this or that lord would join this or that faction as he was moved by family loyalties or his own inclination; and the regent in power might be overthrown and succeeded by another regent of an opposing faction. In these unhappy times names like Albany or Douglas seem to take precedence over the name of the king; and the chroniclers speak of lords who 'worked their will outwith the law'. But another view would point out that the Stewarts had hereditary right, coronation, and unction to exalt their kingship. While the events of the various minorities did indeed lead to inter-baronial rivalries, to the building up of private followings, and even to civil strife, the years of active royal rule show that a king of strong personality had no lack of baronial supporters and that he could command agreement to measures of many different kinds—some very harsh. No king went down before faction, not even the one who showed himself vacillating in government, James III.

Now the truce with England, secured by the treaty of Berwick in 1357, had no firm foundation. It was purchased by tardy payments, always in arrears and never paid in full. Moreover, small parts of southern Scotland were still in English hands—a legacy of Edward Balliol's surrender of 1334. In France, too, much territory was still held by England. Scotland had succeeded in regaining some of her land. So, too, had France. Not unnaturally both countries (allied in opposition to England since 1295) hoped to work together to break the English hold.

With the accession of Robert II in 1371 the alliance with France was promptly renewed—as it was renewed again in 1390 with the accession of Robert III. Moreover, despite the truce for fourteen years which had been agreed in 1369, border warfare had still continued. Berwick had been recaptured by the Scots in 1378; only to be forthwith lost again. In 1380 John of Gaunt had led an English army to the Borders, but had done little more than renew the truce for its remaining period of three years. In 1384 he had again led an army northwards, and had advanced as far as Edinburgh; but he had acted with such restraint (refusing to allow Edinburgh to be burned) that his enemies declared he had inflicted more hardship on his own men than on the Scots.[7]

In 1385, however, with an intensification of French efforts against England, a small force of French knights and men-at-arms, and a fairly large subsidy in gold, were brought to Scotland by John de Vienne. But the French found Scotland poor and backward; there were few comforts, and little save 'hard beds and ill nights'. Nor was their coming wholly popular; and some of the Scots are said to have asked, 'Who needs them? Can we not fight our battles ourselves?' The succeeding campaign, indeed, gave the answer to those questions. There was a typical Border raid into England, in which the French took part; but when Richard II, fearing the threat from the north, led an army into Scotland, the differences between the French and the Scots were clearly revealed. The French knights wanted the glory of war in pitched battle with the enemy; but the Scots, knowing better how to recover their southern lands, preferred harassing tactics and the certainty of regaining a little here and then a little there. In disgust the French had watched the English burn down parts of Melrose Abbey while the Scots, under Douglas, had held aloof and had done nothing; but Douglas, in avoiding battle, had followed the better plan. Although Richard II marched on to burn at Dryburgh, Newbattle, Holyrood, and Edinburgh, his invasion (which had taxed his resources to the utmost) brought no military advantages; and meantime the Scots were recovering Teviotdale from English control.

So the struggle went on. At Otterburn, in 1388, a 'dead Douglas' (James, second earl of Douglas) won the field; but in 1402 a body of Border raiders was defeated on Nisbet Moor and, three months later, at Homildon Hill, in Northumberland, a Scottish army, forgetting the lessons of the past, was heavily defeated when the English archers again won the battle at a distance.

Six months after their arrival the French knights of de Vienne's force, unhappy and disillusioned, had been glad to return to their own country, and, to Scotland's disgrace, had been compelled to pay for all their expenses during their stay in Scotland, leaving behind, as surety for payment, their own leader, de Vienne. In effect, French knights were of little use to Scotland in her well-tried methods of meeting English aggression; though, by contrast, Scottish soldiers, fighting against England in the armies of France on French soil, won much renown.[8] Scots companies played a large part in helping France to win the battles of Liége (1408) and Baugé (1421), and when, at Verneuil (1424), they were cut to pieces, their dead included John Stewart, earl of Buchan (nephew of King Robert III), and Archibald, fourth earl of Douglas. Later, they fought under the banner of Joan of Arc, and, later still, formed the 'Scots Guard' of French kings. Scotland and France, together, were proving too much for the English armies in France; and England's difficulties both at home and in France enabled Scotland at home, despite set-backs such as those of Homildon Hill and the 'Foul Raid' of 1417,[9] steadily to regain her southern lands.

But Scotland's problem was no longer that of resisting England or of striving to regain her southern lands. Now the problem was that of internal order within Scotland itself. The realm was 'nocht governit'. The early Stewarts were strong neither in body nor in character. In 1384, because the king (Robert II, who was then about 68) could not himself secure 'the execution of government and law', his son, the earl of Carrick, was invested with authority to enforce the law 'everywhere throughout the realm',[10] and to give justice to all who were suffering grievance or wrong. Four years later, however, in 1388, the earl of Carrick was likewise relieved of authority because of *his* bodily weakness. And yet, two years later, in 1390, this same earl of Carrick was to become king, at the age of fifty-three, as Robert III.[11]

Now, indeed, under these first two Stewart kings, both old and of little force of character, and both unfitted for strong and active rule, chroniclers and records alike speak of 'horrible destructions, burnings, and slaughters commonly done through all the kingdom', and of a government that cannot govern. In 1389, for example, it is recorded that the king's rents from his burgh of Inverness had not been paid for the last six years owing to disorder in those parts. There, too, in the north, Alexander, a younger son of Robert II, earned the title of 'The Wolf of Badenoch': having incurred the censures of the bishop of Moray for his misdeeds, he retaliated by burning down the bishop's cathedral at Elgin and, for good measure, the burgh as well (1390); and in the preceding month he had burned the burgh of Forres and the church of St. Laurence. Plaintively, under the year 1398, a brief northern chronicle has the entry, 'In those days there was no law in Scotland, but the strong oppressed the weak, and the whole kingdom was one den of thieves. Homicides, robberies, fire-raisings and other evil deeds were unpunished, and justice, outlawed, as in exile, beyond the bounds of the king-dom.' And the ordinances of a general council held in 1404 appear to have been concerned solely with attempts to strengthen the courts of justice and the administration of the law.[12]

In Highlands and Lowlands alike, disorder was rampant, but two events of this time, in relation to the Highlands, stand out. In 1396, in an attempt to settle one Highland dispute, a judicial combat on the grand scale was fought on the Inch of Perth between thirty men of the Clan Hay (Yha) or Kay and thirty of the Clan Quele.[13] The story has been immortalized by Scott in *The Fair Maid of Perth*; but we know little of the background and nature of the dispute. The Exchequer Rolls contain an entry of the expenditure of £14. 2s. 11d. 'for wood, iron, and making the enclosure for sixty persons fighting on the Inch of Perth'; but the sources tell different tales of the outcome of the resulting shambles.[14] The chronicler Bower says that thereafter 'for a long time the north was at peace'; but in truth the 'long time' was very short. In 1411 Donald, lord of the Isles, claiming the earldom of Ross by right of his wife, and possibly fearing the designs of Robert, duke of Albany—who, indeed, awarded the earldom to his son, John, earl of Buchan—advanced with a large force towards Aberdeen, intending to secure the lands of the earldom in the sheriffdoms of Banff, Aberdeen, and Kincardine. Knowing that already he had seized Dingwall and burned Inverness, and knowing that the plunder of Aberdeen was to be a reward for his followers, the burgesses of the burgh, together with the local lairds (Forbeses, Keiths, and Leslies), led by Alex-ander Stewart, earl of Mar, illegitimate son of the Wolf of Badenoch, met Donald's army at Harlaw where, after a bloody battle with great loss on both sides (and the battle became known as the 'Red Harlaw'), they compelled him to withdraw. It has sometimes been maintained that Harlaw was a fight between the civilized parts and the Highland caterans. But Highlanders fought on both sides. Moreover, Donald, lord of the Isles, was no Highland cateran: his mother was a daughter of Robert II, he was an acknowledged scholar, and he had attended the court of Henry IV of England. On the other hand, the earl of Mar could hardly claim 'civility' and is even described by contemporary chroniclers as being himself a 'leader of caterans'.

Into this picture of lawlessness and lack of rule must now be fitted the enigmatic figure of the earl of Fife, the second surviving son of Robert II, the brother of Robert III, and better known by his later title of duke of Albany.[15] In 1388, when the earl of Carrick was relieved of his authority because of bodily weakness, the earl of Fife was made guardian of the realm, to have the power of the king to do justice and maintain the laws: and already he was the chamberlain (the chief financial officer) and the keeper of Stirling Castle. Moreover, in 1390, when the enfeebled earl of Carrick became king as Robert III, the earl of Fife still continued to act as guardian. In 1393, however, he ceased to hold office, and Robert III apparently took the government into his own hands. Certainly in 1399 a general council openly attributed the 'misgovernance of the realm' to the failure of the king and the officers of the law; and it then appointed David, duke of Rothesay, Robert III's eldest son, to be lieutenant throughout the kingdom, 'with full power and commission of the king', for a period of three years. The earl of Fife (now duke of Albany) may well have expected reappointment to an office he had formerly held for so long; and he may have been embittered and jealous of Rothesay. Moreover, Rothesay, who had married[16] Elizabeth, daughter of the earl of March, repudiated her, and 'married' Mary (or Marjory), a daughter of Archibald, third earl of Douglas,[17] only to neglect her and, according to censorious chroniclers, to lead a life of vice and folly. It seems that he abused his authority as lieutenant, by neglecting to consult the council appointed with him, and when his term expired in 1402 possibly Robert III did agree to the arrest of his eldest son, an event soon followed by his death.[18] Inevitably his arresters, Albany and Douglas, fell under suspicion and were formally cleared at a general council in May 1402, where once more Albany was made lieutenant, to rule and govern the realm in the name of the king for two years— a commission which was again renewed in 1404. At the same time it is also obvious that, with the death of Rothesay, only the king's second son, the seven-year-old James, now stood between Albany and the throne. And it is not difficult to guess the suspicions that were in Robert III's mind when, in 1405, he arranged for the young James to be sent to France; but the prince was captured at sea and remained a prisoner in England until 1424.

James's capture took place in March 1406; and in April 1406 Robert III died, giving to those around him his own epitaph: 'Here lies the worst of kings and the most miserable of men.'

An entry in the burgh records of Aberdeen reveals that a general council held at Perth now appointed Albany as governor (*generalis gubernator*), undoubtedly with much wider powers than those of the guardians and lieutenants of the past. The situation was unique, for the heir to the throne was held captive and could neither be crowned nor take the coronation oath. Certainly Albany at once assumed royal powers and a royal style—and even the title of his dukedom (1398) had been royal, for Albany, or Albania, was the old Alba, the united kingdom of the Picts and Scots. A new great seal was struck in his name and charters issued under it also in Albany's name; they were dated, not by the year of the king's

Table 7

HARLAW AND THE EARLDOM OF ROSS

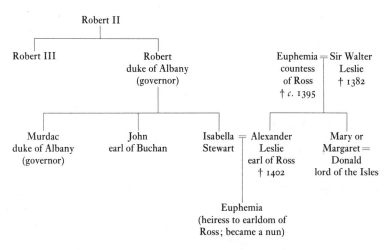

reign, but by the year of Albany's regency; and general councils and exchequers were held in the name and by authority of the lord Robert, duke of Albany, earl of Fife and of Menteith, governor of the realm of Scotland. In 1409, in the Exchequer Rolls, James (who, of course, had not yet been crowned) is referred to, not as king, but as 'the prince, son of the king, now in England'; and in 1410, in a letter to Henry IV, Albany speaks of *his* subjects of Scotland.

It is possible to exaggerate the importance of all this. Wyntoun, writing contemporaneously, seems to stress that although James was recognized as his father's heir he could not be King James I until he had been crowned as such—though Wyntoun may have been excusing Albany's assumption of royal prerogatives. More important, Albany had some knowledge of the disintegration of authority and revenues during his father's lieutenancy in 1346-57, and could reasonably argue that because of the need for strong government after the mismanagement of his brother's reign, it was in the interests of the kingdom and its future king that he should enjoy all the prerogatives of monarchy.

Yet Albany, as governor of the realm, deemed it advisable to enter into a bond for mutual support and defence with the earl of Douglas, itself a clear indication of the Douglas's power. And, if the great feudatories had regarded the first two Stewarts as a feudal house raised to kingship by a lucky chance, what regard could they have for a Stewart acting as governor in the absence of an uncrowned king? Robert II and more strikingly Robert III had weakened the resources of the crown by gifts of pensions from the crown·revenues —some of these pensions even being granted heritably. Individually they were supposed to secure the 'retaining' of the recipient, who was often a kinsman of the king, in his service or that of his heir. That in itself was not necessarily evil, and these 'retainers' were not bribes to procure obedience; rather they were subsidies to cushion the king's friends and relations from the consequences of falling rents and a widespread economic regression. But collectively they were a heavy drain on the finances of the crown. Albany not only continued this weak and unwise policy, but in his regency allowed some of the nobility hitherto not in receipt of pensions to plunder the crown's revenues. More than once we find a Douglas seizing the customs that have been collected in Edinburgh and in Linlithgow, and the earl of Douglas himself seized no less than £5,000 over ten years. It is evident on all hands that Albany, like Robert II and Robert III, was unable to hold the nobility in check, and it is clear that the house of Douglas trod closely on the heels of Albany the governor. Would they dare do so to a king?

Albany died in 1420 and was succeeded as governor by his son, Murdac—we do not know how, or under what authority. Under Murdac, however, lawlessness grew apace; and the governor's own sons were worst of all in their contempt of the law and wrote to England of 'their' subjects and of succeeding to the kingship or at least the governorship. The pillaging of the crown's revenues went from bad to worse. In 1422 a miserable £50 out of a total collection of £1,150 from the customs of Edinburgh reached the central government; and other, though less extensive, losses were recorded from various parts of the realm. Not only was there a growing tide of discontent among the burgesses and the smaller barons and lairds, but even among the more important lords and barons there was apparently a growing hatred of the Albany clan and a desire to bestir them in bringing back the king. The English council governing in the name of the infant Henry VI was not unwilling to allow James to return to Scotland—a ransom would be useful, and possibly Scotland could be weaned from her alliance with France.

So, at last, by the treaty of London (December 1423) James was ransomed for 60,000 merks (euphemistically called the 'maintenance and expenses' of his stay in England) to be paid in six annual instalments of 10,000 merks each, though 10,000 merks were remitted as the dowry of Joan Beaufort whom James married in the February preceding his return to Scotland in April 1424. And the new king's return was one to a grievous inheritance. He returned to find crippled finances, and lawlessness rampant throughout the whole realm: but he returned because his subjects—even the mightiest of them—wanted him back. Men had created disorder in greedy disregard of the common weal, yet none wanted disorder for its own sake.

Yet the governorships of the dukes of Albany were not all loss; perhaps because the first duke held the reins of authority so lightly, the bishop of St. Andrews was able to bring about the founding of Scotland's first university. One result of the war of independence had been that Scottish students had tended to go to the University of Paris rather than to Oxford or Cambridge. With the Great Schism (1378-1417), moreover, when England remained within the obedience of the pope in Rome, and when Scotland and France adhered to the pope in Avignon, Scottish students, more than ever, had gone to Paris or Orleans—for the medieval universities were largely training-centres for appointment and promotion in the church. In 1408, however, France abandoned the Avignonese pope, Benedict XIII, and he was compelled to move to Peñiscola in Aragon. Only Scotland and part of Spain remained faithful to him, and from the French universities the Scots now stood in danger of exclusion as schismatics.

There is evidence that as early as 1410 a number of masters had begun to teach in St. Andrews. There they were joined by other

masters who had felt compelled to leave Paris when France
abandoned the pope. These masters soon attracted students, and
the new school in St. Andrews quickly prospered. In 1412 the
masters and students were granted a charter of incorporation by
Henry Wardlaw, bishop of St. Andrews; and in 1413, at the request
of the church of St. Andrews, of Scotland's prisoner-king, James I,
and of the estates of the realm, the incorporation of masters and
students was granted bulls of privilege and protection, as a university, from Benedict XIII. These bulls gave St. Andrews
recognition as a university with a right to teach and to examine in
theology, canon and civil law, arts, medicine, and 'other lawful
faculties'. The bulls arrived in St. Andrews in February 1414, and
were solemnly promulgated; a *Te Deum* was sung in the cathedral;
and the university of St. Andrews had been founded. Yet there was
probably a more profound reason than the schism for the very
positive steps taken to found the university: the need to combat
heresy.

When Rothesay was appointed to be lieutenant, in 1399, the
oath he was to take, which was based upon the sovereign's coronation oath, included a promise to 'restrain cursit [excommunicated]
men and heretics'. In 1406 or 1407 a certain James Resby was
burned at Perth for preaching the doctrines of Wycliffe in which
he was followed by a Scotsman, Quentin Flockhart, who describes
himself as riding through the countryside to denounce evils in the
church. We hear, too, of Lollards—the people who had embraced
Wycliffe's doctrines, doctrines which called for social as well as
religious change. There was denunciation of the wealth of the
church and the scandalous lives led by some of the churchmen, and
there was the argument that no man could be pope or priest unless
he led a holy life; but there was also a vague theory that the possession of worldly goods was dependent upon 'grace'—a theory that,
for rulers and lords, had dangerous possibilities. Wyntoun, writing
of Albany's appointment as governor, in 1406, includes in his praises

> He was a constant Catholike
> All Lollard he hatyt and heretike.

And in 1416 we find a Congregation of the new university of St.
Andrews enacting that henceforth its Masters of Arts were to swear
to 'defend the church against the insult of the Lollards and to
resist with all their power any who adhered to that sect'. It was surely

with this as its first purpose that the university had been founded. Yet men learned in condemnation of heresy were no less aware of the spiritual perils of schism. And in its very infancy, in 1418, the university of St. Andrews took the initiative in persuading the Scottish estates and the Scottish church to desert Benedict XIII (who had been deposed in 1417 by the council of the whole church at Constance) and to come within the obedience of the new pope, Martin V. This might appear to be ingratitude, as indeed it was; but we must again remember that masters and students in the universities looked for appointments in the church, and that Benedict XIII had practically no benefices in his patronage for, apart from Scotland, the whole of Western Christendom was adhering to Martin. Undoubtedly the masters and students of St. Andrews were influenced by the hard fact that the pope in Rome would be more useful to them than their deserted, isolated, and deposed founder, Benedict XIII. But they also had wit and grit to debate their case before the three estates and to compel the reluctant governor to recognize Martin, as King James had already done from captivity. It is perhaps some small recompense that the arms of the university include a crescent moon to commemorate Pedro de Luna, Benedict XIII.

NOTES

1. A settlement of the throne which Parliament had refused to alter when it rejected the proposals of 1364.

2. And thereby the canon law doctrine of legitimation *per subsequens matrimonium* became accepted in Scottish law. Only in modern times was it accepted in English law.

3. The name of John was possibly considered to be one of ill omen for a king. In France John I was born king and died in a few hours, John II was long a captive of Edward III; also, would the new king be John I or John II?

4. The marriage of Walter, the Steward, to Marjorie Bruce in 1315.

5. James I was eleven years old at his accession; James II was six years old; James III was eight years old; James V was one year old; Mary was one *week* old; and James VI was one year old.

6. Between 1406 (the accession of James I) and 1587 (when James VI attained his majority) there were nearly 100 years of rule by minors and government by regents.

7. But at the time of the Peasants' Revolt in England (1381) he had been given temporary asylum and hospitality in Holyrood, and he had not forgotten.

8. Though, like the French in Scotland, the Scots in France were not always popular. If, in Scotland, it was feared that the French would plunder and spoil the land, in France the Scots were accused of robbing nobles and peasants alike.

It was even argued that, however well-disciplined they might be, the Scottish men-at-arms would be the ruin of the land through their large appetites. In 1385 the French knights under de Vienne had hoped to win fame by knightly deeds; the Scots soldiers in France fought partly to be in active arms against England, but partly also in the hope of winning tangible rewards in pay, booty, and ransoms.

9. When Albany and Douglas collected an army to capture both Berwick and Roxburgh but met with so little success that their attempt was called the 'Foul Raid'.

10. Wording which suggests that the king was still expected to ride throughout his kingdom to execute the royal justice.

11. It should be added, however, that his bodily weakness was due mainly to an injury received from the kick of a horse, though the injury appears also to have affected his character and to have made him timid and retreating.

12. The ordinances of this General Council are printed in *Scottish Historical Review*, xxxv (1956), 132–41.

13. We do not know what this clan was. It occurs as Clanqwheril in 1392 (*Acts Parl. Scot.*, i. 579). In effect neither clan has as yet been identified with certainty.

14. Wyntoun says fifty or more were slain; the *Book of Pluscarden* says seven, wounded, survived; and an entry in the *Register of Moray* says eleven, wounded, survived.

15. In 1398 Robert III's eldest son, David, was created duke of Rothesay, while the King's brother, Robert, earl of Fife, was created duke of Albany. These were the first creations of Scottish dukes.

16. See *Scots Peerage*, iii. 279 note.

17. The earl of March, in anger, deserted to England, became high in the favour of Henry IV from whom he received various grants of land, and fought against the Scots at Nisbet Moor (June 1402) and Homildon Hill (September 1402). See below, p. 218.

18. The story of Rothesay's death from starvation was evidently soon whispered abroad.

CHAPTER 19

The Reign of James I

JAMES I, released in March 1424 from his long captivity, was crowned at Scone on 21 May 1424. He was nearly thirty years old, in the prime of life, and full of vigour; and, in a parliament which he held at Perth within a week of his coronation, he at once revealed his determination to remedy the evils that had recently passed unchecked. Indeed, the early words of its acts, 'That firm and sure peace be kept and held throughout the realm', are eloquent of the resolve traditionally said to have been made by the king immediately upon his return—'If God grant me life, though it be but the life of a dog, there shall be no place in my realm where the key shall not keep the castle and the bracken-bush the cow.' One after another the enactments of parliaments in the first four years of the reign show his determination to secure firm administration of the law under strong royal officials. The use of parliament and of statute on such a scale was new: in 1426 it was enacted that all the king's subjects were to live and be governed by the king's own laws and not by particular laws or privileges (perhaps seeking to limit or abolish methods of trial peculiar to Galloway, or rights of sanctuary, or even the privilege of the clergy to be tried in church courts). Statutes were to be recorded in a register and copies given to the sheriffs to be proclaimed at notable places in the sheriffdoms from which copies were in turn to be provided for other important men. The register was kept and copies made—so we may assume that the rest of the act was carried out. Moreover, the laws in general, 'the books of the law', were to be examined by six wise and discreet men so that they could be 'mended' if in need of amendment; and since some very technical amendments of the law were made, perhaps this 'law reform commission' did sit.

But the statutes which proscribed private wars, rebellion, or aiding rebels, over-large retinues, the importunity of 'valiant beggars', and so forth could only be effective if, as the parliament of 1424 provided

officers of the law shall be appointed who can and may hold the law to the people; that they shall be persons of substance who can be punished in their own goods if they fail to do their duty; and that any now holding office who are incapable shall be replaced by others.

The parliament of 1425 reaffirmed that all judges, including those within regalities, were to do 'full law and justice' as well 'to poor as to rich, without fraud or favour'. But the local courts were apparently still far from being efficient and impartial, and causes, petitions, and complaints were still pouring in to the king in council and parliament. Hence, in 1426, parliament, on the initiative of the king, tried to improve the machinery to cope with this flow: the chancellor and 'certain discreet persons of the three estates chosen by the king' were to sit three times a year in centres that were to be determined by the king and to 'examine, conclude, and finally determine' all causes and complaints that might otherwise come before the king in council—that is, there was to be no appeal from their decisions.

Partly this was an attempt to meet the old difficulty presented by a host of causes and complaints coming before the king in council and in parliament which hindered the progress of the more important work of government and perhaps hindered also the progress of the royal hunt. Partly it eased the burden of seeking the king and council 'wherever they might happen to be'. This new body could sit when parliament was not in session; it could sit in different parts of the realm with prior notice of its sittings; its members were to be chosen by the king and not (as with parliament's judicial committees) by the estates. Its jurisdiction was that of the council and we should be clear what that meant. It dealt only with civil and not with criminal cases (though there was a twilight area in which a civil action could be raised in what was really a criminal matter). It could not use the established procedures of the ordinary courts, especially the assize (jury), because it could not call upon the men of the neighbourhood to give a verdict; it was therefore debarred from dealing with litigation over land-ownership. But it could examine witnesses, discover whether a complaint relating to the possession of *goods* was justified, and it could decree restitution. It was not strictly a court, and only acquired that designation centuries later. Rather it was a tribunal, or, in the fifteenth century word, a sitting, a session.

James I may have been moved by a desire to meet the grievances of his people and to give them justice (and in medieval times the 'good king' was the king who ensured 'good justice'); by a desire to limit the influence of the great lords in their localities (for the new body was to sit 'where the king likes to command'); and by a desire to overcome the rigid rules and procedure of the ordinary courts in providing, more regularly than the council could, the equitable remedies already developed by the council outside or alongside the strict rules of common law. Although we have no record of its sittings under James I, and do not know to what extent it was effective, the fact that in 1439 it was enacted that there were to be only two sessions yearly is a strong indication that there were indeed sessions in many, or perhaps even all, years of James I's reign.[1]

The strengthening of the regular resources of the crown is at once revealed in the rolls of the exchequer. For the whole reign, with but four exceptions, only the accounts of the burghs and the custumars have survived; but practically no grants or pensions from the customs and the burgh fermes were allowed other than certain long-standing royal grants to religious houses; as parliament had said 'all the great and small customs and all the rents of the burgh are the king's for his support. If any man has a claim to any payment from the customs, let him state his claim and the king will give an answer.' And indeed the production of charters was a prerequisite to any payment or allowance from the royal revenues. Nor are there any references to interference with the customs payments which were apparently reaching the royal treasury. As a result, the customs revenue for this first year of James's reign was almost exactly the same as the customs revenue for the *two* years of the audit in 1420. What resulted from another enactment requiring an inquest into crown lands and rents alienated since David II's accession is unknown (unless the case of the earldom of Strathearn was settled in the light of that inquest); it might be inferred that the king's strong hand would result in recovery of lost property—but the precedent of David II's reign suggests that recovery would be difficult and at best partial. As we shall see, crown estates were increased in quite another way.

But the king was also granted in the parliament of 1424 a tax of a twentieth on rents and goods including a levy on corn and reaching down to the meanest landed man, in order to pay the ransom money due to England. A new assessment was to be completed within six weeks and presented to ten named auditors, and if the money was not forthcoming upon demand within fifteen days thereafter 'in gold and silver', then stiff penalties would follow. This twentieth was collected in 1424 and 1425 but aroused much discontent—so much that in the latter year an act was passed threatening with death those scandalmongers who were creating discord between the king and his people. James was revealing that 'cupidity' which led ultimately to his destruction, for he paid only one instalment of his ransom, while holding back enough to pay another. This money was deposited with the burghs and much was sent to Flanders so that it might be exchanged for the English coin in which the ransom was payable; it may be wrong to blame James for defaulting when (to begin with) he was merely seeking a more favourable exchange rate.

For perhaps the greatest puzzle of James I's reign is his relationship with the burghs. Thus at a meeting of the court of Four Burghs in a year given in the record as '1405' it was laid down that from each burgh south of Spey burgess commissioners should come annually to 'the said parliament of Four Burghs'. Now a charter by James II states that his father had granted at Perth that 'the parliament of Four Burghs should be held annually at Edinburgh as it was held from previous times', evidently in October. It seems that the court of Four Burghs became a parliament of many burghs under James I, and that the first stage in this change was the decision of the court held at Stirling on 12 October of '1405', surely a clerical error for 1425. The later development of such burgh meetings is associated with the need to bargain over taxation, and something similar is very likely in 1425, for the legislation of parliaments between 1425 and 1427 shows that within the burghs the struggle of the crafts to control their own affairs became severe in these years.[2] The crafts could only have made their demands of burgh councils, parliaments, and king, where demands (that is for taxation) were being made of them. Exactly how the parliament of four burghs fits into James I's complex dealings with the European money market we do not know, but it is likely that he tolerated or encouraged its evolution for his own financial purposes. Thus the burghs were not called to account for the moneys of 1424-5 until the very end of the reign.

These financial purposes are the nub of our understanding of James I's reign. If we simply accept the records, we chronicle a series of measures which show little common purpose. If we accept that James called parliaments to seek taxation which was refused him and which therefore makes no appearance in the record, much of James's activity becomes policy. Thus in 1426 the two-year tax had ended, and resistance to a renewed grant in the form of individual failure to turn up at parliament (sending instead a procurator with powers to offer views but not promises) would best explain the act that all who held direct of the king—prelates, earls, barons, and freeholders—must attend parliaments and general councils personally, and were to be allowed to send procurators only if they could adduce lawful reasons for their personal absence. Here there was emphasis on the personal attendance of all, including barons and freeholders.

It is possible, but unlikely, that James had in mind that the attendance of small barons and freeholders might help him to check the power of the large feudatories. More probably there was heavy fining in 1427 for continued failure to turn up, and this would fall particularly heavily on the freeholders. Certainly in 1428 there was a further act by which the small barons and freeholders were released from personal attendance at parliaments and general councils provided that each sheriffdom, according to its size, elected two or more 'wise men' to represent them.[3] These commissioners of the shires were to be elected at the head court of the sheriffdom;[4] they were to bring with them their commissions attesting their election, sealed with the sheriff's seal and the seals of the barons of the shire; they were to have full power 'to hear, treat and finally determine'—that is, they were to have full powers, so that their decisions (e.g. to agree to a tax) would be binding on those who elected them; and their expenses were to be met proportionately by those who, by electing commissioners, were thus excused from attendance. Moreover, when they came to parliament, the commissioners of the shires were to choose 'a wise and expert man' to be 'the common speaker of the parliament' to put forward all the 'needs and causes pertaining to the commons'.

Let us note that the whole sheriff court (and not just the small barons) chose these commissioners, and that contemporary England suggests that the baronial voice in any election would be loud and strong. Let us further note that the next parliament consisted of persons summoned as was customary and that in 1430 there were certainly no shire commissioners present. In fact the act was always a dead letter and so we cannot answer all the puzzling questions it raises: why were the shires to elect a common speaker without the burgesses? Was there already a burgess speaker? Was the king

H

conjuring up a commons' estate or even a Commons' House to play off against the magnates?

Now James I had no incentive to relieve the freeholders of fines for non-attendance (which was the aim of the statute) and we might begin with a new assumption—that this legislation was forced through by the magnates at the instigation of their lesser neighbours and dependants. It ended the fining of freeholders but brought (or rather, would bring) to parliament some, in whose election the magnates would have a powerful say. It gave them the right to choose a common speaker without the voice of the burgesses, who were probably much more subservient to the king. And—most telling of all—it was wholly ignored by a king whose legislation is full of revivals and revisions of earlier laws, with dire threats that they be obeyed; but this act was not revived or revised. When we find in the accounts of James I's murder distinct evidence of the existence of a speaker for the barons in parliament refusing the king's demands, we must add this to all the other indications that this act was conceived by those, the prelates and lords, who sought to resist his importunities (especially financial ones) in the hope that an estate of shire commissioners with a speaker would strengthen their hand.[5]

The final section of the act of 1428 provides that the shire commissioners should recover their costs from those of each shire owing compearance in parliament, all bishops, abbots, priors, dukes (there were none in 1428), earls, and lords of parliament, and ban-rents[6] chosen by the king, being excepted (from contributing) and being summoned to councils and parliaments by special (individual) precept; these words seem to imply the continuance for the magnates of an existing practice and are of great interest in revealing the con-solidation of a group of 'lords of parliament'. In the fourteenth century a great landowner was often not merely 'of A' but 'lord of A'. By the end of the century if the title of 'earl' was withheld from the husband of the heiress to an earldom, instead of being called 'earl of B' he was 'lord of B'. Thus the informality of being a lord was achieving a degree of formality, a mark of a place in a hierarchy of men of wealth, such men as would receive individual summons to the king's court of parliament. By 1428 and irrespective of the act under discussion, however, there must have come about (probably in chancery as a matter of convenience) a list of greater barons who always received such summons and were thus lords of parliament, while other barons who might be lords in the eyes of some, were regarded as banrents, receiving individual summons only at the king's discretion. Possibly a banrent might flourish and be added to the list of lords; possibly a lord might lose his fortune and be struck from the list. We cannot say that there was yet a caste of hereditary lords, nor a peerage, and, despite the act of 1428, in parliament the earls and lords formed one estate with such lesser barons as were present.

In some respects the years 1428-9 seem to mark a change in James I's policies. Under the treaty for his release, nobles and heirs of nobles went to England in 1424 as hostages for the payment of the ransom—but they included none of the Albany family. Soon after his return the king arrested Duke Murdac's eldest son; later in the year the earl of Lennox (Albany's father-in-law) and in the March 1425 parliament Duke Murdac and his second son. But none was brought to trial and Duke Murdac was sent to Carlaverock as though to be a participant in the first exchange of hostages, then under negotiation; the arrest of the Albany clan was therefore a move to secure the release of other baronial hostages. But Murdac's youngest son raised rebellion and committed massacre at Dumbarton castle; the king probably changed his plans. All were brought before parliament where an assize of their peers found them guilty (we are not told of what)—and the king hastened them off to execution. Their lands brought him perhaps £1,000 annually— but he did not secure this without judgement and some justification in their behaviour before 1424.

In 1427 another exchange of hostages was arranged, and James, rather than deprive his uncle (and heir) Walter, earl of Atholl, of the earldom of Strathearn (which Albany had given him for life), conferred upon Malise Graham, the heir to Strathearn, the earldom of Menteith which had become crown property in 1425. With that status and income Earl Malise was acceptable to the English as a replacement hostage—and there was nothing sinister in the transaction nor in his going.

But in 1428 the king seems to have decided that parliament would not grant him taxation to build Linlithgow palace, to buy guns in Flanders, to support his extravagant court, and to pay his ransom— and the last now became a matter in which James had little interest, so that his hostages were left to rot in England. The money hoarded since 1425, which could have paid one instalment, was spent recklessly in 1428-31, £500 on Flemish bombards alone, other sums on jewellery, velvet cloth, a company of mummers, and similar marks of James's determination to live like a king. Perhaps in order to increase his income from the fractious Highlanders, James went in 1428 to Inverness, summoning a parliament to meet there; in a display of strength, some fifty Highland chiefs who had evidently turned up in peaceful wise were arrested and imprisoned. Only three appear to have been executed, while the rest were released after a short imprisonment. The king had shown that his authority was to be felt even in the far north, but in the following year, 1429, Alexander, lord of the Isles, who had been arrested in 1428 and released, burned the burgh of Inverness. James immediately marched north again and, somewhere in Lochaber, Alexander was constrained to surrender unconditionally. He was committed to imprisonment in Tantallon. In 1430 Archibald, fifth earl of Douglas, and his cousin Sir John Kennedy were imprisoned 'for certain reasons', probably connected with Douglas's secret negotiations with the English Warden of the West March who had custody of Malise Graham, earl of Menteith. There was probably nothing sinister in any attempt to secure Malise's release, if that was indeed the matter of the negotiations, but they conflicted with James's policy of *rapprochement* with France.

Meanwhile in the absence of Alexander of the Isles the Highlands were ablaze with feud and rebellion. Parliament, summoned to grant the king money for an expedition, first compelled him to release Alexander of the Isles and the earl of Douglas, and then granted a twentieth, to be paid to special treasurers and, unless used for the expedition, to be kept outwith the king's control. The tax was never collected, the king preferring to restore Alexander to his lands and dignities and so to staunch the Highland rebellion, rather than to place taxes raised in his name in the hands of his subjects. The Highland episode reveals the arbitrary streak in James I's political behaviour and his cupidity, but it also shows that his parliaments were not mere servants at his bidding. And for this reason they were less frequent after 1430 than before.

Unfortunately it is not clear beyond a doubt how they functioned. The difficulty of keeping a large number of people together in one place for any length of time had led under David II to the appointment of committees to attend to judicial business, and this continued under James I and his successors. In 1424 the device known under

David II of choosing a number of members to 'hold' the parliament and allowing the rest to go home is *mentioned* for the last time; but it may have continued without mention, or have developed to become the practice of proroguing parliament to a later date (subject to earlier recall by the king) which is found later in James I's reign. When so recalled, was it a 'general council'? Conversely, were all general councils meetings of members of parliament called together again at short notice? There is no evidence to prove that this was so, but nothing to disprove it either; and it was the situation under David II, with whose reign that of James I shows much continuity of institutions and policy.[7]

In the parliament of 1424 (as in those of David II) we read of certain 'articles' (*articuli*, 'points') presented by the king; in 1426 the articles had been put forward by the king to be 'determined by certain persons thereto chosen by the three estates', and thereafter apparently the whole parliament 'answered, ordained, statute and decreed'. It would appear that the king (probably in consultation with his council) had drawn up certain points for consideration by parliament; these points had then been considered by a committee; and parliament had finally legislated according to the committee's recommendations.

From now onwards, indeed, the amount of legislation passed by parliament in a very few days clearly indicates that the 'articles' must have been brought before it in a fully prepared form. But when a whole code of weights and measures is linked to detailed regulations to prevent conflagrations in towns, it is likely that these acts were presented to the committee of the articles already drafted by the burghs; other smaller groups of burgh acts can be identified. Acts regulating the destruction of nesting rooks, or muirburn (which produced a new growth of heath for game), are likely to have come from the estate of barons. In other words the committee of the articles was a useful instrument of government, enabling private interests to have their requests turned into legislation, and enabling the estates to cast a critical eye over the king's legislative proposals. There is no reason to think that the fifteenth-century committee of the articles, which under James I is sometimes found sitting after parliament had been prorogued, failed to give proper attention to its business; it certainly produced an informative corpus of legislation, and the very fact that that legislation was in the vernacular suggests that it had been discussed and was not merely pushed through by the king—as the one or two Latin statutes may have been.

In the effort to establish order and to increase his income, James's legislation is full of fines and forfeitures as sanctions. Although the chamberlain was deprived of all his financial powers except those relating to burghs, the offence of forestalling—of buying before goods reached the market—was made punishable by a fine to the king (not the burgh) and this the chamberlain collected; it almost equalled the other income from burghs. But no sheriffs' or justiciars' accounts survive to tell us how remorselessly the fines and forfeitures introduced for many other offences were pursued: we may surmise that little was forgiven, for in 1434 the king proposed to punish all the sheriffs for their failure to execute justice and the acts of parliament 'up to the exchequer'—i.e. by collecting every penny due—and was dissuaded only by the intercession of the prelates.

The exchequer was merely an audit. What James needed was officers (parallel with the chamberlain for the burghs) to bring to him the money collected by the sheriffs. He simply expanded his own household, allowing and charging four officials of it to handle large sums of money. By 1428 two of these, the comptroller and the treasurer, had taken over the whole task and in the final division of duties, and the one that prevailed, the comptroller was made responsible for all revenue arising from the king's 'property', mainly the rents of crown lands, the burgh fermes, and the receipts of the great customs, while the treasurer was made responsible for all the king's 'casualty', that is chance or casual revenue such as that coming in from the feudal casualties of ward and relief, from judicial amercements and escheats, from payments for respites and remissions, and so forth. In effect, the comptroller and the treasurer soon ingathered all the royal revenue, and the chamberlain (though he was still handling burgh moneys under James I) did little more than preside over the court of the Four Burghs and pass round the burghs on a judicial ayre.

In 1434 James was moving towards an actively anti-English policy; although truces still held, he had renewed the alliance with France and in 1436 his eldest daughter, Margaret, was to marry the Dauphin (Louis XI). It was evidently fear for the security of the eastern approach which led him in 1433–4 to detain the earl of March and seize Dunbar castle. Parliament was persuaded to declare the earldom forfeit on the grounds of the treason of the earl's father in 1400 (and parliament was not always the king's tool), but the king seems to have promised 'Sir George Dunbar', as he now was, the earldom of Buchan. This promise was not fulfilled, perhaps because Dunbar went to England for a visit as 'earl of March' late in 1434. What disquiet this and other arbitrary arrests caused, the sources do not reveal; it is worth remarking that, except in 1425, the arrests were not followed by trials or executions,[8] and the temptation to build up a picture of James's 'tyranny' on the grounds of arrests should be resisted. In the first place such events were probably no more or less frequent than in other medieval reigns: trials and executions, not arrests, were the basis of feuds and rebellions. In the second place it is inconsistent (to say the least) to bewail the 'overmighty subject' and then use the same evidence to bewail an overmighty king.

But we must explain James I's death, which took place after the truce with England had expired and the king had laid siege with his expensive bombards to Roxburgh castle, a siege which ended in an early and ignominious withdrawal. The reasons are obscure and it is tempting to speculate that the army would have preferred to go looting in northern England. But the king was evidently not deterred by his failure and probably in October 1436 (or early in February 1437) was seeking money from the estates to finance another hosting. It seems that the hostility which this conduct aroused provoked into action his bitterest enemy, Sir Robert Graham, who had been arrested in 1424 for a time and who may have fled after being speaker for the estates against taxation in 1436. Who was planned to replace James as king? A later generation accepted that his aged uncle Walter Stewart, earl of Atholl, sought the throne, and modern historians have urged his possible rights as son of Robert II's marriage to Euphemia Ross against the 'illegitimate' line of Elizabeth Mure. But these are *ex post facto* arguments and the earliest evidence is that Graham pursued a personal vendetta and that Atholl (and his family) connived at the murder intending that he should become governor for the young James (II). The murder of James I in the Blackfriars of Perth on the night of 20–1 February 1437 was possible because he was 'acquisitive' and widely unpopular; but he was not a tyrant as Graham claimed, and the murder was not dynastic in purpose.

James I brought law and order to his realm; he was a great innovator in administration; he was fearless and just. Although he was also ruthless, greedy, and spendthrift, nobles and commons alike rallied to the support of the widowed queen, and none hailed the murder of James I as a liberation. Her young son was anointed and crowned as James II on 25 March 1437,[9] and the conspirators were ruthlessly hunted down and put to death with cruelly devised tortures. But, with the death of the strong king, and the accession of his six-year-old son, all that James I had done to bring order into the realm was put in peril. Faction and feud might become the order of the day, and over-mighty subjects were still to seem a danger to more than one Scottish king.

NOTES

1. In the reign of James III, enactments made from time to time ordaining the sessions to be held have an *ad hoc* appearance, and the king's council was again burdened with 'causes and complaints'. Indeed in 1488 it was even enacted that it would be a deferment of justice if parties were to be denied access to the king and council. The problem was not finally solved until the establishment of the College of Justice (the Court of Session) in the reign of James V (below, pp. 305-6).

2. See below, p. 286. The text of the court decision of '1405' is known only from a late-sixteenth-century printed source.

3. In each of the small sheriffdoms of Clackmannan and Kinross, however, only one representative was to be elected.

4. In each sheriffdom there were three 'head courts' a year—at Yule, Easter, and Michaelmas. These were full assemblies of all those in the sheriffdom who held direct of the king and owed attendance at the court. Thus, at a head court, all the small barons and freeholders would be present to elect their representatives.

5. It is possible that the development of a Burgh parliament which, it is suggested, took place in the years after 1425 produced a speaker of the parliament of four burghs and hence encouraged those who drafted the 1428 representation act to include a counterbalancing 'speaker of the parliament', i.e. of the king's parliament. The whole subject is of great interest but is *not* to be explained as an attempt to import English institutions, still less 'the English constitution'.

6. In English 'bannerets', the top rank of knights, distinguished by their entitlement to a small banner.

7. Careful examination suggests that some of the parliamentary terminology of James I's reign, the summoning of burgesses 'ad hoc', the leave to the rest to go home, the articles, may have been due not to the continuous history of these features but to revival by James I's clerks after research in the records of David II's parliaments. Too much should not be read into summoning burgesses 'ad hoc'.

8. Except, of course, for three Highland chiefs (out of fifty) in 1428. When James I was murdered, the first to pursue the murderers was Sir James Dunbar, March's brother.

9. The queen fled to Edinburgh and James II was crowned at Holyrood, the first king not to be inaugurated at Scone.

CHAPTER 20

The Crown and the Black Douglases

ALTHOUGH we cannot put a figure on the population of Scotland in 1400 or 1500, we may perhaps hazard a guess at the trends which a population graph might have shown. The reigns of the earliest Stewarts were probably marked by a decline, the consequence not only of recurrent visitations of the Black Death from 1349 but also, it may be, of over-exploitation of natural resources in the preceding century. What we now know to be the richest soil was too heavy to cultivate, and prolonged cultivation of lighter soil may have taken the heart out of it, lowered productivity, and so yielded less food. If that were true the number of mouths fed must diminish.

Certainly the Scotland of James I was a poorer country than that of David II, and all the indications are that there was little recovery before about 1500. But paradoxically that does not mean that everyone was worse off. On the contrary there is much to suggest that decreased pressure of population upon the land meant a greater sufficiency for those who worked it, and the records of estate management which now begin to survive show that as the fifteenth century progressed it was usual for husbandmen and small tenants, free now of any hint of personal servitude (which had vanished in the fourteenth century), to hold their land on short (e.g. five-year) leases for rents which varied little and were, so far as we can tell, often renewed. There was even the beginning of a movement to allow them a limited security in their holdings, which were often small enough to be worked by the single family. Hence they became 'kindly' tenancies—holdings in which the kin enjoyed some customary rights. In fact there is more likelihood of a 'subsistence economy' in the countryside in the fifteenth century than in the thirteenth.

Thus lairds and great lords who owned their lands heritably became *rentiers* but were unable to increase their incomes greatly so long as population and the demand for land remained stable. Indeed it was probably declining incomes which caused some magnates to prey upon the king's revenues before 1424—and the most notable of those to do so was the earl of Douglas. After 1424 there is reason to think that the income 'differential' between a great magnate and a middling baron was much less than it had once been and that some barons were as well off as some earls. This fact we have already seen leading to discrimination among barons of those who were 'lords'. In 1445 apparently for the first time the king *created* three lords, a circumstance which we can look at in various ways: the king is buying support; the king is taking into his own hands the power to recognize those who have thriven to become lords; the rank of lord is now closed, and includes only those already in and those to be promoted by the king—it can no longer be entered largely by wealth but is carefully exclusive.

In 1452 the king, again doubtless to buy support, promoted some lords to be earls of entirely new earldoms. If we listen we can hear the wealthy baron of 1424 saying 'I am not as other barons; I am a lord'; so now we can hear some lords of 1452 saying 'I am not as other lords but am wealthy and important enough to be accounted an earl to which rank I claim admittance'. And in 1488 the same social ambition forced the politically weak James III to promote an earl to the rank of duke hitherto reserved for the king's sons and eldest brother. Evidently the nobility set great store by rank and title—and indeed showed this by laws to define the clothes to be worn by each rank in parliament. This attitude is best explained as a defence of social position against the inroads of social change at a time of economic stagnation; but the barriers erected merely slowed down change—the number of 'peerages' granted in the fifteenth and sixteenth century shows that honours were even then for sale.

Concern for social position marked by badges of rank—a title, a coat of arms—was the key to many political acts of the fifteenth and sixteenth century. But social position was buttressed not merely by wealth but also by more intangible bonds. The first of these was kinship; it was expected that the kin of a great man, even those distantly related to him, would both receive from him, and help him to give, advice, and, more important, protection and main-tenance. For this was a proud and disorderly society of unlettered men, quick to take offence, descending readily to brawling, violence, and, though this was usually a consequence rather than an aim, killing. From a killing came a feud between the kin of each party and a perpetuation of violence unless the feud could be stanched:

society expected the heads of the respective kin to bring about the stanching. And in the last resort society expected the king to cozen or command the heads of kins into ending their feuds.

The second bond was dependence or 'manrent' from men who were not kin to the great. Living close to a wealthy landowner with numerous kin, like Kennedy in Ayrshire or Gordon in Aberdeen-shire, it was often wise for a lesser man who might himself have a following of kin, to accept the maintenance of the powerful neighbour, to enter his 'allya', enjoy his protection, and increase his power and influence. The motive was not to create disorder but to maintain, by social pressures, a private order presided over by the greatest head of the greatest kin and allya; and significantly we can find these private orders most clearly when they break down and in areas of the country where the king is seldom active: in the south-west, in Moray and the north-east, even in Angus. But not on the whole in Clydesdale, Lothian, Fife, Gowrie, where the king moved from one residence to another and, *so long as he was adult*, maintained reasonable order with no difficulty merely by the respect accorded to his person. Thus it seems that what have been called 'over-mighty subjects' were a useful supplement to, or substitute for, royal authority, in some parts of Scotland.

The third bond might, however, be judged differently: an alliance among two or more of the great. It might often be that a marriage was part of the settlement of a dispute within or between kins. We can see magnates following two policies: marrying into one another's families, as a means of cementing friendships, new or old, more or less precarious; and yet making every possible legal arrangement by entail (or *tailzie*) to exclude females from the family inheritance lest the lands and power of the head of say, the Gordons, should pass through sister or daughter to another family, name, and kin, so leaving headless and destroying the name and kin of Gordon. After all, in the fourteenth century, by a string of marriages, the house of Stewart had swallowed up the earldoms of Fife, Menteith, Buchan, Mar, Ross; marriage into the royal house was a mark of favour but this favour was not to be bought in the fifteenth century at such a price.

All noble families intermarried, and almost every marriage betokened a coming together of two nobles to settle a dispute, or to work for some other common end such as obtaining a favour from the king, or in the ecclesiastical sphere from bishop or pope.

There was nothing inherently sinister in these bonds and alliances, except perhaps on the Borders, where a more violent way of life flourished on the excuse of the Anglo-Scottish war. There is an undischarged burden of proof upon those who see them as a sustained attempt to wreck royal authority; the history of fifteenth-century Scotland can be read in another and more consistent way.

Thus the rise of the house of Douglas first began with the grants of lands and powers that were made to the 'good Sir James' by a grateful Bruce. The earldom, the first earldom since Carrick in the 1220s to take its name from the family lordship, dates from 1358; and William, first earl of Douglas, then added the earldom of Mar to the Douglas lands by his marriage to Margaret of Mar. His son, James, the second earl, was the hero of Otterburn (1388) when, as told in one of the noblest of our ballads, a dead man won a field:

> But I hae dreamed a dreary dream,
> Beyond the Isle of Skye;
> I saw a dead man win a fight,
> And I think that man was I.
>
> My wound is deep; I fain would sleep
> Take thou the vanguard of the three,
> And hide me by the bracken bush
> That grows on yonder lily lee.

And, when the proud 'Hotspur' was compelled to yield—

> Thou shalt not yield to lord nor loun,
> Nor yet shalt thou yield to me;
> But yield thee to the bracken bush,
> That grows upon yon lily lee!

With the death of the second earl, the title and lands (without Mar) descended by an old tailzie excluding females to Archibald 'the Grim', illegitimate son of the 'good Sir James', who already held all Galloway between the Nith and the Cree (granted to him by David II in 1369, and making him lord of Galloway), the earldom of Wigtown (which he had purchased from Thomas Fleming, earl of Wigtown, in 1372), and the lordship of Bothwell (which he gained from his wife, the widow of Sir Thomas Moray of Bothwell). When he was succeeded by his son, Archibald, fourth earl of Douglas, about Christmas 1400, the house of Douglas held the whole of south-west Scotland together with lands in the north and the east,

Table 8. THE BLACK DOUGLASES

EARLS OF DOUGLAS

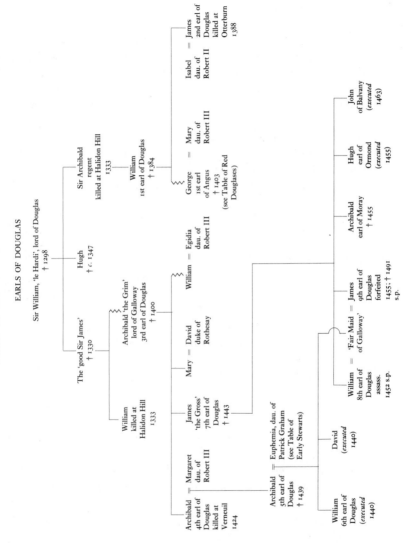

and the power of the 'Black' Douglas in possessions and in followers had become enormous.[1]

Archibald 'the Grim' suppressed a nunnery to found the collegiate church of Lincluden, restored Sweetheart abbey, founded and began to build a collegiate church at Bothwell, and died in the strong castle of Threave which he had built on an island in the Kirkcudbright Dee. His son Archibald, fourth earl, played a leading part in the warfare against England, both on the Borders and in France. When, on the Borders, the earl of March (who had inherited some of Thomas Randolph's possessions in Moray and Annandale), angered by Rothesay's treatment of his daughter, went over to England, Douglas was given his lands and the lordship of Dunbar; and when the earl of March was rehabilitated by Albany, Douglas still retained his lands of Annandale. In search of fame, booty, retainer, and title, he took service in France where Charles VII appointed him lieutenant-general of the French armies and created him duke of Touraine; but, together with his second son, James, and with John Stewart, earl of Buchan (son of the regent Albany), he was killed in the battle of Verneuil (1424).

Archibald, fourth earl, had married Margaret Stewart, the eldest daughter of John, earl of Carrick, afterwards King Robert III. His son Archibald, fifth earl of Douglas, married, in 1424 or 1425, Euphemia, the elder daughter of Sir Patrick Graham, and sister of that Malise Graham, earl of Menteith, sent by James I as a hostage to England in 1427. About Whitsuntide 1430, Douglas and his wife were in communication with the earl of Salisbury, custodian of the imprisoned Malise. It may be that all they sought was the release of Malise, and their negotiations may have had no treasonable intent. But when their negotiations came to the knowledge of the king, the earl was arrested and imprisoned in Lochleven castle, from which he was not released until the autumn of 1431, when the king had a surviving direct heir. The negotiations may have been an excuse to remove an opponent of James I's financial demands.

That Earl Archibald was powerful is beyond question, but he at no time showed ambitions to demolish the king's authority. On the contrary, after James I's murder he was appointed as lieutenant-general of the kingdom, and Bishop Cameron of Glasgow was confirmed as chancellor, obviously to continue the late king's strong government under the queen (as custodian of the young king), Douglas and Cameron. The promise was not fulfilled. Almost at once faction and feud arose to disturb the land, and the magnates who had been curbed by James I turned to strife and disorder in their own parts—perhaps because James I had curbed them too harshly, weakening their traditional local roles. As early as March 1439 we find a general council ordering Douglas, as lieutenant-general, to 'raise the country' and proceed in strength against 'rebels and unruleful men'; and already Sir Alan Stewart of Darnley had been killed by Sir Thomas Boyd of Kilmarnock who, in turn, was later slain by the Stewarts. But Douglas was either incapable of office, or unable to make his office felt; and what little restraint he may have been able to impose was removed by his sudden death, while still in the prime of life, in June 1439.[2]

Almost at once Sir Alexander Livingston, the keeper of Stirling castle, and Sir William Crichton (an able servant of James I), the keeper of Edinburgh castle, strove against each other for the possession of the young king: Crichton endeavouring to maintain the government, Livingston greedy for power. Temporarily coming together in alliance against the Douglas, they killed the new earl, William (aged about sixteen), together with his only brother David, an event picturesquely described much later as the Black Dinner in Edinburgh castle, and denounced in the popular rhyme

> Edinburgh Castle, Toune and Towre
> God grant thou sinke for sinne,
> And that even for the black dinoir
> Earl Douglas gat therin.

Perhaps Crichton and Livingston were in a stronger position with the removal of the young earl of Douglas; but there is a suspicion that one or both of them had acted in secret agreement with, and to win the support of, James Douglas, earl of Avondale, brother of Archibald 'the Grim' fourth earl of Douglas, who now fell heir to the entailed Douglas earldom, while Margaret, the daughter of Archibald, fifth earl, and sister of the murdered Earl William, succeeded to Galloway and to all the unentailed lands which had been acquired through the marriage of Archibald 'the Grim' to Joanna Moray, and so became popularly known as 'the Fair Maid of Galloway'. The earl of March recovered Annandale; and an ungrateful French king had already disposed of the duchy of Touraine. Although James, seventh earl of Douglas, did not long enjoy the fruits of his perfidy when he died three years later, in 1443, and was succeeded in the earldom by his son William, the twelve-year-old 'Fair Maid' was already, or was soon to be, married to the new earl. Thus the Douglas inheritance was satisfactorily reunited.

William, eighth earl of Douglas, now allied with Livingston against Crichton. Crichtons and Livingstons harried each other's land; Crichtons ravaged the Douglas lands in Lothian, and Douglases burned Crichton's castle of Barnton. Bishop Kennedy of St. Andrews, 'whose singleness of purpose and purity of character stand out in bright relief in an age when such qualities were rare', but who was still a man of his time, fearing the growing power of Douglas, his alliance with the Livingstons, and their friendship with the earl of Crawford, gave his strong support to the Crichtons. The followers of Crawford and Livingston ravaged and looted the bishop's lands; in turn, Kennedy excommunicated the earl of Crawford and all his adherents.

Disorder was now rampant. Hepburn of Hailes seized Dunbar and carried off the prior of Coldingham to imprisonment there. Stewarts and Ruthvens fought at Perth, and Sir William Ruthven, the sheriff, was slain. Lindsays and Ogilvies did battle at Arbroath, and the earl of Crawford was mortally wounded when trying (as a great noble) to make peace between the contenders.[3] On the Borders, the Douglases enhanced their prestige by routing an English army at Gretna on the banks of the Sark in 1448, and in the following year the English burned Dunbar and Dumfries while the Scots burned Alnwick and Wark.

Then, in July 1449, James II, nearly nineteen years old, married Mary of Gueldres and, with his marriage, appears to have assumed the government of his kingdom. The Livingstons were forfeited in the autumn of the same year—partly, it would appear, because the king discovered their appropriations of crown finances, but also, and certainly, because of their former ill-treatment of the king's mother and her second husband, the 'Black Knight of Lorn'. And on the other hand the earl of Douglas was given a share of the forfeited lands.

That the royal minority had led to a widespread breakdown in order is beyond question. Yet it is clear that ambitious men sought to use the king's person because the authority of this boy commanded so much respect. They used it to divert money and lands to their own kin, and yet were not powerful enough to use it, as Crawford was using his at his death, to stanch feuds. The Livingstons and other jackals who followed their example were not, as is sometimes said, over-mighty. They were insufficiently mighty, as they discovered in 1448-9 when Douglas left them to the king's mercy. In giving further lands to Douglas, James II was rewarding a man whose equivocal role in preceding events showed shift and drift rather than purposeful ambition or overweening strength.

It was evidently James II who opened the five-year stress culminating in the expulsion of the Black Douglases; his motive was the bankrupt treasury which he inherited and the obligation to provide a large dower, an obligation which he took along with Mary of Gueldres. Douglas like others loaned money to the king; in October 1450, a 'Jubilee' year, he set off to Rome, and in his absence the king moved to treat the unentailed lands (i.e. of the Fair Maid, Douglas's wife) as crown lands, presumably by escheat, aiming probably to confer them upon the queen. There was resistance both before and after Douglas's return—and in the course of that return he visited the English court, so giving colour to charges of treason, though whether justifiably or not is unknown.

In a parliament of June–July 1451 the king climbed down (as James I had had to climb down in 1431), restoring all the Douglas lands save the earldom of Wigtown, which was restored at another parliament later in the same year. When the earl was confirmed in all his lands, offices, and castle in 1451, the charters of confirmation show that he held: the earldom of Douglas, the earldom of Wigtown, the lordship of Galloway, the forests of Ettrick and Selkirk, the lordship of Bothwell, large estates in the sheriffdoms of Edinburgh, Haddington, Lanark, Roxburgh, Linlithgow, Peebles, and Aberdeen, and the offices of sheriff of Lanark and Warden of the West and Middle Marches. Nor should it be forgotten that his brothers, Archibald, earl of Moray, Hugh, earl of Ormond, and John of Balvany, held large extents of lands in the north and northeast. The house of Douglas, it now seemed, bestrode Scotland like a Colossus.

Douglas now made the first move which gave the king grounds to act against him. He 'banded' with Alexander, fourth earl of Crawford (the 'tiger' earl), and John of the Isles, earl of Ross, who had already put the king to defiance. If James II was not blind to the dangers that faced him, Douglas, on his part, had learned reason to fear the king. The 'band' is nowhere quoted in our sources and its terms were therefore probably commonplace and inoffensive enough: undertakings of mutual assistance and advice, saving their faith to the lord king. But the underlying purpose of defending the great Douglas power against royal acquisitiveness was unmistakable, and James II did not hesitate to take up the implicit challenge.

He invited the earl to Stirling castle, under a royal safe-conduct, and there, together, they dined and supped. After their meal, the king bespoke the Douglas, asking him to 'break his band'. When Douglas replied that he 'might not nor would not', James, apparently in sudden anger, stabbed him, and the royal attendants, rushing in, made sure that the earl was dead (22 February 1452).[4] The story is well known; less well known, perhaps, is the fact that, in the following June, parliament exonerated James from all blame, since the earl had entered into treasonable conspiracies against the king and had procured and given grounds for his own death. The king self-consciously turned the blame from where it truly belonged— himself—to the dead man; such self-justification indicates that he was not immune to the force of hostile aristocratic opinion and cohesiveness.

Moreover, following the murder of Earl William, James, his brother, the ninth and last earl of Douglas, came to Stirling with some 600 men, denounced the king as a breaker of his word, dragged the violated safe-conduct through the town at the tail of a horse, and then burned and looted at will. He also made approaches to the English king, and declared his defiance of parliament. In reply, James marched in force through the Douglas lands and, at Douglas castle, in August 1452, received the submission of the earl and his adherents, together with an assurance that Douglas would abandon all rancour and feud for the death of his brother, and would make no band or league against the king in time to come. In January 1453, when the earl bound himself to be faithful to the king, James promised to further a petition for a papal dispensation for the marriage of Earl James to his brother's widow, the Fair Maid of Galloway. The marriage took place, and the vast Douglas lands were united again. Plainly there was little trust between the two men and historians have speculated about the reasons for this strange and agonizing postlude to the 1452 murder. The explanation must surely be the strength of opinion among the Scots, and especially the Scottish nobility, against the destruction of a house and kin so powerful as that of Douglas. For if Douglas should be destroyed without real blame, who would then be safe?

In April 1453, however, the ninth earl of Douglas went to London as a member of a commission seeking to arrange a truce with England, and secured the release of Malise Graham (a man with a possible right to the throne), apparently obtained without James's knowledge or consent. This or other dealings with the unhappy, divided, and powerless English court gave James II his excuse if not his motive. Assembling his forces, he marched against the earl; Douglas showed a singular lack of resolution and, deserted by his more important adherents, fled to England. His brothers were defeated in battle at Arkinholme—Archibald was killed, Hugh was taken prisoner and executed, and John fled to join his brother, the earl, in England. In June 1455 the last earl of Douglas was condemned, and the vast Douglas estates were forfeited to the crown. It was almost certainly the main aim which the king had sought to encompass.

Artillery had given the king a new power over fractious nobility, or, later, Border chiefs. A few small guns were probably imported into Scotland about the middle of the fourteenth century,[5] but the first official reference to royal artillery occurs in the chamberlain's account rendered in 1385,[6] though further payments in the same account, for saltpetre and sulphur for supplying the king's castles, suggest that there were already guns in several royal castles. In 1430, according to Bower, James I imported a great brass bombard from Flanders, and at first most guns, and most of the gunners, came from there. James II used artillery to reduce the castles of Abercorn, Blackness, and Threave. It was he who brought to Scotland one of the greatest of early cannon anywhere—Mons Meg, forged in Malines in Belgium and imported about 1450, doubtless at great expense. Indeed, although James II's accounts are lost, there is more than a suspicion that the extensive foreign debts which drove him to penalize the Douglases, and which remained as a millstone round his son's neck, were incurred in building up an artillery train. It is significant that James sought to do this with the co-operation of the nobility. In 1456 parliament thought it 'speedful that the king make request to certain of the great barons of the land that are of any might to make carts of war, and in each cart two guns, and each of them to have two chambers, with the rest of the

gear that pertains thereto, and a cunning man to shoot them'.
Perhaps the king saw a danger in allowing the nobility to have guns
with 'cunning men to shoot them'; but the act suggests exactly the
contrary—that the king would fain have placed some of the cost
upon his nobility, and that he knew he could rely upon using their
artillery. When later enactments refer only to the provision and
supply of 'carts of war', without any reference to guns, this is surely
because the pieces of artillery were too expensive for earls and lords
to purchase.

Following the forfeiture of the Douglases, and the escheat of their
lands, parliament, in August 1455, proceeded to pass a number of
important acts. Beginning with a general declaration that, since 'the
poverty of the crown is oft-times the cause of the poverty of the
realm' leading to many 'inconvenients' including, certainly, heavy
borrowing by the crown at high rates of interest, therefore, in order
to enable the king 'to live of his own',[7] certain lordships and castles
were henceforth to be 'annexed' to the crown and were to be
inalienable save with the consent of parliament, and then only for
'great and reasonable causes'. Thereafter the annexed lordships
and castles are fully listed. The list opens with 'the whole customs
of Scotland', it includes the strategic castles of Edinburgh and
Stirling, and in it appear many of the lands forfeited by James I,
as well as some of the Douglas lands.

Previous attempts to prevent the alienation of crown lands had
been made in the reign of David II at the time when the realm was
suffering the 'inconvenience' of taxation to meet the king's ransom.
Those attempts had covered *all* the crown lands, none of which
was to be alienated without 'mature advice' or, in a second attempt,
without 'the consent of the three estates'; but they had been in-
operative. Henceforth, however, the crown lands were to be of
two categories—'annexed lands', which were to be inalienable
and were to be retained with the crown for the support of the crown,
and 'unannexed lands', of which the king could dispose at his
pleasure. Moreover, James II was now to swear, and his successors
at the time of their coronations were to swear, to observe and keep
this act. Historians have interpreted this as an attempt to restrain
the king and so to avert taxation. If so, it might not be unreasonable
to see it as a price paid by the king in return for parliament's forfeiture of the Douglases. The pressure under which the king had
acted was that of his overseas debts, and particularly the need to

assign a dower in land to his wife: parliament now sought to put restrictions upon the king's freedom to alienate so that he could never again plead such poverty. Even if the act is to be explained otherwise, even if the king himself had sponsored it in order to hold off importunate supporters, that underlying motive remains the same: the king should never again be in such financial weakness.

In addition to this act prescribing the annexation of lands to the crown, parliament passed other acts which, had they been enforced, would also have strengthened the royal authority. It was decreed, for example, that in future no regality was to be erected without the consent of the three estates—that is, there were to be no more petty kings excluding the royal officers and the royal writ from their lands; and no offices were in future to be granted heritably, the office of Warden on the Border with England being expressly named.

Unfortunately, however, like too many acts of the Scottish parliament, these acts of 1455 were little more than acts of good intention. Although one or two references to the 'annexing' of lands to the crown are later to be found, it is clear that by the beginning of the sixteenth century the principles laid down in 1455 were not being observed. Moreover regalities were still erected without any reference to the estates, and heritable grants of offices were still made.

James II had now made himself master in his own kingdom. But if domestic strife had been settled, relations with England grew steadily worse. Partly England arrogantly renewed the old claim to the overlordship of Scotland; partly Scotland, renewing the auld alliance with France, was determined to regain Berwick and Roxburgh. Periods of uneasy truce alternated with Border raids and forays; but England was torn between Lancaster and York, and the initiative lay with James. Unhappily, when besieging Roxburgh castle in August 1460, he was accidentally killed by one of his own guns which 'brak in the fyring' (3 August 1460).

For the last ten years of his reign James II had followed policies much similar to those of his father. He had striven to strengthen the authority of the crown; he had chosen important ministers from the clerical estate; and his name had become associated with equity and justice. He was only in his thirtieth year when his sudden death fulfilled an old prophecy that a dead king would win the castle of Marchmont (or Roxburgh) from the hands of the English—for, after the death of the king, the siege was still continued and, on 8 August, the castle surrendered and was destroyed. Two days later (10 August 1460) the new king, James III, was crowned in the near-by abbey of Kelso.

Once more Scotland was faced with a long minority, for James III was only eight years old; once more the nobles were freed from the control of a strong and determined king; and once more self-interest might come before service to the realm.

NOTES

1. Black was their heraldic colour; another branch of the family used red and acquired the earldom of Angus under Robert III—hence the Red Douglases, earls of Angus.

2. He died of the plague that was called 'the pestilence but [without] mercy', for those who contracted it never recovered but died within twenty-four hours.

3. It is said that his death took place exactly a year after his excommunication by Bishop Kennedy, and was popularly regarded as a judgement of God. Also, because he died excommunicate, his body is said to have remained unburied until Kennedy lifted his excommunication.

4. And the earl of Crawford was defeated by the earl of Huntly, fighting under the king's banner, at Brechin (18 May 1452).

5. Barbour speaks of 'crakkis of wer' (guns) as a novelty first seen by the Scots in their campaign in Weardale in 1327 (*The Bruce*, book XIX, lines 394-400).

6. *Exchequer Rolls*, iii. 672.

7. That is, to support the expenses of government, and his own personal expenses, out of the revenues of the crown lands and rents, the customs, the profits of justice, and so forth, without recourse to taxation.

CHAPTER 21

James III

I⊤ is sometimes said that James II had attacked Roxburgh castle 'in the Lancastrian interest'. It would be truer to say that he had attacked it in the interests of Scotland. Be that as it may, in December of the same year (1460) Margaret of Anjou, the queen of Henry VI, arrived in Scotland to seek help against her opponents of York. Early in 1461 she led southwards a motley army of 'Scots, Welsh and other strangers and Northernmen' which, plundering as it went, met the Yorkists near St. Albans, won the victory there, and regained possession of the king's person. The way to London lay open; yet, unaccountably, Margaret did not take it. Yorkist forces were able to enter and hold the city; the duke of York assumed the crown as Edward IV; and, in March 1461, the Yorkist king made his title effective by defeating the Lancastrians at Towton near York. Margaret had again to cross the Border into Scotland, this time in company with Henry VI.

Desperate for help, Margaret now surrendered Berwick to the Scots, and made a promise to cede Carlisle. For a brief twenty-one years the gateway of the eastern march returned to Scottish possession. In reply Edward IV used the forfeited and exiled Black Douglas to enter into negotiations with John of the Isles to try to 'stab Scotland in the back with the Celtic dirk'. Early in 1462, by a treaty (which has come to be known as the treaty of Westminster–Ardtornish)[1] John of the Isles, earl of Ross, and his kinsman, Donald Balloch, bound themselves to become and remain liegemen of the king of England and to co-operate with Douglas to conquer and subdue the realm of Scotland. If they were successful, then all Scotland north of the Forth was to be held by them and to be divided equally between the MacDonalds and Douglas as vassals of the crown of England, while Douglas was to enjoy his former possessions in the south-west, to be held in a like way of the English king.

The treaty of Westminster–Ardtornish, however, was of little or no effect. For a time the earl of Ross was able to usurp the royal

authority in the north, gathering in the king's rents and assuming
regal powers; but Douglas's sole success on the Borders appears
to have been the capture of the earl of Crawford, Lord Maxwell,
and 'other noble men' in a raid of March 1463. A little later in the
same year another raid by Douglas was repulsed and his brother
John, Lord Balvany, was captured and executed; and when in
1464 a truce for fifteen years was signed with Edward IV of England,
the earl of Ross apparently deemed it expedient to return to his
proper allegiance to the Scottish king, though that allegiance was
to be of short duration.

During this period the government of the country had been
largely directed by the Queen Mother, Mary of Gueldres, and
Bishop Kennedy. The Queen Mother died in December 1463 however, and James Kennedy, a great churchman, a great statesman,
and the founder of St. Salvator's College at St. Andrews university,
died in May 1465. He had also done his duty by his kin, advancing
their fortunes in a modest way and drawing upon their support.
In consequence they were left by his death in charge of the young
king, and so of the kingdom. But not for long.[2]

In the following year the young king, aged fourteen, was suddenly
seized by a group of lesser nobles headed by the Boyds of Kilmarnock—an old but modest family who for some three years held
all power in their own hands.

At Edinburgh, in October 1466, at a meeting of parliament
following the king's seizure, James III, in what must have been a
prearranged scene, stated that all that had been done by the Boyds
had been done at his command. More than that, Robert, Lord Boyd
was made governor of the king's person and keeper of the fortresses
of the kingdom, until the king should reach the age of twenty-one.
During a royal minority the estates tended to support the faction
that was in power, and which had possession of the king's person.
But the Kennedys and the Boyds were by the standards of their
times honest and well-meaning and the minority of James III saw
no repetition of the chaos of 1439–49. Lord Boyd did not abuse his
newly won power save when, early in 1467, his eldest son, Sir
Thomas Boyd, received in marriage the Lady Mary, the king's sister,
and was created earl of Arran.

In the following year (1468) Lord Boyd concluded the treaty under
which James III married Margaret, the daughter of Christian I of
Denmark, and through which Orkney and Shetland eventually

Table 9. ROYAL STEWARTS, HAMILTONS, AND LENNOX STEWARTS

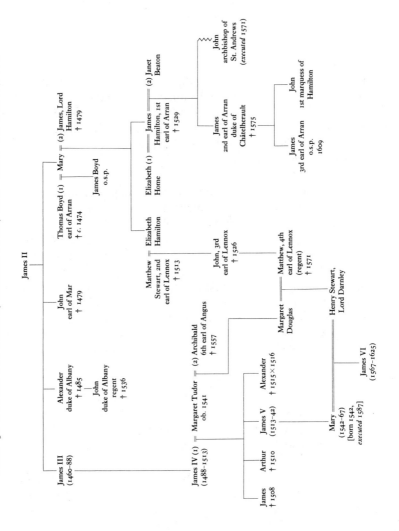

became part of the Scottish realm.[3] He sent his son the earl of Arran to bring the princess to Scotland and, during Arran's absence, with many of his friends and followers, and also during the absence of Lord Boyd himself on an embassy to England, the enemies of the Boyds, jealous of their hold on power, apparently gained the ear of the king. When Arran reached Leith his wife met him on board ship with the news that the king 'had conceived great hatred against him'. The royal bride disembarked with her train, and Arran and his wife at once sailed back to Denmark. At Bruges they were joined by Lord Boyd who had crossed to the Low Countries direct from England; and in Scotland another meeting of the estates, to meet the king's wishes, obligingly found the Boyds guilty of treason and in their absence forfeited them in life, lands, and goods (November 1469).[4]

But James III was incapable of using the power which was his. The enactments of his parliaments now recall very similar enactments during the weak reigns of Robert II and Robert III. Thus, in 1473 the king was exhorted to cease granting remissions and respites for crime and was urged to travel throughout his realm to ensure that justice was done; in 1478 he was again exhorted to cease granting remissions and respites for slaughter and other crimes; and in 1479 it was piously hoped that James would diligently 'put forth justice' throughout all his realm and would hold and set justice-ayres in every part. Moreover the need for royal justice, and the failure of the king to hold the law to the people are amply revealed in the record for the parliament of 1479 which lists feuds between the earls of Buchan and Erroll, between the master of Crawford and Lord Glamis, and between Rutherfords and Turnbulls, and which also speak of 'great trouble' in Ross, Caithness, and Sutherland. It was the king's function to stanch such troubles by firmness and persuasion: James III used neither. Successive parliaments reminded him of his duty to govern and to hold the law to his people, and were particularly outspoken in 1473, 1478, 1479, 1483, 1485, and 1487. James III was lazy and shiftless, selling the true strength of government for the moment's advantage: pardons instead of prosecution. Yet James III also began that policy of *rapprochement* with England for which his son has received so much praise; in 1474 he affianced the young James, later James IV, to Edward IV's daughter, Cecily, and in the following years her dowry was a welcome income-supplement. The policy was sincere enough, but unfortunately James was stranded amid the shifting sands of Anglo-French relations, and was unable to fulfil another part of the rapprochement—an English marriage for his sister, who took a Scottish lover and became pregnant.

In 1479 in a move indicative of his suspicious nature, James III arrested his brother Albany. The charges of violating the Anglo-Scottish truce may well have been justifiable, and Albany was certainly an opponent of the English alliance, perhaps along with other nobles. James could readily arrest his brother, who had only Stewart kin, and the king was head of that kin; but Albany escaped, tried to hold out in Dunbar castle, and fled to France. From 1479 to 1482 Parliament prorogued hearing the charges against Albany, although they were kept alive by committing the power of parliament to a group of lords who moved from one prorogation to another for three years, rehearsing the summons at each brief meeting. The enigma of this procedure has never been satisfactorily explained, and we shall return to it.

Even greater is the enigma of the king's youngest brother, Mar, who (late in 1479 or in 1480) was probably arrested, certainly died, and is said in one royal charter to have been forfeited. Within a short time the accusations levelled by Edward IV of England in 1478 against his brother Clarence of plotting with witches against the king together with Clarence's rumoured death by drowning in a bath or vat,[5] had been transferred to Mar's disappearance. Mar probably died a natural death in prison, but his arrest, following upon that of Albany, shows that the king was subject to morbid suspicions. It is unfortunate that James III's very real failings— and this was one of them—have been obscured by fictitious embellishments.

By 1480 James III's English policy lay in ruins, for Edward IV, who was now a pensioner of Louis XI, did not need a Scottish peace, was angry at the poor return he had had on Cecily's dowry, and was ambitious to recover Berwick. Edward now sent to France for Albany who by treaties concluded at Fotheringhay in June 1482 was acknowledged as king of Scotland, holding his kingdom of the English king; he was to break the old alliance with France and to hand over to England, Berwick and Lochmaben, and the lands of Liddesdale, Eskdale, and Annandale; he was to marry Edward's daughter, Cecily, and, in all this, he was to have English aid and support. In fulfilment of the treaty an English army under

Gloucester (later Richard III) and Albany marched towards the Border. James assembled a Scottish army to meet it although parliament in providing for defence of the Border had laid down that James was to lead the army in person only if Edward IV led the English; but some Scottish nobles, led by the king's half-uncles, seized the king at the muster at Lauder, and led him back to Edinburgh where he was placed in the castle and held prisoner (July 1482), his army disbanded.

Hatred of the king's favourites is the usual explanation of these events. Two very obscure and unimportant men, connected with James's household, Cochrane and Preston by surname, were evidently executed at this time (perhaps even hanged over Lauder bridge and probably for defending the king's person); the analogy of the fate of Louis XI's low-born councillors, executed in 1483, was too much for later writers and the legend of James's low-born and artistic favourites was launched upon its way. Anyone was fair game, so that William Knollis, *knight*, *Preceptor* of Torphichen (i.e. head of the Order of Hospitallers in Scotland), had become by the mid sixteenth century Torphichen, the king's low-born preceptor in knightly pursuits, or even 'fencing-master'. The most unpleasant and time-serving of James III's nobles, the earl of Angus, who joined the king's uncles but played a minor role, was subsequently cast by the sycophantic historians of his family as leader of events, by ascribing to him an old and irrelevant folktale about the bell tied to the cat to warn the mice of her approach.

Were there royal 'familiars' or favourites? Certainly the king promoted William Scheves, a distinguished academic, from membership of his household to the archbishopric of St. Andrews, and during the period of his rise, 1476-9, he appears in one way as uniquely important: he countersigns some letters signed by the king. No other subject did this, and we must accept that he was very influential with the king, whose uncle the bishop of Moray, a leader of the 1482 rebels, did indeed try to have him deposed from the archbishopric in order to succeed to it. Scheves is not named as an unfit counsellor, was not young, nor any more low-born than some other bishops but he was probably defamed (obliquely and unnamed) by hired ballad singers in the streets of Edinburgh and so created the legend of unfit royal familiars, a legend later fitted out with the names of those esquires hanged at Lauder. But Scheves had sat in the council room along with noblemen such as Argyll and Avondale and was to sit there again; he was not a toady of the king's bedchamber. The crisis of 1482–3, therefore, was about James's counsellors only in so far as the 'rebels' sought to replace faithful servants, including Argyll and Scheves, by disappointed uncles. The 'favourites' are largely a fiction of sixteenth-century writers influenced by the 'favourites' of Louis XI and of their own time—Oliver Sinclair under James V and David Riccio under Mary.

Far more real were economic grievances. A recent outbreak of plague and successive bad harvests in 1480 and 1481 brought about famine and dearth, with their accompanying hunger and high prices; and rising prices were attributed (not without justification) to the 'black money', a debased coinage for which the king was held to be responsible and which, immediately after the executions at Lauder bridge, was 'cryit doun', i.e. demonetized.

But the key which will explain these events is neither favourites nor black money, but the arrests of Albany and Mar in 1479. The death of the latter must have confirmed the magnates—even all the estates—in the view that the king had victimized both his brothers. The king's charges against Albany amounted to two: intercommuning with England (which was a vague charge and in any case part of Albany's duties as March Warden) and garrisoning and holding Dunbar castle (which Albany did *after* his arrest and escape). To have forfeited him on these slender grounds would indeed have shown parliament as the tool of a faction, the king's faction. But Albany's peers, the lords in parliament, refused to give the king the judgement of forfeiture which he sought, and for three whole years of prorogations must have insisted that before judgement Albany should be given the opportunity to answer the charges.

In 1482 Albany came north; the king's plan to defend Berwick against Gloucester was also a plan to deny restitution to Albany, and with considerable aristocratic support, the Stewart kin intervened to compel the king (who happened to be head of the Stewart kin) to deal justly with his brother. The king was seized, the army disbanded, and all returned to Edinburgh to await Albany and a parliament which should settle the issue. The only factor which complicated this issue was Gloucester and his determination to retake Berwick and recover Cecily's dowry. James III cared deeply about retaining Berwick, but to his lords this was a small matter when measured against the injustice meted out to a royal duke. For if a royal duke was not safe from the king's arbitrary suspicions, there was no safety for any of them.

And this extraordinary situation was resolved just so. The English, unopposed, besieged Berwick (which thereafter remained in English hands and is still part of England), and marched on to Edinburgh; Gloucester withdrew after a few days at the request of Albany and by the mediating of the burgesses of Edinburgh who promised to see that Cecily's dowry was repaid. The king emerged from Edinburgh castle to preside over general reconciliation and a settlement to be made in parliament which was at once summoned.

Albany, however, was fearful for his position and went too far in seeking protection—he demanded the king's powers. Although he was restored to his lands and honours, and even given the earldom of Mar, the king would not confirm him as lieutenant-general of the realm, as parliament proposed. Amid accusations of attempted poisoning levelled first by Albany then by James, the former fled to Dunbar, plotted against his brother and took refuge over the Border; in his absence he was at last forfeited (1483). Evidently it was felt that Albany had taken enough rope and had duly hanged himself. Gloucester, now Richard III, beset with troubles of his own, made terms of peace with Scotland; and although, in the summer of 1484, Albany and the ageing Douglas led a small force into Scotland in the hope of friends and allies who would support them against the king, they were easily routed. Albany escaped and succeeded in reaching France where he died in 1485. Douglas, who was taken prisoner, was sent into confinement, released on a generous pension by James IV and died in 1491.

But James III's troubles were far from over. He was now to find himself in conflict with the Humes, a powerful Border family that was in close alliance with the Hepburns. At the request of James, the pope had suppressed the priory of Coldingham and had assigned half its revenues to the Chapel Royal at St. Andrews. But the priory of Coldingham had become virtually an apanage of the Humes, who claimed that its revenues were theirs by hereditary right. The quarrel spread suddenly and disastrously from February 1488 when the king's heir James, duke of Rothesay, voluntarily or by persuasion, fled from Stirling castle and its keeper to become a focus of disaffection, seeking to do what Albany has failed to do—become real ruler as lieutenant for a figurehead James III. Angus and Lord Gray were fearful as the only supporters of Albany in 1482 not yet forfeited; Drummond was a newly made lord, but had not been given the coveted office of Stewart of Strathearn, and its profitable pickings; Lyle had supported the king in 1482–3 against his uncles including Buchan with whom he had an old feud and who had been exiled for three years. But as he had opposed King James in 1482 on behalf of the Stewart kin, so now Buchan returned to throw all his weight on the side of King James and against this new threat to James III and the Stewart family—the king's son. And Lyle feared the consequences of the influence of his old enemy with an unstable king. The bishop of Glasgow resented and wished to escape Scheves's authority by having Glasgow made an arch-bishopric, which the king opposed. James sent a royal servant, John Ramsay, recently 'jumped-up' into the peerage as Lord Bothwell, to Henry VII to beg the support of an English army; this was too much for the loyalty of Argyll, a long-standing and faithful royal servant; he deserted in March or April 1488. At the rear and belatedly came the vultures, the Humes and Hepburns, whom posterity credited with originating the king's downfall.

James saw with alarm the growth of adherents to his son, now proclaiming himself 'Prince of Scotland' and piously offering to take over the guidance of his father from evil advisers. The prince did not scruple to tell his uncle the king of Denmark that John Ramsay was responsible for poisoning the late queen—and worse slanders were doubtless circulated in Scotland. It is just possible that some would have dethroned James—but none said so and most intended a less drastic solution. James III went to the faithful northern magnates first, and at Aberdeen his supporters patched up an agreement[6] giving assurances to the prince and his followers. It did not last, for the attempt to secure English help became known and the rebels had to force an issue quickly; similarly James sought to defeat their various forces before they could unite against him. After abortive negotiations at Blackness the two sides met near Stirling on 11 June 1488; the king's army did not do well and the king seems to have pulled back or fled from one part of the engagement. At Bannockburn mill, surrounded by an enemy company which ignored the oath of the rebel lords to do no harm to the king, he was cut down and killed by unknown men of low degree. This was probably his closest association with the low-born whom, in the eyes of posterity, he favoured.

James III was a calamitous failure who always took the easy way out, distrustful and lazy. He was acquisitive, even ruthless, but not, as his father and grandfather, in order to live and govern well. He was a hoarder who raised cash by demoralizing methods: the sale of pardons and debasement of the coinage. He offered neither court life and its perquisites, nor war and its pickings. And he feared to govern.

But we should not take leave of this dismal reign without reflecting upon other aspects of fifteenth-century society, social and cultural. It is perhaps not necessary to stress again the powerful hold upon men's minds of status and kin. Each man looked for guidance and protection to the most influential member of his name and kin next above him in wealth and rank, and thence he might receive not only help but also abasement and punishment in the interest of keeping the peace among kindreds. All of which placed a heavy responsibility upon the nobility who were in general prominent in the leading kindreds of Scotland, and a yet heavier responsibility upon the king who must resolve differences when friends, neutrals, and arbiters alike fail.

Thus the complaints in parliament of feuds are in part a cry for help to the king, and parliament plays a special part with the king in the maintenance of social and political stability. It should not be dismissed as an assembly lacking democracy, lacking shire representatives, and a house of commons on the English model, but judged for what it was—a largely aristocratic assembly in which the most solemn or difficult functions of government were discussed and decided: legislation, taxation, foreign alliances, and the resolution of internal stresses. Instances have been deduced in the reigns of James I, II, and III to show that it would not do the king's will over taxation, that legislation was sponsored by private interests as well as the government, that political victimization by a faction during a minority or by the king in his majority was not easy, and that parliament was a place to seek a constructive political settlement of a tense political crisis. We have assumed too readily that when Albany and Douglas were exonerated of responsibility for the death of Rothesay (1402), or when the Boyds ousted the Kennedys and later were themselves ousted, the approval given by the estates was the craven response of time-servers. There is no evidence that it was so and the forceful behaviour of many lords in other circumstances suggests that it would *not* be so, that they accepted the rule of this or that man during a minority because someone had to do the work, because they trusted this man, and because, if he failed, they could use the king to oust him.

Of course parliament failed: it had a childlike view of economics, and a common reluctance to pay for the means to achieve its aims. It had no executive arm save the king whose powers were as separate as any Montesquieu could conceive, and a magnate seeking to act as its executive became at once a rebel abandoned by his class and (largely) by his dependants. But when all is said, parliament was not and in no way resembled a rubber stamp for the will of a faction. It was an imperfect means of resolving peacefully social and political tensions in a society where recourse to sword, shield, and axe was an equally familiar tradition, but one steadily losing respect because parliament offered an alternative resolution. And this resolution was acceptable just because parliament was so strongly aristocratic in composition and outlook.

The economic stagnation of the mid fifteenth century showed in many ways. Scotland probably had a declining share of the trade of the North Sea zone. The looms of Flanders and Italy were now far fewer in number and had no need of Scottish wool to mix with other finer wools. Home-woven cloth was too coarse to export with success. Thus there seems to have been a chronically unfavourable balance of trade which could only be met by drawing upon the silver reserves of the kingdom. The shortage of bullion in fifteenth-century Scotland in other words was much like our twentieth-century shortage of foreign exchange.

Practically every council and parliament of James III's reign concerned itself with the problem of the 'cunȝie'. More than once a 'royal commission' was appointed to investigate and report, but, as parliament lamented in 1474, 'the matter of the money' remained 'right subtle and great'. To meet the shortage of bullion there were constant enactments designed to prevent money leaving the realm— including one, in 1466, that persons going abroad were to take with them only their reasonable expenses: there were equally constant enactments hopefully designed to bring bullion in. Finally, there was debasement, the coinage of black money, and thereby the provision of a large number of coins to meet a multiplicity of small transactions.

Throughout the whole of the fifteenth and sixteenth centuries there was steady debasement of the coinage, each recoinage being baser than the one before; and naturally each recoinage led to

I

further hoarding of the earlier and more valuable coins. Steadily more and more pennies were coined from the pound of silver; an alloy called 'billon' was soon used; finally the penny contained no silver at all.

In a perfectly pure coinage the pound of silver would be coined into 240 pennies (the 240 pennyweights to the pound of Troy measure), but the king had always been expected to make a small profit from the work of the royal mint. In 1150 David I had coined 252 pennies out of the pound of silver; debasement began in 1367, in the reign of David II, when the number of pennies to the pound of silver was increased to 352. Thereafter further debasement (and the resultant inflation) was rapid. Exact calculations are impossible, but roughly we may say that in 1393 a pound of silver was worth 528 pennies; in 1440 it was worth 768 pennies; in 1451 it was worth 1,152 pennies; and in 1483, the year following Lauder bridge, 1,680 pennies. And debasement still continued. Other countries, including England, were likewise faced with the same problem of a shortage of bullion; other countries likewise debased their coinages; but Scotland's debasement was much heavier than that of England with the result that, whereas up to 1367 the coinages of the two countries had probably been on a parity, in the reign of James III four Scots pounds became equated with one English pound, and by the time of the Union of the Crowns in 1603 one English pound was worth twelve Scots pounds. Nevertheless, the Scottish mint was apparently well run. Its methods, and its coin-types, weights, and denominations, all show continental influences —whereas, until the fourteenth century, it had followed English practice.

A government which debases (or prints more and more pound notes) does so to pay its own bills. More money in circulation pushes prices up and no one is a whit the richer. Debasement of the coinage worked in just this way, that is, it was not the fall in silver content which mattered, for the coin was like a modern note— a mere token. What affected prices was the increased number of coins. Governments understood this well enough: domestically there was nothing to be gained by debasement except a temporary advantage. But the international monetary system worked differently, responding slowly to such changes, so that at the great annual exchanges or clearing houses, rates of exchange would be struck for the penny Scots with the florin, noble, Louis, and so forth, rates which could well persist for a year. What James III did was debase his coinage, save as much of the profit as possible—and he died worth a great deal of money all stored in special treasuries—and use that to settle his foreign debts, possibly with debased coins, before the effects of debasement could work through to lower the exchange rate. His debts abroad were for many things, but probably one figured as more important than all others: ordnance. And to that we must return.

NOTE

James III and his kin

We have seen that James III turned against his brothers. Some more detailed comment may help to throw light upon this and other episodes. Albany had fled long before charges were drawn up against him, first among them the charge of fortifying for war Dunbar castle. But he had been arrested before fleeing and holding that castle, so that the charge was an *ex post facto* justification and not a reason for the arrest. Parliament did not pass judgement upon the charges. Mar was arrested but no charges were framed. He died and the king, referring to him as forfeited, confirmed a grant of lands to St. Salvator's College, requiring in return masses for Mar's soul. This last is strong evidence that Mar had died naturally and not at James's instigation. To pretend that he had been forfeited when he certainly had not been, suggests that in James's view the arrest was tantamount to forfeiture—there was no other point in using the word since the childless Mar's lands fell to James at his death whether forfeited or not. Why was James anxious to forfeit the dead Mar? There is really only one possible explanation: he wanted the forfeiture of Albany and could not obtain the required sentence from parliament—probably because the charges were exaggerated or would not stand up. James had arrested Albany on flimsy grounds and over-abundant suspicion. In his view that royal suspicion should be enough to condemn.

In 1483 the queen and their eldest son James, duke of Rothesay, lived at Stirling apart from the king at Edinburgh. Until the queen's death in 1486 there was no problem. But thereafter the king did a curious thing. The marriage of Rothesay to the Yorkist Cecily planned in 1474, and to Anne de la Pole (planned in 1484) was now impossible and should have been replaced by another betrothal.

In 1487 James III pressed ahead with an English royal marriage
for his *second* son whom, on 29 January 1488, he created duke of
Ross. Four days later the fifteen-year-old Rothesay (James IV) left
Stirling and joined the (as yet) small group of rebel nobles. It seems
an inescapable conclusion that James III became distrustful of his
own heir and was thought to be about to replace him by Ross. Men,
including his son Rothesay, thought James III capable of the wildest
suspicions of, and acts against, his own family. And the evidence,
though circumstantial, suggests that they were right.

NOTES

1. Ardtornish in Morvern was a stronghold of the Lords of the Isles and a
meeting-place of their assemblies.

2. For much of this chapter A. A. M. Duncan is greatly indebted to the
evaluation of the sources in the thesis of Dr. Norman Macdougall on James III.
The interpretation of events offered here, however, differs somewhat from that
of Dr. Macdougall.

3. See above, p. 63. Under James III the Kingdom of Scotland was greater
in extent than at any time before or later; it included Berwick, Orkney, and Shetland, though not the Isle of Man (part of the kingdom from 1265 to 1334).

4. Sir Alexander Boyd, who alone appeared to answer the charge, was attainted
and executed.

The earl of Arran subsequently took service with the duke of Burgundy. His
wife, the Lady Mary, who was greatly attached to him, apparently returned to
Scotland in an attempt to secure a pardon for him from her brother, the king.
In this she was unsuccessful; she was not allowed to return to him; and early in
1474 she was married to James, Lord Hamilton—a marriage which brought the
Hamiltons into the position of heirs presumptive to the Scottish crown (see
below, pp. 331-2).

5. This rumour eventually became drowning in a butt of Malmsey wine for
Clarence, and being bled to death in his bath for Mar. Both tales are later and
fanciful.

6. This is the document named in modern books 'The Pacification of Blackness'—wrongly.

CHAPTER 22

James IV's Scotland

THOSE who had fought for the prince against James III at once issued an 'apologetical declaration' for their conduct. In fact they soon fell out among themselves, and the new king firmly nipped a new rebellion in the bud. He may have come to the throne as their creature but James IV was soon their master. Much has been made of James, the Renaissance prince, but his encouragement of learning and the arts as they flourished in his Scotland have a traditional cast.[1]

The king encouraged learning when a third university, Aberdeen, was founded in 1495, its college in 1505; an Education Act was passed in 1496; and in 1507 Chepman and Myllar received a licence to set up 'ane prent' (a printing-house) in the Southgate (now the Cowgate) of Edinburgh.

The Education Act of 1496, which is popularly attributed to Bishop Elphinstone of Aberdeen—who was also the prime mover in the founding of the university there[2]—endeavoured to ensure that those who administered the law should be trained in a knowledge of the law, though we have no evidence that its provisions were ever effective. The act prescribed that the eldest sons of all substantial barons and freeholders were to be put to school as soon as they had reached the age of eight or nine; they were to remain at school until they were well grounded in Latin; thereafter they were to study 'art and law' for a further three years so that they could acquire 'knowledge and understanding of the laws'. This was to be done under a penalty of twenty pounds; and the whole purpose of the act is revealed in its hopeful statements that thereby 'justice may reign universally through all the realm', that the heritable judges in baronies and sheriffdoms 'may have knowledge to do justice', and that henceforward the poor people would have no need to seek the king's own court for remedy in their own small causes. That is, the intention was twofold: an endeavour to secure a better administration of the law in the localities, and, through that, to relieve the central courts of causes brought by litigants who feared that their own local courts would be unable or unwilling to give them justice.

Again, when Chepman and Myllar received their licence to bring into Scotland the necesssary 'stuff' to set up 'ane prent'[3] they were to print the books of the law and the acts of parliament (which are named first in their licence) together with chronicles, mass-books, and breviaries, and to sell their works 'for competent prices'. Once more there appears to be the same stress upon a knowledge of the law, and once more Bishop Elphinstone appears to have been a prime mover in this new development. But Chepman and Myllar possibly found the law too complex; there is no evidence that they printed either books of the law or acts of parliament.[1] The works that have survived from their press are mainly ballads and poetry, including some poems of Henryson and Dunbar, though by June 1510 they had completed their magnificent printing of the Aberdeen Breviary in two noble volumes—again with the encouragement of Elphinstone.[5]

Robert Henryson (?1430–?1506), who had already written some of his best work in the reign of James III, has been called 'the Scottish Chaucer'. His *Testament of Cresseid* is a continuation of Chaucer's *Troilus*, and much of it, it has been said, 'Chaucer would have been proud to call his own'. But his most characteristic poems are his *Moral Fabillis of Esope* which, set in a Scottish background, are not only delightful to read but also reveal both intimacy with nature and a wide humanity. 'He looks out on the animal world and finds that it is an exact counterpart to the world of men'; his creatures are often 'the poor commons', and his 'morals' denounce oppression and stress the joys of a simple life—

> Blissit be sempill lyfe withouttin dreid;
> Blissit be sober feist in quietie:
> Quha hes aneuch, of na mair hes he neid;　　　[*enough*
> Thocht it be litill in to quantitie.　　　　　　[*though*

William Dunbar (?1460–?1520) was of harder fibre. He can still feel intensely, but in him there is little of Henryson's warm humanity. He is a veritable master of verse, and writes and rhymes for the sheer joy of music in words. 'No other Scottish poet is so sensitive to the magic of words; no other Scottish poet is master of such a range of subtle musical effects.'[6] But unlike Henryson the schoolmaster he is a man of the court; his only compassion tends to be for himself, and he has nothing of Henryson's feeling for his fellow men.

From the poems of Dunbar we gain a far better picture of Scotland in the days of James IV than we do from the oft-quoted 'puff' written to mislead his sovereigns by the Spanish ambassador, Ayala. Dunbar criticizes the delays of justice and the need for a stricter rule of law—in spite of James's attempts to improve the courts and to hold the law to his people; he writes of the low state of morals; above all, his poems contain many lines that give us a picture of the king himself—his early licentiousness, his instability, his liberality, his love of amusement, his dabblings in science, and his desire for military glory and renown. Through this last aspect of James IV's character the field of Flodden brought to an end his patronage of learning and literature.

The political record of James IV is impressive, though it shows him following in the firm footsteps of James I and II, at least in internal affairs. Like them he tackled the problem of the Highlands and Islands. In the official records of the time, we find that he was north of the Mounth in 1490, twice in 1493 he was in the Highland west, while in 1494 and 1495 he was three times in the Isles.

These early expeditions to the west and to the Isles were necessitated by the turbulence of the MacDonalds who, in the Western Isles, had long been beyond the reach of the king's law. In 1491 Alexander of Lochalsh, the nephew of John, lord of the Isles, and his confederates had suddenly marched from Lochaber and, after seizing the royal castle of Inverness, had despoiled the lands of the sheriffdom of Cromarty.[7] Then, turning to ravage the lands of the Mackenzies of Kintail, with whom they were at feud, the MacDonalds were surprised and defeated on the river Conon and driven out of Ross. In turn, the Mackenzies began to harry and to spoil. The end of this story of rapine was the final forfeiture of the lord of the Isles in May 1493 and the annexation of his lands—though James allowed him to remain at the royal court with an 'honourable maintenance'—and thereafter proceeding to the Isles in person, James received one after the other the submission of the chiefs.[8]

Later, there was again trouble in the west. James marched from the south and Huntly from the north, while Sir Andrew Wood and Robert Barton led a naval expedition to the Isles. MacDonalds, Macleans, Macleods, and Camerons, fighting under Donald Dubh, grandson of the lord of the Isles, were only crushed after much fighting; and in 1504, Ross and Caithness were erected into sheriff-doms, and justices-depute and sheriffs-depute were appointed for the Isles both north and south.[9] But, having broken up the confederacy that had been held together by the lord of the Isles, James IV strove hard to secure the friendship of Highland chiefs; and it is probably significant that at Flodden even some of those Highlanders who had earlier fought against the king fought and died by his side. On the other hand, like his predecessors, James, at times, did not hesitate to 'play off' clan against clan, and Huntly and Argyll, as lieutenants of the king, in the north and in the south-west, respectively, were gradually given powers which they used to advance their kin and so perhaps to strengthen the maintenance of order committed to them.

In the reign of James III Edinburgh had come to be regarded as the 'principal burgh' of the kingdom. In the reign of James IV the supreme courts of justice were becoming centralized there; James strove to improve the work of council and session in a multi-tude of ways which are a tribute to the hard work which he obtained from his servants—the secret of a good ruler. In 1501, in prepara-tion for his marriage to Margaret Tudor, the king began to build a new royal residence there—the palace of Holyroodhouse. Edin-burgh was now beyond a doubt the capital of the kingdom.

James dominated in his realm. He held nine parliaments between 1488 and 1496, but thereafter parliament met only in 1504 and 1509. The council, however, was increasingly active both in hearing legal causes and in the administration of the realm, sitting separately, or splitting into two parts, for these two important functions—and in its sittings for administrative and political business we have the genesis of the privy council. Yet in all this James probably played an important personal part, interesting himself in all things. He interested himself in civil justice and its improvement; he rode on the justice-ayres, 'driving the ayres' as they had never been driven before, putting down lawlessness—notably on the Borders—and increasing his revenues through fines and forfeitures. And finance was perhaps the most important aspect of James's government.

By the reign of James IV the balance of the king's income was much changed from that of the time of David II. The customs yielded a modest £3,000 annually (£9,000 in 1371) whereas other sources—taxation of the church, feudal profits, e.g. from ward-ships, profits of justice from pardons and fines, income collected by the sheriffs, and the sale of crown charters of confirmation—each might reach, or almost reach, the same figure. Yet all this was not enough.

Over and above the vast new expenditure arising out of new methods of warfare, which we shall outline in the next chapter, there were also increasing costs in the government of the realm. Not only was there a growing civil service but also, because England and France recovered their stability in the 1460s and by their rivalry drew Scotland more and more into European politics, there were increasing expenses in diplomatic negotiations.[10] Ambassadors were expensive to send and expensive to receive. For example, within the course of a few months in 1512 departing English ambassadors received a present of plate costing £120, a departing French ambassador received plate costing £115, and a departing Spanish ambassador received a purse containing approximately £100.

Then while James III may have amassed treasure and kept it secretly, James IV was openly prodigal. For his marriage to Margaret Tudor his two gowns of cloth of gold, lined with fur, cost over £650 each, and the hangings and canopies of the royal chambers in the new palace of Holyroodhouse cost approximately £1,000. At Stirling castle he built a splendid new hall (often wrongly ascribed to James III), at Edinburgh castle another, and at Holyrood a splendid new palace, as fitting settings for the ostentatious display of his court: their cost is unknown but would certainly run to many thousands of pounds.

On rare occasions a small tax or 'contribution' would be imposed by parliament; but the Scots never suffered taxations gladly, and the collection of a tax was always a slow, difficult, and never-completed task. An occasional forfeiture might help matters for a brief while, and James IV 'drove' the justice-ayres and derived a substantial revenue from their amercements and compositions or pardons. If anything James IV probably sold more pardons than his father who had been bitterly criticized for this activity. But there was this difference: James III sold pardons before trial, so preventing the possibility of trial. James IV brought offenders to book in court, hanged the poor, and, by the implied threat of hanging, raised large sums from the rich. Justice-ayres at Jedburgh in 1498 and 1499, for example, yielded £2,455 and £2,015 respectively; an ayre at Lanark in 1500 yielded £1,750. But many of these amercements were paid in cattle or kind—and we have references to the payment of drovers for driving the cattle to the royal larders. Yet the royal revenue was still far too small for the many calls that were made upon it. In an average year, at this time, the total revenue from all regular sources was probably not more than £30,000 (Scots), or, roughly, £7,500 sterling. It was clear that more money had to be found for the many needs of the crown.

More money was found in two ways—by exploiting the wealth of the Church in the ways described in succeeding chapters, and by increasing the revenue drawn from the crown lands.

The old feudal fighting services contributed nothing to the new financial needs of the crown—though the feudal casualties of relief, wardship, and marriage (or their profitable sale to others) gave the king perhaps as much as a sixth of his income. But obviously the economic position would be vastly improved if the king could increase the rents paid from the crown lands. Money-rents were already paid by many tenants under short tacks (or leases) of three or five years; and in the fifteenth century the names of tenants suggest that even the smallest were in fact given renewed tacks and enjoyed long possession. Their security was not in title deeds which they did not have, but in the sluggishness of the market for land; there was no competition to oust them and little incentive to seek feu-ferme status. Lands held in feu were not only held on a perpetual heritable tenure in return for a fixed annual money-rent, but also, in return for the many advantages of such a perpetual tenure,[11] the tenant could be called upon to pay a goodly sum for the granting of a feu-ferme charter.

In 1458 the king had been urged to ratify sub-infeudations in feu-ferme (provided the ferme was of a reasonable amount and not prejudicial to the crown), and thereby 'give example' to others. In 1504, parliament gave authority to the king to set in feu-ferme the crown lands, both 'annexed' and 'unannexed'. In 1540 a similar act spoke of feuing as being 'to the great profit of the crown'. And in 1584 parliament, considering 'the daily increase of the charges and expenses' of the royal household, ordained that henceforth all lands falling to the crown by escheat, forfeiture, or otherwise were to be annexed to the crown and were to be held of the crown 'only in feu-ferme' for the payment of feu-duties and not otherwise.

The records reveal that James IV soon saw the advantage of the act of 1504, and that from 1508 onwards much feuing of the crown lands took place. The accounts also show that, where lands had previously been held on a short or long tack, and were now feued, the feu-duty was much larger than the old rent; and naturally so, because of the benefits enjoyed by the tenant under a perpetual heritable tenure. Also, because of those benefits, substantial sums in hard cash were paid by tenants for a grant of tenure in feu-ferme. Nevertheless it should be noted that, in different circumstances, of greater demand for land and rising rents, the feu-duties received by the crown, which could never be raised, became gradually of less and less worth. And the warning of this danger was to be seen in those crown lands which were leased for money-rents, for they too had their rents increased (or 'highted').

Thus from the reign of James IV onwards, the crown revenues benefited by the receipt of a greater number of feu-duties, with occasional capital payments for the granting of feu-charters, and by increased rents. And we find that certain of the lords of council were appointed to be 'Commissioners of the Crown Lands', to be responsible for the administration of the crown lands, for the fixing of rents, for setting lands in feu-ferme, and for the collection of rents and feu-duties.[12]

NOTES

1. Dunbar's *Ballat of the Fenyeit Freir of Tungland* is a lampoon on an Italian, Damien (well described in Lesley's *History*), who gained the ear of the king by pretending to be able to multiply gold and to have the secret of the elixir of life. James fell an easy prey to his impostures, made him abbot of Tongland, and, as the *Accounts of the Lord High Treasurer* reveal, spent much money in furthering Damien's experiments.

2. When other prelates were importing luxuries from the continent, Elphinstone was importing wheel-barrows and gunpowder (for quarry-blasting) to further the building of his university.

3. Andrew Myllar, a Scotsman, had learned the art of printing in France. Two books printed by him at Rouen in 1505 and 1506 are still preserved. Walter Chepman was an Edinburgh merchant who, presumably, provided the necessary finance. Scotland, however, was late in the field. Movable type and a press had been used by Guttenberg at Mainz about 1454; there was a printing press in Paris as early as 1470; and Caxton had set up his press at Westminster in 1476.

4. It is perhaps unnecessary to stress that we have no knowledge of books that may have been printed but of which no copies have survived. Nevertheless the first printed acts of parliament were probably those of the parliaments of 1535 and 1540, printed by Davidson in 1541. There was then a gap until 1565 when Lekprevik printed the acts of the parliament of 1563, which were quickly followed, however, in 1566, by a volume of the acts of the parliaments from 1424 to 1564.

5. The licence granted to them had referred to 'mass-books, manuals, matin-books, and portuus books [portable breviaries], after our own Scots use [i.e. as opposed to the Sarum use], and with legends of Scots saints, as are now gathered and eked by the reverend father in God, and our trusty councillor, William [Elphinstone], bishop of Aberdeen'.

6. R. L. Mackie, *King James IV of Scotland*, 172, 174, 181.

7. Some Highland historians say that James, persuaded by interested and partial counsellors, had granted to the Campbells lands which had formerly belonged to the MacDonalds. More likely, however, the MacDonalds were making a new claim, by force, to the earldom of Ross. John, earl of Ross, had been forfeited in 1475 (when his sentence for treason took account of the earlier treasonable negotiations in the treaty of Westminster-Ardtornish), and, when he was restored in 1476 and given the title of lord of the Isles, certain of his lands, including the earldom of Ross, were still withheld by the crown

8. Yet in the summer of 1494, immediately after another royal expedition *apud insulares*, John of Islay seized Dunaverty and hanged the king's governor; but, with four of his sons, he was taken prisoner by MacIan of Ardnamurchan and all five were hanged.

9. Though not until much later did these measures become really effective.

10. The index to the *Acts of the Parliaments of Scotland* under the heading 'Embassy' is eloquent of the sudden increase in diplomatic activity in the reigns of James III and IV.

11. The advantages are sometimes stated in the feu-ferme charter: 'That, from the assured hope to them and their heirs of enjoying and holding a tenure in perpetuity, some reasonable advantages in the increase of "improvement" would accrue—in suitable buildings, lands put under new cultivation, the recovery of "waste", the planting of trees, the raising of fish in fresh water and by means of stanks, the construction of dove-cots, orchards, pleasaunces and warrens, together with the enrichment in movable goods of the tenants holding the same lands thus set in feu-ferme' (cf. *Source Book of Scottish History*, ii (2nd edn.), 241).

12. In miniature all this can be traced in the later administration of the Forest of Ettrick which had fallen to the Crown with the forfeiture of the Black Douglases in 1455.

CHAPTER 23

James IV and Foreign Affairs

IN the international relations of Scotland, James came into conflict with England when he supported the Yorkist pretender, Perkin Warbeck, against Henry VII. Warbeck had arrived in Scotland in November 1495, almost certainly at the invitation of James. James had not hesitated to accept him as Richard, duke of York, and had found a bride for him in Lady Catherine Gordon, daughter of the earl of Huntly; and, in return for Scottish aid, Warbeck had promised the surrender of Berwick. But, when James raided the northern counties of England in the autumn of 1496, there was no rising in support of the Yorkist pretender (as the Scots had been led to expect); in the first two days Warbeck quarrelled with the king over the slaughter of 'my own people' and the seizure of their cattle; he left the Scottish army in dudgeon; and the raid achieved nothing. Thereafter Scottish enthusiasm for the Warbeck cause waned and vanished. Warbeck, accompanied by his wife, left Scotland, sailing from Ayr, in July 1497, in a ship, not inappropriately called the *Cuckoo*, which had been provisioned and equipped by the king—who was now doubtless glad to see him go.[1] After the great raid against Norham at the end of the same month (a raid which was abandoned upon the approach of an English army under the earl of Surrey), a truce was made and, in 1499, was extended to endure until one year after the death of the survivor of the two sovereigns. In 1502 the truce became a treaty of 'perpetual peace'— the first since 1328 and a triumphant vindication of James III's policy of 1474 and later. It was sealed by James IV's marriage, in 1503, to Henry VII's elder daughter, Margaret.[2] That peace, although sorely tested after the accession of Henry VIII in 1509, endured until the eve of Flodden.

In other international relations we find James corresponding with the Emperor Maximilian (who was also a supporter of Perkin Warbeck) and suggesting, at the time of the Warbeck adventure, an alliance between them. In 1502 James sent a small Scottish force to the help of his uncle, Hans, king of Denmark, who was struggling against the rebellious Swedes supported by the Hanseatic town of Lübeck;³ but thereafter, although continually urged by Hans to send further support, James confined himself to diplomatic pressure, though in 1510 he allowed the Bartons to engage in some very profitable privateering at the expense of Lübeck. In another field, in 1506 and 1507, he entered into negotiations to try to prevent the dismemberment of the duchy of Gueldres.⁴

But all international relations were now influenced by the power of France. The Spanish missions to Scotland in 1495 and 1496, and all the English missions sent by Henry VII and Henry VIII had the one aim of detaching Scotland from her old alliance with France. France had become too powerful for the peace of Europe. The great French fiefs of Burgundy, Anjou, and Brittany had fallen to the crown one by one. France had become compact under a strong central monarchy with a developed military organization; and, under Charles VIII and Louis XII, this new France was looking for expansion in Europe, particularly in Italy where she saw many small and weak states. But Spain, too, had changed with the marriage of Ferdinand and Isabella and the union of Aragon and Castile; and Spain also had claims in Italy. As a result, for over fifty years France and Spain fought each other in Italy. England, because of her traditional foreign policy and her strategic interests, could not allow France to become too powerful. And, in Scotland, James IV, bound to England by his marriage to Margaret Tudor, and by a new treaty of 'perpetual peace', but still influenced by the old alliance, found his position gradually becoming more and more difficult. For long he hoped to secure and maintain peace in western Europe by organizing a new Crusade against the infidel Turk, in which England, France, and Spain should all participate—under his leadership. But the Crusade never materialized. And international politics finally compelled James to decide between the new friendship with England and the old friendship with France. He chose the old friendship and died at Flodden.

The road to Flodden began in Italy, where Julius II, 'the warrior pope' who was seeking to unite Italy under his own dominance, formed a league with Louis XII and the Emperor Maximilian— the League of Cambrai (1508)—to crush the strong power of Venice and to seize certain of its territories. Already, in 1507, Julius II had sent a hat and a sword to James IV⁵ and had designated him 'Protector of the Christian Religion'—the pope hoping that, if England

Table 10. THE TUDOR AND STEWART LINES

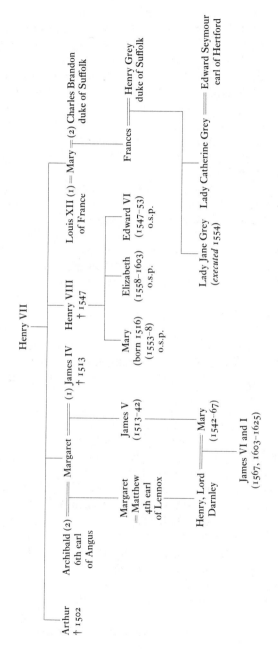

were to attack France, while France was helping the pope against the Venetians, then James, as a faithful son of the church, would attack England—though by the end of 1508 England also had joined the League of Cambrai. The result, however, was disconcerting. The Venetians were defeated by the French; but thereafter the French stayed on, and soon made themselves masters of Milan and northern Italy, which suited neither the pope nor Spain. Moreover, Julius quickly realized that it would be impolitic to ruin Venice, which, as a maritime power, was one of the main defences against the ruthless piracy in Mediterranean waters and against the steadily encroaching Turks.

Accordingly Julius began to look for ways and means to drive out the French; and Louis XII played into his hands by trying, through the French clergy, to summon a General Council of the Church to condemn the temporal warfare of the pope. At once Julius seized his opportunity. Louis was denounced as schismatic; and the pope was able to form a Holy League (1511) against France. The league was 'holy' in little save its name. France was to be crushed by those who feared her power. The league formed by Julius II was joined by Spain, looking for her own gains in Italy, by Venice, hoping to recover something of what she had recently lost, and, a little later, by the Emperor Maximilian, furthering the interests of Spain against those of France, and by England, fearful of French power and traditionally France's enemy.

Meantime, Henry VIII who had succeeded in England in 1509 no less than James IV looked for renown, or was reluctant to tolerate friction. On the Borders, for example, Sir Robert Ker of Ferniehurst, a Scottish Warden of the Marches, had been killed at a 'day of trew' by 'the bastard Heron'; both Henry VII and Henry VIII had declined to take any action; and the affair still rankled in James's mind. Again, in the summer of 1511 when Andrew Barton, James's sea-captain, had been killed in a fight with the Howards and his two ships (the *Lion* and the *Jenny Pirwin*) taken as prizes, and when James had written to Henry demanding the return of the Scottish ships and the trial of the Howards in accordance with the treaty of peace, the English king had sent the arrogant reply that it was not customary to accuse a prince of breaking a treaty simply because he had done justice on a pirate.

In December of this same year James wrote to the pope that

Henry was deliberately making trouble between England and Scotland, attacking 'the Scots by land and sea, slaying, capturing and imprisoning', and that accordingly he presumed the treaty of 1502, renewed upon Henry VIII's accession in 1509, was no longer binding and that the breaking of it was no longer to be followed by the spiritual censures of the church[6]—but the pope did not respond to the appeal.

Henry VIII's accession to the Holy League, and his cavalier attitude towards James IV, had brought the two countries to the brink of war. All the evidence reveals that James was reluctant to take up arms against England. But if a too powerful France was a danger to England, equally a weak France and a too powerful England would be a danger to Scotland.

In the summer of 1512 the old alliance was renewed between Scotland and France, in terms very similar to those of the treaty of Corbeil in 1326 and its confirmation in 1371. Henry, on his side, persuaded the pope to warn James of the consequences to himself and to Scotland should he break the peace with England, and, almost on his deathbed, Julius II issued a bull executorial, authorizing the excommunication of James should he attack England.[7] The crisis was at hand. Henry, having joined the league against France, was anxious to show his prowess on the field of battle. Henry might send his ambassadors in an endeavour to secure peace between the two realms; but Henry had treated James with calculated contempt, had even restated the old English claim to suzerainty over Scotland, and manifestly wanted peace with Scotland only in order to attack France. James knew that if he gave the guarantee not to invade England which Henry sought, he would lose Louis as his ally—though in truth the promises of Louis were as worthless as those of Henry.

In May 1513 the earl of Shrewsbury landed with a small force at Calais, and, on the last day of June, Henry himself landed there with further forces under his own command. On 16 August he defeated the French in the Battle of the Spurs. A week later (22 August) James, against the advice, it was later said, of his councillors, led the Scottish host over the Border to 'the fatal field of Flodden'. Later tales spoke of portents and supernatural warnings sent to James: if we reject these, then we might also reject the tales of the councillors' warnings. The time for invasion—in Henry's absence in France—seemed propitious. But how well prepared was

James IV's Scotland for the aggressive war to which her king now committed her?

In warfare the new and expensive weapon was artillery. Guns were expensive to make or to buy; they were expensive to move and expensive to fire; gunners, smiths, wrights, masons, quarrymen, coopers, and so forth had to be paid money wages. And none of this expenditure could be met from services such as the render of one knight, or an archer, or a sheaf of arrows.

These early guns were of two kinds—*bombards*, or siege guns,[8] of large calibre, firing 'gun-stones',[9] and mounted on iron and wood carriages ('cradles') which were usually drawn by oxen; and 'field guns', called *curtals*, *serpentines*, *culverines*,[10] and a host of other names,[11] the smaller of which were usually carried in 'gun-carts'.

Under James IV some early experiments were made in gun-casting at Stirling castle, and later and apparently more successful experiments at Edinburgh castle, where there was also a powder-factory, and projectiles were made. The larger field-guns fired shot or gun-stones, but the smaller ones fired only iron-shot. In addition there were 'hand-guns'—hackbutts (which, when placed on a forked rest, were called 'hackbutts of croche') and hacks, or demi-hacks, firing 'pellocks' of iron or lead. In 1507 James IV had a 'hand-culverine' and there were shooting-matches at Holyrood and target-practice at Newhaven; once, in May 1508, the king paid 14s. (probably 'danger-money') to a keeper at Falkland to accompany him in stalking deer with his culverine; and gradually, over the next five years, he acquired no fewer than five hand-guns.

When the large bombards were moved from one place to another, squads of men had to be sent on ahead to 'smooth the way', the sheriffs of the shires through which the guns would pass had to be warned to have relays of oxen in readiness, and labourers with picks and shovels, together with smiths and wrights, had to accompany the guns to attend to the various breakdowns that might occur. So, when the guns were moved, we find references in the records to the bell-man being sent through the streets of Edinburgh 'for workmen to take wages'. And the 'wages' were a further heavy burden on crown finance.

The arrangements made to move the king's artillery for the 'great raid' against Norham in 1497[12] are the earliest known in full. In addition to the oxen that would be provided or requisitioned on the way, 179 horses and 110 drivers were also hired 'to draw the artailyerie', at a cost of £114 a week; to smooth the way, 221 men, with shovels, spades, picks, and mattocks, were hired at 6*s.* a week each (making a weekly total of £66. 6*s.*); to fashion and 'correct' the gun-stones, 61 quarrymen and masons were hired at 9*s.* 4*d.* a week each (making a weekly total of £28. 10*s.*); and the wages of twelve wrights, four smiths, and a cooper (for the powder-barrels) came to £8 a week. In addition, Mons Meg had her own team of 100 workmen, and five wrights and smiths, costing £32 a week; and yet, despite a payment of 14*s.* to the minstrels that 'played before Mons down the High Street' of Edinburgh she broke down on the outskirts of the town when seven wrights took nearly three days to make a new 'cradle' for her at a cost of £2. 10*s.*

It might be argued that all this was special expenditure for a raid on England; but, with the steady development of these new weapons of war, the provision and maintenance of the royal artillery in the later years of the reign of James IV was costing well over £5,000 a year. It is scarcely surprising that the artillery captured at Flodden excited the admiration of the English.

Warfare by sea was also becoming more and more expensive, and ships too were armed with guns. In the reign of James III ships like the *Yellow Carvel* were simply armed merchantmen; and 'skeely skippers', though helped to some extent by the king, hoped to recover their outlays by taking the merchantmen of other nations under 'letters of marque', which were authorizations to a merchant-man to recover a loss sustained at the hands of a foreign ship from any ship with the same foreign flag—an invitation to acts of piracy. To police the seas in the Scottish interest James IV, however, spent vast sums on royal men-of-war.

James's first big ship, the *Margaret*, took two and a half years to build and was armed with twenty-one guns. The cost of her building and equipment was about £6,000. But that was a trifle compared with the outlay on the 'great' *Michael*, which took over four years to build[13] and which cost over £30,000. Pitscottie an inveterate romancer who none the less may have derived his figures direct from Sir Andrew Wood, the king's admiral, tells us that the *Michael* was 240 feet long, with walls 10 feet thick, and inside her walls she was 35 feet in beam. His further description (which sounds exaggerated) tells us that her armament consisted of 6 cannons on every side, with 3 great basilisks—2 at her stern and 1 at her prow[14]

—and 300 smaller guns, 'moyen and batterit falcons and quarter falcons, slangs, pestilent serpentines, and double dogs, with hack-butts and culverines'; her complement, over and above her captains, skippers, and quarter-masters, was 'three hundred mariners to sail her, six score gunners to use her artillery, and one thousand men of war'.[15] And he concludes his account with a story characteristic of the king—when the 'great' *Michael* had been launched and was lying off-shore, James tested her by firing a cannon-ball at her, but it 'shook her not, and did her little scathe'.

When James finally broke with Henry VIII, and assembled his host for the ill-fated campaign that ended with Flodden, the *Michael*, the *Margaret*, and at least three other royal ships were victualled[16] and made ready and sailed for France to join the ships of Louis XII; but they sailed under the earl of Arran, and not under one of James's skilled sea-captains, and James's navy, built at great cost, did nothing apart from raiding the English stronghold of Carrickfergus.[17]

But ships, in addition to the wages of carpenters, wrights, and other craftsmen (many of whom came from France), and the cost of their materials and equipment, required docks, repair-shops, warehouses, and other services. Some harbour accommodation for the smaller vessels was already available in the eastern ports; but James IV established new naval dockyards at the Pool of Airth[18] and at Newhaven, where the 'great' *Michael* was built. And when the ships were manned wages had to be paid to both sailors and soldiers. The wages of a sailor appear to have averaged 35*s.* a month; a skipper received £7 or £8 a month. All-in-all, towards the end of his reign James IV was spending well over £15,000 a year on the royal navy.

Further expenditure on the armed forces also arose through the need for extended military service in the field. Unpaid army service was limited to a maximum of 40 days,[19] and all the king's lieges between 16 and 60 were expected to obey the summons to the host,[20] unless they had received royal licences to 'bide at hame'. From time to time parliament had laid down the arms and armour which the lieges were expected to bear when serving with the host, and sheriffs and barons were ordered to hold regular 'wappinschaws' (weapon-showings) to ensure that those within their jurisdictions possessed the weapons that accorded with their status. Much of this, however, was merely paper legislation. When the king called out the host the organization was primitive, the response varied, and those who joined his banner, although undoubtedly brave, and many of them at home in the saddle, had had little or no training as fighting-units.

But such a cumbersome, ill-organized and temporary army, unwilling to leave the demands of steading and farm, was useless for any regular or continuing military duty such as that of garrisoning the Border strongholds. Thus, as early as the reign of James III (and possibly earlier), the government had begun to employ 'wageouris'—regular soldiers receiving wages for their service, usually 2s. or 2s. 6d. a day. Whether James IV had many such with him in 1513 is uncertain, but the army which mustered at Ellem certainly included the local hostings from Fife, Angus, and Lothian, and probably from all southern and many other northern sheriff-doms. The nobility probably brought their own 'wageouris' in small numbers, but the bulk of the army was undoubtedly ill-trained and could have benefited from better arms.

The English army in 1513 was led by the earl of Surrey, who, far more experienced than Henry VIII would have been, also proved to be a better general than the Scottish king; Surrey had spent the early weeks of August in making preparations for a speedy mobilization of the northern levies (should that prove to be necessary) and in moving his artillery to Newcastle.

Having crossed the Border on 22 August 1513,[21] James spent a fortnight in taking the castles of Norham, Wark, Etal, and Ford—profitless work that wasted men and time, though no good general would leave hostile fortresses in his rear; and by then sickness and desertion had already begun to take their toll. That wasted fortnight, moreover, proved the worth of Surrey's earlier preparations. The opening days of September saw his forces from Lancashire and Yorkshire, Cheshire, Durham, Northumberland, and the Borders assemble to the number of nearly 20,000 men. All were well-armed (mainly with bills—eight-foot long axes with curved blades) and well led. At Alnwick, on 4 September, they were joined by Lord Howard with 1,000 men from the fleet. James's host was probably about the same size as Surrey's.

Fearing that James, upon hearing of his approach, might retreat to the Border, and determined to bring the Scots to battle, Surrey now sent a challenge to James, offering to do battle with him on Friday, 9 September, at the latest. It was a move taken in full knowledge of the character of the king: a move well calculated to keep James in the field. James accepted the challenge: he would wait for Surrey until noon on the 9th.

But when Surrey came into touch with the Scottish army he found it on the west side of the valley of the Till,[22] in a well-nigh impregnable position on Flodden Edge, facing east-south-east, and with its guns covering the only approach. Surrey had issued his challenge, but to attack such a position would be to invite almost certain defeat. It was then that the English commander made his risky but brilliant move. Marching past the Scottish position, he crossed to the east side of the Till—unmolested by James, who stayed in his 'fortress' when he might have made a dangerous attack on Surrey's flank or on his crossing of the Till—and, further north, recrossed to the west again by Twizel Bridge and a near-by ford. He had placed himself between James and the Scottish line of retreat. Then, moving south, he made for Branxton Hill, lying to the north-west of Flodden Edge. He, too, would take up a strong position and thereby compel the Scots to fight at a disadvantage when they strove to make their way back to Scotland.

Seeing the peril in which Surrey seemed likely to place him, James left his position on Flodden Edge and, with some difficulty turning his whole army round, moved in haste to Branxton Hill. He was there first, for the English had the more difficult ground to cross, and the encounter began late that same afternoon.

The Scottish guns, bought at such a price, possibly not yet in proper positions, or possibly placed too high on the hill to be sufficiently depressed to reach the advancing English below, had the worst of an opening artillery duel. The English gunners, firing better than their adversaries, soon began to inflict heavy losses in the Scottish ranks. An advance down the northern slope of the hill, and away from that galling gun-fire, became imperative. The issue should be settled by 'hand-strokes'. But it was not in solid phalanxes of spearmen that the Scots moved down the hill to engage the enemy. With their ranks already broken by the English gunfire, and worried by the rough and slippery ground,[23] they moved down the hill in disorder and, without a close formation, had none of the advantages of the old schiltron of spears. More than that, in the 'hand-strokes' that now ensued the Scottish spears, 18 feet long, proved no match for the English 8-foot bills. The bishop of Durham, writing to Wolsey after the battle, says, 'our bills quit them very well . . . for they shortly disappointed the Scots of their long spears wherein was their greatest trust'. Apparently the English bills, with sweeping strokes, broke the Scottish spears; the Scots had then to rely upon their swords; and, in such encounters, the longer bills could beat down upon the Scots before they could reach their enemies with the sword. So, again, the bishop of Durham wrote of 'large, strong and great men that would not fall when four or five bills struck on one of them at once'.

The battle became little less than a massacre. Scotland lost her king, nine earls, thirteen lords, one or more members of almost every important family in the land, and, with them, the thousands of 'mere uncounted folk'. The English reckoned that more than 10,000 Scots were killed, and their reckoning was probably not far wrong; their own losses were probably not more than 1,500, and few of those were men of rank. The 'Flowers of the Forest' had been cut down; and many a family mourned its dead.

Scottish bravery had been proved; and so had that of James IV who, when the infantry battle opened, had rushed upon the enemy and given no further word of command. The contemporary English chronicler, Edward Hall, might write, 'O what a noble and triumphant courage was this, for a king to fight in a battle as a mean soldier', but the king should have directed the battle instead of throwing away his life in the thick of the fight.[24] Had James retained the command, even defeat might not have been disaster. Surrey's men were weary; they had advanced through difficult ground in evil weather; they were short of victuals, and, worse than that, had had no beer or ale for a full three days. To them the victory seemed to be a miracle.

For long in Scotland, the battle was seldom mentioned by name. The official records and registers, when referring to those who died there,[25] say only that they died *in campo bellico*, or 'in the field'. In that field the prime of the land lay, 'cauld in the clay'.

For what end did these men die? James's diplomacy, his hesitations and negotiations with France and England are consistent with his proclaimed purpose: to lead the Crusade against Turkish power, a Crusade which could only be mounted when Italy was stable and France free of English attack. England was invaded to compel an Anglo-French peace, for Louis XII had solemnly (and worthlessly) promised to give James a Crusading army when Henry VIII made peace. That the aim was unrealistic is hindsight; in the mind of

James, with its accumulation of grievances against Henry VIII, the Crusade became irresistibly attractive when, in addition to promises of men and money, Louis seemed inclined towards helping James to secure the succession to the English throne. Such unreal calculations filled the years 1511–13, when James pressed ahead both with preparations for war and diplomatic moves for a general European peace, or at least an Anglo-French one. In one of his last letters to Henry VIII, the king urged that they both adhere to the truce between France and Aragon and, commiserating on the death of the English admiral attacking the French coast, concluded that the 'said umquhile valiant knight's service were better applied upon the enemies of Christ'. The men led to their death at Flodden went there to help France in order that James might save Christendom from the Turk.

Meanwhile Christendom faded into a Europe of ruthless, selfish, and secular-minded princes.

NOTES

1. After his further inglorious adventures in Cornwall and Devon, and his capture and later execution (1499), his wife was courteously entertained by Henry VII, who placed her in the household of his queen, Elizabeth.

2. We are told that, when the marriage was being discussed in the English council, some of Henry VII's councillors objected that if the king's two sons [Arthur and Henry] were to die without issue then the kingdom of England would fall to the king of Scotland; to which Henry replied that, if that should happen, Scotland would be but an accession to England, and not England to Scotland, for the greater would draw the lesser; and the king's answer silenced those who put the question, for it 'passed as an oracle'. There are those who would say that, when James VI succeeded Elizabeth, because of the failure of the English line, the 'oracle' began to prove its truth. It is also to be noted that James IV's marriage to Margaret Tudor brought James IV, and, after his death, James V, close claimants to the English throne from the accession of Henry VIII in 1509 until the birth of Henry's daughter Mary, in 1516.

3. Hans was the brother of James III's queen, Margaret of Denmark. Denmark, Norway, and Sweden had been united under the treaty of Kalmar (1397), but the union was unpopular and unstable, and was particularly resented in Sweden.

4. James II's queen had been Mary of Gueldres.

5. The sword sent to James by Julius is still preserved with the Honours of Scotland.

6. It is important to note that when the treaty of perpetual peace was made in 1502 it was confirmed by the pope (Alexander VI), and the papal confirmation placed the breaker of the treaty under the spiritual censures of the church. This accounts for James's letter to the pope.

7. Because of this, and because of the sanctions laid down in Pope Alexander VI's

confirmation of the treaty of 1502, James died at Flodden an excommunicated king.

8. Hence the word, *bombardment*.

9. The gun-stones were shaped by masons and quarrymen, and in the *Accounts of the Lord High Treasurer* there are many payments to quarrymen for 'correking gunstanis'.

10. It is said that a curtal fired a shot of 60 lb.; a demi-curtal a shot of 35 lb.; a culverine a shot of 20 lb.; a saker a shot of 10 lb.; and a serpentine a shot of 4 or 5 lb.; but there were many variations.

11. In the *Complaynt of Scotland*, in a passage giving commands to gunners, we read of culverine moyens, culverine bastards, falcons, sakers, half-sakers, half-falcons, slangs, half-slangs, quarter-slangs, head sticks, murderers, pasvolans, berses, double-berses, and dogs.

12. Above, p. 257.

13. In the *Accounts of the Lord High Treasurer* we can trace her under construction in 1507 and she was launched, but not completed, in 1511.

14. The *Accounts of the Lord High Treasurer* show that some of her great guns required 6 carts each to carry them.

15. In one official reference the names of 295 'mariners of the great ship' are listed but the gunners number only fourteen.

16. The victualling of the *Michael* included 3,000 gallons of ale, 249 marts, 5,300 'stock' fish, 13,000 loaves of bread, and 200 stones of cheese.

17. The *Michael* never returned to Scotland. In 1514 she was sold to Louis XII for 40,000 francs, and, according to Buchanan, this noble ship rotted away in the harbour at Brest.

18. On the Forth, about eight miles east of Stirling.

19. In 1496 there is a clear reference to the lieges giving 40 days' service in time of war, and serving at their own expense, as had been customary in the past; but service for 20 days appears to have been more common.

20. Such a complete mobilization probably took place only in the immediate neighbourhood of the king's own person. There was no effective machinery for 'shire levies' and much depended upon the action and authority of the local sheriff or lord.

21. In an earlier raid, at the beginning of August, the Scots, under Lord Home, had been badly mauled upon their return from burning and plundering in Northumberland.

22. The Till flows into the Tweed about three miles south of Norham.

23. Many of them had even thrown away their shoes in order to have a better grip on the ground.

24. The story of the dwindling circle around the king is almost certainly legendary. James, brave and impetuous, was probably killed fighting with the foremost.

25. By an act made at Twizelhauch on 24 August 1513, the heirs of those killed in action against the enemy were to succeed without payment of relief and without the king enjoying the casualties of wardship and marriage. A similar concession had been granted to the heirs of those who were slain at Bannockburn, at Harlaw, was later to be granted for the battle of Pinkie, and apparently thereafter became customary.

CHAPTER 24

The Crown and the Church in the Fifteenth Century

WE have already seen that in Scotland towards the end of the twelfth century or early in the thirteenth century a cathedral chapter wishing to proceed to the election of a bishop had to receive prior permission from the king; and in fact the king usually put forward the name to be 'freely elected' and gave his support to the bishop-elect seeking confirmation and consecration from the pope. About this time, however, the pope had begun to assume a right of 'providing' a bishop to a vacant see—notably when there had been a disputed chapter-election;[1] and thereafter, and with increasing frequency during the fourteenth century (especially under John XXII, 1316-34), the pope claimed that certain sees were reserved to him, and that to those sees he himself would provide a bishop whenever a vacancy arose. Except during periods such as 1297-1304, when he might choose between Scottish and English nominees for the same see, the pope had little choice but to accept the government's name. His price for doing so was that the government accept the form or appearance of papal appointment or *provision*, which also obliged the new bishop to pay a tax on his first year's income to the pope.

The reforming councils of Constance and Basle had attempted to curb papal provisions (and the papal taxes that went with them), but they had failed to do so; indeed Pope Martin V (1417-31) had succeeded in establishing a further claim that all bishoprics and abbacies (that is, the 'greater benefices' which, in Scotland, were usually called the 'prelacies') of an annual value of more than 200 gold florins[2] were reserved for papal provision. Reservation and provision carried to this extent not only deprived the cathedral chapters and abbeys of their rights to elect, it also complicated the king's influence in the choice of prelates who, by virtue of their office, were members of his parliament and his council. The man whom the king would prefer might not be the man provided by the pope. Moreover, princes and kings as well as prelates were beginning to grudge the money that went to Rome in payments made upon provision and in other ways. The ending of the Schism in 1417–18 temporarily exacerbated matters since the nominees of the abandoned Benedict XIII were challenged in their benefices by those quick to adhere to Martin V. Prolific litigation at the Curia often ended in one party buying the other off with a pension from the benefice. 'Authority' and 'resources' were both involved—the two major problems that had confronted James I upon his return to Scotland in 1424.

In relation to resources, James I saw much good money going to Rome in support of supplications, in the furtherance of suits, and as payments for provisions or for the right to draw a pension from the revenues of this or that benefice. Any provision to a see, for example, was now subject to a payment known as common services,[3] and common services might amount to 3,300 gold florins for promotion to St. Andrews and 2,250 gold florins for promotion to Glasgow, with proportionate payments for other benefices according to their revenues. And a gold florin was at this time worth about £1 (Scots).

In relation to authority, James was anxious to ensure that the prelates of his realm would be men upon whose support he could rely for he was not indifferent to the kirk's welfare. Thus he was concerned with the decline in discipline within the Scottish monastic houses. In 1425 he addressed a strong letter to the abbots and priors of the Benedictine and Augustinian houses in Scotland urging them to shake off their sloth, to improve their discipline, and to counter- act 'the decline of monastic religion, everywhere defamed and reduced to contempt within our realm'. But the Scottish church, while Holy, Catholic, and Apostolic, was not to be controlled from and by Rome.

James I took action immediately upon his return from captivity— though his moves were directed mainly against the drain of money to Rome and the individual business of Scottish churchmen at Rome. In his very first parliament (1424) it was enacted that clerks (churchmen) or their procurators should not pass overseas without the special permission of the king: that no clerk was to purchase any pension to be drawn from a benefice, or to draw a pension previously granted; and that a duty of 3s. 4d. was to be paid on every £1 of gold or silver leaving the realm. In 1426 parliament confirmed the preventive duty on the export of money; and in

1427 and 1428 it was enacted that clerks wishing to pass overseas were to obtain their foreign exchange in Scotland, were to inform the chancellor of their reasons for wishing to go, and were to undertake that, when overseas, they would do no 'barratry'—that is, they would not 'traffick' in the purchase of benefices or pensions from benefices, or otherwise enter into individual negotiations with Rome.

Naturally these enactments aroused anger in Rome. Scottish clerics were to be denied access to the Roman curia unless they had leave of the chancellor, and money that was Rome's due was to be withheld from her. James's chancellor, John Cameron, bishop of Glasgow, was adjudged to be responsible and, on the orders of Martin V, was cited to the apostolic see (1429). The citation was executed by William Croyser, archdeacon of Teviotdale, who came from Rome as a special nuncio for that purpose, but, on the petition of James to the pope, the citation was withdrawn (1430). In 1433, however, the new pope, Eugenius IV, cited Cameron anew, and on the old charge of promoting legislation against the Holy See. Again Croyser executed the citation, and, this time, Croyser was himself summoned to the next parliament to answer the king's charges of barratry and treason. In his absence he was found guilty and condemned to be stripped of his benefices, while intercourse with him at Rome was strictly forbidden. In letters to the Scottish estates, in 1435, Eugenius asked them to intercede with James for the rehabilitation of Croyser and his restoration to his benefices; and in further letters of 1436, in which he denounced the Scottish bishops as 'Pilates rather than prelates', the pope threatened to exercise the full censures of the church. A few months later, however, both the pope and James I apparently thought it prudent to seek a compromise: possibly, if an impartial nuncio were to be sent to Scotland, some agreement might be reached in personal negotiations. A nuncio (the bishop of Urbino) was accordingly appointed and sent to Scotland where he arrived about Christmas 1436; but, soon after he had opened his negotiations, the king was assassinated.

Undoubtedly James I had been influenced by the efforts of the reforming council of Basle to check both papal provisions and papal claims to annates, and was using the council in his struggle against papal centralization. Undoubtedly, too, James was endeavouring to protect the resources and the authority of the Scottish crown. It should be noted, moreover, that other rulers were striving towards the same end. In 1438 (the year following James's murder)

Charles VII of France, by the Pragmatic Sanction of Bourges, was able to secure some abatement of the papal claims to provisions, to annates, and to ecclesiastical jurisdiction; and in 1439 the Holy Roman Empire was likewise able to limit papal claims. In fact when the pope had successfully withstood the reforming councils, and had succeeded in retaining, and even in extending, his rights of provision (with any accompanying payment of annates), he was able to resume broadly the comfortable working relationship with the monarchy which obtained before the Great Schism.

In Scotland, papal provisions to bishoprics of men certain to be acceptable to the king became so regular that regular communication about any vacancy must have occurred. For example, in 1454, George de Schoriswod, provided to Brechin, was James II's confessor and became the chancellor; and in 1457 Ninian Spot, provided to Galloway, was the comptroller, and Thomas Spens, provided to Aberdeen, was the keeper of the privy seal. It is especially noteworthy that these three bishops were, or became, important officers of state.

James III, however, fell out with Patrick Graham, the unbalanced bishop of St. Andrews, resisting his provision (1466) to the 'commend' of the abbacy of Paisley. In 1469 and 1471, to provide the king with weapons in this struggle, parliament passed acts forbidding what were claimed (with doubtful veracity) to be provisions of a new kind—and abbacies were expressly mentioned. Graham gave up his commend. His successor Archbishop William Schevez received from James III a confirmation of a papal grant once made to Bishop James Kennedy, of the right to approve appointments to abbeys within his diocese. The pope had withdrawn this grant, but it was confirmed by parliament in 1479 and 1482, perhaps because Schevez and James were at odds with the pope over an abbacy. The pope responded in 1483[4] by rejecting two royal nominees to bishoprics and providing other men, and immediately the dispute was exacerbated. In 1484 a spate of legislation against provisions and barratry was moderated by letters and an embassy to Rome. In 1485 parliament sent a petition to the pope that he would delay promotions to benefices for a period of six months, so that the king might have an opportunity of supplicating the Holy See for the promotion of such persons as were acceptable to the king, for the prelates of the realm have the first vote in the king's parliament and secret council. This claim prevailed and in 1487 Pope Innocent VIII granted an indult[5] to James III in which he conceded that promotions to vacant prelacies would be delayed for at least eight months so that, during that period, the king could put forward his supplications (in other words, his suggestions) to the pope.[6]

If, in the past, it had been common practice for the king to make suggestions to the pope, now the king had gained a recognized right to have his suggestions awaited and considered. Moreover, for at least eight months[7] the king could promote to any vacant benefices to which the bishop would have made the promotion,[8] and for at least eight months the king could draw the temporal revenues of the see—mainly the revenues from its endowments of land. The pope, on the other hand, still retained his theoretical right of provision; and, more important, 'common services' were still paid.

The indult was not necessarily a perpetual privilege—though its wording spoke of James III 'and your successors, kings of Scotland'—but, despite some evidence of attempts by individual churchmen to evade both the indult and the acts against barratry, the system of 'recommendation by the king' and 'provision by the pope' was now generally observed.[9] In 1526, moreover, parliament went a stage further and boldly stated that it was the *rule* that 'when prelacies, such as bishoprics or abbacies, fell vacant the nomination [and 'nomination' is far stronger than 'recommendation'] thereof pertained to the king and the provision to the pope'; and in 1535 the pope not only admitted the king's right to *nominate*, but also extended the official period of delay from eight months to twelve months.

In these further concessions granted in 1535, the pope was undoubtedly influenced by Henry VIII's contumacy and the English king's breach with Rome. Scotland, at all costs, had to be kept faithful to the Holy See. But, because of that, the Scottish king, knowing the strength of his position, began to nominate, and the pope, fearful lest Scotland should follow the example of England, began to provide, men who were unworthy of holy office. Steadily in the king's nominations and the pope's provisions there was less and less regard for the spiritual welfare of the church. No longer was it necessary for the king to make a grant of lands as a reward for service, or as a gift to a favourite; all that was necessary was to name his man to the pope so that the pope could provide him to some rich benefice. The officers of state could be paid in a like way.[10] Before the fifteenth century abbacies had been for the most part elective and free of nomination. Under James III, however, began the practice of royal interference, backed by papal provision, in religious houses, and the extension of an earlier abuse whereby the office and revenues of abbot were committed to another ecclesiastic, usually a bishop. He held the *commend* of the abbey or was its commendator. In nomination and provision, promotions to benefices became more and more scandalous. James IV had secured the promotion of his illegitimate son, Alexander, as archbishop of St. Andrews at the age of eleven;[11] but even that paled before James V's supplication to the pope and the pope's provision of three of the king's illegitimate sons, not ecclesiastics, not even adults or adolescents, to the abbeys of Kelso and Melrose, to the priories of St. Andrews and Pittenweem, and to the abbey of Holyrood respectively.[12] Moreover, following the death of James V, the Scottish parliament calmly decreed that, when these sons of the king had drawn from the revenues of their abbeys funds sufficient to maintain them according to their estate, the remaining revenues were to be regarded as available for the general needs of the crown. In effect those important monasteries became, for the time being at least, part of the patrimony of the crown.

One after another, the great abbeys and priories were to fall into the hands of illegitimate sons of the royal house or into the hands of the nobility; their revenues were used solely to support this or that noble lord, at best, in the pursuit of secular ambitions; almost every important monastic house was held by a commendator; high offices in the church were filled by men who had little regard for the care of souls but craved the revenues they could enjoy; once a member of this or that noble family had secured an important office in the church, others of the same family were apt to be given offices both ecclesiastical and secular (e.g. the abbey's bailie) beneath him; and even the episcopate showed a like family connection.[13]

The Roman Catholic historian, Lesley, writing in the second half of the sixteenth century, saw in the indult of 1487 the main cause of the corruption in the Scottish church that led to the Reformation; in truth the indult legitimized the blatant extension of acquisitiveness, of social climbing, of extension of the influence of this or that kin, into the church. The pope could no more have stopped this secularization than Cnut the waves. But he could have tried.

NOTE

The Archbishoprics of St. Andrews and Glasgow

The tradition of parity among the bishops of Scotland remained unbroken until 1472; and when, in that year, Pope Sixtus IV issued a bull erecting St. Andrews into a metropolitan and archiepiscopal see in favour of Patrick Graham and his successors, the pope's action was ill received by the king and the other bishops alike. Patrick Graham, the bishop of St. Andrews, had opposed the royal policy with regard to barratry; in 1466 he had been provided by the pope to the rich abbey of Paisley *in commendam*; and in 1471 he had gone to Rome, obviously to seek papal support. The bull of 1472, undoubtedly granted at Graham's request, not only showed a breach of the acts against barratry, but also, by its very wording, indicated the disfavour with which those acts were viewed in Rome. The king treated Graham as a traitor and ordered the temporalities of the see to be seized into his own hands; an appeal was made to Rome; and Graham was eventually deposed (1478), to die some three or four years later, virtually a prisoner and almost certainly insane.

The erection of St. Andrews into a metropolitan see was, in itself, a desirable step, but it had been too long delayed, and came too late. The other bishops disliked their new status as suffragans of St. Andrews,[14] and succeeding archbishops were not men of the stature required to reform the Scottish church.

Following the final rebellion against James III, and the murder of the king, Robert Blackadder, bishop of Glasgow, was much in favour with the new government, whereas William Scheves, archbishop of St. Andrews, had been a supporter of the opposing faction. That, together with Glasgow's old jealousy of St. Andrews, and her claim to be a 'special daughter' of the apostolic see,[15] may account for a decision of parliament in 1489 that the see of Glasgow should be erected into an archbishopric. The decision was forwarded to Rome; it was followed by direct supplications from James IV himself; and finally, in 1492, Pope Innocent VIII erected Glasgow into an archiepiscopal see, with the sees of Dunkeld, Dunblane, Galloway (Whithorn), and Argyll (Lismore) as its suffragans. The remaining sees remained within the province of St. Andrews.[16]

NOTES

1. A wise move, for, when the members of a chapter had disagreed about their future bishop, concord within the chapter would be better secured by the promotion of someone who had not been one of the original candidates. It should be noted, moreover, that such a 'provision' by the pope was simply an extension of his admitted right to confirm, or quash, a chapter-election, and that sometimes the pope quashed an election and then 'provided' the man who had been elected.

2. In 1431 the gold florin was worth 8s. sterling, or 18s. Scots.

3. At first paid voluntarily as an oblation to the pope when consecrating a metropolitan, it soon became a compulsory payment exacted from all bishops upon their promotion; and no bishop could receive his bull of promotion until full payment had been made. The payment was calculated as one-third of the annual revenues of the see, and was called 'common services' because the moneys so derived were divided *in common* between the Apostolic Camera (the papal exchequer) and the College of Cardinals. When there was provision to lesser benefices half the net revenues of the first year ('first fruits') were paid. Both payments were sometimes given the general term 'annates'.

4. Although in 1483 Pope Sixtus IV had issued bulls commanding the Scottish nobles and prelates to obey the king.

5. A special privilege granted by the pope authorizing something to be done outside the normal law and practice of the church.

6. And, in the preceding year, a legate sent by Innocent VIII had presented the Golden Rose to James as a mark of papal favour and, by using the censures of the church, had striven to support the crown.

7. And the period would usually be even longer than that, for a newly promoted bishop could not exercise authority within his see until he held his bull of promotion which was not until he had paid his 'common services', and the raising of so large a sum was not always easy.

8. In 1450 the bishops had agreed that during a vacancy in any see the king had the undoubted right of filling any lesser benefices normally filled by the bishop of the see; this royal right had been confirmed by provincial councils of the Scottish church in 1457 and 1459; and it had been further confirmed by parliament in 1462 when it was stated to be an 'old and undoubted custom'.

9. After the battle of Flodden, where James IV died excommunicate (above, p. 269), Pope Leo X tried to argue that the indult had ceased to be effective and that Scottish prelacies were now at his disposal; but in 1519 he confirmed the indult by bull.

10. We have already noted this in the reign of James II, and in the reign of James IV the secretary (Patrick Paniter) had been promoted to the abbey of Cambuskenneth and the treasurer (James Beaton) had been promoted to the bishopric of Whithorn and later to the archbishopric of Glasgow.

11. But he was sent abroad to study, at one time reading under Erasmus at Padua and Siena; he did much for the straitened university of St. Andrews; and he fell with his father at Flodden.

12. A fourth illegitimate son was provided to the priory of Coldingham, and a fifth to the Charterhouse at Perth.

13. Three successive Chisholms were bishops of Dunblane from 1487—a

K

brother succeeding his brother, and a nephew succeeding his uncle; and we find Chisholms holding the offices of archdeacon, dean, and subdean. In Dunkeld, Robert Crichton strove to succeed his uncle, George Crichton, and eventually did so; and in St. Andrews, David Beaton succeeded his uncle James Beaton. So also, in the first half of the sixteenth century, we find three Stewarts successively bishops of Caithness, two Gordons bishops of Aberdeen, and two Hepburns bishops of Moray.

14. The bishop of Aberdeen received exemption from the jurisdiction of St. Andrews from 1474 to 1480, the bishop of Glasgow received exemption in 1488, and the bishop of Moray was exempt from about 1509 to 1514.

15. Above, p. 131.

16. At a later date the see of the Isles was also brought within the province of Glasgow, but Dunkeld and Dunblane were restored to the province of St. Andrews.

CHAPTER 25

Burgh Life in the Fifteenth and Sixteenth Centuries

DAVID I's charter to the abbey of Holyrood, granted early in his reign, refers to a 'communio vendendi et emendi' enjoyed by the burgesses of a burgh. Later charters, granted to their burghs by William 'the Lion' and Alexander II, use the Latin word *communicare* when saying that the burgesses who 'participate together' in buying and selling must also 'participate together' in rendering their 'aids' to the king. In exchequer, we frequently find the *communitas burgi* rendering its account. In the records of any burgh the words 'the community' occur on practically every page. Finally, the early burgh court, a gathering of 'all the good men of the community', drew up rules and regulations for the orderly administration and well-being of the community, and enforced judicial sanctions against the transgressor whose actions had hurt the community of his burgh or one of its members.

Throughout, the stress is upon 'the community'. The newly admitted burgess had to take an oath to be 'leel and feel' to the king and also to 'the community of his burgh'; he had to be a 'good neighbour' and observe *vicinitas*. More than that, he had to build his house within a given period of time (usually a year and a day) so that he resided in the burgh—'sleeping there and rising there' as it is sometimes put—in order that he might carry out his duties in return for enjoying his privileges. And, if he offended against the community, his house might be pulled down, so that it became impossible for him to continue to live within the community.

This idea of a community can also be seen in other ways. Outside the burgh there were the 'town's acres', or the 'burgess acres', and the 'burgh muir'—arable land cultivated in runrig by the burgesses and common grazing land upon which they put their cattle to be watched by the 'common herd'. There were 'common' rights of pulling heather (for thatching) and of cutting peats. A burgh on a good river, as, for example, Aberdeen or Ayr, had its 'common fishings'. The burgh had its own burgh mill. And the profits that were made from 'setting' the fishings, the mill, and so forth, and from the 'burgess silver' (which was paid by new burgesses upon their admission), became the 'common good' of the burgh—a fund to be expended upon common causes and common affairs (*communia negotia*).

This burgh community was a trading community, and its trading privileges were likewise enjoyed in common. In the burgh's trade there had to be equal opportunities for every member of the community who had been admitted to trading rights; no one burgess might enjoy special liberties or encroach on the liberties of others. If an unexpected ship arrived in the burgh's haven, the cargo was to be 'loosed' by the burgh officers in such a way that all might have equal opportunities to buy. If the burgh decided upon some 'wild aventure' (the usual term for a ship sailing forth with export goods), the freighting of the ship was done publicly (often at the tolbooth stair) so that all might know and have an equal chance of participating—and, if the offers of freight exceeded the vessel's capacity, then each had to cut his offer proportionately. For both imports and exports, no private bargains could be struck by individual burgesses with the master or crew of a ship.

Again, goods for sale had to be displayed openly for all the burgesses to see; there was to be no secret selling in lofts or cellars, whereby particular persons might benefit. The forestaller, who bought up goods before they reached the market for general sale, and the regrater, who bought more than he required in order to sell again at a higher price, were enemies to the community. At Elgin, Alexander Williamson was found to have done wrong in passing to the sea coast and buying from a French vessel twenty iron pots which had not been offered for sale in the burgh; in Inverness, Robert Reid was found guilty of 'making shoes in quiet places' and selling them to landward 'in hurt of the burgh'. All burgesses had to have an equal chance of any bargain—though one canny exception is to be found in Peebles where, in 1464, it was agreed that burgesses might make private bargains if the chance arose 'suddenly, in time of ganging to the kirk, or on other needful errand'.

The necessity for an open market for all arose particularly in the case of victuals. Although the burgesses were for long farmers (or at least smallholders) as well as traders, growing their crops on the burgess-acres, pasturing their cattle on the burgh muir, and cultivating their own plots (and 'heirship goods', which could not be alienated and which had to descend to the heir, included ploughs, wains and carts, and the crop from any ground already sown with seed), the concentration of so many people in one centre naturally led to a large dependence upon the neighbouring countryside. So arose many regulations to ensure that all foodstuffs were made available in the burgh market and that no one bought before the ringing of the bell. General buying and selling was allowed only when the needs of the burgesses themselves had been met. No burgess was to buy more victual than he required for his own household; the fleshers were not to keep extra meat in their cellars and the bakers were not to buy more flour than they needed for their bakings. Maximum prices for grain and malt were fixed at regular intervals by 'the assize of bread and ale'; tasters of ale and wine (to test the quality) and apprisers of flesh were appointed; and there was strict supervision over measures—the ell-wand, the 'stane wecht', the pint stoup, and the firlot.

In every aspect of its life and work the burgh was always a community. In Dundee, the community was awakened with the hautboy at 6 a.m. in summer; it was put to sleep at 'the usual time of night' by the town's piper, with bagpipe and drum. In Aberdeen this was done with the 'Almany [German] whistle'. The community worked and played between sunrise and sunset. And, after sunset, let no man be found walking the street unless he were an 'honest neighbour' on 'lawful errand', and bearing a light in token thereof— otherwise he would be seized by the watch and 'thrust in the nether-hole, incontinent'.

If the community had its common piper, so also it had its common minstrels for holidays and for special occasions. Dunbar wrote of the common minstrels of Edinburgh that they knew two tunes only; but James IV paid them fourteen shillings for playing before Mons Meg as she was drawn down the High Street on her way to the Raid of Norham. That was an extra payment; for usually common pipers and common minstrels received their 'meitt' (or a small payment in lieu thereof) from the honest burgesses turn and turn about, or, as the Aberdeen records put it, 'circulale throw the nichtbouris'. When James IV left the burgh of Aberdeen in January 1498 he paid that burgh's common pipers 28*s*. We must not assume therefrom that the pipers of Aberdeen were twice as good as those of Edinburgh; but Aberdeen was certainly famed for its minstrels and its pageants, which are praised by Dunbar in *Blyth Aberdein*. And already in 1496, that they might not lag behind the other burghs of the realm, the town council of Aberdeen had caused inquiries to be made into the pageants and processions held in Edinburgh and elsewhere. The answers they received are not recorded; but in Edinburgh, in 1554, the 'play gear' that was then the property of the town included '8 play hats, a king's crown, a mitre, a fool's hood, a sceptre, a pair of angel's wings and hair for two angels'. Dundee was even wealthier, with, among other properties, sixty crowns, six pairs of angel's wings, Abraham's hat, and twenty-three heads of hair.

Apart from pageants like that of Corpus Christi or of the Day of the Holy Rood, summer was brought in by the follies of an Abbot of Unreason, or by Robin Hood and Little John. In Aberdeen, in 1508, the town council ordered all the burgesses to be 'reddy with thair arrayment maid in grene and yallow, [with] bowis, arrowis, brass, and all uther convenient thingis according theirto', so that they could be true 'foresters' to Robin Hood. And although an act of 1555 prohibited the May games of Robin Hood—which often led to 'perturbation' of the burgh's tranquillity—the act was not really effective. Edinburgh, we know, still observed its 'Robin Hood' in 1572; and in that same year, John Knox, aged and enfeebled, watched a play in St. Andrews picturing the siege and fall of Edinburgh castle and the (prophetic) hanging of Kirkcaldy of Grange.[1]

But while Dunbar in *Blyth Aberdein*, which was written to commemorate Queen Margaret's visit there, in 1511, on her pilgrimage to Tain, tells us that their cross, in honour of the queen, 'abundantly ran wine', the evidence of the records soon checks our vivid imagination. In Edinburgh, in 1566, to celebrate the birth of James VI, only one puncheon of wine was run at the cross—its cost being entered in the records at £10 (Scots);[2] and in Aberdeen, at the birth of a son to James VI,[3] the amount of wine to be run at the cross is entered as five gallons—which would certainly not run for long; and, moreover, the provost, the bailies, and the town council would always be first in the queue.

But the burgh was not only a community; it was a close community. The new member had to be *admitted* by the other members and, as we have seen, he had to take the oath of good neighbourhood. There was no automatic succession of son to father, and the early royal writs are addressed, not to the burgesses and their heirs, but to the burgesses and their *successors*. This closeness, this exclusiveness, was furthered by jealousy—jealousy of the town's privileges, and notably its privileges of trade, which were to be enjoyed only by the burgess merchants themselves. Only those could have a share in the burgh's trade, only those could 'pack and peel', who resided in the burgh, who did 'watch and ward', who paid 'scot and lot', and who held 'stob and staik'.

We have already seen that, in the middle of the fourteenth century, when the burghs had to find large sums of money to help to meet the payment of the ransom of David II, the merchants tended to become more important than the craftsmen. Large sums of money could be raised only through the trading activities of the merchants, whereas the craftsmen did little more than serve and satisfy local needs. Thus the merchants, who furnished the greater part of the burghs' contributions to national needs, gradually gained more influence than the craftsmen in the day-to-day administration of burgh affairs.

The Court of the Four Burghs became concerned with the trade of the burghs rather than with burgh law; and its membership increased when, probably under James I, it apparently decided that henceforth two or three burgesses from *every* burgh south of the Spey should attend the Court of the Four Burghs annually so that there they could 'treat, ordain and determine upon all things concerning the utility of the common weal of the king's burghs'. Certainly in 1487 parliament enacted that representatives of all the burghs, both north and south, should meet yearly to treat of 'the welfare of merchants' and 'the common profit of burghs'. In effect, representatives of the merchant oligarchies of the burghs were to meet together regularly, so that they could consider how to advance their prosperity through the advancement of trade.

The Court of the Four Burghs, whether or not still broadly based, disappeared in the early years of the sixteenth century, but its place was soon taken by other, informal, meetings of representatives of the more important burghs. Common discussion, leading to common action to protect and further burgh trade, was too desirable to be allowed to fall into desuetude. And from about 1552 these irregular and informal meetings became regular and formal: they became meetings of the convention of royal burghs, which, from 1587 (if not earlier), sat annually until 1974 to discuss burgh privileges, burgh trade, and burgh policy. (There is now a convention of local authorities.)

The convention of royal burghs contained representatives of all the important royal burghs; so, too, did parliament. And towards the end of the sixteenth century it was apparently customary for a convention of royal burghs to meet just before a meeting of parliament. This was doubly convenient. In their convention the burghs could decide upon a common policy which they would adopt in parliament; also (and a great saving in travelling expenses), the representatives of the burghs who were attending the convention could stay on to attend the parliament.

This convention, however, was dominated by merchant oligarchies to which parliament had, in the second half of the fifteenth century, given practically all authority and power in burgh government. According to the early 'laws' of the burghs the magistrates and officers of the burgh were to be elected annually by the burgesses at the head court held at Michaelmas,[4] and we know that such elections took place in the time of Robert I. By the beginning of the fifteenth century, however, in many burghs the merchants had gained control of the town council to the exclusion of the craftsmen; and in those burghs where the merchants were associated together in a merchant guild, the town council (largely, if not entirely composed of merchants) naturally favoured the interests of the guild. Moreover, in some burghs the guild and the town council worked together so closely that eventually the town council was chosen from the guild and by the guild; and often it becomes difficult to differentiate between council and guild. Thereby the merchants gained an even greater control over burgh affairs to the exclusion of the craftsmen.

Looking at the records, we find that in Edinburgh, in the middle of the fifteenth century, the officers of the burgh were sometimes called officers of the guild, and a sitting of the burgh court was sometimes called a sitting of the guild. In Aberdeen, about the same time, the town council was elected by the merchant guild on the Friday following the holding of the Michaelmas head court: and consequently the craftsmen could have had no voice in the election. At this time, too, in Aberdeen, we find the *council* making burgh regulations (or 'bye-laws') at meetings of the *guild*. Perhaps even more important, we find that the merchants in their guild had complete control over the admission of new burgesses, and that apparently only 'worthy' craftsmen, few in number, were being admitted to burgess-ship.

By this time, however, opposition to such a merchant oligarchy had apparently begun to make itself heard. An act of 1469 instigated by Edinburgh, referring to 'great trouble and contention . . . through the multitude and clamour of common simple persons' at the time of burgh elections, laid down that henceforth the new town council was to be elected by the old town council, and that both councils, sitting together, were to choose the burgh officers— though, as a concession to the craftsmen, each craft was to be allowed to appoint one member to have a voice in the election of the officers. How far such a minority voice, accorded to the crafts, lessened their 'clamour' (and the 'common simple persons' were undoubtedly the craftsmen), we do not know; but, and of importance in another way, the appointment of one member from each craft to have voice in the election of the officers necessarily meant some form of craft organization. Following the act of 1469 a number of crafts in the different burghs obtained from the town councils what were virtually charters of incorporation, and which were popularly called 'seals of cause';[5] and, as we shall see, such 'seals of cause' gave strength and unity to the individual crafts,[6] and increased their bargaining powers.

Then, in 1474, parliament further enacted that four members of the old council were to be chosen to serve on the new council; and in 1504 it enacted that all provosts, bailies, and others 'having office of jurisdiction within burgh' were to be changed yearly, and that no one was to exercise jurisdiction within a burgh unless he 'used merchandise', that is, was a merchant engaged in overseas trade.[7]

These successive acts of parliament, although their intent may have been laudable, and although they did not at once become operative in every burgh, and were in some ways evaded, nevertheless confirmed the powers already gained by the merchants, and also concentrated power in each burgh in the hands of a small merchant group. In Aberdeen, for example, the act of 1504, prescribing that the burgh officers were to be changed yearly, was disregarded until 1590. Moreover it was easy to argue that the act of 1474 did not say that 'four *and four only*' of the old council were to be elected to the new council; the act said 'four', which could mean 'at least four'. And if at least four members of the old council were to be elected to the new council, why should not the whole of the old council, or at any rate a majority of the old council, be elected to the new? From that, the final step was easy. In some burghs, the council re-elected itself to office, year by year; in other burghs, the old council (council *A*) elected the new council (council *B*), and then, at the end of its year of office, council *B* elected council *A* to serve again—and so on, thereafter, year by year. Thus a small group of merchants could gather and retain all power in its own hands, and burgh offices could be held by the same men, or at least the same families, year after year. In 1590, for example, complaint was made to the privy council that in Aberdeen the provostry and chief offices had been held by the same men, their kin, friends, and allies 'these fourscore years bygone', and it was notorious that in most of the burghs the retiring council, in choosing the new council, tended more and more to re-elect a majority of themselves.

Such a monopoly of power, moreover, inevitably led to corruption. The burgh's common lands or common fishings, for example, could be leased, or even set in feu-ferme, to a councillor, or some member of his family, or even some friend, at a figure much below the real value;[8] indeed, the small clique who had secured control of the town council could manage to its own advantage the whole of the common good of the burgh—that is, all the property and all the funds belonging in common to all the burgesses. This is well illustrated in a complaint made to the privy council by the burgesses of Cupar in 1567 which reveals what had happened in that burgh and was undoubtedly happening elsewhere: 'The old council having always faculty to elect the new, they choose men of their faction and so hold the public offices and the council among a certain [number] of particular men, from hand to hand, using and disponing the common good of the burgh at their pleasure.'

Quite apart from the control of burgh government and burgh property which, in each burgh, was thus gained by a small group of merchants, parliament had attempted in other ways to place the craftsmen under the direction of the merchants. In the reign of James I, after the crafts had won the right to choose their own deacons in 1425, the merchants evidently won back their preponderance, and in 1426 and 1427 craft meetings had been denounced as 'conspiracies'; craft organizations had been condemned as tending to raise prices to the hurt of the lieges; and power had been given to the town councils (already, as we have seen, largely composed of merchants) to fix the prices to be put upon craftsmen's work, and the wages to be paid to craftsmen who, like wrights and masons, used materials supplied by others. Steadily, moreover, there had been legislation throughout the fifteenth century against craftsmen 'using merchandise' unless they had 'renounced' their craft.

Occasionally, but only occasionally, there is record of a crafts-man renouncing his craft and being admitted to the ranks of the merchants. Sometimes this occurs because of some special service rendered to the burgh—perhaps the craftsman had put new windows into the town church, or had been particularly helpful in repairs to the tolbooth. But transition from craftsman to merchant was apparently rare; and it became more difficult still as the distinc-tion between merchant and craftsman became a social one. To rise from craftsman to merchant was to climb the social ladder. In 1588, for example, when an Edinburgh skinner was admitted as a guild brother he not only renounced his 'trade' but also he undertook that his wife and servants would use 'no point of common cookery outwith his house', would not carry 'meat dishes or courses through the town', and would not appear in the streets 'with their aprons and serviettes'.

But, although in the reign of James I parliament (presumably at the instigation of merchants) had denounced craft organizations, the act of 1469, as we have seen, had encouraged incorporation under seals of cause; and, although from time to time the govern-ment still forbade craft associations, incorporations under seals of cause quickly multiplied. Under its seal of cause a craft could now draw up rules to ensure good workmanship for the honour of the craft, to regularize apprenticeships, and to exercise discipline over its members. In addition, the incorporated craft could raise funds from its members (usually in the form of a 'weekly penny' from each craftsman) to maintain an altar to its patron saint and to care for 'decayed brethren' and for the widows and orphans of brethren who had untimely deceased.[9] So arose the 'incorporated trades', of which the numbers varied in the different burghs: in Edinburgh and Glasgow there were finally fourteen incorporated trades;[10] in Ren-frew there was only one. Each incorporated trade, with its deacon, could hold an assembly, or court, to enforce the rules and regula-tions of the craft; and, in due course, in the case of disputes between different crafts a decision could be given by an assembly or court consisting of representatives of all the incorporated trades within the burgh sitting under a 'deacon-convener'.

Such incorporations enabled each craft to ensure that, within the burgh, the work of the craft was done only by its own members:

a position similar to the 'closed shop'; and James VI was later to complain in his *Basilikon Doron* that 'the craftsmen think we should be content with their work, how bad and dear soever it be, and if they in anything be controlled, up goeth the blue blanket [the Edinburgh craftsmen's banner]'. But such incorporations also increased the bargaining power of the crafts and placed them in a stronger position to contend with the merchants for a share in burgh government and administration.

The many references to 'risings' and 'commotions' within the burghs in the first half of the sixteenth century possibly indicate agitation by the crafts for a fuller participation in burgh affairs— both in administration and in trade—and in 1555 parliament returned to the repressive policy of the reign of James I. The choosing of deacons of crafts (which had proved to be 'right dangerous') was forbidden, and craft meetings and the drawing up of craft rules were proscribed; but the act also laid down that two craftsmen were to be admitted to the council of every burgh and were to take part in the auditing of the burgh's common good.[11] In the following year, however, the queen regent, Mary of Guise, granted a general charter to the craftsmen which, after referring to 'dissensions and contentions' between merchants and craftsmen in all burghs, virtually revoked the act of 1555, restored to the crafts the right to choose deacons (who, in accordance with the act of 1469, were to take part in the election of the burgh officers), gave them a right to meet and to make craft rules, and even empowered the craftsmen to 'use merchandise'.[12]

It is probably significant that the craftsmen do not appear to have taken advantage of this last privilege, and almost the only reference to it comes from a complaint of the craftsmen of Stirling in 1579. More generally, 'common agreements' were now being reached between merchants and craftsmen, in the different burghs, under which 'merchandise' (overseas trade) was reserved to the merchants while the craftsmen were given a local liberty to trade freely in their own wares. In effect, the craftsmen, again in a position of strength, and in many cases prosperous, were apparently content to leave overseas trade in the hands of the merchants and were more intent upon gaining a share in burgh administration.

Matters came to a head in 1582. A riot in Edinburgh, at the time of a burgh election in that year, was followed by an inquiry, presided over by the precocious sixteen-year-old James VI; and the findings of the inquiry were confirmed by an act of parliament in 1584. Edinburgh was given a 'set' (or constitution) of a provost, four bailies, a dean of guild, and a treasurer (all of whom, according to the act of 1504, were to be merchants), together with eighteen other town councillors of whom ten were to be merchants and eight craftsmen. Merchants and craftsmen were to share in the administration and auditing of the common good, and they were to share the privilege of representing the burgh in parliament and in the convention of royal burghs.

Somewhat similar sets were gradually adopted by the other royal burghs; but it is noticeable that the merchants still retained their control. Merchants still filled all the offices, and merchants outnumbered the craftsmen on the town council.

Above all, corruption still continued. Theoretically, there was supervision—for what it was worth. By acts of 1535 and 1567 the administration of the common good of the burghs was placed under exchequer control, and books of the common good were certainly produced in exchequer; but it is evident on all hands that that was little more than a formality. In 1590, for example, there was a complaint in the convention of royal burghs that for the last thirty years the common lands of Aberdeen had been held in the hands of the magistrates and their friends; and later reports, down even to the nineteenth century and the era of burgh reform, reveal a sorry tale of private bargains at the expense of the common lands, fraudulent contracts for the carrying out of common works, and deliberate disregard of the welfare and solvency of the community in the selfish interests of the magistrates and councillors themselves.

Whatever the tensions within the burgh there was always deep distrust of the stranger, particularly on the part of the merchants. in the so-called 'Laws of the Four Burghs' no burgess could harbour a stranger for more than one night, unless he were willing to become pledge for him. In the Aberdeen records, in 1402, pledges are to be found that certain English sailors, whose ship had come to trade, would not be allowed to spy out 'the secrets of the town or the state and converse of the burgesses'; and, again in the Aberdeen records, in 1442, we read that 'no man of this town, whatever he be, harbour any man of without the town, but incontinent he shall come to the Alderman, and let him wit of how many persons and what persons they are, under the pain of law and banishing'. Above all, there was deep distrust of 'outside lords'. No member of the community could solicit the support of a lord 'dwelling to landward', or support the request of a lord for a place in the town.[13] In Aberdeen, in 1447, when the town council agreed that a burgess could assign his lease of one of the burgh fishings, it was careful to add, 'except [to] lordis'. And, if there were to be no outside lords poking their noses into burgh affairs, there were to be no outside lawyers either. In Peebles, in 1555, it was laid down that in all time coming no neighbour, under pain of losing his freedom for ever, was to solicit or cause men of law to come into the burgh to act as procurators, save only for brieves of heritage.

The community of the burgh protected its own interests in its own court (which had special laws and special procedures to meet its own special needs) and protected itself by physical defences and by the watch and ward of its own burgesses. In this latter respect the Scottish burgess was for long a man-at-arms as well as a merchant or craftsman; and in many burghs one of the conditions of admission of a burgess was the possession of suitable and sufficient armour and weapons 'for serving the king's grace and the town'. In Peebles, in 1462 and 1463, we find newly admitted burgesses paying 'a bow and a sheaf of arrows' for the town's armoury, in place of the usual burgess silver; and in Edinburgh, as late as 1565, an English arrow-maker was admitted to burgess-ship in order that he might stay within the burgh to instruct others in his craft.

In Aberdeen, in 1412 (when the ordeal of Harlaw was still fresh in the memory of the burgh), it was laid down that every burgess must 'stand guaird' and help to protect his neighbours 'fra schaith and surprice' under pain of banishment and the destruction of his house. In Edinburgh, in 1513, when the rumour of Flodden reached the burgh, we read in the records that those burgesses who were still left in the burgh were ordered to look to their weapons of war and to be ready to gather at the sound of the common bell for the defence of the town; and, continues the order, sternly, let no women be seen clamouring and crying in the streets, but let them pass to church for prayer or busy themselves at home with their domestic tasks.

Upon such occasions many a worthy burgess doing his watch must have felt, as honest Simon Glover felt on the walls of Perth, 'a strange breathlessness and some desire to go home for a glass of distilled waters'. But such occasions became less and less frequent—save perhaps on the Borders where, for example, as late as 1540 a charter granted by James V to the burgh of Selkirk spoke of it as 'often burned, harried and destroyed' because of its proximity 'to England, Liddesdale, and other broken parts', and granted to it a right to have 'walls and water-ditches'; while upon another occasion the king enjoined it to choose a 'warlike' man to be its provost.

With more settled times, however, many a burgh had allowed its early defences to fall into disrepair. In Edinburgh, in 1559, three of the gates were reported to be 'auld and failyeit'; in Dundee, as in many other burghs, fines were prescribed for those who entered the burgh by climbing over the back-dykes of the tenements; and at Peebles, in 1572, the defences were in such a state that punishments were laid down for those found guilty of leaping the wall.

By now, too, the burgesses frequently paid out sums of money to be relieved of their military services. In national mobilizations, when the king's host was called out, many a burgh secured an arrangement whereby the burgesses could 'bide at hame' by paying a fixed sum to the lord treasurer or by furnishing a quota of mercenaries ('wageouris') who were to be paid by a local stent[14] upon the town. In 1494 the burgesses of Aberdeen were allowed to 'reman at hame fra the passage in Ingland' by paying a lump sum of £100 and providing five shillings and fourpence a day for the space of a month for the maintenance of eight Englishmen in Perkin Warbeck's force. For the Raid of Norham, in 1497, the community of Perth paid £150 and the community of Dundee £225 for the right to 'bide at hame'—and James IV appears to have preferred the money (which he could use for the 'forthcoming of the artillery') to the somewhat doubtful military prowess of the burgesses. It is to be noted, however, that occasionally some burgesses, bolder than their fellows, preferred to serve personally rather than contribute to the local stent. In Aberdeen, for example, in 1522, six burgesses refused to pay their share of a local stent for a licence to 'bide at hame' from the muster at Roslin Muir and declared that, instead of paying, they would themselves 'pass furth to the said oist'.

Another picture, of a somewhat different kind, comes from Edinburgh, in 1559, when the town council, hearing of the approach of the army of the congregation, and remembering what had happened at Perth and Dundee, dispersed the vestments and the precious altar vessels of St. Giles among individual burgesses for safekeeping, hid the town's evidents,[15] and also hired three score 'men of war', paying each man thirty pence a day, to defend St. Giles and its choir-stalls. A little later we read that the walls and gates were hastily repaired; six gunners 'well qualified and of good practice' were hired 'to handle the town's artillery'; 'cut-throats' (weapons, not assassins) were placed in position; and 6s. 8d. was ordered to be paid to Willie Thompson, the whistler, for his labours in playing for two nights upon his whistle at the watch—doubtless to keep up their spirits when the danger was most threatening.

The general plan of almost every Scottish burgh was one main street—the High Street, or Market Street—with a number of smaller and narrower streets, or perhaps only closes or vennels, running off it at right angles. This plan, as we have seen, goes back to the time when the burgh served the castle: when it was a supply-centre for the castle and a market-centre for the sheriffdom. Then the main street of the burgh ran direct to the castle-gate.

In this High Street everyone tried to keep to the crown of the causeway—for middens would be piled high on either side; fore-stairs jutted out; and, to add to the strong scent, the forestairs of the furriers and skinners would be hung with what the records aptly term their 'stinking goods'; while dogs and swine would be roaming freely around. Where the street widened out for the markets, these conditions were only intensified: the wider the street the more refuse it could hold. The fleshers and fish-dealers threw their trimmings on the street and, despite many statutes of the town to the contrary, it was apparently difficult to say them nay. In Edinburgh in 1511 it was even deemed necessary to enact that, whenever the bailies visited the fishmarket 'for the execution of the statutes of the town' (presumably on this very matter of trimmings), one or two of the sergeants were always to accompany them so that, in the mild words of the record, the bailies would not 'be destitute in time of need'.

Admittedly from time to time the mess in the streets would be cleared: labourers would be hired and paid by the rood; but in general it was safer, and more comfortable, to keep to the 'crown of the causeway'. And, since everybody wished to do the same, one result, in the words of Dunbar, was 'cries and debates'—or, in the words of the records, 'tulyies'. Hence all merchants and craftsmen had to keep their weapons ready by them in their booths, to come to the aid of the burgh officers in time of 'sudden tulye or bargaining'—and the weapons were to be sufficient in number for themselves and all their servants. An act to this effect is to be found in the records of almost every burgh; though with frequent re-enactments we gradually notice a tendency to prescribe 'long

weapons' such as 'pike, spear, and other fencible long armour'—
the most useless type of weapon for close fighting in the street, but
possibly the ideal type of weapon for separating contestants.

Naturally, too, this general filth and squalor, and also the primitive materials used for the construction of most of the houses
(encouraging rats and vermin to flourish there), resulted in frequent
outbreaks of plague. Then, remarkably, the burgh adopted measures
which were advanced and efficient in their nature and compre-
hensiveness. A standstill order was placed on all persons and cattle;
severe penalties, such as branding, were decreed for any who entered
the burgh by back posterns or open places in the wall; children
were to be kept off the streets; markets were closed; dogs and swine
were to be kept 'in band'; special places were laid down for the
washing of clothes, and special cleansers were appointed for the
affected streets and houses. But also, and with a failure to understand the real nature of the outbreak, we generally find that all
doors and windows were to be 'steikit up' and opened 'only upon
reasonable cause'.

In the High Street were usually to be found the tolbooth, the
church, and the market-cross. The cross was the symbol of the
burgh's jurisdiction and its market peace, and was thus its legal
centre: the usual place for proclamations, for executions, and for
the display of the dismembered limbs of traitors and criminals. At
the market-cross the enemy to the community might be condemned
to sit, with a paper on his head bearing the nature of his offence—
as in Edinburgh, in 1585, when two fleshers were so punished for
'misusing' an honest woman who had criticized their meat.[16] That
may sound vastly different from today, but in other respects many
traders' tricks of today were known in earlier times. In Dundee, in
the reign of Mary, cadgers were not to sell their fish in bundles, so
that good and big fish showed on the outside, whilst within there
were only rotten fish, or small codlings and ling. Similarly, no man
was to sell victual which showed good in the mouth of the sack,
but which was bad and worse in the middle and bottom thereof.
Nor was a black market in cattle and poultry unknown. Because of
the many cattle that were stolen, killed, and then brought to market,
the fleshers were forbidden to buy carcases unless in the hide, with
the head thereon, and the lugs with the head;[17] nor were geese to
be bought if they had been plucked and were wanting the head.

Usually the church was in fairly good repair, for the merchants took pride in keeping it so. The dean of guild was sometimes 'kirk-master', or master of the kirk fabric, and it was common for each craft to maintain an altar to its patron saint. But the tolbooth was another matter; there are constant references in all records to the necessity for repairs. At Edinburgh, in 1555, the lords of council, sitting in the tolbooth, took 'ane effray', and masons and wrights were quickly called in; but their repairs were apparently not extensive enough for, seven years later, in 1562, we find the queen writing to the town council, calling their attention to the condition of the tolbooth as being ruinous and 'abill haistelie to dekay and fall doun', and ordering its immediate demolition.

The tolbooth served the burgh for all its public affairs—the burgh court was held there, the council sat there, it was used as the burgh prison, and public intimation to the burgesses might be made at the tolbooth stair or at the market cross. Here, however, we must distinguish between two kinds of imprisonment—warding in the tolbooth being vastly different from being put into 'the netherhole, incontinent'. The distinction was partly a social one and partly one between civil and criminal offences. A person '*entered* himself into ward'—he was not *put* there. Admittedly, like a baker of Canongate, he might answer that 'devil a foot wald he gang to his waird'; but the records do not suggest that that was a common reply. Warding was often 'open and free ward', when the door was not locked; and in the Paisley and Stirling records we read of the offender being given the key of the tolbooth and told to go and lock himself in. At Elgin a man warded in the tolbooth was later pursued 'for taking away the lock of the tolbooth', and presumably departing with it; and at Inverness an unfreeman, warded for trafficking in timber, was reported to have kept himself warm by burning the common firlot (the wooden standard measure) which was kept in the council house—thus showing that he could pass freely about the building from one room to another.

But the tolbooth was so often in disrepair that it was common for the church to be pressed into service for public business. The court might be held in it (despite all canons to the contrary), and its steeple might be used as a prison. In Dundee the steeple was generally used for offenders against ecclesiastical discipline; and this was also the case in St. Andrews where, in 1582, a woman who had been placed in solitary confinement in the steeple, by order of the kirk session, was released before the completion of her term 'in respect of the

vehemency of the storm of weather' which made the steeple so to
rock as to put her in terror of her life. In Peebles, as late as 1652,
the town miller, who had rejected the council's scale of payments
with the opprobrious words 'Deill nor he break his neck if that he
served upon those terms', was ordered into 'close prison within the
steeple for abusing the magistrates and council to their face'.

While the 'kirk dykes and kirk yard' provided convenient places
for the fullers to 'hang their gear', the kirk and the kirkyard were
also the haunt of beggars (of whom there were always plenty),
lovers, mischief-makers, and the general rag-tag and bob-tail of the
town. The kirkyard was regarded not only as a common meeting-
place for sports and dancing, but also as a common pasture, and
a common dumping-ground and sanitary convenience. At Peebles,
in 1468, in an attempt to protect the decency of the graves, the parish
clerk was authorized to take 4*d*. for every head of cattle found
pasturing there, and to kill all swine. But that was the least of the
abuses. If the middens in the street tended to grow too quickly,
the kirkyard provided a convenient place for the overflow, and a
place of large capacity. This was particularly the case after the
Reformation, and the general decay of most of the ecclesiastical
buildings not used as parish churches. Then the vast utility of old
kirkyards is aptly revealed by an entry in the Aberdeen records in
1606, when a certain Alexander Davidson asked for permission
to build a ship in the kirkyard of the Trinitarians, arguing that it
was a most suitable and convenient place for 'bigging of the said
bark', and that at present it was merely 'filthilie abusit be middingis'. The council granted his request, finding the desire 'verie
reasonable', and ordered all those who had middens in the said yard
to remove them within eight days.

In his strictures upon Edinburgh, Dunbar complains of the many
'fensum flyttingis of defame'. And certainly, if we are to trust the
records, outspokenness was a characteristic of the burgesses, and,
apparently, particularly the women. Acts innumerable were passed
against flyting, backbiting, slandering, oaths, and opprobrious
words; and the punishments included the pillory, the stocks, the
cuck-stool, the branks,[18] and whipping. In Stirling and in Ayr, the
unfortunate culprit might be 'creeled', which meant suspension in
a creel or cage hung by a rope from a projecting beam near the top
of the tolbooth—much like the washing hung out from high
tenements even today.

These 'acts innumerable' were acts of the town council—our modern bye-laws—and, later issued as 'proclamations', they covered every phase of burgh life. Some of them, such as those relating to prices and to trading regulations, or against forestalling and regrating, or against flyting and oaths, were passed annually; others were passed as the need occurred. For example, in Dundee, parents of children were to see that their bairns did not play, cry, or otherwise disquiet the preacher in the kirk and, above all, that they did not break the glass windows; and, in the period immediately following the Reformation, the acts of almost every burgh included one against leaving the kirk before the end of the sermon and prayers.

In all records, however, the entries that predominate are those relating to trade; for the burgh was essentially a community organized for trade. Yet the burgh court also exercised an ordinary civil and criminal jurisdiction, and it was a court of record, that is, registration could be made in the court books and the authority of the court interponed for enforcement. Usually registration was that of some contract or agreement; one, in Edinburgh, in 1491, relating to the work of the masons on St. Giles, reveals the long hours then worked in the building trade. But registration might also take other forms. In Inverness, in 1560, a burgess registered an entry that he would no longer be responsible for debts that were incurred by his wife, and the record was thereafter proclaimed by the bell-man throughout the burgh that none might pretend ignorance thereof. In Peebles, in 1559, we find a wager solemnly recorded—ten merks to a tar-barrel against Queen Elizabeth marrying the king of Sweden within a year.

In its civil jurisdiction the court could impose fines or the loss of burghal privileges; in criminal causes it could, in some burghs, impose the death penalty, though banishment from the burgh, often to the accompaniment of whipping or branding, or nailing by the ear to the tron[19] (with other variations) was more frequent. Here, again, we have the idea of a close community. As long as the burgh got rid of the undesirable, that was all that mattered: let others look out for themselves. But when we constantly find this or that undesirable person sentenced to be banished perpetually 'like as she was of before', or to be banished 'because she has been oft banished before' (and it is usually a woman), we begin to wonder how effective banishment from the burgh really was.

Probably banishment was more popular with burgh bailies and

town councils because it was simpler, and also cheaper, than the penalty of death. Hanging an undesirable was a costly business with little or nothing to be gained in return by way of escheats or otherwise. In 1593 'Jonet Smyth the hussie that was execute' cost the burgh of Ayr £1. 11s. 4d.; and the burning of a witch in 1587 had cost the same community £7. 3s. 8d. in 'candles, her meat and drink, pitch-barrels, coals, resin, heather, trees and other necessaries'. But both those executions were cheap. In Edinburgh, the new-fangled Maiden[20] was an expensive luxury—always needing to be sharpened, or to be oiled (the usual entry is 6s. 8d. for oil and soap to 'cresche' her); and whenever she was brought into action a scaffold, resting on puncheons, had to be constructed at varying cost—the nobler the victim, the higher the scaffold—ranging from a humble 7s. to as much as £4. 10s. for Patrick Stewart, second earl of Orkney, executed in 1615. Nor did the expenses end there. In 1619 the cost of the execution of two simple Highlanders, 'born thieves' we are told, came to more than £30, which included their winding-sheets and payment 'to the women that wind thame'.

But what the burgh lost through criminal justice it more than made up in the general business coming before its court. And here again we see how all the activities of the burgh were woven together. For fines went to the common good (that is, the general funds of the burgh), or to specific common works, such as the repair of the tolbooth, the upkeep of the haven, buying a new town clock, or repairing a bridge. And sometimes it is impossible to avoid the suspicion that fines were always more strictly imposed whenever the burgh had some new and expensive common work on hand for which otherwise it would have been difficult to find the necessary funds. And, if the unfortunate had no money to pay his fine, then, more often than not, he was sentenced to give his labour, for perhaps a week or ten days, at the common work then on hand. So, in the end, the offender against the community assoiled himself by a community service.

NOTES

1. It is perhaps as well to record that the Roman Church on the eve of the Reformation tried to suppress plays and pageants because they had become too biting in their criticism of ecclesiastical corruption and clerical pretensions. The Reformed Church did not denounce them until the seventeenth century when their growing lewdness called for condemnation.

2. Roughly £1·66 sterling.

3. Henry, born in February 1594; predeceased his father in 1612.

4. Above, p. 109.

5. They were so called because they were sealed, not with the burgh's common seal, but with its court seal, its seal of causes.

6. There is evidence that in some burghs some of the crafts were already well organized at the time of the act of 1469, but, after that act, seals of cause followed thick and fast.

7. This act was re-enacted in 1535. It has been argued that it was directed against the holding of office by local lords and lairds, but, even if that were so, the act still placed office in the hands of the merchants and excluded the craftsmen.

8. The burghs had long been leasing or setting part of their common lands in private holdings and placing the revenues derived therefrom to their common good, and it is apparent that this setting or disponing of the 'common geir' was known to be liable to grave abuse. The setting of common lands or common fishings in feu-ferme (a heritable *perpetual* tenure) was particularly ill-advised and liable to abuse.

9. In this the craft incorporations closely followed the pattern of the merchant guilds.

10. The number of incorporated trades (crafts) in both Edinburgh and Glasgow varied from time to time but, with amalgamations and other changes, the final number appears to have been fourteen.

11. Three years earlier the convention of royal burghs had ordered the constitutions of all the royal burghs to be modelled upon that of Edinburgh; and in Edinburgh two craftsmen sat on the town council.

12. This general charter was confirmed by Mary in 1564 and by James VI in 1581.

13. This, moreover, was to be carefully inquired into and enforced by the chamberlain on his ayre.

14. That is, a local taxation.

15. That is, its legal documents which were 'evidence' of its possessions.

16. And as late as 1738 a 'fishwife' was condemned to stand there with two dozen herrings about her neck and with a label, noting her offence, on her breast.

17. Possibly indicating an early use of ear-markings.

18. Scold's bridle.

19. The public weighing-beam.

20. A type of guillotine (now in the National Museum of Antiquities) popularly said to have been introduced into Scotland by the earl of Morton who himself perished by it in 1581.

CHAPTER 26

The Reign of James V

SCOTLAND was in no immediate danger after the disaster of Flodden. The earl of Surrey was short of supplies; the weather was appalling; and, above all, Henry VIII, whose chief interest lay in his campaign in France, realized that the Scots, with their heavy casualties, and with an infant king, could be of no further trouble for some time to come.

Yet, if Scotland had been drawn into the tangle of European politics in the reign of James IV, now, more than ever, Scottish politics were to be influenced by events in Europe—notably the rivalry between the French king, Francis I, and the Emperor Charles V, the preaching of Luther, and the German Reformation, and, finally, Henry VIII's breach with Rome.

Charles V, who became emperor in 1519 (against the strong candidature of Francis I), was the grandson of Maximilian. When he succeeded to the Habsburg lands, however, he was already ruling Spain, Naples, and Sicily, and drawing upon the wealth of the New World overseas (as the grandson of Ferdinand and Isabella), while from his father, Philip of Burgundy, he had inherited the Netherlands. The ramifications of his wide empire extended further still through marriages: two of his sisters married the kings of Denmark and of Portugal; Catherine of Aragon, Henry VIII's first wife, was his aunt, and much later his son, Philip of Spain, married Mary Tudor.

But, if the once-powerful France was now encircled, Charles V's empire was widely scattered and not easily held. For example, the emperor needed the friendship of England if he was to use the English Channel for easy communication between Spain and the Low Countries. Moreover, although France was England's traditional enemy, Henry VIII would not necessarily ally with the emperor against France, and Henry's divorce from Catherine of Aragon tended to throw Henry and the emperor into opposite camps.

All this affected Scotland; and, at a later stage, European politics were reflected in the various negotiations for the marriage of

Scotland's king. France still wanted the 'auld alliance'; England still wanted to be safe from an attack from the north; and England, France, and the emperor all negotiated for Scotland's friendship and support.

James IV had named his queen as regent in the event of his death; and, within a fortnight of Flodden, she was duly appointed as guardian of the infant king and regent of the kingdom. The king was crowned at Stirling, and the earls of Angus, Arran, and Huntly, and James Beaton, archbishop of Glasgow, were associated with Margaret as her councillors. Yet it would appear that, almost at once, certain of the nobility sent secret letters to France, to John, duke of Albany,[1] inviting him to come to Scotland to take over the regency; and when, in August 1514, the queen mother (who was still only twenty-four years old) married Archibald Douglas, sixth earl of Angus (who was about the same age), the invitation to Albany was urgently renewed. The Red Douglases were powerful enough already without the young king being in Douglas hands. And at last, in May 1515, Albany arrived in Scotland; he was confirmed in his regency, he was made guardian of the king, and the two offices were to be held by him until James V reached his eighteenth year.

The new regent was virtually a Frenchman, speaking only French[2]—a severe handicap for that tactful handling of jealous and headstrong nobles which had always been necessary in the Scottish council and court but, with the death of the king's young brother, Alexander, towards the end of 1515 or early in 1516, he was next in succession to the throne. Naturally Henry VIII, anxious to wean Scotland from the auld alliance, disliked the idea of a Scottish regent who was a Frenchman and also next in succession to the Scottish throne. He had made peace with France in August 1514, and thereafter both Henry and the French had done all they could to prevent Albany leaving France—and, when Albany sailed for Scotland, Henry had even tried to intercept him on his way. In fact Scotland was adrift internationally until 1520 when the Anglo-French accord broke down.

At first Albany showed both energy and ability. The young king was taken from his mother and entrusted to the keeping of a small group of nobles who supported the regent; the queen mother fled to England;[3] and an abortive resistance-movement headed by Arran and Lennox was easily crushed. Henry VIII, striving to oust

Albany from the regency, now informed the Scottish estates that if they wished to have peace with England they must send Albany back to France; but the English king's imperious message merely strengthened the regent's position and party and, in November 1516, parliament formally declared Albany to be the 'second person of the realm'—that is, heir presumptive to the crown.

In the following summer Albany returned to France to arouse support for the Scots in their difficulties with Henry VIII. The treaty of Rouen (1517) reaffirmed the old arrangements for mutual help against English aggression, but, in addition, it was agreed that James V should marry a daughter of Francis I—a clause in the treaty which was not fulfilled until twenty years later when James married Madeleine de Valois. But when he sought to return home, Albany was detained—for four years—by the French, anxious to please Henry VIII.

Before his departure, Albany, not unsuccessful in the arts of government, had appointed a council of regency, which, in an endeavour to secure some order of tranquillity, he had made a council of all parties (including Huntly, Argyll, Angus, and Arran), while, as a gesture to Henry VIII, the queen mother had been allowed to return to Scotland. But all these endeavours were useless. Almost at once one of Albany's lieutenants, the Sieur de la Bastie, whom he had made Warden of the East March in succession to Lord Home,[4] was ruthlessly murdered by the Homes of Wedderburn; the queen mother began proceedings of divorce against Angus; and a long-standing feud between Angus and Arran came to a head in a street fight in Edinburgh (1520), when the Hamiltons, striving to oust the Douglases from the capital, were themselves driven out—a fight which became known as 'Cleanse the Causeway' or, in other words, 'cleanse the streets of Edinburgh of all the Hamiltons'.[5] From France Albany suggested how these feuds might be ended, but without his presence no one had the authority to make Angus and Arran behave themselves.

With the outbreak of war between France and the emperor in the autumn of 1521, however, and with France becoming apprised of a treaty that had been concluded between Henry VIII and Charles V, the auld alliance once more appealed to the French king. After all, in any war between Charles V and Francis I, England was almost bound to be on the side of the emperor, partly because of her long-standing tradition of war with France, and partly because of her cloth trade with the Netherlands. Albany returned to Scotland (November 1521) with the task of encouraging an attack upon England.

In July and August 1522 English forces raided and harried the northern coast of France, and in September, in fulfilment of the treaty of Rouen, Albany led the Scottish host to the western march for an invasion of England. But, at the Border, the Scottish nobles refused to invade England. Albany in one of his letters to France, complained that the Scots lords were saying their wars with England were merely in the interests of France and they were weary of fighting for others. Certainly Henry VIII exploited Scottish divisions, and the defection of Angus and others, his allies, gave the appearance of the build-up of a pro-English party.

The refusal of the Scottish lords to march into England was a clear indication of a changing attitude towards the old alliance; and Albany, whose position had been rendered difficult, and who saw that he could do little in Scotland to help France, returned thither in October 1522. Again Henry tried to have Albany removed from the regency. In January 1523 he offered, in return for the removal of Albany, a long truce and the marriage of his daughter Mary to James V. His offers, however, were mistrusted and rejected. Turning again to force, Henry sent the duke of Norfolk (the son of 'old Surrey' of Flodden) over the Scottish border to ravage and to waste. Kelso was burned in June and Jedburgh in September, and 'the scourge of the Scots' left 'neither house, fortress, village, tree, cattle, corn nor other succour for man' in his wake. On the day of the burning of Jedburgh, however, Albany once more landed in Scotland, bringing with him men and guns. Again the Scottish host was led to the Border—this time on the east—and again the Scottish nobles refused to cross into England. This second refusal convinced Albany of the hopelessness of his task. In May 1524 he once more returned to France—this time on the understanding that if he did not return to Scotland before September 1524 his regency would be at an end. But it was ended by a coup long before that.

With Albany's return to France, and with the earl of Angus still in France (whither he had gone after 'Cleanse the Causeway'), the earl of Arran now patched up an alliance with the queen mother, making a party favourable to an alliance with England rather than with France. In July 1524 they arranged for the 'erection' of the king—James, then twelve years old, was brought from Stirling to

Edinburgh, placed on a throne, and publicly invested with crown, sword, and sceptre. A guard of 200 men was sent by Henry to act as a bodyguard for his nephew; in August the officers of state who had been appointed by Albany were discharged; a parliament held in November confirmed the appointments made by the queen mother and Arran; and James Beaton, now archbishop of St. Andrews, and always a supporter of the old alliance and of Albany, who remained James V's heir, was placed in confinement. The 'English faction' was, for the time being, supreme. In June of the same year, moreover, the earl of Angus had arrived in London from France, and in October he returned to Scotland—also in favour of an alliance with England. In February 1525 he was confirmed by parliament in all his former dignities, offices, and lands, and in March he was made Warden of the East and Middle Marches.

All seemed to be going well for the English faction; but Angus and Arran were still at feud, and Angus and Margaret, once married, now bitter enemies, were wholly unable to work together. The English faction was divided within itself—Arran, next in succession to the crown after Albany, must not have too much power; the headstrong Margaret was always in opposition to Angus, now the leading pro-English magnate. So Margaret became a Francophil sighing for Albany's return and opposing the agent of her brother, Henry VIII! When Francis I was defeated and captured at Pavia (1525), there was again the fear that a weak France might mean a too-powerful England, even though Wolsey, anxious to redress the balance of power, now made an alliance with France against the emperor. Indeed, at this stage, both parties in Scotland were at a complete loss in their diplomacy; if, indeed, it can be said that the leaders of either party had a policy that was dictated by considerations other than personal ones.

Because of the divisions, parliament, in July 1525, agreed that the king should remain 'in company' with certain lords and prelates, 'quarterly', according to a system of rotation. Those for the first 'quarter' were the earl of Angus and Gavin Dunbar, archbishop of Glasgow; and Angus, having secured the person of the king, 'would in no wise part with him'. Thus, in June 1526, when the estates declared that since James had now reached the age of fourteen his royal authority should henceforth be in his own hands, that meant, simply, that royal authority was in the hands of Angus. And likewise, when the same parliament declared that the king should appoint royal officers as he thought expedient, that meant as Angus thought expedient, and the Red Douglas, keeping the king in his own hands[6] and filling the offices of state with his kin and friends, virtually ruled Scotland until the king's escape in the spring of 1528. The cost was apparent: at first Arran made terms with the all-powerful Angus, but as Douglases filled every office in the household, Arran, Lennox, Argyll, and others, most of them anxious for a stable government, withdrew from the court, and Scotland became the Douglas's kingdom, ruled by fear of the harm he might do to the king.

James V escaped, was joined by his mother and the nobility and with easy unanimity the Angus Douglases were forfeited. For a while Angus successfully defied the king at Tantallon; but he was compelled to take refuge in England, and he did not return to Scotland until after Solway Moss and the death of James V.

These had been troubled years, yet again the great kins of the north (Huntly) and west (Argyll) had used their influence on the side of order whatever faction ruled the High Street of Edinburgh and Lothian. There is a measure of unreality about the jockeying for power, which even Angus must have realized would end as the king matured: experience of these factions taught James V to be master in his own house, where he should manifestly set his royal majesty far above their jealous ambitions.

In the tangle of European politics, Scotland was once more a pawn which the rivals—the emperor, France, England, sought to play. Perhaps the emperor might even be able to find a bride for James V and so seal the alliance. But the emperor's suggested match—his sister Marie, the widowed queen of Hungary[7]—was attractive to neither party, and, as soon as Francis I heard of the emperor's approach, he again suggested a French marriage, though this alliance with England against the emperor (if it could be relied upon) was more valuable to him than alliance with Scotland, and the treaty of Rouen had faded into the background.

Brides had now been suggested for James V by France, England, and the emperor. James, it may be said, was being courted in high quarters. But James was bankrupt;[8] he was determined that when he did marry he would marry a well-endowed bride; and, while the rich bride who would not upset European diplomacy was difficult to find, James's financial difficulties were becoming more and more pressing. There was only one other source of money—the church.

In 1531 James approached the pope for a permanent and swingeing subsidy of £10,000 a year from the revenues of the church in Scotland 'for the protection and defence of the realm'.

The European situation was favourable to James's request. The pope was still virtually in the emperor's power, and the emperor, trying to wean Scotland away from the old alliance with France, had just concluded a treaty with Scotland furthering her commercial relations with the Netherlands. Above all, Henry VIII, demanding a divorce from Catherine of Aragon (the emperor's aunt), was putting the pope to defiance, and in Europe heresy was spreading apace. It was essential that Scotland should remain true to Rome. Yet £10,000 a year was a startling demand.

At first the pope temporized. Then he granted the imposition on the church of a tenth for three years. Finally, when it was urged that the £10,000 a year was to be used to establish a College of Justice[9] (half of whose members would be churchmen), and that the Roman Church in Scotland could survive the assaults of heresy only if law and order were maintained, he agreed. In September 1531 Clement VII issued a bull authorizing an ecclesiastical subsidy of £10,000[10] a year for the maintenance of a College of Justice in Scotland as long as James and his successors remained true to Rome. And in the following year (1532) James undertook in parliament to establish the College and also to maintain the authority of Rome and the freedom of the church.

In other words, James had bargained to remain true to Rome provided he was allowed to use part of the church's revenues for state purposes. The precedent was dangerous. But the prelates, aghast at a standing contribution of £10,000 a year, were well aware of James's pressing needs, and now entered into an agreement with the king that, instead of this heavy annual subsidy, they would pay to him £72,000 in eight half-yearly instalments over the next four years, which the king could use as he wished, and thereafter would provide, for the endowment of the College of Justice, £1,400 a year, in perpetuity, which should be met from certain benefices assigned for that purpose. How and with what effect the £72,000 was raised, we shall see later.[11]

In 1535 the succeeding pope, Paul III, issued a bull confirming the erection of the College (and also confirming the agreement with the prelates whereby £1,400 a year was to be provided from benefices within their patronage); and in 1541 parliament ratified the institution of a College of Justice to consist of fourteen judges (seven churchmen and seven laymen), to sit under a President (who was to be a churchman), and with power to the king to add 'extraordinary lords'.

The limited finance of £1,400 a year was, from the very first, inadequate; it meant less than £100 (Scots) a year for each of the judges; and further provision had eventually to be made. But, for the first time, Scotland's central civil court, the Session, had a paid judicial bench.[12] The erection of the College of Justice was a financial expedient in every respect for even the College of Justice freed the king from the need to give pensions and places to those serving on the Session.

In relation to law and order, James did not neglect the difficult parts—the Highlands and the Borders. An attempt by the earl of Argyll, the king's lieutenant in the west, and James Stewart, earl of Moray, the king's lieutenant in the north, to advance their own interests at the expense of the MacDonalds, had led to a gathering in arms of the MacDonalds of Islay and the Macleans of Duart, and there had been much mutual ravaging and wasting of Campbell and MacDonald lands.[13] In the spring of 1531 the king determined to lead his army northwards in person; but, when the chiefs had laid their cause before him and had voluntarily come into his will, it appeared that Argyll and Moray had determined upon a 'danting of the Isles' largely for their own ends. With justice, Argyll was deprived of his office and temporarily imprisoned, and, for the rest of his reign (and largely through the loyal efforts of the Macdonalds of Islay), James had no further trouble in the southern isles.[14] Further north, however, in 1539, Donald Gorm of Sleat, chief of the MacDonalds of Skye, in alliance with the Macleods of Lewis, once more strove to regain the lost earldom of Ross, but when, at the outset of his campaign, he died of a wound received in the siege of Eilean Donan, the attempt collapsed.

James now determined upon a display of force. In May 1540, with a large and well-armed fleet, he sailed from the Forth to Orkney and thence to Lewis, Skye, Mull, and Islay, and by Kintyre back to Dumbarton. From every disaffected part he brought back with him the local chiefs: some were released upon promise of obedience and the giving of hostages; others were still in confinement at the time of his death. So, we are told, there was as 'greit quietnes and obedience' in the Isles as in any other part of the realm, and 'gude compt and payment' was made of the king's rentals there.

On the Borders, always a difficult part of the land, the Armstrongs of Liddesdale had long defied the wardens of Scotland and England alike, and had boasted that they would be ordered by neither king. Nor were some of the Border lords and lairds—Bothwell and Home, Maxwells, Johnstons, Scotts, and others—any better. Some were certainly intriguing with England; and, quite apart from the maintenance of law and order, and the pacification of the Border lands, there was the danger that Border incidents might give Henry VIII an excuse for Border devastation. In 1530 James placed a number of these march lords and lairds in close ward and, leading a veritable army to the Border, hanged 'Johnnie Armstrong' of Gilnockie and some forty of his followers. Johnnie Armstrong may have been 'nane the waur o' a hanging',[15] but he was probably more of a nuisance to England than to the Scottish king. The ballad makes him a hero; tradition accused a 'graceless' king of treachery for Armstrong came to him under safe-conduct; and it was said that the trees upon which he and his followers were hanged[16] withered away in manifestation of the injustice that had been done.

Yet it should also be noted that, seeking to hold the law in the 'broken parts' of his land, James was strengthening the government. Argyll and Moray and the Border lords were reminded of the power of the king; and when, in 1536, James left Scotland to bring back a bride from France, the government, in his absence, stood firm.

As we have seen, James, in 1532, declared his determination to maintain the Roman Church. Henry, on the other hand, had already broken with Rome, and the breach quickly widened with his marriage to Anne Boleyn, the Act of Supremacy, and the suppression of the monasteries. Henry strove hard to persuade his nephew to follow his example; but James refused and, in addition to remaining true to Rome, remained true also to the old alliance.

James was still unmarried, and was still being courted in high quarters. In 1532 the emperor sent him the Golden Fleece; in 1534 Henry VIII sent him the Garter; and in 1536 Francis I admitted him to the Order of St. Michael. There was a possibility, as late as 1534, that he might marry Mary Tudor; a little later, the emperor suggested marriage into the royal house of Denmark, and then into that of Portugal; and although, in 1536, James contracted to marry

Mary of Bourbon, daughter of Charles, duke of Vendôme—at the same time stipulating the 'wealth' she was to bring with her—he was so bitterly disappointed when he saw the lady that he at once broke off the match. At last, however, James married. On 1 January 1537 he married Madeleine, the eldest surviving daughter of Francis I with 100,000 livres and the income from a further 125,000 livres.

A marriage with Madeleine had been discussed at intervals since 1530, but the poor health of the princess had made Francis reluctant to agree. And only eight weeks after she had bent down to kiss the soil of her husband's kingdom, the young queen, 'of pleasand bewtie, guidlie favour, luffing countenance and cumly manners', died (7 July 1537). Again James sought a bride in France; and in June 1538 he married Mary of Guise-Lorraine, the eldest daughter of the duke of Guise, with 150,000 livres.

As he squeezed the church and touted for a rich bride, James V set about showing his subjects how a king should reign. In a mere fourteen years he lavished upon palaces probably as much as his four predecessors put together. Attached to his father's palace of Holyrood he built a new tower and completed a quadrangle by the building of two ranges. Beside his father's Gothic hall at Stirling he built a courtyard palace, its royal presence-chamber decorated with elaborate carvings in wood; the outside, French in inspiration, carries a range of statues including the bearded king himself. At Falkland French architects built one range which shows more clearly than anything else surviving in Britain the impact of Francis I's patronage of architecture. This range is linked to a gate-house, markedly more old-fashioned in appearance, and akin to the tower of the palace of Holyroodhouse: all these, too, were built by James V. At Linlithgow he altered and improved: the result was said by his wife to be worthy of comparison with a French palace. Apart from Falkland these works cost at least £26,000, and probably the total building expenditure for the reign was something nearer £50,000. And in any of these palaces King James could display himself wearing the crown with imperial arches (signifying sovereignty) carrying the orb of heaven above his head, a crown completed for him in 1542, and still to be seen as part of the Honours of Scotland— one of the trappings of a Renaissance prince.

There can be little doubt that James V deserved that description far more than his father or grandfather. The scale and style of his palaces indicate an exalted view of the majesty of kingship which had shifted markedly from the position of earlier kings. The ruthlessness which James showed on many occasions, with several arbitrary executions among the nobility, had a financial purpose, as when in 1537 he made the usual revocation of grants in his minority and followed it not by the recovery of occasional lands but by swingeing levies for confirmation of earlier titles. The streak of cruelty in his character which grew plainer as he aged, was the consequence of indulgence of an arbitrary temperament by the obsequious with whom he surrounded himself. The progressive alienation of James V from his nobility may be ascribed to these characteristics and in part to the emerging religious issue. But James V was no more a good Catholic than he was a good Christian; he showed none of his father's devotion to the saints (although he built a chapel at Holyrood), and he both recognized and ignored the failings of the clergy.

His adherence to Rome may be ascribed to his sense of the community of interest between his and the church's authority as established institutions, and to the willingness of pope and prelates to pander to the arbitrariness of his will (which another age would call absolutism).

The literary renaissance of James IV's reign which was indeed a remarkable cultural flowering is not to be confused with the autocracy of Francis I, Henry VIII, and James V which has earned them the description of 'Renaissance' rulers. They sought to employ scholarship and the printing press in exalting not their effectiveness at home, but their status abroad. To this end the national histories of France and England were rewritten by Italians who brought to them the Latin vocabulary, syntax, and rhetoric of Classical Roman authors and so made them esteemed works of scholarship. Hector Boece, principal of Aberdeen University, sought to do the same for Scotland when, between 1517 and 1525, he invented a history for Scotland up to 1437, which was provided not merely with a fictitious ancient history stretching back for centuries before the establishment of Dalriada, but also with drama (including supernatural wonders) and rhetoric throughout. From this, Shakespeare's tale of Macbeth, with the witches, Banquo, Macduff, and Birnam wood, is derived—and it is all the work of Boece's powerful imagination. But it is fiction upon a model, Livy, and with a purpose, to give Scotland a history in classical Latin, its substance parallel with,

L

akin to, but independent of, the history of the Rome, as chronicled
by Livy. It seeks to show the antiquity of the Scottish monarchy
and its development alongside classical Rome (when, it was
admitted, France and England did not exist) as well as its persistence
into modern times.

For this opportune scholarly propaganda King James gave Boece
a pension. But he also paid handsomely to have made and to publish
translations into Scots of Boece's *Scottish History* and Livy's *Roman
History*, which together underlined the king's claims for his kingship: its antiquity, its imperial (or as we should say, sovereign)
character, and its right to a place in European esteem beside the
successor-states of the Roman empire: 'the Empire' (Germany),
France, England, Spain.

James's declared intention to maintain the Roman Church, his
adherence to the old alliance, and his successive French marriages
roused the anger and fear of the English king.[17] Henry, denounced
as a heretic, an adulterer,[18] and a despoiler of the church, saw facing
him the possibility of attack from a league of the Roman Catholic
powers; and in the north lay Scotland, true to Rome, and united by
marriage with one of the greatest houses in France. Striving to
persuade James to adopt Protestant policies, Henry secured a
promise from him that he would meet him at York (September
1541); but, although Henry made the long journey, he journeyed
in vain. James's privy council, and notably the churchmen had
feared the possibilities of such a meeting and had dissuaded the
king although a simultaneous Scottish embassy in France failed to
secure any assistance for Scotland. Angered, and determined to
teach James a lesson, Henry now loosed the northern levies on Scotland. In August 1542 Sir Robert Bowes crossed the Border to raid
Teviotdale, but was heavily mauled by the earl of Huntly at Haddon
Rig. The duke of Norfolk was more successful—and Roxburgh,
Kelso, and a number of smaller places were burned.

In reply, James assembled the Scottish host; but at the muster
at Fala Muir many lairds from the east coast did not appear, and
those nobles and lairds who did attend refused to march further—
they would not march to the Border, much less cross it into England.
The old argument that the war was a war for France was scarcely
valid; there was a new argument that, if James were to be killed,
he had no child to succeed him.[19] But the refusal at Fala Muir was
made only some three weeks before the attack on England which

met with disaster at Solway Moss: and the reason for those two different events lay in other factors that were now at work. A war against England was a war against reforming opinion, and so many would not go, and some went reluctantly, to the muster at Fala.

And after Fala Muir the king's ruthlessness and unpopularity with at least the nobility came home to roost. They would not fight the campaign on which he had determined and they were excluded from his counsels in favour of David Beaton (who had succeeded his uncle, James Beaton, as archbishop of St. Andrews), a staunch upholder of the old faith and the auld alliance. James collected another army—apparently with help from the church—and part of it, commanded by Oliver Sinclair, the king's favourite (who was captured 'fleeing full manfully'), caught in marshy ground between the Esk and the Sark, suffered an ignominious and overwhelming defeat. It is said that some of the nobles took umbrage at the assumption of command by Sinclair and that some of those who were inclined to the new faith suspected that they had been put in the forefront of the battle to be smitten there. There may have been deliberate betrayal by Borderers alienated by James's harsh policies. But the Scottish staff-work was incredibly bad, and the Scottish host had little heart for the fight to which it had been led.

Solway Moss was fought on 24 November 1542. On 7 or 8 December 1542 Mary of Guise gave birth to a daughter, Mary. On 14 December 1542 James V died.

Mary, now queen of Scots, was one week old.

NOTES

1. Son of Alexander, duke of Albany, the second son of James II (see the Table on p. 237).

2. The Scottish chronicles were translated into French for him so that he could know something of the history of the country of which he was now regent.

3. She was at Harbottle, Northumberland, in October 1515 when she gave birth to a daughter, Margaret Douglas, who was to marry Matthew Stewart, fourth earl of Lennox, and to become the mother of Darnley.

4. Lord Home had been executed by Albany, in 1516, for treasonable intrigue with England.

5. Pitscottie's account of this affair contains one of his best stories. He relates that Gavin Douglas, bishop of Dunkeld, and uncle of Archibald, sixth earl of Angus, striving to bring the Hamiltons and Douglases together in peace, called on James Beaton, archbishop of Glasgow, a supporter of the Hamiltons, and asked

for his help as mediator. But when the archbishop, striking his breast, declared on his conscience that he knew nothing of the intentions of the Hamiltons, his own armour rattled beneath his vestments. Whereupon Gavin Douglas replied, 'Faith, my lord, but yours is a poor conscience, for I heard it clatter'.

6. An attempt by Scott of Buccleuch to free the king was defeated; and in a further attempt Lennox was slain.

7. Her husband had been killed on the bloody field of Mohacs (1526), vainly fighting against Suleyman the Magnificent.

8. As we have seen, James IV had spent recklessly on the army and navy, and the period 1513–28 had been ruinous for government.

9. In effect a supreme central civil court. A 'college' is a society instituted for certain common purposes and possessing special rights and privileges; and the name is still used in that sense in, for example, the College of Surgeons.

10. Strictly, 10,000 ducats *auri de camera*, equivalent, roughly, to £10,000 (Scots).

11. See below, pp. 320–1.

12. For later changes in the constitution of the College of Justice (the Court of Session), see *Source Book of Scottish History*, ii (2nd edn.), 52.

13. In the case of the Macleans there was also a background of feud. Lachlan Maclean of Duart had married Catherine, daughter of Archibald, second earl of Argyll, and, tiring of her, is said to have had her placed on a rock (still called 'the Lady's Rock'), which was exposed only at low tide, intending to drown her (1523). She was luckily rescued by a passing boat; but, in revenge, her brother, Sir John Campbell of Cawdor, later murdered Duart in Edinburgh.

14. For a detailed account of these troubles, see Gregory, *History of the Western Highlands and Isles* (1836), pp. 132–43.

15. *Anglice*, 'none the worse of a hanging'.

16. At Caerlanrig, about ten miles south-west of Hawick on the road to Langholm.

17. It is also interesting to note that Henry had thought of Mary of Guise, a lady of 'majestic stature and graceful proportions', as a possible fourth bride for himself.

18. Catherine of Aragon had been divorced; Anne Boleyn had been beheaded; and Jane Seymour had died a few days after giving birth to Edward (VI).

19. Two sons, James and Arthur, born of Mary of Guise, had both died in infancy; Mary had not yet been born.

CHAPTER 27

Religion and Society before the Reformation

WHAT is 'the richt way to the Kingdome of Hevine'? From the end of the fourteenth century until the mid sixteenth the church in Western Europe was increasingly troubled by its inability to give a clear, consistent, and readily intelligible answer to this layman's question. Learned men in the fourteenth-century universities argued for a sharp distinction between reason and faith and removed from the former the attributes of God, the central dogmas of the Trinity, the Incarnation, and the Resurrection, though continuing to employ (in increasingly arid fashion) the methods of scholastic philosophy in theology. John Wycliffe reacted against this distinction and, rejecting much of the elaborate doctrinal superstructure of medieval theology as contrary to reason, accepted only what was revealed in the Bible. Fifteenth-century churchmen repressed such radical criticism, condemning as heretical this or that Lollard teaching and in England driving underground this fundamentalism and anti-clericalism. We have seen how in Scotland St. Andrews university was founded to combat heresy and there were indeed two burnings for Lollardy in the twenty years thereafter. But when Glasgow university was founded in 1451 and Aberdeen in 1495 there was no word of heresy, and Lollardy has left no further traces in Scotland until the year 1494 when a group of Ayrshire gentlefolk was accused of fairly typical Lollard heresies. All-in-all this episode makes only the most modest reservation to the generalization that Scotland was a country of orthodox beliefs before 1520.

And although there was no systematic and agreed exposition of catholic teaching, there was much that was general catholic practice, much that is found in Scotland, revealing common religious attitudes and beliefs, however unsophisticated. At the heart of these practices was a conviction of the dependence of man's spirit upon God's grace for redemption from the terrible pains of the hereafter.

Men feared the Doom (day of Judgment), the Devil, and the pains of Hell as much as they sought the love of God.

> Jesus on thee with peteous voce I cry
> Mercy on me to haif on domisday[1]

And the beginning of that fear was fear of death:

> Sen he hes all my brether tane,
> He will nocht lat me lif alane,
> On forse I man his nyxt pray be;
>   *Timor mortis conturbat me.*

> Sen for the deid remeid is none,
> Best is that we for dede dispone,
> Eftir our deid that lif may we;
>   *Timor mortis conturbat me.*[2]

'That after our death, we may live.' The promise of that life was contained in Christ's sacrifice upon the cross, every detail of which was dwelt upon in private devotions and public worship. Thus despite the bonfires of devotional literature, and the whitewashing of 'holy' pictures, after 1560, the surviving poems of Dunbar include 'Of the Passioun of Christ' and a poem on the Resurrection, while a collection made later by the Catholic Howard family in England includes cycles of prayers in Scots: to the Crown of Thorns, the Jesus Psalter, the Golden Litany, Remembrance of the Passion, the Hours of Our Lady's Dolours (at the Passion), prayers based upon the Seven Words, the Five Wounds, and so forth—all dwelling upon the Passion in detail which becomes obsessive.

Where printed, such texts were accompanied by crudely executed Crucifixion scenes; were such scenes common in Scottish churches? Within a few miles of each other in Midlothian are the collegiate churches of Crichton and Roslin, mid-fifteenth-century simple vaulted structures. But while the former is bare and stark stone, Roslin is a riot of carving which seems to have survived because largely botanical in inspiration. Yet there too are the apostles and martyrs, the Doom (in the form of the dance of death, the seven sins, and the seven virtues), the Passion, and the Resurrection, scenes the like of which would have been probably painted on plastered walls at Crichton. We offer this conjecture with confidence because two collegiate churches of the same date in Angus have preserved pre-

Reformation scenes painted on wood there: on the roof at Guthrie the Doom on one side, the Passion on the other; on the rood screen at Foulis Easter the Passion on one side, the other side being lost; on the lost rood screen at Elgin, the Passion was paired with the Doom.

These depictions in word, stone, and paint are revealing not so much of what the church wanted to stress in religion as of what men wanted to find there: a meaning for death. The understanding which they took away was of a life after death in which the suffering of Christ on the cross offered to each man God's grace (including the avoidance of purgatory and ultimately salvation) earned in this life by faith and works. And the most effective of those works was thought to be the sacrament of the altar, whereby through the mediation of the priest and with the 'instrumental cause' of saying the words of consecration, the body and blood of the Redeemer, portrayed so vividly on the crucifix, were really present in substance though not in appearance (transubstantiation) in the wafer which acted as 'host' to them. Each mass was a means of grace through the body and blood of Christ, obtained only through the priest; the mere contemplation of the host was itself an act of devotion, and in the minds of the unlettered the miracle of transubstantiation might permit further miracles performed by the consecrated host. Thus the wish to reserve the host for devotion and at the same time to protect it from superstitious use led to the incorporation of lockable 'sacrament houses' in many churches: they are still to be seen at some fifteenth-century kirks.

Confession, penitence, and communion as means of access to grace were certainly important. Dunbar has left two poems on confession which, however, suggest that for most they took place only annually—at Easter, the feast of the Passion. The layman sought access to Christ through another mediator—the Virgin Mary. Here the iconographic evidence in Scotland is very slight and does not assign great prominence to the cult of the Virgin which was greatly elaborated at this time, for example through the rosary. Yet the rosary appears on a fifteenth-century tombstone in remote Iona, in a manuscript Book of Hours for Arbuthnot church in Mearns, in the *Acts of Parliament* printed in 1541, and on the banner embroidered about 1520 for the Confraternity of the Holy Blood of Edinburgh. And the literary evidence supports this visual material. All Scottish rulers from James III to Mary possessed rosaries, and many traces of it appear in the surviving devotional literature:

> I enterit in ane oritorie
>   And knelit doun with ane *pater noster*
> Befoir the michtie king of glorie
> Haveing his passioun in memorie
> Syne to his mother I did inclyne
>   Hir halsing with ane *gaude flore*³   [*embracing her*]

Robert Henryson's *Annunciation* is a beautiful salutation to the queen of Heaven (the commonest portrayal) while Dunbar wrote two rhapsodical 'ballads' of Our Lady with stress upon Christ's suffering for the sins of mankind:

> O madyn meike, most mediatrix for man,
>   O moder myld, full of humilite!
> Pray thy sone Jhesu, with his woundis want,
>   Quhilk denyeit him for oure trespas to de,
>   And as he bled his blude apon a tre,
> Us to defend fra Lucifer oure fa,
>   In hevyne that we may syng apon our kne:
> O mater Jhesu, salve Maria!⁴

Other aspects of devotion and belief are less easily recovered. Thus the efficacy of pilgrimages was still widely accepted, though there was distinctly 'nationalist' shift in popularity to the shrines of St. Ninian at Whithorn, St. Adrian [Ethernan] on the Isle of May, and St. Duthac at Tain, while St. Andrew and St. Kentigern slumped. Relics were certainly collected—in 1455 William Preston of Gorton bequeathed the arm-bone of St. Giles (which he had obtained in France) to the kirk thereof, and it was thereafter carried in the saint's procession in Edinburgh on his annual feast day until the riots of a century later. But on the whole contemporary evidence does not bear out the criticism of some reformers (perhaps borrowing their words from Luther's Germany) of a widespread reliance upon the efficacy of relics. Nor is the pardoner with his remissions attested in the records.

Indeed it is possible that devotion to the saints and relics was a diminishing force in late medieval religion. They tend to be mentioned in the devotional literature in a perfunctory manner, if at all, and the Legends (a word meaning 'things to be read') of the

Saints which were widely circulated in earlier centuries have not survived from the Reformation century to suggest much faith in intercession by the saints. The lives of the saints printed in the Aberdeen Breviary may represent an attempt by Bishop William Elphinstone to reverse this trend.

The evidence of a few poems, prayers, and pictures may not seem weighty, but it complements and explains other long-recognized features of the century or so before 1540: the many foundations by laymen of collegiate churches, hospitals, and altars. By 1500 there were twelve collegiate churches in Lothian alone; in Lanarkshire by 1560 five, in Angus two, in Perthshire three. In each there ministered canons and chaplains—their number varied greatly— whose function was to say masses for the family or (in those founded by town councils) the brotherhood of the founder. In some ways the towns were even more remarkable patrons of religion than the lords and lairds who built collegiate kirks. Municipal pride doubt- less encouraged the diversion of resources into St. Giles at Edin- burgh with its fine late-fifteenth-century stone crown, into St. Michael's at Linlithgow, St. Mary's at Haddington, the Holy Rood at Stirling, the Holy Trinity at St. Andrews, St. John's at Perth, St. Mary's at Dundee, St. Nicholas' at Aberdeen, all built or in large measure rebuilt after 1400. But all was not for external show; within the walls the number of altars multiplied—some thirty-two at Holy Trinity, St. Andrews, forty-four at St. Giles, Edinburgh— each served by a chaplain maintained in his altarage by the town council or by a craft. And the function of these multi-aisled multi- altared kirks? To multiply the saying of masses for the redemption of the souls of the faithful.

The religious concerns which we have outlined are striking in their churchliness. It is not the case that men were abandoning the church in a spirit of criticism or disgust for other forms of piety, for more radical or fundamentalist beliefs. On the contrary, there seems to be concern with salvation and an attempt to bring the means of it, the mediators between God and man, within man's control, as a guarantee of it. The priesthood, the mass, the cult of the Virgin, all within the Church, all served to give man that access to grace which he craved and which seemed to be freely offered. Yet was it offered in sufficiency? The terrible dilemma was quantifi- cation, a mechanistic redemption which required faith as a pre- condition but which must yet be the free gift of God to those who

have further earned it by repentance—confused with penances—
and works.

So far we have written of 'men' who sought grace. Late medieval
religious life was formed as a response to the needs of the laity; but
although swiftly destroyed by the Protestant reformation, it had
been formed over a long period, and in so far as it was related
to the structure of society, that relationship was deeply founded.
The complex theological debates, the universities which framed
them, the orders of friars who conducted them, these were all
products of the rapid social evolution of the thirteenth century
when economic change made towns catalysts in creating both
a small 'middle class' of rich merchants and a large 'middle class'
of free landowners. The church, dominated intellectually by
the universities, sought to explain salvation for these men in
a way which would bring it within their grasp (financially and
intellectually), a way which stressed means and attitudes different
from those stressed by the great monastic leaders of the early
twelfth century to feudal rulers. In response the lairds put their
money and faith in collegiate churches, the burgesses in town
altars.

But the church could not speak plainly to those who asked: surely
with these masses I have found the right way to the Kingdom of
Heaven? Is it enough? For the church had doctors, masters, and
opinions, but it did not have a doctrine of justification (salvation)
which showed the essential relationship of man to God through
Christ uncluttered by inessential pardons, pilgrimages, and invocation of the saints. When a new theology was offered by Luther, and
another, more radical, by Calvin, there was no agreement on what
was essential Catholic doctrine to be defended.

Throughout the two centuries before the Reformation literacy
spread more widely, increasing the size of the market for reading
matter and stimulating the development of printing, or, in Scotland,
the importation of printed works. Yet on the whole the fourteenth
and fifteenth centuries were times of economic stagnation and social
consolidation—times in which the middling men in country and
town sought to protect their place in society by, for example,
legislation. Thus there were laws about what might be built, what
hunted, what worn, who summoned to parliament, who elected to
the town council: and all these show a society with well-developed
formal hierarchies, a society, that is, untroubled by innovation,

social tension, rapid economic development. From about 1500 it would no longer be possible to describe society as untroubled by these things; there was no revolution, but there was movement, pressures in both town and country which encouraged not new social structures, but greater activity within existing structures.

In sixteenth-century Europe there has been discerned a marked rise in population, uneven in pace from one decade to another, one region to another, but none the less general. Towns grew most rapidly in size: and so did the Scottish towns, many of whose sixteenth-century dwellings still survived in the early nineteenth century; but the rural population also increased. We do not know why the demographic plateau of the fifteenth century should change so, but without doubt the increasing number of mouths to be fed stimulated economic activity, especially agricultural production, through the obvious response to increased demand—rising prices for corn paid to the agricultural producer, and rising prices for bread paid to the baker. Land therefore was a source of profit again, and the demand for land began to rise.

It is in this light that we must see the movement to feu. Many fifteenth-century crown lands were occupied by a laird or administrator who had an arrangement without security of tenure, to pay a rent to the king. That rent did not vary. In his turn he collected rents from occupiers of the soil, many having tacks for a few years, some leases for life with the custom of their family's labour on, and occupation of, that land. These tacksmen for life were perhaps recorded in a rental: they were 'rentallers'. Their kin had been there beyond memory: they were 'kindly tenants'.

From the mid fifteenth century the king was adjured by parliament to a policy of feuing crown lands. This policy was vigorously followed by James IV and V in order to raise money, because a lump sum or grassum was paid to the king when the feu-charter was granted and because the feu-duty payable annually to the king was higher than the former rent; in return the feuar obtained a secure, heritable, title to the land. It was now his so long as he paid his feu-duty.

It seems likely that most feuars of crown lands were nobles, lairds, or verging thereupon. There has been no close study of their social composition nor of the extent to which they had previously been occupants of the land at rent. More important we do not know what became of the men with short leases and the kindly tenants during the reign of James V: did they in turn become feuars? Not if we are to believe the comment of social critics of the day, like Sir David Lindsay, who are unanimous in condemning the evils of insecure tenure and rack-renting which are stereotypes in their writings. We should certainly expect that rents would go up if only so that the new feuar could pay his feu-duty; but one way of raising the new grassum and feu-duty was to grant feus in turn to rentallers.

In the case of kirklands, however, the evidence is better. It shows that the fifteenth-century short-term tacksmen enjoyed considerable freedom in exchanging and conjoining their property—there was (as we have seen) little pressure of demand for land. During the reign of James V, however, there is a marked and dramatic swing away from five-year to nineteen-year or life tacks, a swing which can best be explained as a move towards greater security for the tacksman in conditions of rising demand for land. In the reign of Mary the process of giving security to some—apparently a majority —of occupiers of the land was taken a step further by the rapid development of feuing of kirklands.

Just as in England Henry VIII dissolved the monasteries and threw on to the land-market their vast properties, so James V carried out the same task in different fashion and to preserve Catholicism. To raise the great 'finance' agreed in 1532, monasteries and other corporate bodies had no alternative to realizing some of their landed capital; in May 1543, just before the treaties of Greenwich were negotiated by the Regent Arran (who was then leaning towards an Anglophil and Protestant policy), a meeting of the clergy at St. Andrews (called by Cardinal Beaton) resolved to raise £10,000, by a tax upon prelacies and benefices, 'to maintain the liberty of the Church and to preserve the State'. The church had to find half of taxes of £20,000 for defence (1555), £60,000 for the queen's marriage, and £48,000 to pay the regent's troops. All these forced the religious corporations to sell land.

Canon law forbade such outright alienation, and this has been called the reason for the form which realization of assets took— grants in feu-ferme tenure; there is, however, little reason to think that canon law by this time commanded so much respect as to be an effective safeguard, and the move to feu-ferme tenure should be looked at in a wider context than taxation of the church. We have seen that the nobility (including the crown for its illegitimate sons) had moved into monastic offices in the wake of the system of commends which first spread as a means of increasing episcopal incomes. True, the Beatons were a non-noble family promoted by James V, and enjoyed not merely the archbishopric of St. Andrews but also the commend of Dunfermline. But Hamiltons succeeded Beatons at St. Andrews and engrossed Paisley and Arbroath abbeys; the Erskines for example took Dryburgh and Inchmahome, and the Kers Newbattle. Other abbeys were held as commends by bishops until the Reformation and even later; but these bishops were of noble families, and it made little difference to the dispersal of monastic property whether the commendator was ecclesiastic or lay. Moreover, feuing of kirklands took place on the baronies of bishops and cathedral chapters as well as of monasteries in the two decades on either side of 1560. Who, then, were the beneficiaries of this movement?

Some nobles took feus but in the vast majority of cases the feuars were lairds and a multitude of small kindly tenants who replaced their rents by feus and remained tenants of land already theirs. The nobles and lairds who individually took substantial amounts of land at feu seem in many cases to have granted feus to the kindly tenants, so that in the end the effect was the same as direct feuing to these tenants, and far from revolutionary. On the contrary the occupancy of land was in general stabilized and its ownership was widely diffused. Legislation or even taxation were no more than minor factors in this movement; far more important were market forces— the advantages of security, the terrors of insecurity. Thus when a feu charter was granted an important financial transaction took place. The laird and the rentaller taking a feu had to find their grassum, and there is evidence that a commendator or laird giving the feu would lend the grassum to a small feuar, that is collect it on an instalment plan (including interest), the instalments being added to the feu-duty. It was certainly well worth while for a laird to take land at feu and then feu it out in turn to the kindly tenants, for he could make a substantial profit on the transaction, and draw in perpetuity feu-duties less than the feu-duty he had to pay in his turn.

In so far as the leaders of the reformers were noblemen, it is impossible to show that 'greed for church lands' was a significant motive for their behaviour. On the contrary, the scattered records would probably show that they were feuing out their lands to lairds and kindly tenants, just as the king and the church, whose records survive, certainly did. Where the nobility benfited was in the final secularizing of abbeys after 1560; the commendator was thereafter always a member of a prominent family, no longer a bishop, and therefore receiver of a substantial income from feu-duties. It is perfectly true that much church property was already secularized, much church land already feued out by 1560, but there remained the ownership of feu-duties. A nobleman was a *rentier*, receiver of feu-duties; he could acquire for himself or for his close kin more feu-duties. And the validity of that concern as a motive for joining the attack on the old church in the 1550s is demonstrated by the sensitiveness of the issue of secularized church lordships as late as the 1630s.

Secondly there is a coincidence in time between the rise of the reform movement and the growing activity, and presumably importance, of lairds in the land-market. Many, it is quite clear, made a pretty penny from their deals, and many became owners of rather wider estates and hence men of greater social consequence. They had an undoubted interest in participating in the feuing process (including the feuing of crown lands), and may even have been hostile to the anxiety of the better ecclesiastical landowners to grant feus direct to kindly tenants. This interest and hostility shows up in the strong local pressures exerted upon ecclesiastical landowners to appoint lairds as bailies of their lands, bailies who could influence the choice of feuars. The social and economic rise of the lairds suggests that they may in individual cases have persuaded a nobleman to whom they looked as lord, to join the Protestant lords (and Protestant nobles were few and hesitant until the 1550s). It explains why in 1560 they were willing and able to demand a voice at the Reformation parliament. But it does not explain why in the 1540s some were active and committed Protestants, and many were indifferent to the distress-cries of the old church. No simple economic motive will link the rise of lairds to the rise of Protestantism.

NOTES

1. Robert Henryson, *Ressoning betwix Deth and Man.*
2.   Since he has taken all my brother [poets]
                He will not let me alone live on
                With care I must his next prey be;
                    The fear of death betroubles me.

                Since for death there is no remeed
                Best is that we prepare for death
                That after our death live may we;
                    The fear of death betroubles me.

   William Dunbar, *Lament for the Makaris.*
3. William Dunbar, *Of the Passioun of Christ.*
4. William Dunbar, *Ros Mary: Ane Ballat of Our Lady.*

CHAPTER 28

The Reformation—I

IN 1549 the Scottish churchmen, assembled in their own provincial council, declared that there appeared to be two main causes of 'heresy', namely, 'the corruption of morals and profane lewdness of life in churchmen of almost all ranks, together with crass ignorance of literature and of all the liberal arts'. Therefore, in their council, they set themselves to remedy those abuses within their church. The statutes then passed are eloquent of the crying need for reform. We find statutes against the incontinence of the clergy, and against their intemperance and negligence; statutes forbidding them from using the revenues of the church to endow their illegitimate children; statutes commanding the examination of priests in their ability to read and to expound the Scriptures, and ordering parsons and bishops to preach in person at least four times a year; together with other, more general, statutes for the amendment of life and morals so that 'those who correct others be not themselves guilty'. That such statutes were long overdue is evident from contemporary writings. That unfortunately they remained paper-statutes, and were not observed, is clear from a report made to Pope Paul IV by Cardinal Sermoneta in 1556 in which a number of these abuses, together with others, were once more denounced, and the pope was urged to take measures to secure correction and reform; while in 1559 many of these statutes were passed again, in even stronger terms, in what was to be the last provincial council of the unreformed Scottish church.

Through the appropriation of parish churches—and nearly nine-tenths of the parish churches in Scotland had been appropriated by 1560—the great wealth concentrated in the higher offices within the church had led to a neglect of the parishes and of parish work. The larger part of the revenues of the appropriated parish churches was now being taken by cathedrals, monasteries, and collegiate churches; the 'living' was impoverished; and, as a result, many a parish became ill-served by an illiterate and underpaid priest who, needy and greedy, pressed for offerings which his poor parishioners could ill afford. The exaction of mortuary dues (the cow and the 'upmaist cloth') was denounced by James V and scathingly satirized by Sir David Lindsay in his play, *Ane Pleasant Satyre of the Thrie Estaitis*, written for the court;[1] the feeling of the common people was aptly expressed in their saying, 'Nae penny, nae paternoster'; and, through this, there had grown up an anti-clericalism which was both widespread and deep.

This drawing away of the revenues of the parish churches had two other ill-effects. Little or nothing was available for the poor of the parish, and little or nothing for the repair of the parish church. A statute of the provincial Council of 1549 enjoined that, where churches had been appropriated, alms were still to be distributed as of old, and the churches were to be kept in repair; but that was merely reiterating a law which in many parts had long been flouted. In 1556, when Archbishop Hamilton wrote to the dean of Christianity of the Merse calling his attention to the ruinous state of a number of parish churches within his deanery, in many cases English armies must have been responsible for the damage; he complained that, in a great many, 'choirs as well as their naves were wholly thrown down and as it were levelled to the ground; others were partly ruinous or threatening collapse in respect of their walls and roof; they were without glazed windows and without a baptismal font, and had no vestments for the high altars and no missals or manuals, so that their parishioners could not hear the divine services or masses therein as befits good Christians, neither could masses be celebrated nor the church's sacraments administered'.

Already, in 1541, an enactment of parliament had spoken of the 'unhonesty and misrule of kirkmen both in with knowledge and manners' as being the reason why the kirk and kirkmen were despised and contemned.

It is small wonder that prelates who were laymen and politicians were divorced alike from the impoverished lesser clergy and from the laity, especially the literate laity of the towns who had for long supported their own kirks and their own clergy. If they had little need of prelates, did they need the pope; or the mass?

Contempt for corrupt churchmen was quickened with the public performance of morality plays and with the circulation of books and broadsheets now made possible by the growth of printing. In 1543, 1549, and 1552 we read of slanderous bills, writings, ballads, and books which were circulating to the defame of the church and churchman. None of these early broadsheets has survived, but some indication of their contents may perhaps be gathered from Lindsay's *Thrie Estaitis*, and from the collection of *Gude and Godlie Ballates*, made by the brothers Wedderburn of Dundee,[2] in which, in addition to metrical vernacular versions of a catechism, the creed, the commandments, and certain psalms, there are also lampoons on the state of the church and on its priests.

Yet much of this criticism was not only age-old (and therefore not an adequate explanation of the Reformation); it was also misplaced. Of the worldliness of most of the prelates there can be no doubt. But when the reformed kirk recruited its ministry, there are to be found among its numbers former parish priests, friars, and religious, particularly from the Augustinian order which allowed its canons to serve parishes. The cathedral priory of St. Andrews was also the faculty of theology in the university and its canons teachers of the doctrine and theology of the medieval church. Almost to a man they entered the reformed ministry. Were they illiterate men or in any other way unworthy? At the other end of the hierarchy the ill-paid parochial chaplain may have lived in concubinage with his housekeeper; this was sinful, but in the reformers' eyes it was sinful that they might not marry. The lechery of some notorious ecclesiastical rakehells and the greed of others were weaknesses in the church, but they do not convince as reasons for the attack upon the church, which, while demanding reform of life also demanded reform of doctrine and institutions. It was a cardinal error of the church to think that it could remove criticism by burning the critics; but it was no less hopeless to seek to meet them half-way by commanding removal of the external blemishes which were only symptoms of the internal canker.

In January 1552 a provincial council of the Scottish church had openly admitted that neither the prelates nor the inferior clergy had, as a rule, 'such proficiency in the knowledge of the holy Scriptures as to be able, by their own efforts, rightly to instruct the people in the Catholic faith and other things necessary to their salvation'; and accordingly, to combat such clerical ignorance, the council had decreed that a Catechism in the Scots tongue, which had already been prepared and approved, should be printed and put in use. *Hamilton's Catechism* was published and distributed to the churches in the following August. Its publication was significant. Described on its title-page as 'ane commone and catholik instructioun of the

christin people in materis of our Catholik faith and religioun', and
written in simple and moving language, it reveals, in places, a spirit
of compromise, an attempt to meet some of the doctrinal points
raised by the reformers. Indeed, one notable passage on justification by faith was little different from the declarations of Martin
Luther and from the views for which Patrick Hamilton had been
burned.[3] And it nowhere mentions the pope.

But, admirable as it was, this attempt at instruction and reform
came too late. The *Catechism* itself helped to call attention to the
issues which reft the church, while the compromises offered
belonged to a stage of the debate long past.

For criticism of the clergy was essentially criticism of a mediating
priesthood and any of the explanations of the Reformation should
make central a rejection not of the men but of the claims for their
office. In the renewed economic and social liveliness of the sixteenth-
century burghs, in the adjustment and change implied by the feuing
movement, in the changes taking place within the structure of
sixteenth-century society, we should discover the conditions in
which reformed opinion took root. The quest of lairds and merchants
for 'the richt way to the Kingdome of Hevine', their religious pre-
occupation, remained the same. But their improved economic
security and social status coincided with—and we cannot show that
they caused—alternative routes to the spiritual assurance which
a man of business required as he went about his affairs.

The influence of Luther was already clear when in 1525 and 1535
acts of parliament had condemned the 'damnable opinions of the
heretic Luther' and had striven to prevent the entry into the realm
of Lutheran books and writings. With Luther had come a new
reliance upon faith: 'If a Christian has faith he has everything . . .
Faith unites Man to God.' In 1528 Patrick Hamilton, a grandson of
James, first Lord Hamilton, and of royal descent, was burned at St.
Andrews for maintaining 'divers heresies of Martin Luther and his
followers'. Patrick Hamilton had reaffirmed that faith brought
'Man and God together'—and 'the reek of Master Patrick Hamilton
infected as many as it blew upon'.

As in other movements of criticism, the early reformers were
clear about much that should be swept away but disunited about
what should be retained. Lutherans, though they rejected much
Catholic doctrine, preserved many of the outward usages of
discipline and worship, and to these a new generation of reformers

took exception. Where should criticism end and constructive acceptance begin? Thus George Wishart, martyred at St. Andrews in 1546, had been influenced by the preaching and work of the Swiss reformers at Zürich, and laid stress upon the rejection of all beliefs, practices, and institutions for which no warrant could be found in the Word of God. That reliance upon scriptural warrant was henceforth to be a cardinal point in the preaching of the Scottish reformers and was to be central in their Confession of Faith.

Yet how were the people to know the story revealed in the Gospels if the Word of God was denied to them except as an integral part of a doctrine including many things—the saints, the seven sacraments, the priesthood—which were in fact later accretions to Christ's teaching? By 1530, however, copies of Tyndale's translation of the New Testament were reaching Scotland through the east-coast burghs; and, with the reading of the Gospel, arose a great yearning for 'the unsearchable riches of Christ'; the Reformers could justify their preachings by the printed Word.

If the church was prepared to dally with justification by faith in Hamilton's *Catechism*, it could have no truck with the anti-sacerdotal views which by the 1550s were widely held in the towns and among some lairds, views asserting the priesthood of all believers, and hence the direct access of each individual to the Grace of God. From the assurance which an increasing number of confident, well-read, and prosperous townsfolk derived from that promise sprang the 'privy kirks', gatherings of Protestant believers, in towns—though how many towns we do not know. From that assurance came the desire for a church to preach the faith, pure and undefiled and free from all man-made ceremony and invention. Where in the Word of God was there warrant for the ceremonies of the Church of Rome, the authority of the pope, and the invocation of saints? Above all, the mass of the Roman Church, said in a tongue unknown to most of those who attended, was held to be far different from Christ's words and actions in the Last Supper as they were recorded in the Gospels. More important, the mass was celebrated as a propitiatory sacrifice for the sins of the living and the dead, and, in the mass, the priest was interposed between God and his people; but a true 'communion' meant the full participation of the people in the 'Lord's Table', there to break bread and to take the cup in remembrance of Christ and therein to renew their faith and find union with God. Only thus could Christ's command be obeyed by men.

The numbers of lairds and townsfolk who took to this faith renewed is unknown until the Reformation itself was accomplished. It would be misleading, however, to claim that there was a popular following for the reformers in either town or country, or even that a majority of lairds were inclined to the new faith. We might claim that the minority so inclined were often firm in their convictions, whereas a majority viewed the old church and the reformers alike with indifference, even selfish indifference. The reformation need have been no more than a movement of 'enthusiasm', limited socially and geographically as were the Huguenots in France or the Puritans in Elizabethan England, though perhaps ultimately (as in both those countries) provoking civil war. That did not happen in Scotland where, as in the Netherlands, the old church was protected and supported by a government misguidedly relying for its authority upon the presence of foreign troops. And so, as a new faith formed the anti-clericalism of some men, in others there stirred xenophobia and fears of political repression. And from the marriage of these attitudes was born the Scottish Reformation.

NOTES

1. We do not know when the *Satyre* was first printed, but we know that it was performed before James V, his queen, and the lords of council at Linlithgow on Epiphany 1549, and it has been persuasively argued that much of it was written for a young king recently freed from evil advisors—James V in 1528. In his works Sir David Lindsay (*c.* 1490-*c.* 1555) attacked corruption in both church and state: in the church, in his *Satyre*; in the state, in his *Testament of the Papyngo*. In his *Supplicatioun anent Syde Taillis* he even attacked absurd female fashions. His *Historie of Squyer Meldrum*, on the other hand, is a long epic of its hero's many adventures, military and amatory.

2. Again, we do not know the date of the first printing. The earliest surviving edition is that of 1578, though there is reference to an earlier edition of about 1570.

3. See *Source Book of Scottish History*, ii (2nd edn.), 145-50. Archbishop Hamilton was certainly not opposed to some measure of reform, but it should be noted that tradition ascribed the authorship of the *Catechism* to John Winram, sub-prior of St. Andrews, who later joined the reformers and took part in drafting the Confession of Faith and the Book of Discipline.

CHAPTER 29

The Reformation—II

JAMES V had died in December 1542, three weeks after the rout at Solway Moss. Mary, queen of Scots, was exactly one week old. For a brief period there was a struggle for the regency between Cardinal Beaton, archbishop of St. Andrews, the advocate of the old faith and the old alliance, and the unstable earl of Arran, heir presumptive to the throne, who had leanings towards Protestantism and who favoured a new alliance with England and with an English king who had broken away from Rome. Thus the struggle for the regency had both a political and a religious aspect. Henry VIII, moreover, quick to seize his chance, had promptly sent back to Scotland a number of the Scottish lords who had been captured at Solway Moss and who, moved by bribes and promises, had entered into assurances with him to further the cause of the English alliance and to secure the marriage of the infant Mary to Henry's son, Edward, later Edward VI.[1] And with these 'assured lords' came also the forfeited Douglas, earl of Angus, a strong supporter of an alliance with England.

Arran soon won the struggle for the regency. Beaton was seized and imprisoned by the Douglases, and, in the middle of March 1543, a parliament formally declared Arran to be the governor of the realm. The same parliament also passed an act permitting the lieges to have and to read the bible in English translation (though it forbade 'disputes' or the 'holding of opinions'), and ambassadors were sent to England to discuss the English marriage.

For those who favoured the old alliance and the old faith the position was critical. The imprisoned Beaton contrived to send messengers to France representing the danger to the church and the peril to French interests; and, regaining his liberty, by bribery or connivance, towards the end of March, at once conspired with John Hamilton, abbot of Paisley, half-brother to Arran, a man of far stronger character than the governor and a devoted member of the Roman Church. A little later, and possibly as a result of Beaton's urgent communications, Matthew, fourth earl of Lennox, returned to Scotland from France—and Lennox could claim to be next in succession to the crown if the divorce of the first earl of Arran were to be proved invalid. Moreover, that both France and the papacy realized the danger of the events then taking place in Scotland is clear from the appearance in Scotland, a few months later, of two French envoys, La Brosse and Ménage, and a papal legate, Grimani.

Meanwhile the negotiations with England still went on. On 1 July 1543 two treaties (the treaties of Greenwich) were agreed—a treaty of marriage: on the conclusion of her tenth year Mary was to marry Edward; and a treaty of peace: there was to be peace between Scotland and England until a year after the death of either Mary or Edward. These treaties with England, the 'old enemy', were nevertheless far from popular. Arran was accused of having 'sold the young queen to the English'; the 'assured lords', who had taken Henry's money, did little in return to help the English cause; Beaton and Hamilton actively urged the old alliance and the old faith and Henry VIII alienated the Scots by his overbearing attitude. He assumed the air of an overlord, demanding the custody of Mary and the succession in the event of her death, and he seized, in breach of the treaty, a number of Scottish merchantmen. As he 'promised' to send troops to 'help' Arran, the latter wavered and then changed. Little more than a week after the treaties had been solemnly ratified at Holyrood (25 August 1543), Arran suddenly re-embraced the Roman faith, did penance for his apostasy, and made Beaton and Mary of Guise, the queen mother, members with him in a new council of government.

It is possible that Beaton and Hamilton had reminded Arran in no uncertain terms that his legitimacy, and thereby his position as heir presumptive to the throne, depended upon the validity of his father's divorce.

The table on p. 237 shows how this proximity of the Hamiltons to the Scottish crown came through their descent from the *son* of the marriage of Mary, daughter of James II, whereas the Lennox Stewarts were only the descendants of the *daughter* of that marriage. On the other hand, James, first earl of Arran (who died in 1529), had been married twice—first to Elizabeth Home, and second to Janet Beaton. He was married to Elizabeth Home from about 1490 until 1504, when he secured a divorce; but he still lived with Elizabeth Home until 1510, when the sentence of divorce was renewed; and, six years later, in 1516, he married his second wife,

Janet Beaton. James, second earl of Arran, the heir presumptive to the throne from 1536 until his death in 1575, was the son of the second marriage. If, however, as the Lennox Stewarts maintained, the first earl of Arran's divorce and his second marriage were unlawful, then James, second earl of Arran, was illegitimate; and, in that event, the heir presumptive to the Scottish throne was a Lennox Stewart, namely Matthew, fourth earl of Lennox (1526-71).

This nearness of the Hamiltons and the Lennox Stewarts to the Scottish throne, and the question of the legitimacy of James, second earl of Arran, explains to some extent the policies followed by Arran and Lennox during the period 1542 to 1567—and even thereafter. If indeed the Reformation and the establishment of the Protestant faith were to result in the deposition of Mary, a Roman Catholic queen, then James, second earl of Arran, could expect to wear the Scottish crown. Perhaps we need not be surprised that he became the titular head of the Protestant forces during the brief struggle of the Scottish reformation-rebellion and that during the course of that struggle he was more than once accused of aiming at the throne. A Hamilton was heir presumptive to the Scottish throne for virtually the whole of the period 1536 to 1594; but only if the first earl's divorce was valid. Beaton may now have pointed out that a divorce granted by the church could be rescinded by the church; and that, if the divorce were to be rescinded, Matthew, fourth earl of Lennox, would become heir presumptive to the throne. Certainly in December 1543 a new parliament annulled the treaties of Greenwich, renewed the alliance with France, and reaffirmed the laws against heresy. Beaton was reinstated as chancellor. The cardinal had not laboured in vain; but, while the Scottish parliament had shown itself to be little more than a gathering of the faction then in power, it is also clear that the English ambassador was right when he wrote that the people 'hated England and stood by France'.

This complete reversal of policy, however, meant that Henry VIII, denounced by the pope, soon to be again at war with France, and devoid of friends and allies, had once again to reckon with a hostile Scotland in the north. Cheated of the prize which he thought was in his grasp, angry and disillusioned, Henry determined to teach the Scots a lesson. And the lesson took the form of the destructive invasions by the earl of Hertford in 1544 and 1545. Possibly these invasions could be called 'actions for breach of promise'—for the marriage of Mary to Edward had been broken off; certainly the

'English Wooing' was a brutal attempt to bully the Scots into marrying their queen to a suitor of England's choosing.

In 1544 Hertford burned Edinburgh, Holyrood, and Leith; and in 1545 he boasted of the burning of seven monasteries (including Dryburgh, Melrose, and Kelso) and over 240 villages and towns. Lennox, in opposition to Arran, and active in Henry's interests, also harried in the West Marches and Annandale; and the MacDonalds entered into treaty with Henry, swearing allegiance to him and binding themselves to do all they could to the annoyance of the regent.

When they saw their burning houses the women of Edinburgh might well cry out, 'Woe worth the Cardinal',[2] and lament a policy that had brought such ruin in its train; if Hertford's devastations were hardly likely to commend an English alliance, they did cause all parties save Lennox to pause and form a united government of sorts. In this government Mary of Guise for the first time played a leading part, but it showed its internal divisions by irresolutely permitting Protestant preachers (encouraged by Henry VIII) to work in Scotland. Beaton alone took a stand, arresting George Wishart, whose martyrdom (1 March 1546) had a political as well as a religious aftermath. It showed that if the new faith were to be embraced by many, and if a united Protestant party were to arise, that party could look only to England for support. And 'the sword of the Lord and of Gideon' had already been seen: at the seizure of Wishart, the 'servant of the Lord' had caused a two-handed sword to be taken from one of his followers, called John Knox.

The martyrdom of Wishart, together with a 'deadly feud' against Beaton, led to the assassination of the cardinal in his castle at St. Andrews less than three months later (29 May 1546). Knox insists in his *History*[3] that Beaton was slain in vengeance for 'the shedding of the blood of that notable instrument of God, Master George Wishart', and because Beaton had been, and remained, 'an obstinate enemy against Christ Jesus' (which, to Knox, meant an enemy to the new faith); but, significantly, the Leslies played a leading part in the murder, and there was old feud between the Leslies and the cardinal, who may have been planning action against them.

With the help of Mary of Guise, Beaton had successfully opposed the scheming of Henry VIII and had maintained the old policies and the old faith. His murderers, on the other hand, proclaimed themselves to be the upholders of the 'true faith' and, fortifying themselves in the murdered cardinal's castle, looked to England for aid. Opposing parties in Scotland were taking shape; and the 'Protestants', or 'Reformers', holding a strong castle in arms, were there steadily joined by others of the Protestant faith—and also by some of little or no faith at all. Thither, to St. Andrews, in the Easter of 1547, came John Knox, looking for security; there Knox received a call to become the castle's minister. But the looked-for English aid came too late; in July 1547 the 'Reformers' in the castle were compelled to surrender to a French attack. Some were placed in French prisons; others, including John Knox, were put to row in the French galleys.[4]

With the death of Henry VIII, in January 1547, Hertford, now the Protector Somerset, continued the policy of 'rough wooing'; and, although at one time he suggested safeguards for Scottish independence if only the Scots would agree to the marriage of Mary and Edward, his campaign of September 1547, which included the rout and massacre of the Scottish army at Pinkie, served to show the queen mother that the interests of her daughter came last in the calculations of Hertford, Arran, and many other Scots.

After their success at Pinkie, the English seized and fortified Haddington, only 18 miles from Edinburgh and a strategic centre which commanded Lothian. After their defeat at Pinkie those Scots who did not run to deal with Hertford for the sake of the reformed religion or English money, appealed to France for the protection of their kingdom.

Scotland's appeal was answered—but there were conditions. France would defend the liberties of Scotland, but Mary was to be sent to France so that, in due course, she could be married to the Dauphin. This was formally agreed in the treaty of Haddington (July 1548), concluded with the French plenipotentiaries in the camp of the Scottish army then besieging the town; and, a few weeks later, Mary set sail for France. Meantime Arran still remained regent. In 1549 he was further bought by the queen mother by being granted the French duchy of Châtelherault. In the same year his half-brother, John Hamilton, succeeded the murdered Beaton as archbishop of St. Andrews.

With the treaty of Haddington the five-year-old Mary had been committed to the 'faith and credit' of the French king, and France, for the defence of Scotland, soon established there a force of some

6,000 or 8,000 well-trained soldiers led by officers who had gained experience in the wars in Italy. The treaty of Haddington, in effect, had given France a double hold over Scotland. We are told that when Henry II heard of it he 'leaped for blitheness, and was so blithe that it seemed incredible'; yet naturally so, for, as the queen mother wrote, the decision to send Mary to France 'put all things into the hands of the French king'.

Henry II certainly hoped that if an English army could be committed to Lothian he would be able the more easily to recover Boulogne.[5] That, indeed, happened. England lost on both fronts. There was a first, unsuccessful assault on the English garrison holding Haddington—unsuccessful, if we are to believe Knox, mainly because of two miraculous shots from the English ordnance[6] —but that was only a check; Haddington soon fell, and the English were 'clean dung out of Scotland'. On the other front, France regained Boulogne. In 1550 Scotland was included in the treaty of peace (the treaty of Boulogne) between England and France.

But, if France had saved Scotland from English designs, who was to save Scotland from the designs of France? Henry II undoubtedly had hopes far beyond the recovery of Boulogne. We are told that when he heard of the arrival of Mary in France he declared 'France and Scotland are now one country'; and in 1550, with the conclusion of the treaty of Boulogne, he was speaking of 'maintaining the kingdom of Scotland in the obedience of our son the Dauphin'. With the treaty of Boulogne, Scotland was freed from the English, but the French forces, steadily reinforced, still stayed on.

It is possible that, in the period immediately following the treaty of Boulogne, Arran (now duke of Châtelherault, and still regent) and his half-brother, Archbishop John Hamilton, were quick to see that the sending of Mary to France and the continued presence of French troops on Scottish soil might result in an alliance between the Protestants and those who, for various reasons, feared or disliked the increasing influence of the French. Thus the issue of *Hamilton's Catechism* may have been part of an endeavour to meet the danger by trying to satisfy some of the demands for reform within the church.

Mary of Guise, devoted to her daughter's interests, remained in ungrateful Scotland, though she visited France in 1550–1, taking with her a group of Scottish nobles whom the French thought to attach to their interest with pensions and payments. Ready takers, ready promisers, the Scots kept no better faith for French bribes than for English.

In December 1553 Mary, queen of Scots, entered her twelfth year. The French court soon found lawyers to maintain that, being in her twelfth year, the queen of Scots was virtually twelve years old and was therefore legally of age to govern in her own name. That, in effect, meant that, while Mary would continue to reside in France, Scotland would be governed in her name by her own delegates. And who could be more suitable to govern Scotland in the queen's name than the queen's own mother, Mary of Guise? In a parliament of April 1554 the regency was formally transferred from Arran to the queen mother. Technically Arran resigned; but he was certainly not anxious to demit office, and pressure (or bribery) was brought to bear upon him—in particular, he was freed from accounting for all his intromissions with crown property (including the crown jewels and furnishings) during the period of his regency.

With Mary of Guise as regent, there was an immediate increase of French control. Frenchmen were appointed to offices of state, Scottish fortresses were garrisoned by French soldiers, and the French 'began to think themselves more than masters in Scotland'. As early as 1555, amid murmurings of lords and commons alike, it was necessary to pass an act against speaking evil of the queen regent and the French; and undoubtedly there was a steadily growing antipathy to both the French officers and the French soldiers, some of whom were guilty of outrage and excess. Nevertheless, because England from 1553 to 1558 was ruled by a persecuting Catholic queen in alliance with Catholic Spain, France's enemy, the queen mother judged that a policy of toleration would win her and the French friends among those who had embraced the new faith. English Protestants were allowed to find refuge in Scotland; and in the autumn of 1555 John Knox visited Scotland from Geneva and stayed preaching and exhorting for well-nigh a year, though often in secret. The queen regent was endeavouring to avoid serious trouble in Scotland and a possible French succession to Queen Mary; for Mary, before her marriage in 1558, and Mary and Francis after their marriage, entered into solemn agreements to observe and keep the laws, liberties, and privileges of Scotland; and, later, both Henry II and Francis (as king of Scots) bound themselves to maintain the immunities and ancient liberties of the

Scottish realm. We now know, however, that, three weeks before her marriage, Mary had signed secret documents of a vastly different purport, whereby, in the event of her decease without issue, she made over to the king of France her kingdom of Scotland and such rights as she had or might have to the kingdom of England.

John Hamilton, archbishop of St. Andrews, whose half-brother Arran should succeed to the throne if Mary were to die without issue, may also have wished to be 'well thought of', and hence abstained from persecution in 1553–8. So with toleration in Scotland and the inept persecution in England the numbers of the Reformers steadily increased. Already they were strong in the east-coast burghs and in the south-west; many lairds and barons were embracing the new faith; and now even some of the nobility were supporting the Protestant preachers.

Early in 1557 there was apparently some hope of a rising, both political and religious. In March a number of Scots lords wrote to John Knox at Geneva inviting him to return to Scotland where he would find the faithful 'ready to jeopard lives and goods in the forward setting of the glory of God'; then they decided that the time was 'not yet ripe', and Knox, having reached Dieppe in October, received there further letters advising him to stay awhile. In the following December (1557), however, some of the leading Protestant nobles, calling themselves the 'Congregation of Christ', subscribed a Common Band (which, being a religious band, was later called a 'Covenant'), binding themselves to 'apply our whole power, substance, and our very lives, to maintain, set forward, and establish the most blessed word of God' and to 'labour at our possibility to have faithful Ministers purely and truly to minister Christ's Evangel and Sacraments to his people'. And thereafter, as Knox admits in his *History*, 'the Lords and Barons professing Christ Jesus', that is, the Protestants, frequently convened in council, and their discussions in council covered both religion and 'policy'.

The face of a reformed church was revealing itself. Some of the Protestant lords openly associated themselves with the preachers; some maintained preachers in their own households; and the leading preachers found that more and more they could rely upon temporal support.

Some time in the following year a number of the 'temporal lords and barons' who desired reform presented certain 'articles' to the queen regent. They spoke of the ungodly and dissolute lives led by spiritual men, and the failure of provincial councils to secure reform; they asked for the sincere preaching of God's word in parish churches on Sundays (or at least on every third or fourth Sunday), for more qualified curates and vicars, for the sacraments to be administered in the English tongue, and for the common prayers and litanies also to be said in English. They also asked for some mitigation of clerical exactions at Easter-time and at the time of burials, and some reform in the 'long process' and 'exorbitant expenses' of the consistorial courts. The queen regent passed these articles to Archbishop Hamilton and, at his instance, they were considered at the provincial council held early in 1559—again an indication of the queen regent's desire for an understanding and of Hamilton's interest in reform. Some reforms were attempted— clerical exactions were to be mitigated,[7] and there was to be more efficient supervision of the parishes and of the lives and qualifications of parish priests; the request for services and the administration of the sacraments in the English tongue was refused but the *Twopenny Faith*—a moving statement, in the vernacular, of the nature and meaning of the 'Sacrament of the Altar' which was to be read to the people at the time of the sacrament—was published in 1559.

Meantime in France, in April 1558, Mary had married the Dauphin, Francis, and in England, in November 1558, Mary Tudor had died and had been succeeded by Elizabeth. And, with the accession of Elizabeth, most of the anti-papal legislation of Henry VIII's reign was renewed and the prayer-book of Edward VI brought back into use.

But Elizabeth, Henry VIII's last surviving child, was the daughter of Anne Boleyn and in the eyes of Rome she was neither a legitimate daughter of Henry VIII nor legitimate queen of England; but, recognizing the fact of her authority, the pope and Spain treated with her as a lawful sovereign. France, however, did not temporize: the rightful queen of England was Mary, queen of Scots, the direct and lawful descendant of the marriage of James IV and Margaret Tudor, even though Henry VIII had endeavoured to cut out the descendants of his elder sister Margaret in favour of the descendants of his younger sister Mary.[8] Within two months of Elizabeth's accession, Francis and Mary, king and queen of Scotland, and the future king and queen of France, had assumed the title of King and Queen of England and Ireland. The policy of France was abundantly clear, and for Elizabeth, as for the Protestants in Scotland, politics and religion were inseparably intertwined.

And, at this very juncture, Mary of Guise, the queen regent, appears to have decided that the days of toleration and compromise were over. To maintain English and Scottish Protestants in Scotland no longer embarrassed England. With the agreement of the first draft of the treaty of Cateau-Cambresis (which brought the war between France and Spain to an end) France was no longer in military danger. So, like Henry II of France, she now threatened the Protestants with a policy of repression (and already in 1558 Archbishop Hamilton had resumed persecution by the burning of the aged Walter Myln). According to Knox, in his hatred of the regent and of all her actions, she now began 'to spew forth and disclose the latent venom of her double heart'. Certainly there was a change in her attitude when an 'intercession' on behalf of the Protestant preachers was received with the forthright answer that they would be 'banished out of Scotland, albeit they preached as truly as ever did St Paul'.

But the Protestants were not browbeaten. To the poor, and they were many, the church was no longer the supporter of those in distress. On 1 January 1559 the 'Beggars' Summonds' mysteriously appeared on the doors of friaries and hospitals in towns. It ordered the friars to quit their houses, which had been endowed for the maintenance of the poor, so that on 'flitting Friday',[9] 12 May, the poor could enter into possession of foundations which were theirs by right. This notice of imminent revolution is one of the most remarkable features of the Reformation. We may be sure that whoever paid for and synchronized the posting of the 'Summonds', it was not the poor—just as it was not the poor who eventually took possession of the friaries. But the middle classes of the towns were prepared to sound a note of class war in order to rouse the urban mob to do their 'reforming' work for them; this is striking evidence of the strength of anti-clerical feeling in the towns, where already the merchant oligarchies (who controlled the burgh church as well as the town council) were stopping the saying of mass and inaugurating kirk 'sessions', bodies 'sitting' to manage the burgh church.

The preachers continued to preach, and the more important of them were summoned to Stirling 'to underlie the law' (10 May

1559); whereupon the 'brethren', the Protestant lords and lairds, assembled at Perth, though without armour, to support their preachers. And 'in this meantime that the preachers were summoned', John Knox again returned to Scotland (2 May 1559). At Perth, on 11 May, the eve of 'flitting Friday', he preached a sermon 'vehement against idolatry'. A boy threw a stone; an image was broken; a riot broke loose; and the houses of the Black Friars and the Grey Friars, together with the Charterhouse, were looted and despoiled.

No government could allow such lawlessness to pass unchecked. The regent assembled her forces and marched towards Perth. The Army of the Congregation gathered in arms. The reformation-rebellion had begun.

There was some marching and counter-marching, but little fighting. The queen regent was largely dependent upon her small force of trained French troops, who had earned for her an increasing unpopularity and encouraged the fear, which we now know to be justified, that she would hand Scotland over to become an appendage of France as the Low Countries were of Spain. The Reformers, on the other hand, had no forces comparable with the trained French levies. Nevertheless, by the end of June the Army of the Congregation had succeeded in occupying Edinburgh, while the regent and her French troops fortified themselves in Leith—a useful strategic base for the recapture of Edinburgh as well as a port to which French supplies and reinforcements could be sent.

A series of useless challenges and answers between Edinburgh and Leith now ensued. Wearying of these, the Lords of the Congregation 'deposed' the queen regent, in the names of Francis and Mary (thereby assuming a delegated authority which they did not possess), but also indicating that they had a political motive—to ensure that control of Scotland would remain in Scotland even though (as seemed very probable) the queen of Scots and future kings of Scots lived as French kings in French royal palaces. They transferred the government of the realm to a new 'Great Council', and were joined in September 1559 by an important recruit, the Hamilton heir presumptive, Châtelherault, who had feared to move so long as his son Arran was a 'guest' in France. On his way north from his escape Arran met Cecil and Queen Elizabeth. It was becoming clearer that some at least of those in the Army of the Congregation were fighting to replace a personal union of France and Scotland by at least a permanent Hamilton governorship. Accused by the watchful queen mother of attacking 'authority', they preferred to stress their religious motives and to sharpen their arms for an assault on Leith (October 1559). But the long period of 'challenges and answers' had enabled the French to fortify Leith to some purpose. The assault was repulsed; more than that, the French issued out of Leith and so harassed the Reformers that 'many fled away secretly, and those that did abide (a very few excepted) appeared destitute of counsel and manhood'. The Army of the Congregation retreated in disorder from Edinburgh to Stirling—part going thence to Glasgow and part to Fife.

Now, more than ever, English aid was essential to save the Reformers from disaster and utter defeat. And now, at last, Elizabeth, who had hitherto confined her help to smuggling small sums of money across the Border—some of which had been intercepted—actively intervened. In January 1560 an English fleet under Admiral Winter anchored in the Forth, and so cut the French sea-communications. No further supplies and reinforcements could reach either the regent in Leith or the French troops who had set out to engage the forces of the Reformers in Fife. At the beginning of April an English army, under Lord Grey, crossed the Border, and combined English and Scottish Protestant forces began a second siege of Leith held mainly by the troops of Roman Catholic France.

Hitherto, for many reasons, Elizabeth had been reluctant to intervene openly in the Scottish struggle. If she helped rebellious subjects in another realm might not rebellious subjects in her own realm seek outside help in a like way? One of the leading Scottish reformers was that John Knox, who had written a book against women rulers; and although Knox's book—*The First Blast of the Trumpet against the Monstrous Regiment of Women*—had been directed against the rule of Mary of Guise and Mary Tudor (both Roman Catholics), and although he later wrote to Elizabeth grudgingly conceding that if she humbled her heart she could yet prove herself to be exceptional—like the blessed Deborah in Israel—many of the statements in his work had aroused her natural resentment.[10]

Elizabeth intervened solely in her own interests. Her belated decision to send the much-needed help to the Army of the Congregation—a step that had been constantly urged by Cecil—was dictated by the danger of French support for, and acquisition (by marriage)

M

of, Mary's claim to the English throne. Francis and Mary 'queen of England, Scotland and Ireland', had assumed the English royal arms; and, in July 1559, Francis and Mary had become king and queen of France. To fail to intervene might well give France a control over Scotland that would imperil Elizabeth's throne.

Thus Elizabeth's intervention could be regarded as a purely defensive move; and the treaty of Berwick (February 1560), whereby English aid became a reality,[11] was little more than a treaty of mutual defence. It declared that because the French intended to conquer Scotland and to unite it to the crown of France, therefore Elizabeth, at the request of the Scots, took Scotland under her protection and maintenance, but only for the preservation of its freedoms and liberties and to save it from conquest, and only during the time of the marriage of Francis and Mary and for one year thereafter. English forces were to be sent with all speed into Scotland; and the Scots, in turn, promised to send support to England should England be invaded by France. Finally, and because Elizabeth did not relish the thought of aiding subjects who were in rebellion against their lawful rulers, the Scots testified and declared their due obedience to their queen provided that she and her husband, the king of France, did nothing that tended to the subversion and oppression of the just and ancient liberties of their kingdom. In the whole treaty there was not a word about religion. To Elizabeth the crisis was a political one; and Knox was later to speak of her as 'neither good Protestant nor yet resolute Papist'. It has been well said that English forces took part in the final battle of the Scottish reformation–rebellion purely because Elizabeth was not sure of the validity of her mother's marriage certificate.

Leith, although stoutly defended by the French troops of the queen regent against a new assault and siege by combined English and Scottish forces, was at last starved into surrender. Mary of Guise, mortally sick, had entered the castle of Edinburgh on 1 April for greater security and medical attention, and had died there on the night of 10-11 June. With the arrival in England of commissioners from France authorized to negotiate a peace, who travelled north with similarly authorized English commissioners, the Scottish reformation–rebellion came to an end with the treaty of Edinburgh (July 1560).

The treaty of Edinburgh between England and France recognized Elizabeth's right and title to the English throne; Francis and

Mary were to abstain from using and bearing the title and arms of the sovereign of England and Ireland; the French and the English forces were to be withdrawn from Scotland; and there were to be no future warlike preparations in England against France, or in France against England. Again not a word was said about religion. The treaty was the natural corollary to Elizabeth's defensive intervention; by it she secured the withdrawal of the French forces from Scotland and her recognition, by France, as the lawful queen of England.

In addition to the treaty, by the mediation or pressure of the English representatives certain 'Concessions' were granted to the Scots by the French commissioners in the name of Francis and Mary to settle essentially Scottish questions. By the Concessions the fortifications of Leith were to be destroyed; the French troops there were to be sent home[12] and no French forces were again to be brought into Scotland; no stranger (in effect, no Frenchman) was henceforth to hold office under the crown; there was to be a general act of oblivion, and Francis and Mary were to take no action against any who had joined the Congregation; the estates of Scotland were to meet in August 1560; and finally, on the question of religion, it was granted that, 'Whereas on the part of the nobles and people of Scotland there have been presented certain articles concerning religion and certain other points in which the lords deputies [the French commissioners] would by no means meddle, as being of such importance that they judged them proper to be remitted to the king and queen; therefore the said nobles of Scotland have engaged that in the ensuing convention of estates some persons of quality shall be chosen to repair to their Majesties and remonstrate[13] to them the state of their affairs . . . and to understand their intention and pleasure. . . .'

Thus, while Elizabeth had gained the security and recognition for which her English contingents had fought, the whole question of religion, for which alone many of those in the Army of the Congregation had fought, was left undecided—to be submitted to Francis and Mary for their consideration. But, for Knox and his fellow-preachers, and for many of the lords, lairds, and burgesses who had joined the Army of the Congregation, the whole struggle had been one to secure the 'true religion'. To them, this happy victory, this glorious end, had shown 'how wondrously the light of Christ Jesus had prevailed'. Hence, although religion had been passed by in the treaty of Edinburgh, and virtually passed by in the Concessions, the Reformers were quick to turn a political victory into a religious victory also. To them it was essential to establish the true religion forthwith. There were too many risks inherent in delay: notably, there could be little doubt about the answer that would come from Francis and Mary—if, indeed, they deigned to send any answer at all.

The estates met in August 1560, in accordance with the Concessions, and forthwith, despite the wording of the Concessions, the authority and jurisdiction of the pope were abolished, the celebration of the mass was forbidden, a Confession of Faith (a full statement of Protestant doctrine, drawn up by the ministers and engrossed in the register of parliament) was approved, and all doctrine and practice contrary to the Confession were condemned.

This meeting of the estates (called the 'Reformation Parliament') was attended by over a hundred small barons and lairds—many fervent Protestants—who claimed a right to sit as freeholders of the king, although, as we have seen, neither the act of 1426 nor that of 1428 had ever been fully operative.[14] But the actual wording of the Concessions had been, 'the estates shall be summoned to the parliament according to custom: and it shall be lawful for all those to be present at that meeting who are in use to be present . . .'. Were these small barons and lairds 'in use to be present'? Was the parliament of August 1560 a lawful parliament? More than that, in the Concessions the whole question of religion was to be remitted to Francis and Mary for *their* decision. But parliament itself had legislated in matters of religion. Were these Protestant enactments of the Reformation parliament lawful and valid?

Mary never ratified either the treaty of Edinburgh or the enactments of the Reformation parliament.[15] Thus, throughout the whole of her personal rule from 1561 to 1567 the religious question remained unsettled in law. Shortly after her abdication (or deposition) in 1567, however, another meeting of the estates re-enacted the anti-papal legislation of 1560 and again engrossed the Confession of Faith in the register of parliament; and this time the royal assent was given by the Regent Moray in the name of the one-year-old King James VI. More than that, when the infant king was crowned, the earl of Morton, in the name of the king, took a new coronation oath which included a clause that the sovereign would maintain the true religion and would preserve it to the utmost of his power.

A Protestant church had supplanted the church of Rome; the old alliance with France had been broken; and a new alliance with England had been born. Two Protestant countries, Scotland and England, were drawing together, and the way was being prepared for James VI to succeed Elizabeth and to rule over both realms as a Protestant king.

Nevertheless the Reformation had fallen far short of all that Knox and his fellow ministers had hoped and prayed for. While the Confession of Faith had been engrossed in the register of parliament, the *Book of Discipline*—a plan, drawn up by Knox and others of the ministers, for the establishment of the reformed church, and its endowment out of the wealth that had been bestowed upon the Church of Rome[16]—had been passed by. The old church still retained the larger part of its revenues; its prelates and priests remained undisturbed in their benefices; its structure was still intact. A new faith had been accepted; but the new church had been given neither establishment nor endowment for the furtherance of the faith.

NOTES

1. They had agreed to do all they could to break the alliance between France and Scotland; to hand over Mary into Henry's hands, to be brought up by him until she could be married to Edward; and to help Henry to become the 'director and protector' of the realm of Scotland. Some of them had even signed secret articles that, in the event of Mary's death, they would help Henry to take over the government of Scotland. But although they had taken English gold, Henry was soon to complain that they did little in return.

2. 'Woe be to the Cardinal.'

3. A vivid account of the Reformation by one who played a leading part in the struggle. Although its bias is obvious, it is, nevertheless, remarkably trustworthy in detail.

4. Released early in 1549, Knox became a preacher in England under the Protestant Edward VI. With the accession of the Roman Catholic Mary Tudor he fled to the continent and became a preacher to Protestant congregations—first at Frankfurt-am-Main, and then at Geneva. At Geneva he was attracted by Calvin's religious and political doctrines which were henceforth to influence all his work.

5. By a treaty of 1546 England was holding Boulogne as guarantee for the payment of a French indemnity.

6. 'Which God so conducted that . . . the bullets rebounded from the wall of the Friar Kirk to the wall of Saint Katherine's Chapel, which stood direct foiranent it, and from the wall of the said Chapel to the said Kirk wall again, so oft, that there fell more than an hundred of the French at those two shots only' (*History of the Reformation in Scotland*, ed. Dickinson, i. 106).

7. Notably those at burials—'the corpse present', the 'kirk cow', and 'the grey cloak that haps the bed'; exactions which James V had tried in vain to end or to reduce.

8. See the Table on p. 259.

9. 'Flit' is the Scots word meaning 'remove from a house'.

10. Three brief passages will suffice to explain that resentment:

'To promote a Woman to bear rule, superiority, dominion or empire above any realm, nation or city is repugnant to Nature; is contumely to God, a thing most contrarious to his revealed will and approved ordinance; and, finally, it is the subversion of good order and of all equity and justice.'

'Where Women reign or be in authority, vanity must needs be preferred to virtue; ambition and pride to temperance and modesty; and, finally, avarice must needs devour equity and justice.'

'As for Woman, it is no more possible that she, being set aloft in authority above man, shall resist the motions of pride, than it is able to the weak reed or to the turning weathercock not to bow or turn at the vehemency of the unconstant wind.'

11. Winter's fleet had entered the Forth *before* the conclusion of the treaty of Berwick; but the English army, under Lord Grey, entered Scotland only after the treaty had been signed.

12. A letter from Cecil to the English council tersely comments that the French were glad to be gone; the English were glad to carry them (in English ships); and the Scots were glad to curse them on their way.

13. Represent.

14. Above, pp. 213-14.

15. To have ratified the treaty of Edinburgh would have meant abandoning her claim to the English throne; to have ratified the enactments of the Reformation parliament would have meant abandoning the practice of her religion.

16. See below, p. 368.

CHAPTER 30

Mary Queen of Scots

FOR a whole year—from August 1560 to August 1561—the government appears to have been largely in the hands of the Lord James Stewart, Mary's half-brother, and of the duke of Châtelherault, both important leaders of the victorious Congregation, together with the Secretary, William Maitland of Lethington.

Probably neither the Lord James Stewart[1] nor Châtelherault desired or expected the return of Mary, though if she were to bear a child to Francis the problem of the Scottish succession would become acute. The Lords of the Congregation had thought in 1559 of transferring the crown to Châtelherault—and Knox's *First Blast* may have sought to justify the act; now the conservatives and the Lords united in stressing Châtelherault's rights. Following the meeting of the Reformation parliament, an embassy was sent to England to propose the marriage of Queen Elizabeth to his son, Arran, and stress was laid on the fact that the Hamiltons were heirs presumptive to the Scottish crown; but Elizabeth replied that she was 'not at present disposed' to marry.

In any case these hopes were rudely shattered by the unexpected death of Mary's husband, Francis II, in December 1560, and by Mary's resolve to return to her own country. No longer queen of France, she was still queen of Scots. And what would be the outcome when Mary, brought up in the Roman church, returned to govern a nominally Protestant realm? Châtelherault and Knox were not slow to see the advantages of marrying Mary to Arran and Protestantism.

Lesley states that a number of the Roman Catholic bishops and lords, knowing of Mary's intention to return to govern her own kingdom, sent messengers to her, urging her to land in the north where she would find faithful and true service from all. But the story typifies the attitudes of a later decade. A staunch Catholic like Archbishop Beaton had fled; those supporters of Mary of Guise still left had no stomach for further struggle in defence of Catholicism, though they would join conservative Protestant lords in resisting the claims of Knox and a few other radicals. From a government, and therefore Protestant, Convention the Lord James Stewart went to France to give counsel to the queen; his counsel was that she should 'press no matters of religion'. Perhaps, too, he promised that she could have her own mass privately in her own chapel.[2] On 19 August 1561, Mary, not yet nineteen years old, landed at Leith to take over the government of her native realm.

According to Knox, 'the very face of heaven, the time of her arrival, did manifestly speak what comfort was brought into this country with her, to wit, sorrow, dolour, darkness, and all impiety. For, in the memory of man, that day of the year was never seen a more dolourous face of the heaven than was at her arrival . . . The sun was not seen to shine two days before, nor two days after. That forewarning gave God unto us.' The six years of Mary's personal rule were to close tempestuously, with 'sorrow and dolour' for the queen herself, but she did little that touched reformed religion, or indeed, apart from her private mass, that showed she was a Catholic. Our views of Mary have been too strongly influenced by Knox's determined and misleading harping upon her religion.

On the very first Sunday after Mary's landing a riotous demonstration broke out at Holyrood against the mass that was celebrated in the chapel royal for the queen and her household:[3] and then it was the Lord James Stewart, seeking to compromise, or merely fulfilling a promise he had made to the queen, who held the door against the angry mob. On the following day Mary—probably on the advice of the Lord James—issued a proclamation in which she ordered the state of religion which she found 'publicly and universally standing' at the time of her arrival to be maintained, but in which she also forbade all tumults and interference with her servants and household for any cause whatsoever.

There were murmurings among 'the godly'; but Maitland of Lethington, now Mary's secretary, argued that, with time, Mary might yet be brought round to 'sweet reasonableness'; and a calmer atmosphere soon prevailed. As one ardent reformer declared, 'At the first I heard every man say, "Let us hang the priest"; but after that they had been twice or thrice in the Abbey [of Holyrood, at the queen's court], all that fervency was past. I think there be some enchantment whereby men are bewitched.' And the enchantment was undoubtedly the queen.

It worked because the young queen had enough political sense to accept as her leading counsellors these two men, James Stewart and William Maitland, leading Protestants who, however, rejected the ambitious importuning of Châtelherault and the extreme Protestants. For four years Scotland was governed by a Catholic queen whose exercise of her religion was tolerated by her subjects while she tolerated the establishment of a Protestant church by act of privy council and even of parliament. Too much has been made of her failure to confirm the acts of the Reformation parliament; to refuse to approve the abolition of papal authority and the mass was, despite Knox's dark fears, worlds away from an intention to restore them.

In February 1562 there was compromise with the demands of the leading Reformers, probably supported by lairds, when the privy council agreed to some financial provision for the urgent needs of the reformed church. Hitherto, with the rejection of the *Book of Discipline*, the unreformed clergy, still in legal possession of their benefices, had continued to enjoy their revenues, while the ministers of the reformed church had had no assured incomes and some were living as 'poor amid the poor', dependent upon the benevolence of others. Now, by an act of the privy council, one-third of the revenues of all benefices was to be collected annually and used partly to provide stipends for the ministers and partly for the 'support of the Queen's Majesty'. To Knox this was to give the reformed church only part of one-third of all that which it should enjoy of right. His comment was, 'I see two parts freely given to the Devil [the two-thirds still retained by the holders of Roman benefices— though some had embraced the reformed faith], and the third must be divided between God and the Devil [the one-third to be divided between the ministers and the queen]. Well . . . ere it be long the Devil shall have three parts of the third;[4] and judge you then what God's portion shall be.' Certainly as the years passed by, the queen took more and more of the one-third and less and less was available for the stipends of the ministers.[5] But that was a continuation of the extortionate policies of James V.

When, in 1562, during a progress in the north, the queen met with 'manifest tokens of disobedience' from the Gordons, she allowed the Lord James Stewart to crush the most powerful Roman Catholic family in Scotland. The Lord James, to whom Mary had recently granted the earldom of Moray (though the grant was then kept secret), defeated Huntly (who probably still held the earldom of Moray *de jure*) in a pitched battle at Corrichie. Huntly died on the field, possibly from apoplexy; the Gordons were forfeited; and shortly thereafter the Lord James received a further charter of the earldom of Moray, the grant being now made public. Mary elevated her Protestant half-brother at the expense of the Catholic Huntly because she had relied upon the former to hold in check the radical Protestants, to secure more of the church's wealth for the crown, and to pursue with England the question of Mary's rights there. Only on the last had Lord James and Lethington failed to guide the queen through her difficulties to marked success. In the following year (1563), moreover, Archbishop Hamilton and a number of the Roman clergy were warded for celebrating mass in violation of the proclamation of August 1561. There seemed little to be feared from a queen who crushed Huntly and who allowed the priests of her own church to suffer for their faith.

By the treaty of Edinburgh, Elizabeth had secured France's recognition of her right and title to the English throne. Mary, however, had refused, and continued to refuse, to ratify that treaty, thereby maintaining her claim to be recognized as Elizabeth's rightful successor, a claim which Elizabeth, on her part, equally consistently refused to acknowledge.[6] The attitudes of both queens were natural. Mary regarded herself as the rightful queen of England; if she was willing to accept Elizabeth as the *de facto* queen, surely she could be given recognition of her right, *de jure*, to be Elizabeth's successor. Elizabeth, on the other hand, feared that to acknowledge Mary as her successor would be to strengthen Roman Catholic opposition to her own rule; it might even encourage some zealot to cut short her life and thereby hasten the accession of the legitimist Roman Catholic queen. Slightly to vary her own words, an acknowledgement of Mary's right might be tantamount to wrapping herself in her own winding-sheet.

Thus it is easy to understand why Lethington and Lord James Stewart were unable to secure any form of reciprocal recognition between the two queens. Moreover the difficulties of Lethington and the Lord James lay not only in trying to curb Mary's ambitious claims by some form of compromise agreement, but also in trying to restrain a strong Protestant faction which demanded that Mary should be compelled to embrace the new faith and rule a Protestant country as a Protestant queen.

Preaching at the time of the Parliament in 1563, Knox did not spare his words:

> The Queen, say ye, will not agree with us. Ask ye of her that which by God's word ye may justly require, and if she will not agree with you in God, ye are not bound to agree with her in the Devil. Let her plainly understand so far of your minds; and steal not from your former stoutness in God, and he shall prosper you in your enterprises.

That outspoken passage was evoked by the current rumours of a marriage for the queen. For if Mary were to marry into one of the great Roman Catholic houses—if she were to marry Don Carlos of Spain, as was then bruited, or any of 'the children of France, Spain or Austria'—then the Protestant faith in Scotland (and in England also) might well be gravely imperilled. So, in the same sermon, Knox sounded the warning,

> This, my Lords, will I say, . . . whensoever the Nobility of Scotland professing the Lord Jesus, consents that an infidel (and all Papists are infidels) shall be head to your Sovereign, ye do so far as in ye lieth to banish Christ Jesus from this Realm; ye bring God's vengeance upon the country, a plague upon yourself, and perchance ye shall do small comfort to your Sovereign.

For this sermon Knox was summoned before the queen;[7] and when, angrily, she demanded, 'What have ye to do with my marriage? Or what are ye within this Commonwealth?' there came the quick reply, 'A subject born within the same, Madam. And albeit I neither be earl, lord, nor baron within it, yet has God made me (how abject that ever I be in your eyes), a profitable member within the same.'

Knox's fears were not without foundation. In western Europe the Wars of Religion had begun. The Netherlands were held down by a Spanish army; in France the Huguenots were fighting to avoid suppression. At Trent a General Council of the Roman Church, while calling for reform in the church and a higher zeal for the Roman faith, had also rejected all Protestant doctrine and had called for the extirpation of heresy.

Elizabeth, too, was not blind to the dangers that threatened. She left Mary in no doubt that any marriage with France, Spain, or Austria would inevitably mean hostility between England and Scotland. And yet the only alternative that Elizabeth proposed was marriage to her own favourite, Lord Robert Dudley, earl of

Leicester—whom she was probably reluctant to lose, and to whom, as merely a newly elevated subject, Mary was not in the least attracted.

For a whole year the marriage of the queen of Scots was the subject of diplomatic activity, rumour, and counter-rumour. Then, in the autumn of 1564, Elizabeth persuaded Mary to allow the forfeited Matthew, fourth earl of Lennox, to return to Scotland;[8] and his son, Darnley, followed early in 1565. What Elizabeth's motives were, we shall never know. The Lennox Stewarts were suspected of trafficking with Papists, and, for a time, the earl and his wife had been imprisoned on that suspicion. If Mary (now twenty-two) were to fall in love with 'the long lad' Darnley (aged twenty), a marriage between Mary and Darnley would unite the two nearest claimants to Elizabeth's throne:[9] and both were Roman Catholics—but better a marriage with Darnley than a marriage into one of the great continental Roman Catholic houses.

Or was Elizabeth's anger after the marriage genuine, because it had strengthened the claim of Mary and Darnley to her throne? Certainly by announcing that she would not nominate her own successor, Elizabeth had yielded the reins on Mary which she had held, and left the queen free to choose her own fate. We shall never be sure of Elizabeth. But Darnley arrived in Scotland in February 1565 and on 29 July 1565 Mary married him according to Roman Catholic rites.[10]

Between these dates there was more than an onset of infatuation. Men would obey a queen only when she was advised by men. And so for four years James Stewart, earl of Moray, had been able to act as quasi-king in Scotland; marriage with Darnley represented freedom from that dependence on Moray, the chance for Mary to confer the crown matrimonial upon Darnley, and to govern as 'Henry [Darnley] and Mary King and Queen of Scots'. For months Mary hesitated over the step, yet each week of doubt and each sign of affection for the sick Darnley served to weaken the loyalty of Moray (who now made a 'band' with Châtelherault) and Lething-ton. Withdrawing from court, they sought armed support for a demonstration against the match.

To allay alarm and to disarm opposition, Mary issued two proclamations stating that she had no intention of molesting her good subjects in the freedom of their consciences and religion.

Urged by Moray a number of the Protestant lords none the less convened at Stirling, in arms, determined to demand complete assurances for the maintenance of the reformed faith before they would give their consent to the queen's marriage. Mary, however, had no intention of asking for their consent: and forestalled their demand (and the arrival of a papal dispensation for the marriage) by a decision that the deed had best be done quick. She did not wait for a parliament to authorize a title for her husband but issued a proclamation, by heralds, that Henry, Lord Darnley, should be 'named and styled' king; on the following day she married her Henry; and on the next day the proclamation was made again when, of all those who were present, not one so much as said 'Amen', save only Darnley's father, Lennox, who cried out, 'God save his Grace'. That prayer was to be unanswered.

These details are significant. It was not simply, as Buchanan avers, that heralds had been given the functions of council and parliament. Nor was it simply the old jealousy of a noble house raised to kingship. There was something more. The sudden marriage with Darnley, taking place within six months of his arrival in Scotland, affected too many interests, and too many persons and parties. The queen had married a Lennox Stewart, and the Hamiltons saw an end to their long-held hopes of kingship. For the Lord James Stewart, earl of Moray, and for Lethington, the marriage spelled the end of compromise, the end of their wishful thinking that Mary could be 'allured into sweet reasonableness', the end, too, of their 'guidance' of the queen. For Knox and all those who were fervent for the Protestant faith, the marriage was a union of Papists, and was to be feared for all that might follow. But, for Mary herself, her marriage meant a new chance—a chance to take everything into her own hands, to be free from the old restraints of Moray and Lethington, and from the unwelcome advice of Knox.

But no longer were the Protestant lords united as of old. Moray and Lethington, by their previous policy of appeasement and compromise, had split the ranks of the Army of the Congregation of Christ Jesus. Some had supported them; others had opposed them, foretelling that no good would come from shaking hands with the Devil. Long, long ago, Moray had guarded the chapel door of the queen's mass; long, long ago, Knox had urged that the queen should be compelled to embrace the new faith. Knox had claimed the right of subjects to resist the idolatry of their rulers; Moray had opposed him. Knox and Moray had become strangers to one another.

And now two armed forces were in the field—one led by Moray, the other by the queen. On 26 August 1565 those Protestant lords and lairds still willing to fight under Moray and Châtelherault (though not solely for the old cause of the 'true Evangel') rode into Edinburgh. They were only some 1,200 strong. Hearing that the queen with her supporters was riding to meet them, they beat a hasty retreat. Then followed the 'Chase-about-Raid' when, however much her followers might weary, 'the queen's courage increased man-like, so much, that she was ever with the foremost'. And the end of the queen's chase was that Moray and his associates were compelled to flee into England, where, later, Elizabeth, still fearful of subjects in rebellion against the lawful authority, and yet probably angry because in this instance they had failed, gave them a scolding reception and refused their request for aid.

Mary was now supreme, with all power in her own hands. And now, tragically, she discovered that Darnley was not fit to be a king. Devoid of manly qualities, inconstant, unstable, and weak, he was also headstrong, intolerant, and proud. Bitterly disappointed, Mary refused to give him any royal authority for to confer the 'crown matrimonial' which was the sign that he was truly king would have meant that, if Mary predeceased him and left no issue, Darnley would continue to reign as king. And, in discovering the mistake of her marriage, she found herself deprived of the guidance of Darnley and the nobility alike.

A proclamation issued at Dumfries by Moray and his associates during the Chase-about-Raid had declared that they were moved to take action because of the evident danger to the Protestant faith and also because of Mary's neglect of the advice and counsel of her nobility and her reliance upon 'strangers . . . men of base degree'. Those strangers of base degree included her musician-secretary, David Riccio ('her trusty servant Davy', or 'that poltroon and vile knave Davie', as Knox called him); and Riccio was now viewed with a suspicion probably greater than he deserved. To the Protestants he was a papal agent; to the nobility he was an upstart whom they found 'always speaking with her Majesty'; to Darnley he was a rival, the man to whom the queen gave confidences which she denied to her husband.

Darnley had even baser thoughts. Jealous, jaundiced, and unstable, he entered into a plot with the Protestant lords who had been driven out in the Chase-about-Raid and who were due to be forfeited in life, lands, and goods in a parliament that was to be held on 12 March 1566. A 'band' was made: the Protestant lords were to be pardoned and allowed to return to Scotland; 'the religion' (that is, the Protestant faith) was to be maintained; Darnley was to be given the crown matrimonial and, if Mary were to die without issue, Darnley was to succeed to the throne; if necessary, the queen was to be coerced into agreement; and, as a first step, Riccio was to be murdered.

How far the Protestant lords were sincere in their promise of the crown matrimonial is doubtful; but the first step was duly taken on the evening of Saturday, 9 March 1566. James Douglas, fourth earl of Morton, secured the approaches to Holyrood; and Darnley, Lord Lindsay of the Byres, Lord Ruthven and his son, and others associated with them (but not the careful Moray) gathered within the palace itself. Then, when Mary was at supper in her private chamber, they burst into the room, dragged the doomed Riccio from behind the very skirts of the queen and, to the accompaniment of angry recriminations between Mary and Darnley, stabbed him to death in an adjoining chamber, the king's own dagger (said to have been used by Ruthven) being left sticking in the dead man's breast. On the following day, Sunday 10 March, Darnley, by proclamation, discharged the parliament which was due to meet on the Tuesday to pass doom of forfeiture on Moray and those who had been with him in the Chase-about-Raid; and, on the evening of the same Sunday, Moray and his friends rode into Edinburgh.

So far all seemed to have gone according to plan. On Monday 11 March, Mary, virtually a prisoner in her own palace, received Moray and his adherents. Openly she promised forgiveness; secretly she vowed revenge. She planned escape. She easily persuaded the cowardly and unstable Darnley to desert his fellow-conspirators and to take her part. In the early hours of Tuesday 12 March, Mary and Darnley slipped out of Holyrood and rode to Dunbar—a castle belonging to James Hepburn, fourth earl of Bothwell. From there the queen quickly rallied her supporters. On Sunday 17 March, in face of the forces she had gathered, Moray and his friends retreated from Edinburgh; the murderers of Riccio—Morton, Lindsay, and the Ruthvens—fled to England; Knox fled to the west country; and on Monday 18 March Mary made a triumphant re-entry into the capital.

For a second time two armed forces had opposed each other; and for a second time Mary had prevailed, cleverly dividing her enemies by pardoning Moray and the other lords of the Chase-about-Raid while Morton, Lindsay, and Ruthven were proclaimed traitors.

To the queen, Darnley had denied all knowledge of the plot that had led to the murder of Riccio, and had confessed only to being 'art and part' in the home-bringing of Moray without Mary's knowledge and consent. But Darnley had deserted his fellow-conspirators and had connived at the queen's escape; nay more, he had fled with her. His fellow-conspirators retaliated by revealing to Mary his full complicity in the plot. Mary, who had previously guessed all, now knew all. And that meant that she knew not only of Darnley's complicity in the death of Riccio but also of his endeavour to gain the crown matrimonial by murder and coercion. Perhaps, too, she wondered how far her brutal husband had hoped to go. At the time of Riccio's murder, and that terrifying scene when armed men with drawn daggers had broken into her private room, she was six months pregnant.[11] Had Darnley, the desirer of the crown matrimonial, basely hoped for a miscarriage that might result in a still-born child, her own death, and kingship for himself? Hitherto she had simply despised Darnley. Now she hated him.

It is not difficult to sympathize with the unhappy queen. Young—she was not yet twenty-four years old—proud, and gifted, she found herself in an environment that had taxed the strongest kings. To old contentions was now added that of religion. Mary had need of a consort who was strong, trustworthy, and wise: a consort who could give her sound advice in difficulty, and comfort and strength in time of need; but also a consort who would temper any headstrong ambition and youthful pride. Instead, she had married Darnley, who was cowardly and callous, brutal and base.

Henceforward in the tangled skein of evidence that has come down to us there is one continuous thread—Mary's loathing and hatred of Darnley: increased, perhaps, by the knowledge that his body was now diseased through licentious indulgence. But a divorce might affect the legitimacy of her infant son; and she is said to have bewailed that she saw 'no outgait'. Nor was the queen alone in her hatred. Darnley was hated by well-nigh everyone else. By Moray,

Lethington, Bothwell, and many another lord he was hated for his insolence and arrogance; by the fugitive murderers of Riccio he was hated for betrayal. Certainly another plot was hatched; and, although we may never know the truth of all its ramifications, there was now a suspicious sequence of events.

On 20 December 1566 the queen, by act of council, showed a new tenderness towards the ministers of the reformed church, assigning towards their stipends a definite portion of the 'thirds' and giving to the reformed church the right of collection. On 23 December, by a grant under the privy seal, she restored to John Hamilton, archbishop of St. Andrews, his old consistorial jurisdiction—a jurisdiction which included marriage cases—and discharged the commissary courts which had been established in 1564 from exercising their jurisdiction with the diocese of St. Andrews. The next day, 24 December, Mary pardoned Morton and a large number of those who had been associated in the murder of Riccio, allowing them to return to Scotland.

At this time Mary was probably hoping to end her marriage by act of parliament or consistory. In January, however, she revoked the archbishop's powers, evidently despairing because divorce (i.e. annulment) would bastardize her son. It has been argued that the queen had taken Bothwell as an adulterous lover and, discovering that she was again pregnant, hastened to cover her tracks by a reconciliation with Darnley; but the balance of evidence seems to be against the pregnancy and Bothwell was as yet no more than one of the ambitious men, Moray among them, by whom she was surrounded.

And so we do not know, and shall never know, who laid the powder and who twisted the garrotte on the night of 9–10 February 1567, when Kirk o' Field, where Darnley was lodging, was 'blown up wi' pouder' and the king was found, strangled to death, in the adjoining gardens. There may even have been a plot to blow up the queen; but it seems that contemporaries were agreed that Bothwell was guilty, and the politic thing to do was to try him. Yet to Mary that would probably be the final deliverance of power back into the hands of Moray and Lethington, and, reluctantly or with growing willingness, she drifted into dependence upon the man whose coarse vigour marked him out as her husband's murderer. He was acquitted of the murder by the device of preventing Lennox from prosecuting the case, and on 19 April 1567 he openly canvassed the nobility

(Moray was carefully in London) for their consent to his marriage to the queen.

On 24 April, when Mary was on her way back to Edinburgh from Stirling (where she had been to see her infant son) she was intercepted by Bothwell and taken to his castle at Dunbar. Whether or not she was taken willingly we shall never know. Her friends, equally with her later accusers, had noted an undue familiarity towards Bothwell in recent months, and the evidence relating to her 'abduction', although contradictory, suggests willingness rather than the reverse. Thus though it seems likely that the twins of whom Mary miscarried in July were conceived at this time, all that can be said with reasonable certainty is that Mary, in her reaction against Darnley, had been attracted to Bothwell, whose divorce from his wife was completed early in May.

On 6 May Bothwell rode back into Edinburgh with the queen, 'leading the queen's Majesty by the bridle as captive'. John Craig, Knox's colleague in Edinburgh, was asked to proclaim the banns of marriage between Mary and Bothwell, but refused to do so without written warrant from the queen. When Mary's warrant was brought to him, charging him to make the proclamation, he did so but, at the same time, publicly denounced the marriage he proclaimed.[12] On 15 May 1567 Mary and Bothwell were married at Holyrood by the bishop of Orkney according to Protestant rites.

This hasty marriage, three months after Darnley's murder, shocked public opinion. Whether or not Mary knew of the plot that had culminated in Darnley's murder, and whatever that plot was, and whether or not Bothwell had seduced her and placed her under constraint, she had married the man whom popular opinion had branded as the murderer of the king, and the man who, within the last fortnight, had been divorced in an Edinburgh court for adultery. Even the pope, in the following month, gave his decision to have no further communication with the queen of Scots 'unless, indeed, in times to come he shall see some better sign of her life and religion'.

Mary undoubtedly married Bothwell of her own will but at his persuasion, and perhaps hastened by pregnancy. Yet she might surely have found another—perhaps even a Hamilton—father for her new child, and the truth seems to be that she chose the unseemly Bothwell not because, or not only because, she was in love with him, but because he seemed to stand firm against the jostling of Lennox, Hamilton, Moray, and those others who would not accord to a queen the respect and obedience given to James V and James VI.

And so for the third time in Mary's brief personal reign two armed forces opposed each other. The 'Confederate Lords' declared that they were in arms to deliver Mary from Bothwell and her enemies, to secure the person of the young prince, and to prosecute the murderers of the king. Exactly one month after her marriage to Bothwell, Mary surrendered to the Confederate Lords at Carberry, as her army melted away (15 June 1567), and after urging Bothwell to make good his escape.[13]

The queen was imprisoned by the lords in Lochleven castle, and there, on 24 July 1567, not long after her miscarriage, she was compelled to demit the crown to her infant son James, to appoint her half-brother, the earl of Moray, as regent, and to appoint certain lords to act until Moray could be recalled from France.[14] Five days later (29 July 1567) the one-year-old James VI was crowned, and in December 1567 a parliament, held by the regent Moray, ratified the action taken by the lords at Lochleven.

Less than a year later, on 2 May 1568, the queen escaped from Lochleven and made her way westwards to the Hamilton country, where she hoped for Hamilton support against the Lennox Stewarts now represented by the infant king.[15] Defeated at Langside (13 May 1568), she fled over the Border into England, expecting Elizabeth's assistance in procuring her restoration.

Naturally Elizabeth found Mary's presence in England disconcerting. But Mary was a sister-sovereign who sought asylum from rebellious subjects—and it made little difference that they were Protestant while Mary was—what? She dare not allow Mary to travel to the continent to raise the Catholic powers, and yet could not well detain her without some action on her behalf. This move, undertaken at Mary's request, was an inquiry into the actions of the 'rebellious' Scots. At York, and later at Westminster and Hampton Court, commissioners appointed by Elizabeth heard at wearisome length the charge of 'rebellion' brought by Mary against her subjects, and the defence by Moray and his adherents that Mary was unfit to rule her kingdom. Now, suddenly, the casket-letters between Mary and Bothwell were produced; but, since the originals 'disappeared' a few years later, leaving us with translations only, and since it is impossible to check their statements against evidence that we know to be trustworthy, the question as to whether or not they were genuine must still be held 'not proven'. The production of the letters, however, so besmirched Mary's character that it was virtually impossible for Elizabeth to intervene to restore her former honour and estate—an inevitable outcome of which Moray cannot have been unaware. Finally, on 10 January 1569, Cecil made a non-committal statement on behalf of Elizabeth which gave leave to Moray and his adherents to return to Scotland 'in the same estate' as that in which they were when they came to England—that is, Moray was to return as regent for the infant James VI: and that meant that Mary was to remain in England, to all intents and purposes a prisoner.

Yet she was not without hope of reconciliation and release, for many who were moderate Protestants and who had risen against her marriage, had not wished her deposition. She came to accept the need for a divorce from Bothwell, and even made Protestant devotional gestures. Thus, despite the rising of the English northern earls in October 1569, which included among its aims the release of Mary, Elizabeth was no warm supporter of the devious Moray. The queen's supporters still held some strongholds and the regent was performing an elaborate political balancing act when in January 1570 he was assassinated by a Hamilton in Linlithgow; a small English force, in retaliation for a Border raid, seized the opportunity to harry the Hamilton lands; and Archbishop Hamilton, taken prisoner at the capture of Dumbarton castle (held by Lord Fleming in the name of the queen), was hanged, without respect to his office or his age, for art and part in the murder of Moray (April 1571). Now open civil war was raging between the 'king's-men' and the 'queen's-men'. In an attempt by the queen's men to break up a convention of the king's men, at Stirling, in September 1571, the new regent, the earl of Lennox (Darnley's father), was killed. His successor as regent, the earl of Mar, died just over a year after his appointment, and was succeeded by the earl of Morton (1572). There was little quarter on either side, though gradually the king's men prevailed until at last Edinburgh castle, held by Kirkcaldy of Grange, was the only important stronghold still in the hands of Mary's supporters.

Then, once more, as in 1560, Elizabeth actively intervened. Mary had lost patience and looked now for release to English Catholics and to Philip II of Spain; the Ridolfi plot of 1572 brought home to

Elizabeth some apparent dangers of a successful bid for power by the queen's men in Scotland. And so for a second time an English army crossed the Border to help in the siege of a Scottish stronghold. In May 1573 English artillery helped to batter down Edinburgh castle; and Kirkcaldy of Grange, a brave soldier, an old companion with Knox in the French galleys, but now too loyal to a doubtful cause, was hanged.

Elizabeth's decision to intervene, and her subsequent support of Morton in the regency, up to the very time of his execution in 1581,[16] were clear pointers that she had determined to keep Mary in England. A friendly north was essential. On the continent, the wars of religion were being fought with bitterness and no mercy. Already the pope had declared Elizabeth excommunicate and deposed, thereby encouraging rebellion against her authority and an attack upon her realm, and in 1580 another pope gave a ruling that the assassination of the English queen would be no sin. Thus, when William of Orange, the Dutch Protestant leader, was assassinated in 1584, excitement in England, and fear for the life of Elizabeth, led to the Bond and Act of Association for the safety of the queen. If there were to be an attempt on Elizabeth's life, then the person in whose interest the attempt was made, or who was privy to the attempt, was to be pursued to death.

Mary was now more strictly guarded, but still hoped for release. After sixteen years of imprisonment it is little wonder that she clutched at any scheme that offered her a chance of freedom again. In 1585 Anthony Babington held out that prospect of release. His plot was stupid, he himself the most stupid of conspirators. Walsingham played with him as a cat plays with a mouse; but, in the intercepted correspondence, Mary had approved of the assassination of Elizabeth. Her fate was sealed. Elizabeth might say she would have been glad of 'some other way' of dealing with the unhappy Mary Stewart; but parliament, council, and people demanded justice, and Elizabeth finally signed the death warrant. On 4 February 1587 (unknown to the still wavering Elizabeth), the English council sent the warrant to Fotheringay, and on 8 February Mary died on the scaffold there. It was the only solution. Mary was too dangerous to be alive. Roman Catholic might was gathering for its greatest trial of strength with Elizabeth and England. Whether or not justice was served at Fotheringay, expedience demanded the death of Mary Stewart.

James VI, approaching the manly age of twenty-one, played an ignoble part. He was determined to succeed Elizabeth on the English throne, and he had her vague promise that she would not prejudge his title. Although in turns he both prayed and threatened, in the end he silently acquiesced in his mother's death. James could not forget that Mary's claim to the English throne came before his own; more than that, the success of a Roman Catholic invasion (for which the Spanish shipyards were known to be already at work) might even restore Mary to the throne on which he sat. With James VI also, expedience prevailed.

NOTES

1. He was a natural son of James V by Margaret Erskine, daughter of John, fourth Lord Erskine.

2. See the account of the instructions given to Lord James (Knox's *History*, ed. Dickinson, i. 354–5); though that account may have been coloured by the light of subsequent events.

3. Possibly a Protestant service had been or was being held in the adjoining Abbey church which was then in use as a parish church for Canongate.

4. That is, none of the one-third would be available for the ministers.

5. The total of the one-third varied from year to year, owing to deductions, remissions, and exceptions; roughly, it amounted to about £72,000, of which at first about £26,000 was allowed to the ministers. The latter sum steadily decreased, and, moreover, the diminishing sum had to be allocated to an increasing number of ministers, exhorters, and readers.

6. By Henry VIII's will, and by act of parliament, the succession went to the issue of Henry's younger sister Mary, and not to the issue of his elder sister Margaret. If Elizabeth were to die without issue, then the crown of England was due to pass to a Seymour (see the Table on p. 259). Or was Henry VIII's will, with its accompanying confirmation by parliament, irrevocable? Could not the throne of England pass to Mary, queen of Scots, the descendant of his elder sister Margaret? The situation was complex and dangerous; and, had Elizabeth not recovered from an attack of small-pox in 1562, England might have been torn by a civil war between those who favoured the Seymours and a Protestant succession and those who favoured Mary Stewart and a return to the Roman faith.

7. This was Knox's fourth and final interview with Mary. Although the accounts all come from Knox's own pen (in his *History*) certain notable passages in the earlier interviews deserve quotation. In the first interview (4 September 1561), after Knox, in the pulpit of St. Giles, had thundered against the mass, he had argued that subjects might resist their Princes in matters of religion; to which Mary, 'amazed', had answered, 'Well, then, I perceive that my subjects shall obey you [Knox], and not me; and shall do what they list, and not what I command: and so must I be subject to them, and not they to me.' To which came Knox's reply that he sought only 'that both princes and subjects obey God', which, to

him, meant 'embrace the Protestant faith'. The second interview (15 December 1562) came after Knox had preached against the vanity of princes and the danger that they were more exercised in their delights (including the queen's dancing) than in reading and hearing God's word; and when, at his dismissal from the interview, some had muttered, 'He is not afraid', he had answered, 'Why should the pleasing face of a gentlewoman effray me? I have looked in the faces of many angry men, and yet have not been afraid above measure.' At the third interview (in April 1563), when the queen had asked Knox to use his influence to prevent the Roman Catholics in the west from being punished for observing their own rites, Knox had reminded her that princes and subjects alike were bound to observe the laws, that the 'Sword of Justice is God's', and that if the ruler failed to do justice, then the servants of God [the Protestants] could do so.

So far as is known Knox never preached before Queen Mary in St. Giles; though he did preach at Darnley there.

8. Lennox had gone to England in 1544 where, later that year, he married Margaret daughter of Archibald, sixth earl of Angus, and Margaret Tudor (see the Table on p. 237). He had remained in England, had entered Henry VIII's service, and had been given English estates. As a result, he was declared guilty of treason and forfeited.

9. See the Table on p. 259.

10. Mary and Darnley were both grandchildren of Margaret Tudor (see the Table on p. 237), and, since they were so closely related to one another, a papal dispensation was necessary to enable them to marry. Mary, however, was so anxious for the marriage of her choice that she could not wait for the dispensation and, when it was granted, it had to be antedated. It is also to be noted that the dispensation was granted on a promise by Mary and Darnley that they would defend the Roman faith to the utmost of their power, but, as it happens, their marriage and its aftermath actually freed Scotland from the danger of a counter-reformation supported by France or Spain.

11. Her son, James VI, was born on 19 June 1566.

12. The fearless Craig also denounced Bothwell before the privy council, referring to the laws relating to adultery and ravishing, the suspicion of collusion between Bothwell and his wife (the Lady Jean Gordon), the sudden divorce, the new proclamation of marriage to the queen, and lastly the suspicions that had been raised in connection with Darnley's death which Mary's marriage to Bothwell would confirm. His account can be read in the record of the General Assembly for 30 December 1567 (*Booke of the Universall Kirk*, i. 115).

13. Bothwell fled north and was sheltered for a while in Spynie Castle by his kinsman, the bishop of Moray. Thence he made his way to Orkney and to Shetland and from there to Norway. Having no papers, his ship was taken and he was placed in custody as a privateer. Taken to Bergen, he was confronted by the Lady Anne Throndssön, whom he had married in Denmark in 1560, and who now accused him of desertion. The authorities, not knowing what action to take, kept him in confinement. He died in prison, in 1578, after a long illness and with his mind deranged.

14. He had left Edinburgh for St. Andrews the day before Darnley's murder — possibly knowing that the king was to be killed, but possibly not knowing the manner of the killing. Although he later returned to Edinburgh, he left Scotland

for France about the middle of April. It is impossible not to be suspicious of Moray, who was so conveniently absent at every crisis.

15. It should be remembered that, if Mary were not restored, and if James VI died, as lawful king of Scotland, without an heir, the crown would pass to Darnley's brother, Charles, to the exclusion of the Hamiltons.

16. Morton was regent from 1572 until 1581, though with diminished authority after 1578. He ruled with 'a judicious mixture of severity and conciliation' maintaining good relations with England, but failing to stifle the Melvillian movement in the church (see below, p. 370), and to restore the disordered finances of government (G. Donaldson, *Scotland, James V-James VII*, 166–70).

CHAPTER 31

The Crown and the Kirk

I T may be said that Mary's brief personal reign was little more than an interlude which has acquired unwarranted attention from the fast-moving drama of its closing months. An interlude: for, with the deposition of Mary in 1567, the reformation settlement of 1560 was at once confirmed, and the Confession of Faith was re-engrossed in the register of parliament.[1]

Yet although in 1567, as in 1560, the Confession of Faith was approved, the *Book of Discipline*, which had been drafted by Knox and his fellow ministers in 1560 and examined by a General Assembly in 1560 and by a Convention of the Lords in January 1561,[2] was passed by in both 1561 and 1567. The *Book of Discipline*, which would have devoted the wealth of the old church to the work of the church reformed—in stipends for the ministers, in the furtherance of education, and for the relief of the poor—did not commend itself to the greater part of the lords. We may say that 'faith' was not followed by 'works'; we may agree with Knox that 'avariciousness would not suffer this corrupt generation to approve . . . the Policy . . . of the godly ministers'; and yet, looking back, we can now see that the schemes advocated in the *Book of Discipline* were so far-reaching as to be impossible of immediate achievement. The wonder is that so much of the Book was realized in the long run.

Like the Confession of Faith, the *Book of Discipline* claimed to be firmly based on the Word of God.[3] In it, Knox visualized church and state working hand-in-hand. With the people 'all professing Christ Jesus' and all subject to a ruler who would rule 'according to the law of God', church and state would be the twin pillars of God's house on earth. The state must bring the laws of the land into conformity with God's Law revealed in Scripture, supporting the church by punishing adulterers, profaners of the sacraments and of the Sabbath, as well as by supporting education. Yet the difficulties in fulfilling the Book's 'Policy' showed that in Scotland, as in the 'perfect city' of Geneva, a harmonious Christian commonwealth was not to be easily created.

The foundation of the Reformers' thinking in the *Book of Discipline* was the church as it really existed for the Christian believer—not a great international organization, but a local congregation to which must be ministered the Evangel (the Bible) and the sacraments. And so each minister was to be elected by the congregation of the church he was to serve, and was to be examined in 'life and manners, doctrine and knowledge'. To assist each minister (and principally in maintaining religious discipline), elders chosen from the congregation of the church, were to be elected annually. For collecting and administering the revenues of the church, deacons were to be elected similarly. And the elders and deacons were to report on the life, manners, study, and diligence of the minister, once a year, to the Superintendent. The Superintendents were nominated in 1561 by the state,[4] but the office was that of minister and future Superintendents were to be elected. There has been much controversy over the intention and practice of this office which was well known in Reformed churches on the continent, and yet which seems to savour of a lingering episcopacy. The facts seem to be that by 1559 there were well-established Reformed kirks in the large towns attracting townspeople and near-by lairds. But rural parishes were unreformed and unlikely to be reformed except by vigorous initiative from the ministers of these burgh churches—and in revising the *Book of Discipline* in 1560 the problem was met by recourse to the principle of supervision (*episkope*) for which there was ample New Testament authority, and the office of Superintendent introduced. The countryside was to be assigned into dioceses within each of which a minister from a leading town as Superintendent was to plant and erect churches; he was to be a preacher, expounding in the different churches within his diocese; and, as he passed from place to place in his diocese, he was to examine 'the life, diligence and behaviour of the ministers, the order of their churches, and the manners of the people', and to consider the provision for the poor and the instruction provided for the youth.

There is much, too, in the Book which supplements the Confession of Faith in prescribing the 'policy' or conduct of the minister and his congregation in matters spiritual: the hours and manner of daily prayer, of preaching, catechizing, and ministration of the sacraments. Thus the Lord's Table was to be administered four times yearly (to avoid superstitious confusion with the mass) after examination of those admitted, who should be able to recite the Lord's Prayer, the Creed, and the Ten Commandments; in similar way there is provision for the seemly conduct of marriages and burials, and for the 'prophesying or interpreting of Scripture', the weekly public 'exercise' at which ministers and other learned men might elucidate by exposition and discussion (but not contention) the meaning of God's Word. This reformed church is no silent witness to His truth; before all things the minister must proclaim and preach the Evangel. To Knox and his colleagues the worst of all the offences of the bishops of the unreformed church was that they were '*dumb* dogs'.

In its sections dealing with education, the Book stressed the necessity for the education of youth under the supervision of the church. Every church (that is, every parish) was to have a school-master able to teach at least grammar and the Latin tongue. In rural parishes, where this might not be possible, the minister or reader was to give elementary education and to act as schoolmaster. In 'notable towns', and especially in the head burghs of dioceses, there were to be 'colleges', with paid teachers, providing courses in Latin, Greek, Logic, and Rhetoric. The three existing universities—St. Andrews, Glasgow, and Aberdeen—were to be maintained and endowed; and the existing degree courses were to be revised so that students, having gained a background in Arts, could specialize in divinity, medicine, or law. In the home there was to be systematic reading of the Bible, while every head of a household was to ensure that his children, family, and servants were instructed in the principles of the Christian religion. And the whole object of educa-tion was clearly defined: that men might be the better able to serve the church and the commonwealth.

The proposals relating to the poor were left somewhat vague and ill-defined, but the relief of poverty was clearly laid upon the church. The poor were to return to their native parishes and there the deacons of the parish churches were to make arrangements for their support.

Thus there was sensible attention to social needs. There were to be variable stipends for the ministers—for, while all of them would require money for books, some would be bachelors while others would have wives and families, and some would need to travel more than others; there were to be 'educational allowances' for the children of ministers, and pensions for ministers' widows and orphans; there were to be variable university fees, according to the rank of the parent and his capacity to pay; and there were to be university bursaries for the poor.

All this, however, could be done only through the transfer of the vast wealth of ecclesiastical benefices. The stipends of the Superintendents and the revenues of the universities were to come from the rents and feu-duties derived from the land-holdings of the bishoprics. The ministers, the schools, and the poor were to be supported by the teinds (or tithes) which were still to be paid, but which were now to be 'reasonably taken' and paid direct to the parish, and not to some 'appropriator' such as a monastery. The rents and feu-duties of the monastic houses were not included in the scheme—because they had already largely fallen into the hands of the laity and were now largely irrecoverable.

But these essential financial proposals were undoubtedly the main reason for the failure of the state to accept the 'godly policy'. In most instances a bishopric or monastery had arranged with a 'tacksman' that, in return for paying a lump sum, he could collect both its teinds and its land-rents in this or that district. Moreover, hundreds of parish churches (each with its teinds and often with land-endowments as well) had been assigned to cathedral chapters or monastic houses. Thus the problem of separating the teinds (for the payment of ministerial stipends and the maintenance of the schools and the poor) from the land-rents (for the support of the superintendents and the universities), and the further problem of ensuring that local teinds were paid direct to the local parish minister, were probably beyond the administrative capacities of the time. Even some seventy years later, in the opening years of the reign of Charles I, a statesmanlike scheme to evolve some order in the payment of teinds brought upon the king the odium of ministers and laymen alike.

In 1560 the jurisdiction of the pope was abolished, the mass proscribed, and a Protestant Confession of Faith accepted; but bishops and priests were still left undisturbed in their benefices and the monastic houses were not dissolved nor were the monks dispersed. Too many of the lords were busy becoming commendators of monastic houses, or had other interests at stake. Thus, while the bishops, abbots (laicized as commendators), and priests of the Roman church performed no spiritual office but still drew all, or, after 1562, two-thirds of, the revenues of the benefices, the ministers of the reformed church preached the new faith but lived largely on the 'benevolence of others'. In effect, two churches existed side by side—one, silenced and well-endowed; the other, active and miserably poor. And the active reformed church was steadily multiplying its ministers and kirk sessions.

Despite the financial obstacles and the refusal of the government to nominate more than five Superintendents (leaving bishops who had accepted reform in charge of their dioceses), much of the *Book of Discipline* was put into effect. Ministers were gradually found from the ranks of the old clergy (including unbeneficed chaplains), from the universities, and from the educated laity. They were indeed on occasion disciplined by their congregations; the 'exercises' were held. Elders and deacons were elected and met in session to do the work outlined for them in the Book. This Kirk Session is very occasionally mentioned in the Book as the church council, though by 1559 it was integral to the life of the local church. In the same way the council of the national church, sketchily referred to in the Book, was assumed to be a part of the harmonious commonwealth envisaged in 1560. The first such General Assembly seems to have met in July 1560, and certainly from December 1560 the kirk met twice annually in Assembly for the rest of Mary's reign, taking to itself, for example, the appointment of 'commissioners' where the state would not appoint Superintendents. It was a council of those in the church and not merely of ministers or ministers and elders; the lords and lairds who came did so, it seems, as lords and lairds, just as they came to parliament.

Not until Mary had been deposed and Moray was regent were steps taken to ensure that as the benefices of the old church fell vacant they would be filled by ministers of the church reformed.[5] Accordingly it was enacted that as parish churches fell vacant their patrons were to present 'qualified persons'—that is, ministers of the reformed faith—for examination and admission by the Superintendents, thus drastically amending the rights of congregations in favour of the rights of property. Four years later, in January 1572, by what has been called the 'Concordat of Leith', it was agreed that henceforth as episcopal sees fell vacant they were to be filled by bishops nominated by the crown but examined and admitted by a 'Chapter' composed of ministers; but the new bishops were to be subject to the General Assembly in all things spiritual.

The Concordat of Leith received the qualified approval of Knox, and yet, even before he died that same year (November 1572), he had seen that the appointments of these new reformed bishops could be subject to abuse. And, under the regent Morton (who assumed office on the day of Knox's death), the appointments of the new bishops were blatantly accompanied by agreements under which part of the episcopal revenues were diverted to secular purposes or secular pockets, while rural ministers were still living as 'poor amid the poor'. There may have been little new in this, but it was the setting which the academic Andrew Melville found' in Scotland upon his return from Geneva in 1574; with others he drew up a second *Book of Discipline* in which we find a condemnation of episcopacy and, with it, the doctrine of the parity of ministers —the groundstone of Scottish presbyterianism.

This second *Book of Discipline* again stressed that all its claims were based on the Word of God. Like the first *Book of Discipline*, but departing from the compromises made since 1560, it demanded that the *whole* 'patrimony' of the church should be devoted to the ministers, the schools, the poor, and 'other affairs' of the kirk, so that those who served God could be 'provided for without care or solicitude'. But in addition it also declared that bishops with authority over their brethren, 'pastors of pastors', were unlawful before God, for all God's ministers were equal, one with another. Authority and discipline were to be maintained, not by dignitaries, but by a hierarchy of church courts, including elders as well as ministers, and later defined as the kirk-session, the presbytery (originating in part in the 'exercises'), the synod (in existence since 1561, formerly presided over by the Superintendent or commissioner, but now to have an elected Moderator), and the General Assembly. The examination and admission of ministers was to be by presbyteries. The General Assembly was to be essentially a gathering of ministers and elders, representing the lower courts in the hierarchy, and it was to have authority over all men, lay as well as spiritual, in 'ecclesiastical causes'. This authority of the Assembly, moreover, derived from the authority of the church which was 'different and distinct' from the authority of the state. For, as the Book laid down at the very beginning, the kirk 'has a certain power granted by God' and flowing direct from God; the kirk has no head on earth—its only head is Christ, the spiritual king and governor. So, if the civil magistrate transgressed 'in matters of conscience and religion', he had to submit to the discipline of the kirk; and it was the duty of the kirk to 'teach' the civil magistrate how to exercise his civil authority 'according to the Word'.

Here was far more than a renewed claim to the wealth of the Roman church for the work of the church reformed. Here too, there was far more than a condemnation of bishops and a claim that all God's servants were equal. Here, in effect, was a threatened theocracy: a kirk that would 'teach' (which might well mean dictate) a policy to the state. With the kirk claiming a right to instruct the civil authority in those matters that were of 'conscience and religion', and with the kirk claiming to be the judge of what those matters were, the authority of the king could be heavily invaded. Indeed, to drive the argument to its logical conclusion, where lay the need for a king's council when the ministers claimed that they were in counsel with God?

The Regent Morton and James VI were quick to perceive that the kirk and its ministers could soon be claiming to control almost every aspect of royal policy; on the other side, Andrew Melville was fearless in asserting an authority for the kirk that was separate from, and above, the authority of the state. In 1584 he did not hesitate to tell the king's privy council that they 'presumed over boldly' to 'control the ambassadors and messengers of a king and council greater than themselves and far above them'; and in 1596 he told James VI that church and state were twin jurisdictions, and that there were two kings and two kingdoms in Scotland; one was 'Christ Jesus the King, and his Kingdom the Kirk, whose subject King James the Sixth is, and of whose kingdom [he is] not a king, nor a lord, nor a head, but a member'. It is not surprising that James was later to declare that Scottish presbytery agreed 'as well with monarchy as God and the Devil', or that he roundly asserted 'No bishop, no king'. And that axiom, 'No bishop, no king', provides the key to James's policy in his ensuing struggle with Melville and the kirk.

Taking his cue from England, James saw that in episcopacy, with bishops chosen and appointed by the crown, lay his only hope of royal control over the church, perhaps even his only hope of some royal control over the state. So, in the contest between the crown and the kirk, James strove for the supremacy of the crown, supported by an episcopal church; Melville strove for a church which contained no bishops, who might be tools of the king, and a church which, under its General Assembly, was independent and free from any control by the state.

This struggle between the king and the kirk first came into the open in the events that followed the arrival in Scotland (in 1579) of Esmé Stewart, Lord d'Aubigny.[6] D'Aubigny, ingratiating and handsome, had at once become a close favourite of the thirteen-year-old James. He was created earl of Lennox in 1580, and duke of Lennox in 1581; he was given command of the king's bodyguard; and the uncompromising regent, the earl of Morton—who had brought stability to the realm—was accused by Captain James Stewart[7] for art and part in the murder of Darnley, was imprisoned and later executed (June 1581). And Captain James Stewart had by now been created earl of Arran.

But the ministers strongly suspected Esmé Stewart of being a papal agent; rumours of Roman Catholic plots and conspiracies were rife; and even Elizabeth had thought it wise to send warning letters to the young king. To lull these alarms and suspicions, James, Lennox, and the members of the royal household had subscribed, in January 1581, a Confession of Faith (known as the 'King's Confession', or the 'Negative Confession'—because of its denial of all religion and doctrine that was not in accord with the Confession of 1560), and in March 1581 had given orders for this Confession to be subscribed throughout the whole realm.[8] The ministers, however, were alienated by the king's refusal to set up presbyteries by act of parliament (though he had done so by act of privy council) and offended by the appointment of an archbishop to the vacancy at Glasgow; evidence of Roman Catholic intrigues and plots, however shadowy, deepened their suspicions of Lennox. Nor were the ministers without the support of a number of the nobility who disliked the sudden ascendancy of Lennox and Arran and their influence over the king, and who were perturbed by the undoubted plots that were afoot, including plots for the restoration of Mary to the Scottish throne.

In August 1582 the earls of Mar and Gowrie, with Lord Lindsay and Lord Boyd, seized James at Perth and compelled him to accompany them to Ruthven castle. Arran was seized soon afterwards; Lennox was compelled to obey an order to leave Scotland (December 1582);[9] and the 'Ruthven Raiders' held the young king in their power for some ten months until his escape in June 1583. Meantime in October 1582 the General Assembly of the kirk had given its approval to the 'Raid of Ruthven' (an approval which James never forgot or forgave), regarding it as an 'act of reformation' that had delivered 'the true religion . . . from evident and certain dangers', and had preserved the person of the king from 'no less peril'.

With James's escape in June 1583, however, Arran was at once restored to favour, and Andrew Melville, accused of treason, took refuge in England. A second plot, in which the earls of Mar, Gowrie, and Angus played the leading parts, and which was directed against Arran, failed. Gowrie was executed; Mar and his associates fled to England; and to England also fled a number of the leading ministers who had supported both the Ruthven Raiders and this second plot.

Arran was now in complete ascendancy, though hated more than ever by nobility and ministers alike; and James, taking his revenge for the approval given by the General Assembly to the Raid of Ruthven, now struck at the roots of all that Melville had claimed for the kirk. In May 1584 the so-called 'Black Acts' affirmed the king's authority over the 'spiritual estate' as well as the temporal; affirmed the right of parliament to legislate for all persons both spiritual and temporal; discharged all judgements of the church that were not approved by king and parliament; forbade any assembly of the church to be held without the king's permission; forbade the preaching of any sermon in contempt of the king or of the proceedings of the king's council; and, denouncing presbyteries, laid down that the government of the church was to be by bishops responsible to the king.

Little more than a year later, however, the killing of Lord Russell, son of the earl of Bedford, at a Border 'day of trew', enabled Elizabeth to demand the surrender of Arran as the instigator of Russell's death. Elizabeth, who did not realize the challenge of presbyterianism till 1590 or later, and who was anxious for a Protestant league with Scotland,[10] not only distrusted Arran but also wished to effect a reconciliation between James and the 'Protestant Lords' who had taken refuge in England. In October 1585, after ineffective diplomatic exchanges, she 'let slip' these 'Banished Lords'; they recrossed the Border and were at once joined by their friends. For a time it looked as though armed conflict was inevitable, but Arran's courage failed him and his ascendancy was at an end.[11]

N

Andrew Melville and the other presbyterian ministers now returned to Scotland, and in February 1586, at a conference of councillors and ministers at Holyrood, agreement was reached on a compromise intended to reconcile the rival claims of the crown and the kirk. Henceforth bishops were to be presented by the king to the General Assembly for election and admission; each bishop was to be appointed to a particular kirk which he would serve as a minister; he was to be subject to a presbytery or 'senate', chosen from the ministers within his bounds, through whose advice he would appoint to vacant parish churches; and in 'life and doctrine' he was to be answerable to the General Assembly. This compromise was accepted by the next General Assembly—though not without much discussion—and a scheme of presbyteries, twenty-two in number, was drawn up, each of which was to have a 'moderator' who would be either a bishop or a commissioner.[12] But the compromise, mainly owing to the Act of Annexation in the following year, never became effective.

By his Act of Annexation (1587), which he later bitterly regretted, James, possibly trusting too much to the advice of his chancellor, John Maitland,[13] unwittingly struck a severe blow at the episcopal system which he was striving to erect. As was to be constantly the case, the king was spendthrift and short of money; accordingly, on the argument that former royal endowments of the church had seriously impoverished the crown, and to avoid placing unbearable taxations upon the people, the crown now resumed, by annexation, all the temporalities still pertaining to any 'archbishop, bishop, abbot, prior, prioress' and 'whatsomever other prelate'. The manses and glebes of the parish churches were left untouched; but, for the rest, the 'possessors of great benefices' were stripped of everything save their principal dwelling-places. Who now would want to be a bishop? There was a 'temporary eclipse of episcopacy'; and the ministers shrewdly forgot the compromise of 1586.

Then, once again, extraneous events played a part—this time greatly to the advantage of the kirk.

In February 1592 the Catholic earl of Huntly slew the 'Bonnie earl of Moray' at Donibristle. There was feud between Huntly and Moray, but the latter was the son-in-law of the 'Good Regent' Moray. Worse still Huntly after a brief imprisonment was released and not brought to trial.

Amid a general outcry, notably in the sermons of the ministers, that James's royal authority was 'contemptible', that he allowed the earl of Bothwell[14] to put him to defiance and Huntly to commit murder with impunity, and that he even favoured Huntly as a Roman Catholic, James, again on the advice of Maitland, now Lord Thirlestane, agreed to an act of parliament which has been called the 'Golden Act'. By this act, James ratified all the liberties and privileges previously granted to the reformed church, gave to the kirk the right of calling General Assemblies (though at each General Assembly the king or the royal commissioner was to name the date and place of the next meeting),[15] granted the right of synods and presbyteries to meet, declared that the acts of 1584 (the 'Black Acts') were not to take away 'the privilege that God has given to the spiritual office bearers in the kirk' in matters of religion and discipline, and finally declared that henceforth presentations to benefices were to be directed to presbyteries.

Yet James was still a hater of presbyterianism and of the independence asserted by the ministers. To James, parity of ministers was 'the mother of confusion'; and the independence asserted by the ministers was little short of an attempt to govern the government. Then, for a third time, unforeseen circumstances affected the course of the conflict between the claims of the ministers and the king's insistence upon some royal authority over the church.

In March 1596 the king's continuing leniency towards the Roman Catholic earls, Huntly and Erroll,[16] had been criticized in the General Assembly, and the ministers had not spared their words; in September of the same year Melville had taken the king by the sleeve and called him 'God's sillie[17] vassall'; and in November, David Black, minister in St. Andrews, had refused to acknowledge the jurisdiction of the privy council when charged with uttering 'unreverent, reproachful and infamous' words in a recent sermon. Then, in December, came a sudden and unexpected tumult in Edinburgh, the cause of which is not known with certainty, but which gave James his chance. Denouncing both the burgesses and the ministers, James left Edinburgh and by act of council proclaimed it to be no longer the capital of the kingdom.

Edinburgh, it is true, was soon able to recover its status and privileges by payment of a fine of 20,000 merks, but, touched in their pockets, its burgesses were henceforth more wary in their support of the ministers. Moreover, by making generous grants from the temporalities of the bishoprics and abbacies which he had annexed to the crown, James was able to secure the support of many of the nobility—support from those who received as well from those who hoped they might receive.

The ministers were now fighting their battle almost alone. And James had already seen that not all the ministers were as unyielding and resolute as Andrew Melville. By taking advantage of the clause in the act of 1592 which enabled the king or his commissioner to name the date and place of the next meeting of the General Assembly, James now began to summon Assemblies to meet in places like Dundee, Perth, and Montrose, where opinion was less radical than in the south, and where the atmosphere was likely to be less perfervid.

And now, by a combination of astuteness, subtlety, and plain common sense, as well as by bribes, flattery, threats, and some chicanery—all of which is sometimes called his 'kingcraft'—James was able gradually to graft an episcopal form of government upon a presbyterian church.

His first step was to persuade a General Assembly, held at Dundee in May 1597, to appoint commissioners 'to give advice to his majesty in all affairs concerning the welfare of the kirk'. Andrew Melville had given the king advice enough; but, as Calderwood records,[18] the commissioners 'being exalted so high as to have access to the king when they pleased' soon became the 'king's led horse' and concurred with the king by giving him the advice he wanted. In December 1597, when they had recommended that the ministers should have representation in parliament, James at once agreed and, in the same month, secured an act whereby ministers whom the king pleased 'to provide to the office, place, title and dignity of a bishop, abbot or other prelate' should have seat and vote in parliament, and that accordingly vacant bishoprics, now and to come, should be filled by ministers of the kirk.

The king astutely professed that his sole desire was to give the kirk a voice in the government of the realm; he denied any intention to introduce 'papistical or Anglican bishopping'; but the supporters of Melville's true presbyterianism saw here the thin edge of the wedge.[19] Moreover the king had not disguised his views in *Basilikon Doron*;[20] his opponents had secured a copy of the book; and they had noted that in it the king had written that there were some among the ministers who were learned and modest and who, if preferred to bishoprics, would not only re-establish the old spiritual estate in parliament, but would also defeat the demand for parity, 'which I can not agree with a monarchy'.

A cautious General Assembly, meeting at Montrose in March 1600, resolved that the representatives of the kirk in parliament should be chosen by the king out of a list drawn up by the kirk, and could be deposed by the kirk; that they were to be responsible to the General Assembly; that they were to discharge no episcopal functions, and were to be called 'commissioners' and not 'bishops'; and that they were to be continued in office from year to year. James's answer (October 1600) was to appoint ministers of his own choice to the vacant sees of Ross, Aberdeen, and Caithness, paying no regard to the safeguards laid down by the General Assembly; and these three bishops, together with a fourth bishop appointed to the see of Moray, sat and voted in a parliament held in November 1600. The king had firmly inserted the thin end of the wedge. Here was the beginning of an episcopal church.

Admittedly these bishops had as yet no place in the government of the kirk; but by further 'kingcraft' James was eventually able to secure a church controlled by bishops who presided over synods, who admitted ministers, and who enjoyed a consistorial jurisdiction. All that, however, came only after his accession to the English throne and was itself a temporary gain.

James VI struggled long and hard against Melvillian claims, and it is likely that many, perhaps a silent majority, of the ministers, liked them little more than he did. What James heard was the noisy preaching and denunciations of the kirkmen of Edinburgh and other Lowland towns, influential out of all proportion to their numbers—but it was these men he had to answer. He chose to do so not by burnings, for he hated violence, nor even by imprisonment, but by his writings. It was as an answer to the Melvillian claims for the ministry that the king evolved and eventually published his theory of the Divine Right of Kings. The argument was trite and sounded bombastic when used in lectures to the English parliament after 1603, but in the context of Scotland in the 1590s it must have sounded like a moderate statement of the theory behind the traditional authority of, and respect due to, the state. That authority was being challenged by clerical pretensions as great as ever were those of medieval popes, and it is much to James VI's credit that he answered them by the pen.

NOTES

1. Above, p. 344.

2. A first draft of what is now known as the *Book of Discipline* had been drawn up between 29 April and 20 May 1560. That is, it was a 'blueprint' of the policy to be adopted when victory had been won.

3. 'Protesting, that if any man will note in this our Confession any article or sentence repugning to God's holy word . . .' (the Confession of Faith). 'For as we will not bind your Wisdoms to our judgments further than we be able to prove the same by God's plain Scriptures . . .' (the *Book of Discipline*).

4. 'By the consent of the kirks of Lothian and by the commandment of the nobility, I am appointed superintendent over the same [i.e. Lothian] and by virtue thereof by the lords of secret council [i.e. the privy council] . . .'. From a letter of John Spottiswoode, 22 March 1561.

5. Not until 1573 was it enacted that all those who held benefices, or who enjoyed any church revenues, and who refused to accept the Confession of Faith, were to be deprived of their benefices or holdings; and under this act a few ejections at last took place. Their fewness is a mark of the disappearance of committed Catholics.

6. Esmé Stewart was the son of John Stewart, Lord d'Aubigny, and grandson of John, third earl of Lennox. He was thus a cousin of James VI. Moreover, with the forfeiture of the Hamiltons, and with the death in 1576 of Darnley's brother Charles, sixth earl of Lennox, who left only a daughter, Arabella Stewart, Esmé Stewart was a near heir to the Scottish throne.

7. This adventurer, hand-in-glove with Lennox, was the second son of Andrew, Lord Ochiltree, and, strange as it may appear, John Knox had been his brother-in-law.

8. This 'Negative Confession' was later made the basis of the National Covenant of 1638.

9. He retired to France and died there shortly afterwards (May 1583).

10. Below, p. 381.

11. In 1595 he was killed by James Douglas of Parkhead, a nephew of the Regent Morton, in revenge for his denunciation of Morton which had led to Morton's imprisonment and execution.

12. Originally a 'commissioner' was a minister commissioned to carry out the functions of a Superintendent; here the commissioner in a like way was to be a minister commissioned to carry out the functions of a bishop.

13. Younger brother of William Maitland of Lethington. Their father, Sir Richard Maitland (1496-1586), was a competent poet (his best work is probably his *Solace in Age*) who, however, also collected specimens of early Scots poetry. In the Maitland MSS., and in the equally valuable Bannatyne MS. (the collection of George Bannatyne, 1545-1608), much early Scottish vernacular poetry has been preserved.

14. The son of John Stewart, a natural son of James V, and Jean Hepburn, the sister of Mary's Bothwell. He had been created earl of Bothwell by James VI in 1587. In 1591 Bothwell had repeatedly put the king to defiance and revealed the weakness of the royal authority. He had broken into the tolbooth of Edinburgh and carried off a prisoner; he had escaped from his ward in the castle of Edinburgh;

had been outlawed and twice thereafter had appeared in Edinburgh and insolently challenged the authorities; and finally he had made his way into Holyrood and into the king's own chamber.

15. But no provision was made whereby a General Assembly could be called if the king or royal commissioner, being present, did *not* name the date and place of the next meeting—a loophole of which James took advantage in his continued struggle with the kirk after his accession to the English throne.

16. Below, pp. 384–6.

17. *Sillie*: not in its modern sense of *foolish*, but in its earlier sense of *feeble* and *frail*.

18. *History of the Kirk of Scotland*, v. 644. Calderwood (1575–1650) wrote as a perfervid presbyterian.

19. One minister even compared the act to the wooden horse of Troy.

20. A book of advice for his son, Prince Henry, which James had just written and which was printed for private circulation probably towards the end of 1598 or early in 1599.

CHAPTER 32

The Rule of James VI and the Accession to the English Throne

IN August 1560 over 100 small barons and freeholders (many fervent Protestants) had thronged the 'Reformation Parliament', vaguely relying upon an ancient right but also claiming that, as there was no better place than parliament in which they could serve the commonwealth, they ought to be present there to 'be heard, to reason, and to vote'. Their attendance had been accepted, but it had conflicted with the terms of the Concessions, and the validity of the parliament had been called in question.

Again, in December 1567, when Mary had been deposed, and when affairs once more were critical, a number of small barons had presented themselves at the parliament held by the Regent Moray in the name of the one-year-old James VI—doubtless to demonstrate their support of the new government. And now, in 1567, an attempt was made to regularize the position. By one of the articles put forward 'for the common weal of the realm', and said to have been 'approved', it was declared that since by 'law and reason the barons of this realm ought to have vote in parliament as a part of the nobility' henceforth, whenever a parliament was summoned, the sheriff of each shire was to call together the barons of the shire so that they could choose one or two commissioners to represent the shire; and the expenses of the elected commissioners were to be met by the rest of the barons whom they represented. Significantly this system of representation was recommended 'for safety of numbers at each parliament': the small barons were mainly Protestants, and the regular attendance of shire commissioners (rather than the haphazard presence of those who decided themselves to come) would give the Protestant party steady support for its political programme. It could rely upon a safe majority. On the other hand, there is no mention of freeholders; and it looks as though the freeholders were now to be disfranchised.

Owing to the defective nature of the parliamentary records, it is impossible to say whether or not this 'approved article' became

statute law. Certainly there is no record of the election of shire commissioners, or of the attendance of shire commissioners at parliaments and conventions of estates (these, attended by all three
estates, gradually replaced the conventions of lords found earlier
in the sixteenth century). Certainly, too, at times of crisis—as, for
example, at the election of the Regent Mar (September 1571) and
the election of the Regent Morton (November 1572)—the small
barons still turned up in 'goodly numbers' to support the government: but they turned up as individuals and not as representatives
of the shires.

Yet clearly it was essential that the composition of parliament
should be known and definite. More than that, uncertainty in its
composition might mean uncertainty in the furtherance of a
Protestant policy. And the need for a strong Protestant government,
with certainty in its retention of power, was one of the factors leading to the county franchise act of 1587.

In March 1585 Philip II of Spain and the duke of Guise proclaimed their 'Catholic League' for the extirpation of all heresy.
Most of the Netherlands, 'a pistol pointed at the heart of England',
had already fallen into the hands of Spain; the fate of Protestant
Europe appeared to hang in the balance; and Elizabeth sent hastily
to James asking him to conclude with England a Protestant League,
offensive and defensive, to combat the threat from Roman Catholic
might.

A league with England was accepted by a convention of estates
in July 1585, although it was not finally concluded until July 1586[1]
when Arran had been overthrown.[2] Meantime, in a parliament held
in December 1585, a petition had been presented to the king and
the estates representing the need for both king and parliament to
be 'well and truly informed of the needs and causes pertaining to
his loving subjects in all estates, especially the commons of the
realm', and asking for the revival of the 'good and lovable' act of
1428. And out of this petition came the franchise act of 1587 which,
with only a few later modifications, determined the county franchise
until the Reform Act of 1832.

The act of 1587, which recited James I's act of 1428 in full, was
little more than a straightforward re-enactment of that measure.[3]
Commissioners (two from each shire—but only one from each of
the small shires of Clackmannan and Kinross) were to be elected
by the freeholders (small barons were evidently understood to be

included in that term), and the expenses of the commissioners were to be met by those whom they represented. The commissioners were to have votes in both parliaments and conventions of estates, and their representatives on the committee of the articles were to be equal in number to the representatives of the burghs. Finally, the voting qualification suggested in 1585 (those small barons and freeholders who held land, direct of the king, of the annual value of at least 40s.) was now regarded as part of the act itself.[4]

The small barons and freeholders undoubtedly represented a strong Protestant group, at a time when a strong Protestant government was essential, but the background to this county franchise act is also interesting in other ways. Parliament was largely an assembly of the greater landowners. The burghs tended to prepare their own business in their own convention of royal burghs and their influence was upon the king through his financial needs rather than upon the nobility. The theory of a clerical estate was still maintained, but the clerical estate was virtually non-existent. Only four or five bishops sat; and the abbots and priors were nearly all commendators who, although forming part of the spiritual estate, were 'of the nobility' and thought and acted like the nobility.[5] In effect parliament contained many great lords, only a few burgesses, and no real clerical estate. To bring in the small men would help to offset the power of the great lords.

In another aspect, the king, always short of money and always spendthrift, could the more easily secure the ingathering of a taxation (and taxations were already multiplying) if the small men, as well as the great lords, had agreed to its imposition. Equally, if the small men were present in parliaments and conventions they could strive to protect their fellows by opposing any exaggerated demands from the king.

Finally, it is significant that the small men, eager and anxious to have voice and vote in parliament, now regarded representation as a privilege whereas, in 1428, it had probably been regarded as a burden. This was part of a new political consciousness which had been stimulated by the Reformation movement; and its strength is to be seen in the fact that, in order to further their petition of 1585, the small men were willing to make a 'handsome contribution' of £40,000 to the king. Because of some delay in the forthcoming of this 'contribution', the act of 1587 did not become effective until 1594; and, even then, not all the shires elected commissioners.

Gradually, however, in steadily increasing numbers, shire commissioners took their places in parliaments and conventions of estates.

Nevertheless James VI, in another aspect of his 'kingcraft', was soon able to use the method of electing the committee of the articles to gain control of that committee and, therewith, control of the legislation put before the parliament. In 1467 we have record of a committee, nine in number, chosen from the three estates *ad formandos articulos*—to put the articles into shape. In 1469 parliament met on 20 November, elected a 'committee of the articles' on 21 November, and passed its legislation on 27 November. Evidently expedition has been achieved. But, as the decades pass, it is borne in upon us that expedition has been achieved at a price: the price of parliament's initiative. The step from 'putting the articles into shape' to 'deciding upon the articles' has been only too easy. In due course we find that parliament meets and elects the 'Lords of the Articles'—a certain number from each estate; it then disperses and, say, a fortnight later meets again to say 'yes' to the legislation that is placed before it. Parliament, in effect, has become little more than a rubber stamp to endorse conclusions reached by its committee. There is no debate, there is no legislation other than that which is drafted by the committee of the articles. In 1587 parliament elected the committee of the articles on 13 July, and on 29 July (sixteen days later) gave its assent to no less than 136 Acts, some of which were both lengthy and involved. We know, however, that by then it was customary for the king's privy council to draft the legislation for the lords of the articles to consider; and thus, if the king (or the faction that was in power) could control the membership of both the privy council and the committee of the articles, the king (or the faction) had complete control over all legislation. After his accession to the English throne James VI secured a close relationship between the lords of the articles, the privy council, and the court of session, and, with the 'king's men' dominating those three bodies, James could ensure that the legislature, the executive, and the judiciary did all things according to the king's own pleasure. The committee of the articles which had begun as a convenient device was in the end to be denounced as a 'great grievance to the nation'.

In the background to the act of 1587, as we have seen, lay the Roman Catholic League between Philip II and the duke of Guise, and the Protestant League between Elizabeth and James. The act was passed in July 1587; and, a year later, in August 1588, most of the surviving galleons of Philip's 'Invincible Armada', striving desperately to round the northern capes, were broken to pieces on Scottish and Irish coasts. But there were still a number of Scottish lords—notably the earls of Huntly and Erroll in the north, and John, Lord Maxwell, in the south-west—who, remaining true to the Roman faith, continued to intrigue for its restoration. Moreover, according to a contemporary estimate, the majority of the people in the northern counties, as well as in Dumfriesshire and Wigtown-shire, were favourable to Rome. And James himself, while willing to enter into a Protestant League with Elizabeth (and to receive for his 'support' a pension of £4,000 a year), was for a time anxious to carry an insurance policy lest she be defeated by Spain. Yet with the death of his mother (1587) and the defeat of the Armada (1588) he became more plainly intent upon the succession to the English throne and had little incentive to pretend to Catholic sympathies.

In February 1589 Elizabeth's agents intercepted a packet of letters from Huntly, Morton (that is, John, Lord Maxwell), and Lord Claud Hamilton, which, written to Philip in the name of the Roman Catholics in Scotland, expressed regret at the failure of the Armada and suggested that in any future enterprise a Spanish force should be landed in Scotland whence it could easily make trouble in England. 'Good Lord, methink I do but dream', wrote the English queen, when forwarding the letters to James, 'no king a week would bear this'; the traitors must be forthwith 'clapped up'. Faced by Elizabeth's angry letter, and by the clamour of the ministers, James had perforce to take some action. Huntly was warded in Edinburgh castle, and yet, on the day following his ward, the king, who had a 'tenderness' for him, dined with him, 'kissed him often, and protested he knew he was innocent'; and within a few days the earl was free again. King James was perfectly well aware that these plottings with Philip were against the queen of England and not the king of Scots.

Huntly and Erroll now entered into a band with Crawford, Bothwell, and Montrose to move on Edinburgh from both the North and the Borders. James, learning that the earls were march-ing against him, summoned his lieges. The move from the south petered out. Bothwell, Huntly, and Erroll retired northwards, and James came up with them and their followers (who are said to have

numbered 3,000) at the Brig o' Dee. There the earls, losing the
courage to do battle against their sovereign, surrendered. Yet James
still avoided strong measures. Although the earls had plotted against
the person of their king, and had risen in arms against the royal
authority, thereby incurring the penalties of treason—namely,
forfeiture of life, lands, and goods—again they were merely warded,
and again, within a few months, they were released. Huntly was
again released after the murder of Moray (February 1592)[6] yet
within a few months was again intriguing.

In December 1592 a number of letters and certain blank documents (the 'Spanish Blanks') signed by Huntly, Erroll, and Angus,
were seized in the possession of George Ker (younger brother of
Lord Newbattle) just as he was about to sail from the Firth of Clyde.
According to a royal proclamation, issued on 5 January 1593, the
letters revealed a treasonable conspiracy to bring strangers and
Spaniards into the realm of Scotland to overthrow the monarchy
and the true religion; but thereafter James strove to parry the loud
demands of the ministers and the people of Edinburgh for action
rather than proclamation. There was a strong suspicion that the
king himself was not averse to the use of Scotland for a Spanish
invasion of England—provided Philip II did not take the English
crown for himself—and that among the intercepted letters there
had been one 'which tuiched the king with knowledge and approba-
tioun of the traffiquing'.[7] It is possible, but hardly likely, that James
may have toyed with the idea that, if England were to be conquered
by Spain, and a heretic Elizabeth overthrown, he could then be
'converted' to the Roman faith and rule both Scotland and England
as a Catholic prince. Certainly in a document drawn up about June
1592 James had weighed up the pros and cons of the conquest of
England by a Spanish force with Scottish help, and the wording
of his 'reasons' suggests that the crown of England meant more to
him than the religion of its ruler and its people.[8] On the other hand
the character of the argument indicates that this was an 'academic
exercise' and little more.

For their treasonable conspiracy in the affair of the 'Spanish
Blanks' Huntly and Erroll finally appeared before the king in
October 1593 and offered to submit themselves to trial, but, a few
weeks later, James came to an agreement with them that if they
renounced the errors of popery or, alternatively, left Scotland, no
action would be taken against them. Neither earl took advantage

of this agreement and both were forfeited. Yet they paid little heed to that; and when, in July 1594, the good burgesses of Aberdeen arrested a known papal agent and, with him, three strangers also 'suspect to be papists' on a ship that had arrived from Calais, they were compelled to deliver their prisoners to Angus, Huntly, and Erroll under the threat that otherwise the 'gryt forcis of the saidis erlis . . . lyand about the toun' would 'invaid and persew the samen with fyre and sword'. Word soon reached James of the arrest and the release, and, in the face of this affront to the royal authority, the king once more summoned the lieges to accompany him to the north. Before he could march, the young earl of Argyll had rashly opposed Huntly and Erroll at Glenlivet, and had been heavily defeated (October 1594); but when James, with his stronger forces, and accompanied by Andrew Melville and others of the ministers (whom he took with him to give them proof of his zeal against papists), arrived in the north-east, Huntly and Erroll, for the second time, shrank from battle against their king. Their houses of Strathbogie and Slains were destroyed, and the earls were compelled to observe the earlier agreement and to retire abroad. They were back again in Scotland in 1596, when they were favourably received by James and their forfeitures soon reduced (1597); but thereafter the northern earls took no further part in Catholic intrigues. In the south-west, moreover, John, Lord Maxwell (and titular earl of Morton), who had apparently ceased to be an active 'trafficker' in the cause of Rome, had been killed in a 'clan battle' with the Johnstones, near Lockerbie (December 1593).

There has been little understanding of James VI's relations with his nobility; in particular his handling of the erratic or even insane Bothwell and of Huntly has been thought to show that they were over-mighty and he a scared coward. But the Scottish crown had long relied upon certain territorial magnates, notably Argyll in the west and Huntly in the north-east, to maintain order on the king's behalf through the network of their kin and dependants. In the Lowlands the king was his own man, but the problems which he might have had in the north were well illustrated by the disorderly kindreds of the Border region, whose shifting feuds were a constant danger to trade and to Anglo-Scottish relations, who would obey neither king nor magnate. Huntly was certainly a necessity, and probably an advantage, in the north.

But Moray had ambitions to replace him and set about suborning

Huntly's dependants, thereby provoking the disorder which Huntly was commissioned to repress. In so doing he killed Moray— an event which was presented from a hundred pulpits as barbarous, and a popish plot to boot. In traditional manner Huntly offered amends, and the king was well within his rights in deciding that the balance of political advantage, both within Scotland and in relations with Spain, lay in releasing the Catholic earl.

Armies cost money for which James had other uses, defeat and punishment left scars of resentment and even feuds; infinitely preferable were the arts of conciliation and the middle way. In international relations James was in consequence all things to all kings, the carrier of insurance against every eventuality. But at home, where his right and left hands were both of necessity visible, James's policies were realistic and on the whole successful—and it was better to free Huntly to plot another day than to punish him, spilling blood, raising feuds in the north, vaunting the already tiresome ultra-Protestant ministers, and losing insurance with King Philip.

Such a judgement accepts Scottish society (at the political level) as it was—an elaborate network of kindreds with alliances in uneasy equilibrium.

In burghs and landward areas alike, loss of equilibrium through breaches of the peace was of constant occurrence. The local lord was still often a law unto himself; nobles and their followers were the cause of many a fracas in the burgh's streets;[9] the royal authority was frequently put to defiance; and more often than not the royal officers were partial and venal. Central and local records are full of references to 'murder, burning, ravishing of women, violent reif, slaughter, common theft and reset of theft', or, more frequent still, 'wrangous, violent and masterful spoliation'—though we should always remember that this last was the claim made by one party in a legal action. 'Deadly feuds' were still too common. They were denounced by James VI in his *Basilikon Doron*, and upon at least two occasions the king showed his true political philosophy by trying to end them. On Sunday 14 May 1587 he invited all the nobles who were then attending a convention of estates in Edinburgh to a banquet at Holyrood, where, after drinking to them thrice, he solemnly exhorted them to maintain friendship with one another, and threatened to be an enemy to the one who first broke the peace. Not content with that, on the next day, in the evening, he led a procession of his nobility through Canongate to the market cross of Edinburgh, two abreast, each holding another by the hand, and each a mortal enemy to his companion. At the market cross a table was laid with wine and sweetmeats, and there, once more, the young king made his nobles drink to each other and to peace and happiness. Again, in December 1595, grieving that deadly feuds had 'altogether disordered and shaken loose' the realm, and that slaughter had become a daily occurrence, James summoned over thirty of the nobles and barons who were at feud with one another to wait upon him at certain days and places so that, with the advice of their friends, their quarrels might be reconciled. Little success attended an attempt in 1587 to re-establish the justice-ayres and to supplement them by appointing in every shire certain 'honorable and worthie personis being knawin of honest fame' to be 'kingis commissioners and justices in the furtherance of justice peax and quietness', similar to the English Justices of the Peace.

In the Highlands and on the Borders where, owing to the difficulties of communication and access, the royal authority was less effective still, James also tried to find new methods of securing some measure of control. In 1587 parliament enacted that, under a 'General Band', all chiefs of clans and all 'landlords and bailies of the lands on the Borders and in the Highlands where broken men have dwelt or presently dwell' were to find sureties (landed men in the Lowlands) for the peaceful conduct of those on their lands. Anyone thereafter suffering injury from 'broken men' could pursue the surety who had been found, and the 'chief' or 'landlord' in addition to being bound to satisfy his surety was to be mulcted in a heavy fine. The 'Band', however, was no more successful than similar earlier expedients.

Ten years later, in 1597, all 'landlords, chieftains and leaders of clans, principal householders, heritors and other possessing, or pretending right to possess, any lands in the Highlands and Isles' were ordered to produce their titles before the lords of exchequer before 15 May 1598. They were then to find sureties for regular payment of their rents and services to the crown, and for the observance of law and order within their lands, with the penalty that those who failed to produce their titles and to find sureties would forfeit their holdings. Since it was well known that few Highland chiefs would be able to produce titles for their lands, this act gave the king an opportunity to forfeit and to regrant in those cases where he thought such action desirable. And, when certain of the MacLeods failed to produce their titles, the Isles of Lewis and Harris and the lands of Dunvegan and Glenelg were declared to be forfeit and at the king's disposal. These lands were now granted by James to an association of Lowland lairds which, since its members came mainly from Fife, became known as 'The Gentlemen Adventurers of Fife'. The 'Adventurers' were to hold the lands free of crown rents for a period of seven years, so that they might develop and improve them; but thereafter they were to pay rental in money and victuals to the crown.

There is evidence that James had exaggerated ideas of the 'incredible fertility' of these outlying parts of the realm, and that, through the 'Adventurers', he hoped to secure not only law and order but also a considerable increase in crown revenue. The 'Adventurers' (accompanied by artificers and labourers) first endeavoured to 'colonize' Lewis (October 1599); but disease, insufficient supplies, and the natural hostility of the Lewismen forced them, after three attempts, to abandon the project,[10] and the 'Adventurers' were gradually absorbed into Gaelic society, or returned to the Lowlands.

In the case of the MacGregors who, largely through the high-handed actions of Campbell of Glenorchy, had become a 'landless clan' and 'broken men', James did not shrink from a policy of attempted extirpation. In 1590, certain of 'the wicked clan Gregor', continuing in 'blood, slaughters, herschips, reifs and stouths', had murdered the king's forester in Glenartney, and then, according to the accepted account, had cut off the dead man's head and had carried it to their young chief in Balquhidder. There, the whole clan being assembled, each man had laid his hands upon the bloody head, had avowed his approval of the deed, and had sworn to defend those who had done it. The privy council granted 'letters of fire and sword' to the earl of Huntly to be used against the Mac-Gregors, but, through the influence of Campbell of Cawdor, the chief and his clan escaped destruction. Early in 1603, however, and again through Campbell cunning, the MacGregors took part in a raid upon the Lennox when the Colquhouns of Luss were defeated with great slaughter at Glenfruin and much spoil was carried away. This time there was to be no escape: the MacGregors were to be extirpated; and the task was entrusted to Argyll who had persuaded them to attack the Colquhouns. All who had fought at Glenfruin were outlawed; the name of MacGregor was proscribed; their chief, Alasdair, was hanged; and Argyll, for his services in hunting down the clan, was rewarded with a grant of Kintyre. Later, the privy council decreed that no former member of the clan might carry any weapon save only a pointless knife for his meat, and that not more than four of them might meet together at any time for any purpose.[10]

In his attitude to political problems James VI could be ruthless with those of whom he had no understanding. Misguided and wretched as his solution of Highland disorders seems now, it certainly commended itself to most of his subjects, Lowlanders, and it reflects the social attitudes not merely of the king but of the nobility, showing, as does so much else of James's reign, that the monarchy was but the most prominent thread woven into the fabric of aristocratic society.

This integration is illustrated in a different way by the strange episode known as the 'Gowrie Conspiracy'. In August 1600, when James was hunting near Falkland, he was persuaded by Alexander, master of Ruthven, and brother of the earl of Gowrie, to ride to Gowrie House in Perth to interview a man who, according to Ruthven, had been seized with a pot full of coined gold. At Gowrie House the king was led through various chambers, each carefully locked behind him, until he was brought to a small turret room where he found himself confronted by an armed man. In a struggle that then ensued, James managed to reach the window and to give the cry of 'Treason'. Those who had ridden with him to Gowrie House rushed to his rescue and both the earl of Gowrie and his brother were slain. The story of the armed man in the turret room, and what happened there, rested solely upon James's own account which was clearly improved in order to anticipate criticism from the pulpit by the ultra-Protestant clergy with whom the Ruthvens were associated. It is difficult to believe that James endangered his own life in a plot against Gowrie, and more natural to accept that Gowrie tried to constrain the king—perhaps only to secure payment of the large sum owed to him. James walked into a trap because he did not fear his nobility; yet he clearly felt that having procured the death of an earl he must 'explain' events fully in order to reassure others.

Like his ancestors James employed a few magnates in important offices of state and like his ancestors he found them none too efficient. Bureaucrats drawn from the class of lairds and burgesses were important agents in that development of administration which marked James's rule. Thus the exchequer which had been an occasional sitting of men drafted in from other tasks became a permanently staffed office as part of the attempt to improve the king's income. Despite a 'dig' at his employees—that he wanted hangable men, not nobles (a significant contrast)—neither James nor his nobles saw anything reprehensible in the rise of 'new men' through service to the king.

From 1596 James began to devote all his attention to the 'great prize'—the succession to the English throne. Elizabeth had told him she would not prejudge whatever 'right, title or interest' he might have or claim to have; but beyond that she would not go. She would not name him as her successor. Moreover, although James was the obvious Protestant successor, the line of Henry VII's daughter Margaret was still excluded by Henry VIII's will which had been confirmed by the English parliament, nor was it clear whether the Bond and Act of Association precluded James from the succession as a result of his mother's complicity in the Babington plot.

In 1589 James had committed himself to a Protestant marriage with Anne, daughter of Frederick II of Denmark, and, in romantic fashion, sailed from Scotland to bring home his bride from across the sea (May 1590). Still not certain that Protestantism would prevail, James did not hesitate to make careful diplomatic approaches to the pope. How far he was prepared to go, however, is another matter; he may merely have been calculating that Roman Catholic help (or perhaps an absence of Roman Catholic opposition) might be his if he held out a vague prospect of emulating Henry IV who became king of France as a Protestant in 1589, but in 1593 became a Roman Catholic in order to unite his realm. In politics, the 'auld amitie' with France was renewed, and James's agents were busy in the minor courts of Europe. Above all, James entered into an important secret correspondence with Cecil. He was convinced that Cecil could secure his accession; and Cecil's letters were certainly encouraging and full of wise advice.

Although in 1598, 1599, and 1600 James had taken measures indicative of a determination to use force of arms in support of his claim, everything moved steadily in his favour. During the years from 1601 to 1603 Cecil was definitely on his side, even indicating, in his letters, an acceptance of James as Elizabeth's successor; the

English armed forces were controlled by Cecil's supporters; and there was no real rival to James's claim. In Scotland, Roman Catholics and Protestants alike wanted James, a Scot, to succeed to the English throne; in England, Protestants looked for the maintenance of the 'true religion', and Roman Catholics could expect toleration. In the closing months of 1602 the English council was ready to proclaim James as king.

On 24 March 1603 Elizabeth, the last and greatest of the Tudor line, died; and less than three days later, on the Saturday night, Sir Robert Carey, travel-stained and weary, brought the news to Holyrood. James VI of Scotland had become also James I of England.

In a message to his people the delighted king told them that 'where I thought to have employed you with some armour, now, I employ only your hearts, to the good prospering of me in my success and journey'. London and Edinburgh were not far apart: 'I shall visit you every three years at the least, or oftener, as I shall have occasion.'

James lost no time in assuming his inheritance. He left Edinburgh on 5 April 1603 and reached London on 7 May. He was to reign until 1625; but the year 1617 was to be the one solitary 'occasion' when he visited his native realm, a misfortune alike for England, which he ruled ill, and Scotland, which he had governed well.

NOTES

1. For its details, see *Source Book of Scottish History*, iii. 441–3.

2. Above, p. 373.

3. Above, p. 213.

4. So arose the 'forty shilling freeholder'. So, too, those holding land, direct of the king, of a lesser value were now definitely disfranchised.

5. When, after the act of annexation, James began to erect the lands of the monasteries and priories into 'temporal lordships', the 'lords of erection' sat as lords temporal.

6. See pp. 374–5, 386–7.

7. Calderwood, *History of the Kirk of Scotland*, v. 251.

8. See 'The Spanish Blanks and the Catholic Earls' in *Collected Essays and Reviews of Thomas Graves Law* (ed. P. Hume Brown), 244–76, and, particularly 268–71.

9. Edinburgh, indeed, where rival houses frequently met at councils or at court, was said to have been 'the ordinary place of butchery, revenge, and daily fights'.

10. In 1607 they finally sold their 'rights' to Mackenzie of Kintail.

CHAPTER 33

Scotland in the Time of James VI

THE account of an English traveller, Fynes Moryson, who visited Lothian and Fife in 1598, confirms the impression gained from other sources that in many respects Scotland was still a poor country, with a still primitive economy. Usually there was a sufficiency of plain food—salt meat, wild fowl and game, fish, oats and barley, kale, peas and beans; but a backward agriculture and poor communications meant that periods of dearth (and even starvation) were not unknown, and according to Moryson there was 'no Art of Cookery'.

The methods of working the land had hardly changed from early times. Oats or bere (an inferior barley) would be grown on the 'in-field' for three or four years with steadily diminishing yields; the land would then lie fallow for three or four years or more (and, in that time, become choked with weeds), and a patch of almost equally poor 'outfield' would be brought into cultivation. The old heavy ox-plough still ploughed the rigs that were separately owned and were divided by ditches or baulks; while 'community working' made it difficult, if not impossible, for any one member of the community to introduce improvements in method. There were practically no hedges enclosing 'fields'. Much of the land was wet and sour—mainly because it was ill drained—and accordingly the hillsides, where there was natural drainage, were brought into cultivation to such an extent as to surprise English travellers. Thomas Morer, visiting Scotland in 1689, found it 'incredible' how much of the hill-sides were ploughed when 'to our thinking, it puts 'em to greater difficulty and charge to carry on their work than they need be at in draining the valleys'. Feuing, with its benefit of perpetual heritable tenure, had encouraged some improvement, but more than 100 years were still to elapse before there were outstanding changes in Scottish farming.

Communications were still difficult: the roads were little more than beaten tracks, leading from burgh to burgh, or from bridge to bridge. These 'roads' were almost impassable for wheeled vehicles and difficult to traverse, but there were apparently many wooden bridges and the stone bridges were often graceful and well built. In effect, however, the transport of goods had to be by pack-horse, with all the limitations of quantity implied thereby. When one part of the country was afflicted by bad harvests, and the price of grain rose through scarcity, the obvious means of relief—supplies attracted from outside by high prices—was rarely operative to a sufficient degree since neither roads nor vehicles existed to bring relief in large quantity. On the other hand every commentator remarks upon the abundance of domestic animals—cattle, sheep, and goats—and of fish, and the facts of large Scottish exports of fish and hides confirm the accuracy of travellers' impressions. Thus protein was perhaps not in short measure in the diet of many Scotsmen, and, we might further guess, increased the expectation of adult life and so the numbers of children born. There is much to suggest that from the 1560s until 1621 the population of Scotland was increasing, supported by a precarious improvement in food production, but increasing only slowly, and creating stiff competition for the means of sustenance—land—essential to such a primitive economy.

The relative poverty of the country can be illustrated from the top of the social structure to its base. The king's palace of Holyroodhouse was sparsely furnished, and strenuous efforts were made to improve both the building and its furnishings in readiness for Anne of Denmark. At that time too, the begging letters sent out by James VI to meet the expenses attendant upon the queen's arrival reveal the poverty of the Scottish court. Not only does the king beg for money, which is 'scarce in these parts', but also from the laird of Barnbarroch he begs for 'such quantity of fat beef and mutton on foot, wild-fowls and venison, or other stuff meet for this purpose, as possibly ye may provide and furnish', from the laird of Caldwell he demands 'a hackney for transporting of the ladies accompanying the queen . . .', and from the earl of Mar he solicits the loan of a pair of silken hose for his own person.

In the countryside the baron would have his 'ha' house', built of well-dressed stone, and the laird and tenant-farmer might have a 'fair dwelling'.[1] A royal rental of 1541 had stipulated that the king's tenant in feu-ferme had to have an 'honest mansion', containing hall, chamber, pantry, and kitchen, with barn, byre, and dovecot, and with a garden well hedged in—though it may be questioned how often the stipulation was observed. We can see throughout Scotland small and middling-sized stone dwellings of the barons and lairds, usually built 'vertically', room upon room, a sure sign (illustrated also by the gun-loops around the door) that security was still an important consideration. The greater baron sometimes built a noble house with spacious windows, within the security of a medieval castle's curtain wall (as at Caerlaverock), evidence that he craved light and spaciousness where it could be had securely; such houses might be ostentatious and occasionally downright incongruous, as in the Italian façade and colonnade constructed triumphantly within the cramped courtyard of Crichton castle. The small baron and laird in the Border shires would still live in a grim tower bristling with the defences needed in that disturbed region of rieving. But further north the defensive features of tower houses often turn out on closer examination to be skeuomorphs—imitations of the real thing, retained for reasons of fashion but incapable of being put to their apparent purpose. Security mattered, for the sixteenth century had its thieves and vandals; but save in the Borders and western seaboard, 'defence of war' was a declining source of concern. Within, although the furnishings were scanty, plain, crude even, there might be decorative work in the new fashion—a board ceiling painted in tempera with classical or allegorical figures framed in a border or columns which would often display the initials of the laird and his wife responsible for this modest ostentation. Such men gave their patronage to the first Scottish portrait painter of merit to find customers in Scottish society, George Jameson, or to the smiths who made the cups of wood in gold or silver settings, called mazers and apparently unique to Scotland.

The houses of the common folk were roughly built of stone and turf, or of turf alone, low and squat, with a ridged or crutched roof thatched with heather or turfs. There would be a hole in the roof to act as a chimney for the central hearth, one window at the most, and a doorway probably hung with a hide. Even in the middle of the seventeenth century an English traveller in Scotland, Richard Franck, was amazed to see sheep grazing on the roofs of these low houses; and, a little later, another traveller, Thomas Kirke, spoke of the houses of the common people as 'very mean, mud-wall and thatch', and added that 'in some parts, where turf is plentiful, they build up little cabins thereof, with arched roofs of turf'.[2] These primitive dwellings had usually only one room, or two rooms at the most, with a floor of beaten earth. Their plenishings were practically non-existent: a stool perhaps, an iron pot, and a few wooden platters and spoons. In winter, the cattle shared the limited accommodation with the human occupants. Filth predominated, as also did disease —notably the 'itch'.

In the burghs, stone houses were now steadily replacing houses built of wood, though the many burgh 'acts' made in 'feir and dreddour' of fire—notably that heather, broom, whins, and 'other fewall' must not be stacked in closes, and that naked lights must be shielded in a 'bowet'—indicate that wood was still widely used in house construction, for the panels which divided rooms as well as for floors, roofs, and occasionally staircases. Within his house, how-ever, the wealthier merchant might have better furniture and more comforts and luxuries than many a baron or laird. Most barons had lands but little pence, for their rents were largely paid in victual; but the merchant had money through trade and, with trading con-nections overseas, could import continental luxuries for his own use. His house, usually reached by a 'forestair' running up from the street, might consist of only two or three rooms above his booth, but those rooms were often well furnished: a settle perhaps, one or two carved oak chairs, one or more oak aumries (or cabinets), oak chests, a bed fitted with curtains, and perhaps a small table. The solar (or principal room) and the bedchamber would probably be hung with arras, or have carved panelling, and the ceiling might be painted with a repeating pattern. There would be comfortable cushions; a good supply of napery; probably some of the spoons and table-ware would be of silver and others of pewter; and the kitchen would be well supplied with pots, cooking utensils, and dishes. But in all burghs sanitary arrangements were still non-existent. Even in Edinburgh, 'the cheif and principall burgh of the kingdome', the privy council in vain ordered the magistrates to take action to prevent the streets, vennels, wynds, and closes from being 'over-laid and coverit with middingis and with the filthe and excrementis of man and beast'. Disease must have taken a heavy toll of the urban population, yet when we look at old prints of the centres of our towns made before the mid nineteenth century, they show us 'ludgings' in streets unmistakably built in the reign of James VI or soon thereafter. The towns were prospering, developing rapidly even, though in an unsophisticated economy, and in comparison with the cities of England or France they were derisory in size and economic endeavour.

None the less many a merchant throve enough to invest in land, to build his own rural tower house, and to marry into a lairdly or baronial family, while many barons took an eager interest in the affairs of their local towns—though whether to improve the market for their rural produce, or to raise money for 'conspicuous consumption'—extravagance—it would be hard to say.

Perhaps the most interesting evidence of the growth of population and the availability of some scanty resources of capital is to be found in the industrial developments of the period. Industrial undertakings in towns were discouraged by the jealous monopolistic practices of gild and crafts, but there was one exception to the general rule in Scotland of shoddy manufacturers from poor quality materials, exported to wherever the lower end of the market would absorb Scottish goods such as poor cloth. This exception was metalwork both in quite homely commodities like iron hinges and door 'snecks' and in silverware such as simple communion vessels or elaborate mazers. Most remarkable of all, however, was the preeminence of Dundee as a centre for the manufacture of pistols and (though only two survive) guns. Elaborately chased brassware pairs of pistols from Dundee workshops are found in royal collections abroad, presentation pieces from one king to another, and clear evidence that for a period Dundee enjoyed European fame and preeminence in this field. Was this extraordinary, specialized masterwork the 'luxury' end of large-scale production of steel pistols and guns of simple design and unmarked by their makers' identifying tags? We do not know.

Much more important for the evolution of the Scottish economy was the industrial exploitation of coalworks especially in the Forth estuary. The revival of coalworks involved the digging of pits and mines on a scale far greater than the heughs exploited in medieval times, and as the seams disappeared under the Forth, added problems of flooding to those of ventilation. One of the great native entrepreneurs, George Bruce, came of burgess stock, but leased the Culross colliery and installed a horse-powered bucket-and-chain drainage system, building an artificial island at spring low-water mark (it can still just be discerned) from which a shaft led to the mineworkings. Coal was brought to the surface there to be loaded directly on to ships for the market abroad, or to fire the many salt-pans worked on the shores of the Firth. Bruce was knighted, doubt-less because of his skill at flattery, but his enterprise and willingness to innovate earned him no less. His success was limited only by the materials available for his innovations—the theory and plans for more advanced methods were doubtless there in Bruce's mind,[3] but wood, leather, and iron simply would not bear the stresses which must needs be put upon them to advance productivity further. The only alternative recourse was to use more labour and, since mining was dangerous, to compel that labour if necessary—hence, from 1606, the acts reintroducing serfdom for miners and colliers and their families.

Other industrial enterprises can be traced in the shifting bloomeries to make iron from bog-ore with whatever timber might be available. There was assiduous mining for precious metals, for which a string of foreigners was imported in the hope that they would find an eldorado on the moors of Dumfriesshire. A glass-works was opened at Wemyss and flourished for a time until closed by the efforts of a London monopolist.

That coal-mining was the most successful industrial enterprise in James VI's Scotland is made abundantly clear by the many ship-loads arriving not merely at London, but in the Low Countries and the Baltic. Salt was also exported, for the coal-masters had an economic grip upon the saltpans fired by their coal; exports of yarn are particularly interesting since it is clear that in addition to native flax, regular imports of raw flax from the Baltic were spun and re-exported to be woven abroad. Thus Scotland had a reservoir of labour (obviously female) so cheap that it was worth the haulage costs to bring the raw materials to it.

In fact it is doubtful if Scotland's exports paid for her imports in more than a minority of years. A developed trade with the Baltic in importing grain (from Gdansk), copper and iron (from Sweden), and timber (from Norway) is well attested for the 1590s, and is justified by some at least of the uses—the industrial uses—to which these materials were put. But wine from France was also a significant import, along with other luxury goods which raised the expectations of living-standards among lairds and barons, and so should have encouraged them to more careful and intensive husbandry to pay for their luxuries.

The extent to which it did so seems to have been slight. Admittedly when in 1603 the Borders became effectively the Middle Shires, the export of cattle to England took on a new lease of life and may have increased many baronial incomes. But other and more sinister exports are also found—men. From the 1570s, irregularly at first, but after 1600 with increasing frequency, the younger sons of barons and lairds hired themselves as captains to the recruiting agents, a few Scottish nobles and gentry, of the Baltic rulers. In their turn the captains levied companies of men from among the tenantry and landless of their families' estates and neighbours, shepherding them to Dundee (and we remember the possibility of armaments made there), or to Leith, whence they sailed to the disease-ridden siege camps or bloody battles of Livonia, Prussia, or Scania. The captains often returned to Scotland, the men seldom. Whether it was better that the Scot should die in the quarrels of the Swede rather than in his own debates over political and ecclesiastical authority is perhaps a question for the moralist rather than the historian.

James VI's Scotland lacked neither moralists nor historians— the king was not averse to being lauded for his scholarship in both fields, and many continental scholars regarded Scotland as a home of erudition, or so one might think from the 'Edinburgh' imprint put upon many Protestant works which were in fact printed on the continent.[4]

Although the first *Book of Discipline*, with its comprehensive proposals for education in school, college, and university, had been rejected, the Reformed Church still strove to 'plant' schools as well as kirks. In the landward areas many ministers acted as school-masters in their parishes; in the burghs the kirk sessions co-operated with town councils in the furthering of burgh schools; and the church never abandoned Knox's concept of a school for every parish. The university of Glasgow was given new life under Andrew Melville who introduced there a new curriculum and new methods of teaching which constituted so radical an improvement as to be known as the *nova erectio* (1577); the university of St. Andrews was reorganized and reformed, likewise with a 'new foundation and erection' (1579), and Andrew Melville's acceptance of the office of principal of St. Mary's College meant that the reforms were given full effect; and at Aberdeen, where King's College apparently resisted reform, George, fifth earl Marischal, founded a new university (Marischal College), in 1593, in which the 'order' was to be similar to that established by Andrew Melville in Glasgow.[5] In Edinburgh, James VI granted a charter to the town council in 1582, giving it leave to erect a college and making available the lands and buildings of the collegiate church of St. Mary in the Fields,[6] and the 'Town's College', at university of Edinburgh under the control of the town council, opened its doors in 1583.

In the realm of learning, George Buchanan, who had been James's tutor, was accounted the finest Latin scholar of his time. He was no mean dramatist, and his *Rerum Scoticarum Historia*, despite its early legends and its later denigration of Mary, was a remarkable work for its time, going through many editions and remaining the best history of Scotland until the works of Thomas Innes, William Robertson, Lord Hailes, and John Pinkerton appeared in the eighteenth century. Sir John Skene of Curriehill had prepared his editions of *The Lawes and Actes of Parliament* (covering 1424-1597), and of *Regiam Majestatem*, and had published his valuable law dictionary, *De Verborum Significatione*. John Napier of Merchiston was already at work on many inventions including his 'artificial numbers' which we now know as logarithms. While the king himself, pedant and poet, furthered a proposal made in a General Assembly at Burntisland in 1601, for a new translation of the Bible—a proposal that eventually led to the Authorized Version of 1611.

A statement made in 1572 by an English agent in Scotland has often been quoted: 'Methinks', wrote Sir Henry Killigrew to Lord Burghley, 'I see the noblemen's great credit decay . . . and the barons, boroughs and such-like take more upon them.' One of the unresolved historical problems of sixteenth- and seventeenth-century Scotland is the accuracy of this assessment. We have seen that James VI lived in harmony with aristocratic ideas and most aristocrats, and the fact that he recruited to the nobility and knightly caste men of bourgeois origins was no more than a recognition (paralleled among his ancestors) that these men had indeed risen in the social scale. Certainly many nobles became courtiers after 1603, sycophants at Theobalds, neglectful of their retinue and influence at home in Scotland. But much work remains to be done upon the lairds and tenantry of the countryside, and on the complex social structure of the towns before we can know whether the great Reformation in religion was accompanied by a revolutionary shift in the basis of economic power and political importance. These are large questions but they may not be avoided by anyone who would study seventeenth-century Scotland.

On the other hand the departure of James VI for London in 1603 and his continued absence from Scotland, the administrative structures which he left in Scotland, the ending of centuries of Border warfare and reiving, these in themselves justify the wise judgement with which previous editions of this book closed: the old order was changing; a new order was slowly taking shape.

NOTES

1. The bedsteads were 'like Cubbards in the wall, with doores to be opened and shut at pleasure'; and early in the seventeenth century we are told that Gordon of Abergeldie had 'ane clos kaisset bed, lokkit and bandit' in which, presumably, he felt secure from draughts and enemies alike.

2. Houses built of turf could still be seen in some parts of the Highlands in the second half of the nineteenth century. It should be noted, however, that turf roofs are still sometimes used on modern houses in the Faeroes and Norway where they have proved to be well adapted to climatic conditions.

3. As they are in abundance in the drawings of Leonardo da Vinci.

4. Of course this deception was practised largely to avoid the hostile attentions of Catholic city or state authorities, searching for Protestant printers.

5. A year earlier, in 1592, a charter had been granted to Sir Alexander Fraser enabling him to erect a university in his burgh of Fraserburgh (Faithlie), and a small college eventually took shape there. But the competition from Marischal college was too strong; Fraserburgh was small and remote and was strongly presbyterian; and, with James VI's establishment of episcopacy, the college of Fraserburgh lapsed after a tenuous life of some eight or nine years.

It should also be noted that in 1581 we have reference to an article before parliament 'for erection of ane college in Orkney'; but nothing more is known of this project.

6. The 'Kirk o' Field' of Darnley's murder.

Select Bibliography

A. RECORD PUBLICATIONS

Livingstone, M., *A Guide to the Public Records of Scotland*. 1905.

Accounts of the Lord High Treasurer of Scotland, 1473-1566. Edited by Thomas Dickson and Sir James Balfour Paul. 11 vols. 1877-1916.

Accounts of the Masters of Works, 1529-1615. Edited by Henry M. Paton. 1957.

Acts of the Lords Auditors of Causes and Complaints, 1466-1494. Edited by Thomas Thomson. 1839.

Acts of the Lords of Council in Civil Causes, 1478-1495. Edited by Thomas Thomson. 1839.

Acts of the Lords of Council in Civil Causes, 1496-1501, with some *Acta Auditorum et Dominorum Concilii, 1469-1483*. Edited by George Neilson and Henry Paton. 1918.

Acts of the Lords of Council in Public Affairs, 1501-1554. Edited by Robert Kerr Hannay. 1932.

Acts of the Parliaments of Scotland, 1124-1707. Edited by Thomas Thomson and Cosmo Innes. 12 vols. in 13. 1814-75.

Border Papers. [1560-1603.] Edited by Joseph Bain. 2 vols. 1894, 1896.

Calendar of Documents relating to Scotland, 1108-1509. Edited by Joseph Bain. 4 vols. 1881-8.

Calendar of State Papers relating to Scotland, 1547-1603. Various editors. 13 vols. in 14. 1898-1969.

Chronicles of the Picts, Chronicles of the Scots, and other Early Memorials of Scottish History. Edited by William F. Skene. 1867.

Documents and Records illustrating the History of Scotland. [1237-1307.] Edited by Sir Francis Palgrave. 1837.

Documents illustrative of the History of Scotland, 1286-1306. Edited by Joseph Stevenson. 2 vols. 1870.

Exchequer Rolls of Scotland, 1264-1600. Various editors. 23 vols. 1878-1908.

Foedera. Edited by T. Rymer. 4 vols. 1816-19, 1869.

Hamilton Papers. [1532-90.] Edited by Joseph Bain. 2 vols. 1890, 1892.

Ledger of Andrew Halyburton, Conservator of the Privileges of the Scotch Nation in the Netherlands, 1492-1503. [Edited by Cosmo Innes.] 1867.

Letters of James V. Edited by Denys Hay. 1954.

National Manuscripts of Scotland. Facsimiles. [1094-1649.] 3 vols. 1867-71.

Register of the Great Seal of Scotland, 1306-1668. Various editors. 11 vols. 1882-1914.

Register of the Privy Council of Scotland. First Series. 1545-1625. Edited by John Hill Burton and David Masson. 14 vols. 1877-98.

Register of the Privy Seal of Scotland, 1488- . Various editors. 7 vols. 1908- . In progress.

Rotuli Scotiae. [1291-1516.] Edited by D. Macpherson and others. 2 vols. 1814, 1819.

B. NARRATIVE AND LITERARY SOURCES

Adomnan, *Life of Columba*. Edited by Alan Orr Anderson and Marjorie Ogilvie Anderson. Edinburgh, 1961.

Barbour, John, *The Bruce*. Edited by William Mackay Mackenzie. London, 1909.

[Bower, Walter,] *Scotichronicon Johannis de Fordun cum supplementis et continuatione Walteri Bower*. Edited by Walter Goodall. 2 vols. Edinburgh, 1775. [See also *Liber Pluscardensis*.]

Calderwood, David, *History of the Kirk of Scotland*. [1524-1625.] Edited by Thomas Thomson and David Laing. 8 vols. Wodrow Society, 1842-9.

Chronicle of Melrose. Edited by Alan Orr Anderson, Marjorie Ogilvie Anderson, and William Croft Dickinson. Facsimile edition. London, 1936. [*The Chronicle of Melrose*, translated by Joseph Stevenson. London, 1856.]

Chronicon de Lanercost. [1201-1346.] Edited by Joseph Stevenson. Bannatyne and Maitland Clubs, 1839.
[*The Chronicle of Lanercost, 1273-1346*, translated by Sir Herbert Maxwell. Glasgow, 1913.]

Complaynt of Scotland. Edited by James A. H. Murray. Early English Text Society, 1872.

Diurnal of Remarkable Occurrents. [1513-75.] Edited by Thomas Thomson. Bannatyne and Maitland Clubs, 1833.

Dunbar, William, *Poems*. Edited by John Small and Æ. J. G. Mackay. 3 vols. Scottish Text Society, 1893.

Fordun, John, *Chronica Gentis Scotorum*. Edited and translated by William F. Skene. 2 vols. Edinburgh, 1871, 1872.

Fragments of Scottish History [edited by Sir John Graham Dalyell]. Edinburgh, 1798.
[Contains the 'Diary of Robert Birrel' (1532-1605), 'The Late Expedition in Scotland under the Earl of Hertford, 1544', and Patten's 'Account of the Expedition into Scotland under the Duke of Somerset, 1547'.]

Gray, Thomas, *Scalacronica*. [1066-1362.] Edited by Joseph Stevenson. Maitland Club, 1836.
[*Scalacronica*, translated by Sir Herbert Maxwell. Glasgow, 1907.]

The *Gude and Godlie Ballates*. Edited by David Laing. Edinburgh, 1868.

Henryson, Robert, *Poems*. Edited by G. Gregory Smith. 3 vols. Scottish Text Society, 1906-14.

Knox, John, *History of the Reformation in Scotland*. Edited by William Croft Dickinson. 2 vols. Edinburgh, 1949.

—— *Works*. Edited by David Laing. 6 vols. Edinburgh, 1895 [Reprint].

Lesley, John, *History of Scotland*. [1437-1561.] Edited by Thomas Thomson. Bannatyne Club, 1830.

Liber Pluscardensis. Edited and translated by Felix J. H. Skene. 2 vols. Edinburgh, 1877, 1880.
[The *Liber Pluscardensis* is largely founded upon Bower's *Scotichronicon* (q.v.), which is still untranslated.]

Lindsay, Robert, of Pitscottie, *Historie and Cronicles of Scotland.* [1437-1575.] Edited by Aeneas J. G. Mackay. 3 vols. Scottish Text Society, 1899-1911.

Lyndsay, Sir David, of the Mount, *Poetical Works.* Edited by David Laing. 3 vols. Edinburgh, 1879.

Major, John, *History of Greater Britain.* Edited and translated by Archibald Constable. Scottish History Society, 1892.

Melville, James, *Autobiography and Diary.* [1556-1601.] With a 'Continuation' called *A True Narratioun of the Declyneing Aige of the Kirk of Scotland.* Edited by Robert Pitcairn. Wodrow Society, 1842.

Melville, James, of Halhill, *Memoirs of his own Life.* [1549-93.] Edited by Thomas Thomson. Bannatyne and Maitland Clubs, 1827.

Moysie, David, *Memoirs of the Affairs of Scotland.* [1577-1603.] Edited by James Dennistoun. Bannatyne and Maitland Clubs, 1830.

Orkneyinga Saga. Translated and edited by A. B. Taylor. Edinburgh, 1938.

Pitscottie, see Lindsay, Robert.

Spottiswoode, John, *History of the Church of Scotland.* [To 1625.] Edited by M. Russell and Mark Napier. 3 vols. Bannatyne Club and Spottiswoode Society, 1847-51.

Vita Edwardi Secundi. Edited by N. Denholm-Young. Edinburgh, 1957.

Wyntoun, Andrew, *Orygynale Cronykil of Scotland.* Edited by David Laing. 3 vols. Edinburgh, 1872-9.

C. GENERAL HISTORIES AND WORKS OF REFERENCE

Anderson, Alan Orr, *Early Sources of Scottish History, 500-1286.* 2 vols. Edinburgh, 1922.
—— *Scottish Annals from English Chroniclers, 500-1286.* London, 1908.

Black, George F., *The Surnames of Scotland.* New York, 1946.

Brown, Peter Hume, *History of Scotland.* Library edition. 3 vols. Cambridge, 1911.

Burton, John Hill, *History of Scotland.* Second edition. 8 vols. and Index. Edinburgh, 1873.

Chalmers, George, *Caledonia.* New edition. 7 vols. and Index. Paisley, 1887-1902.

Craigie, Sir William (editor), *A Dictionary of the Older Scottish Tongue from the Twelfth Century to the end of the Seventeenth.* Chicago and Oxford, 1931- . In progress.

Dalrymple, David, Lord Hailes, *Annals of Scotland.* [1057-1371.] Third edition. 3 vols. Edinburgh, 1819.

Dickinson, William Croft, Donaldson, Gordon, and Milne, Isabel Arnot, *A Source Book of Scottish History.* Second edition. 3 vols. Edinburgh, 1954, 1961.

Donaldson, Gordon, *Scotland, James V-James VII* (Edinburgh History of Scotland, vol. iii). Edinburgh, 1965.

O

Donaldson, Gordon, *Scotland, Church and Nation through Sixteen Centuries.* Second edition. Edinburgh, 1972.
—— *Scottish Historical Documents.* Edinburgh, 1970.
Dowden, John, *The Bishops of Scotland.* Glasgow, 1912.
Dunbar, Sir Archibald H., *Scottish Kings.* Second edition. Edinburgh, 1906.
Duncan, Archibald A. M., *Scotland, The Making of the Kingdom* (Edinburgh History of Scotland, vol. i). Edinburgh, 1975.
Easson, David Edward, *Medieval Religious Houses: Scotland.* London, 1957.
Hailes, Lord, see Dalrymple, David.
Keith, Robert, *An Historical Catalogue of the Scottish Bishops down to the Year 1688.* Edited by M. Russell. Edinburgh, 1824.
Lang, Andrew, *History of Scotland.* Third edition (vols. i and ii). 4 vols. Edinburgh, 1903–7.
Menzies, Gordon, *The Scottish Nation.* London, 1972.
Nicholson, Ranald, *Scotland, The Later Middle Ages* (Edinburgh History of Scotland, vol. ii). Edinburgh, 1974.
Paul, Sir James Balfour (editor), *The Scots Peerage.* 9 vols. Edinburgh, 1904–14.
Scott, Hew (editor), *Fasti Ecclesiae Scoticanae.* Revised edition. 8 vols. Edinburgh, 1915–50.
Scottish Historical Review, vol. i (1904–   ). In progress.
Smout, T. C., *History of the Scottish People, 1560–1830.* London, 1969.
Thomson, J. Maitland, *The Public Records of Scotland.* Glasgow, 1922.
Tytler, Patrick Fraser, *History of Scotland.* [1249–1603.] Second edition. 9 vols. Edinburgh, 1841–3.
Watt, Donald E. R., *Fasti Ecclesiae Scoticanae Medii Aevi.* St. Andrews, 1969.
Webster, Bruce, *Scotland from the Eleventh Century to 1603.* [Discusses the sources.] London, 1975.

D. PARTICULAR PERIODS

Prehistoric Times

Childe, Vere Gordon, *Prehistoric Communities of the British Isles.* Edinburgh, 1940.
—— *Prehistory of Scotland.* London, 1935.
—— *Scotland before the Scots.* London, 1946.
Fox, Sir Cyril, *Personality of Britain.* Fourth edition. Cardiff, 1952.
Piggott, Stuart, *British Prehistory.* Oxford, 1949.
—— *Scotland before History.* Edinburgh, 1958.
Rivet, A. L. F., *Iron Age in Northern Britain.* Edinburgh, 1967.

Roman Times

Burn, A. R., *Agricola and Roman Britain.* London, 1953.
Collingwood, R. G., *Roman Britain.* Second edition. Oxford, 1937.
Crawford, O. G. S., *Topography of Roman Scotland.* Cambridge, 1949.
Frere, S., *Britannia.* London, 1967.
Haverfield, F. J., *Roman Occupation of Britain.* Edited by Sir George Macdonald. Oxford, 1924.

Macdonald, Sir George, *The Roman Wall in Scotland*. Second edition. Oxford, 1934.

Miller, S. N. (editor), *The Roman Occupation of South-Western Scotland*. Glasgow Archaeological Society, 1952.

Richmond, I. A., *Roman Britain*. Harmondsworth: Penguin Books, 1955.

—— (editor), *Roman and Native in North Britain*. Edinburgh, 1958.

Celtic Scotland

Anderson, Joseph, *Scotland in Early Christian Times*. Edinburgh, 1881.

Anderson, Marjory O., *Kings and Kingship in Early Scotland*. Edinburgh, 1973.

Bannerman, John, *Studies in the History of Dalriada*. Edinburgh, 1974.

Chadwick, H. M., *Early Scotland*. Cambridge, 1949.

Chadwick, Nora K., and others. *Celt and Saxon*. Cambridge, 1963.

Dillon, M., and Chadwick, N. K., *Celtic Realms*. London, 1967.

Duke, John A., *The Columban Church*. Edinburgh, 1957 [Reprint].

Dumfriesshire and Galloway Natural History and Antiquarian Society, *Transactions*, Third Series, vol. xxvii (1948–9). 'Whithorn Volume'.

Henderson, Isabel, *The Picts*. London, 1967.

Jackson, Kenneth, *Language and History in Early Britain*. Edinburgh, 1956.

—— *The Gaelic Notes in the Book of Deer*. Cambridge, 1972.

Laing, Lloyd, *The Archaeology of Late Celtic Britain and Ireland, 400–1200*. London, 1975.

MacQueen, John, *St. Nynia*. Edinburgh, 1961.

Skene, William F., *Celtic Scotland*. Second edition. 3 vols. Edinburgh, 1886–90.

Stenton, Sir Frank, *Anglo-Saxon England*. Third edition. Oxford, 1971.

Thomas, Charles, *Early Christian Archaeology of North Britain*. Oxford, 1971.

Wainwright, F. T. (editor), *The Problem of the Picts*. Edinburgh, 1955.

Watson, William J., *History of the Celtic Place-Names of Scotland*. Edinburgh, 1926.

Medieval Scotland

Balfour-Melville, E. W. M., *James I, King of Scots*. London, 1936.

Barron, Evan Macleod, *The Scottish War of Independence*. Second edition. Inverness, 1934.

Barrow, G. W. S., *Feudal Britain*. London, 1956.

—— *Acts of Malcolm IV* (Regesta Regum Scottorum, vol. i). Edinburgh, 1960.

—— *Acts of William I* (Regesta Regum Scottorum, vol. ii). Edinburgh, 1971.

—— *Robert Bruce and the Community of the Realm of Scotland*. London, 1965. (A new edition is promised, 1976.)

—— *The Kingdom of the Scots*. London, 1973.

Cooper, Thomas Mackay (Lord Cooper), *Supra Crepidam*. Edinburgh, 1951.

Coulton, G. G., *Scottish Abbeys and Social Life*. Cambridge, 1933.

Dunlop, Annie I., *The Life and Times of James Kennedy, Bishop of St. Andrews*. Edinburgh, 1950.

Fergusson, Sir James, *William Wallace*. New edition. Stirling, 1948.

Lawrie, Sir Archibald Campbell (editor), *Annals of the Reigns of Malcolm and William, Kings of Scotland*. Glasgow, 1910.

—— *Early Scottish Charters, prior to 1153*. Glasgow, 1905.

Nicholson, Ranald, *Edward III and the Scots*. Oxford, 1965.

Origines Parochiales Scotiae. Edited by Cosmo Innes and others. 2 vols in 3. Bannatyne Club, 1851–5.

Powicke, Sir Maurice, *The Thirteenth Century*. Oxford, 1953.

Ramsay, Sir James H., *The Genesis of Lancaster, 1307–1399*. 2 vols. Oxford, 1913.

Ritchie, R. L. Graeme, *The Normans in Scotland*. Edinburgh, 1954.

Stenton, Sir Frank (editor), *The Bayeux Tapestry*. London, 1957.

Stones, E. L. G. (editor), *Anglo-Scottish Relations, 1174–1328*. London, 1965, Reprinted 1970.

From 1488 to 1603

Black, J. B., *The Reign of Elizabeth*. Second edition. Oxford, 1959.

—— *Andrew Lang and the Casket Letter Controversy*. Pamphlet. Edinburgh, 1950.

Brown, P. Hume, *George Buchanan*. Edinburgh, 1890.

—— *John Knox*. 2 vols. London, 1895.

Bruce, John (editor), *Correspondence of King James VI with Sir Robert Cecil and Others*. Camden Society, 1861.

—— *Letters of Queen Elizabeth and King James VI of Scotland*. Camden Society, 1849.

Buchanan, George, *Rerum Scoticarum Historia*. See Gatherer, W. A.

Cameron, James K., *The First Book of Discipline*. Edinburgh, 1972.

Clifford, Arthur (editor), *The State Papers and Letters of Sir Ralph Sadler*. 2 vols. Edinburgh, 1809.

Cowan, Ian B., *Enigma of Mary Stewart*. London, 1971.

Dickinson, Gladys (editor), *Two Missions of Jacques de la Brosse, 1543, 1560*. Scottish History Society, 1942.

Donaldson, Gordon, *The Reformation in Scotland*. Cambridge, 1960.

—— (editor), *Accounts of the Collectors of Thirds of Benefices, 1561–1572*. Scottish History Society, 1949.

—— *The First Trial of Mary Queen of Scots*. London, 1969.

—— *Mary, Queen of Scots*. London, 1974.

Fleming, David Hay, *Mary Queen of Scots*. Second edition. London, 1898.

—— *The Reformation in Scotland*. London, 1910.

—— (editor), *Register of the Minister, Elders and Deacons of the Christian Congregation of St. Andrews, 1559–1600*. 2 vols. Scottish History Society, 1889, 1890.

Fraser, Antonia, *Mary, Queen of Scots*. London, 1969.

Gatherer, W. A., *The Tyrannous Reign of Mary Stewart*. [A translation, with editorial notes, of George Buchanan, *Rerum Scoticarum Historia*, Books XVII–XIX.] Edinburgh, 1958.

Henderson, T. F., *Life of Mary Queen of Scots*. 2 vols. London, 1905.

Keith, Robert, *History of the Affairs of Church and State in Scotland, 1527–1568*. 3 vols. Spottiswoode Society, 1844–50.

Lang, Andrew, *James VI and the Gowrie Mystery*. London, 1902.

—— *John Knox and the Reformation*. London, 1905.

—— *The Mystery of Mary Stewart*. New edition. London, 1901.

Lee, Maurice, *James Stewart, Earl of Moray*. New York, 1953.

—— *John Maitland of Thirlestane.* Princeton, 1959.

McCrie, Thomas, *Life of Andrew Melville.* New edition. 2 vols. Edinburgh, 1899.

Mackenzie, William Mackay, *The Secret of Flodden.* Edinburgh, 1931.

Mackie, J. D., *The Earlier Tudors.* Oxford, 1952.

Mackie, R. L., *King James IV of Scotland.* Edinburgh, 1958.

—— (editor), *Letters of James IV, 1505-1513.* Scottish History Society, 1953.

Mathieson, William Law, *Politics and Religion.* 2 vols. Glasgow, 1902.

Percy, Lord Eustace, *John Knox.* London, 1937.

Pollen, John Hungerford (editor), *Mary Queen of Scots and the Babington Plot.* Scottish History Society, 1922.

—— *Papal Negotiations with Mary Queen of Scots.* Scottish History Society, 1901.

Reid, W. Stanford, *Trumpeter of God.* [Biography of John Knox.] New York, 1974.

Robertson, Joseph (editor), *Inuentaires de la Royne d'Escosse.* Bannatyne Club, 1863.

Shaw, Duncan (editor), *Reformation and Revolution.* Edinburgh, 1967.

Smith, Alan G. R., *The Reign of James VI and I.* London, 1973.

Smith, G. Gregory, *The Days of James IV.* London, 1900.

Teulet, A. (editor), *Papiers d'État . . . relatifs à l'histoire de l'Écosse au XVIe siècle.* 3 vols. Bannatyne Club, 1852-60.

—— *Relation Politiques de la France et de l'Espagne avec l'Écosse au XVIe siècle.* 5 vols. Paris, 1862.

Thomson, Thomas (editor), *Acts and Proceedings of the General Assemblies of the Kirk of Scotland, 1560-1618 (Booke of the Universall Kirk of Scotland).* 3 vols. Bannatyne and Maitland Clubs, 1839-45.

Tough, D. L. W., *The Last Years of a Frontier.* Oxford, 1928.

Willson, D. Harris, *James VI and I.* London, 1956.

Winzet, Ninian, *Certain Tractates.* Edited by James King Hewison. 2 vols. Scottish Text Society, 1888, 1890.

E. LEGAL AND CONSTITUTIONAL STUDIES

Cooper, Thomas Mackay (Lord Cooper), *Select Scottish Cases of the Thirteenth Century.* Edinburgh, 1944.

—— *The Scottish Legal Tradition.* Pamphlet. Edinburgh, 1949.

Dickinson, William Croft (editor), *Court Book of the Barony of Carnwath, 1523-1542.* Scottish History Society, 1937.

—— *Early Records of the Burgh of Aberdeen, 1317, 1398-1407.* Scottish History Society, 1957.

—— *Sheriff Court Book of Fife, 1513-1522.* Scottish History Society, 1928.

Hannay, Robert Kerr, *The College of Justice.* Edinburgh, 1933.

Innes, Cosmo, *Lectures on Scotch Legal Antiquities.* Edinburgh, 1872.

Mackenzie, William Mackay, *The Scottish Burghs.* Edinburgh, 1949.

Mackie, J. D., and Pryde, G. S., *The Estate of Burgesses in the Scots Parliament and its relation to the Convention of Royal Burghs.* St. Andrews, 1923.

Murray, David, *Legal Practice in Ayr and the West of Scotland in the Fifteenth and Sixteenth Centuries*. Glasgow, 1910.

Neilson, George, *Trial by Combat*. Glasgow, 1890.

Pagan, Theodora, *The Convention of Royal Burghs of Scotland*. Glasgow, 1926.

Pitcairn, Robert (editor), *Ancient Criminal Trials in Scotland*. 3 vols. in 4 (11 parts). Bannatyne and Maitland Clubs, 1829-33.

Pryde, George S. (editor), *Ayr Burgh Accounts, 1534-1624*. Scottish History Society, 1937.

—— *Burghs of Scotland*. Oxford, 1965.

Rae, Thomas I., *The Administration of the Scottish Frontier, 1513-1603*. Edinburgh, 1966.

Rait, Robert S., *The Parliament of Scotland*. Glasgow, 1924.

Stair Society. *An Introductory Survey of the Sources and Literature of Scots Law*. Various contributors. Edinburgh, 1936.

—— *An Introduction to Scottish Legal History*. Various contributors. Edinburgh, 1958.

Thomson, J. Maitland, *The Public Records of Scotland*. Glasgow, 1922.

[*Note*: Scottish feudalism, early land tenures, and the organization of society in the twelfth and thirteenth centuries must be studied in the charters. Most of the surviving monastic and episcopal cartularies have been printed by historical clubs and societies; and there are many charters in the family histories edited by Sir William Fraser. A list (complete up to 1935) of manuscript charter collections, of printed cartularies, and of family histories and other works containing printed charters is given by William Angus in *Sources and Literature of Scots Law* (ut supra), pp. 259-64.]

F. ECCLESIASTICAL HISTORY (GENERAL WORKS)

Bellesheim, A., *History of the Catholic Church in Scotland*. Translated by D. O. Hunter Blair. 4 vols. Edinburgh, 1887-90.

Burleigh, J. H. S., *Church History of Scotland*. London, 1960.

Cowan, Ian B., *Parishes of Medieval Scotland*. Edinburgh, 1967.

—— and Easson, David E., *Medieval Religious Houses: Scotland*. Second edition. London, 1976.

Cunningham, John, *The Church History of Scotland*. Second edition. 2 vols. Edinburgh, 1882.

Dowden, John, *The Bishops of Scotland*. Glasgow, 1912.

—— *The Mediaeval Church in Scotland*. Glasgow, 1910.

Grub, George, *An Ecclesiastical History of Scotland*. 4 vols. Edinburgh, 1861.

Hannay, Robert Kerr, *The Scottish Crown and the Papacy*. Historical Association: Pamphlet, 1931.

Henderson, G. D., *The Claims of the Church of Scotland*. London, 1951.

Herkless, John, and Hannay, Robert Kerr, *The Archbishops of St. Andrews*. 5 vols. Edinburgh, 1907-15.

Innes Review, i (1950-   ). In progress.

MacEwan, Alexander R., *A History of the Church in Scotland* [to 1560]. 2 vols. London, 1913, 1918.

Patrick, David (editor), *Statutes of the Scottish Church, 1225-1559.* Scottish History Society, 1907. [See also Robertson's *Concilia.*]

Robertson, Joseph (editor), *Concilia Scotiae: Ecclesiae Scoticanae Statuta, 1225-1559.* 2 vols. Bannatyne Club, 1886. [See also Patrick's *Statutes.*]

G. SOCIAL AND ECONOMIC CONDITIONS

Brown, Peter Hume (editor), *Early Travellers in Scotland.* Edinburgh, 1891.

—— *Scotland before 1700 from Contemporary Documents.* Edinburgh, 1893.

—— *Scotland in the Time of Queen Mary.* London, 1904.

Chambers, Robert, *Domestic Annals of Scotland.* Third edition. 3 vols. Edinburgh, 1874.

Franklin, T. Bedford, *A History of Scottish Farming.* Edinburgh, 1952.

Grant, I. F., *The Social and Economic Development of Scotland before 1603.* Edinburgh, 1930.

Innes, Cosmo, *Scotland in the Middle Ages.* Edinburgh, 1860.

—— *Sketches of Early Scotch History.* Edinburgh, 1861.

Lythe, S. G. E., *The Economy of Scotland, 1550-1625, in its European Setting.* Edinburgh, 1960.

—— and Butt, J., *Economic History of Scotland, 1100-1939.* Glasgow, 1975.

Shrewsbury, J. F. D., *History of the Bubonic Plague in the British Isles.* London, 1970.

Symon, J. A., *Scottish Farming, Past and Present.* Edinburgh, 1959.

Warrack, John, *Domestic Life in Scotland, 1488-1688.* London, 1920.

H. THE HIGHLANDS AND ISLANDS; ORKNEY AND SHETLAND

Adam, Frank, *The Clans, Septs and Regiments of the Scottish Highlands.* 4th edition, revised by Sir Thomas Innes of Learney. Edinburgh, 1952.

Clouston, J. Storer (editor), *Records of the Earldom of Orkney.* Scottish History Society, 1914.

Darling, F. Fraser, *Natural History in the Highlands and Islands.* Glasgow, 1948.

Donaldson, Gordon (editor), *The Court Book of Shetland, 1602-1604.* Scottish Record Society, 1954.

—— *Shetland Life under Earl Patrick.* Edinburgh, 1958.

Goudie, Gilbert, *The Celtic and Scandinavian Antiquities of Shetland.* Edinburgh, 1904.

Gregory, Donald, *History of the Western Highlands and Isles.* Second edition. London, 1881.

Innes, Sir Thomas, of Learney, *The Tartans of the Clans and Families of Scotland.* Revised edition. Edinburgh, 1950.

Kermack, W. R., *The Scottish Highlands: A Short History.* Edinburgh, 1957.

MacDonald, Colin M., *The History of Argyll.* Glasgow, 1950.

Mackenzie, W. C., *The Highlands and Isles of Scotland: A Historical Survey.* Revised edition. Edinburgh, 1949.

Simpson, W. Douglas (editor), *The Viking Congress, 1950.* Edinburgh, 1954.

Skene, William F., *The Highlanders of Scotland.* Edited by Alexander MacBain. Stirling, 1902.

I. EDUCATION, LITERATURE, ART AND ARCHITECTURE

Cant, R. G., *The University of St. Andrews: A Short History.* Second edition. Edinburgh, 1970.

—— *The College of St. Salvator.* Edinburgh, 1950.

Cruden, Stewart, *The Scottish Castle.* Edinburgh, 1960.

Dunbar, John G., *The Historic Architecture of Scotland.* London, 1966.

Finlay, Ian, *Art in Scotland.* Oxford, 1948.

—— *Scottish Crafts.* London, 1948.

Grant, Sir Alexander, *The Story of the University of Edinburgh.* 2 vols. London, 1884.

Grant, James, *History of the Burgh Schools of Scotland.* Glasgow, 1876.

Hannah, Ian C., *Story of Scotland in Stone.* Edinburgh, 1934.

Hannay, Robert Kerr, 'The Universities of Scotland' in H. Rashdall, *The Universities of Europe in the Middle Ages.* New edition, edited by F. M. Powicke and A. B. Emden. Oxford, 1936.

Henderson, G. D., *The Founding of Marischal College, Aberdeen.* Aberdeen, 1947.

Henderson, T. F., *Scottish Vernacular Literature.* Edinburgh, 1910.

Herkless, John, and Hannay, Robert Kerr, *The College of St. Leonard.* Edinburgh, 1905.

Kinghorn, A. M., *The Chorus of History.* London, 1971.

MacGibbon, David, and Ross, Thomas, *The Castellated and Domestic Architecture of Scotland.* 5 vols. Edinburgh, 1887–92.

—— —— *The Ecclesiastical Architecture of Scotland.* 3 vols. Edinburgh, 1896–7.

Mackenzie, Agnes Mure, *An Historical Survey of Scottish Literature to 1714.* London, 1933.

Mackenzie, William Mackay, *The Mediaeval Castle in Scotland.* London, 1927.

Mackie, J. D., *The University of Glasgow, 1451–1951.* Glasgow, 1954.

Millar, J. H., *A Literary History of Scotland.* London, 1903.

Rait, Robert S., *The Universities of Aberdeen.* Aberdeen, 1895.

Scott, Sir Walter (editor), *Minstrelsy of the Scottish Border.* Revised and edited by T. F. Henderson. 4 vols. Edinburgh, 1932.

Scott-Moncrieff, George (editor), *The Stones of Scotland.* London, 1938.

Wittig, Kurt, *The Scottish Tradition in Literature.* Edinburgh, 1958.

[*Note*: The county inventories published by the Royal Commission on the Ancient and Historical Monuments of Scotland are invaluable for the study of ancient and historical monuments—prehistoric, Roman, medieval, and early modern up to (and where there are special reasons later than) 1707.]

J. ATLASES, MAPS, AND GAZETTEERS

Bartholomew, John (editor), *Survey Atlas of Scotland.*
—— *Survey Gazetteer of the British Isles.*
Groome, F. H. (editor), *Ordnance Gazetteer of Scotland.* 6 (or 6 in 3) vols.
Johnston, W. and A. K., *Gazetteer of Scotland.*
McNeill, Peter, and Nicholson, Ranald (editors), *An Historical Atlas of Scotland,* c. *400-c. 1600.* St. Andrews, 1975.
Ordnance Survey. Map of Britain in the Dark Ages—North Sheet.
　　　　　　　　Map of Britain before the Norman Conquest.
　　　　　　　　Map of Monastic Britain—North Sheet.
　　　　　　　　Map of Roman Britain.
Royal Scottish Geographical Society, *Early Maps of Scotland.* Edinburgh, 1936.

K. BIBLIOGRAPHIES

Black, George F., *List of Works* [in the New York Public Library] *Relating to Scotland.* New York, 1916.
Ferguson, Joan P. S., *Scottish Family Histories held in Scottish Libraries.* Edinburgh, 1960.
Hancock, P. D., *A Bibliography of Works Relating to Scotland* [published in the years] *1915-1950.* 2 vols. Edinburgh, 1960. [See also Mitchell and Cash.]
Matheson, Cyril, *A Catalogue of the Publications of Scottish Historical and Kindred Clubs and Societies, 1908-1927.* Aberdeen, 1928. [See also Terry.]
Mitchell, Sir Arthur, and Cash, C. G., *A Contribution to the Bibliography of Scottish Topography.* 2 vols. Scottish History Society, 1917. [See also Hancock.]
Stair Society. *An Introductory Survey of the Sources and Literature of Scots Law.* Various contributors. Edinburgh, 1936.
Stuart, Margaret, *Scottish Family History: A Guide to Works of Reference on the History and Genealogy of Scottish Families.* Edinburgh, 1930.
Terry, Charles Sanford, *A Catalogue of the Publications of Scottish Historical and Kindred Clubs and Societies, 1780-1908.* Glasgow, 1909. [See also Matheson.]

P

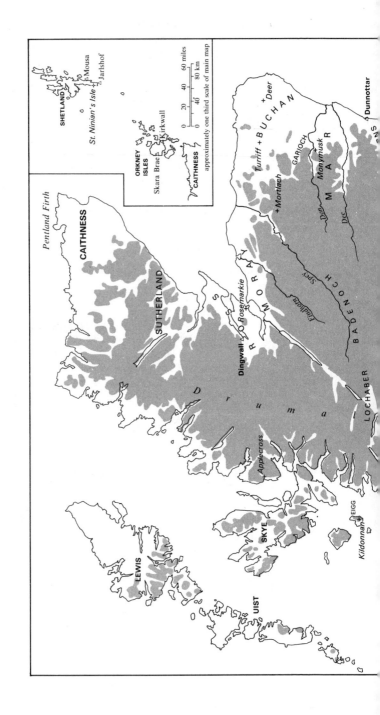

SHETLAND

St. Ninian's Isle

Mousa

Jarlshof

ORKNEY
ISLES

Skara Brae

Kirkwall

CAITHNESS

0   20   40   60 miles

0   40   80 km

approximately one third scale of main map

Pentland Firth

CAITHNESS

SUTHERLAND

Druma

Applecross

LEWIS

UIST

SKYE

EIGG

Kildonnan

Dingwall

Rosemarkie

R   O   S   S

M   O   R   A   Y

Spey

Findhorn

BADENOCH

LOCHABER

BUCHAN

Deer

Turriff

Mortlach

GARIOCH

Monymusk

M   A   R

Don

Dee

Dunnottar

NS

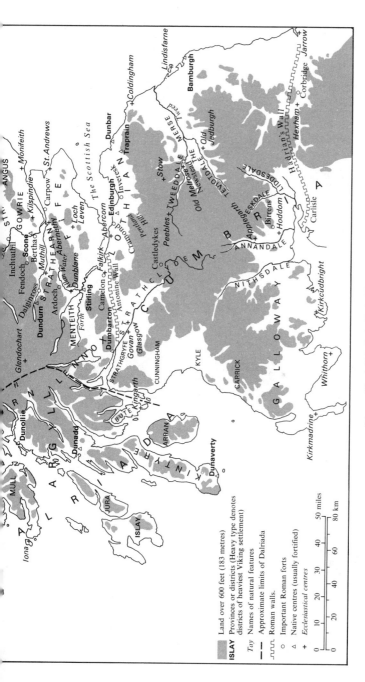

Map 1. North Britain in Early Times

ISLAY Land over 600 feet (183 metres)

ISLAY Provinces or districts (Heavy type denotes districts of heaviest Viking settlement)

Tay Names of natural features

— — Approximate limits of Dalriada

〰〰 Roman walls.

○ Important Roman forts

△ Native centres (usually fortified)

+ *Ecclesiastical centres*

0   10   20   30   40   50 miles
0   20   40   60   80 km

Map 2. Kingdom of Scotland (without the Northern Isles)

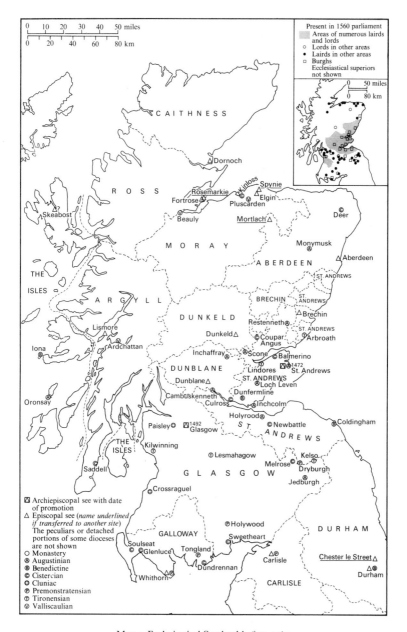

C A I T H N E S S

△Dornoch

R O S S

Kinloss△ Spynie
Rosemarkie△ △ Elgin
Fortrose△   Pluscarden
          Beauly   Deer ©

Skeabost △?

M O R A Y

Mortlach △

Monymusk
△ Aberdeen
A B E R D E E N

THE
ISLES ○

A R G Y L L

ST. ANDREWS

BRECHIN   ST.
          ANDREWS
△Brechin

D U N K E L D

Restenneth△ ST. ANDREWS
Lismore   Dunkeld△ ©Coupar   ©Arbroath
                        Angus
Ardchattan   Inchaffray△ ©Scone ©Balmerino
Iona   Lindores ▨△1472
         D U N B L A N E ST. ANDREWS St. Andrews
                     Dunblane△ ●Loch Leven
Oronsay   Cambuskenneth△ Dunfermline
              Culross© ®Inchcolm
                 Holyrood△
         Paisley○ ▨1492   ©Newbattle
THE   Glasgow   S T   A N D R E W S ©Coldingham
ISLES Kilwinning
         ⑦   ⑦Lesmahagow   Kelso○
Saddell©   Melrose©© ⑦
         G L A S G O W   Dryburgh
                          △
                     ©Crossraguel   Jedburgh

℗Holywood   D U R H A M
Sweetheart©
GALLOWAY
Soulseat©   △®
©Glenluce Tongland   Carlisle   Chester le Street △
              ℗
Whithorn△© Dundrennan©   △®
                                  Durham
              CARLISLE

Map 3. Ecclesiastical Scotland before 1560

Index

The dates within brackets are the dates of tenure of office or title